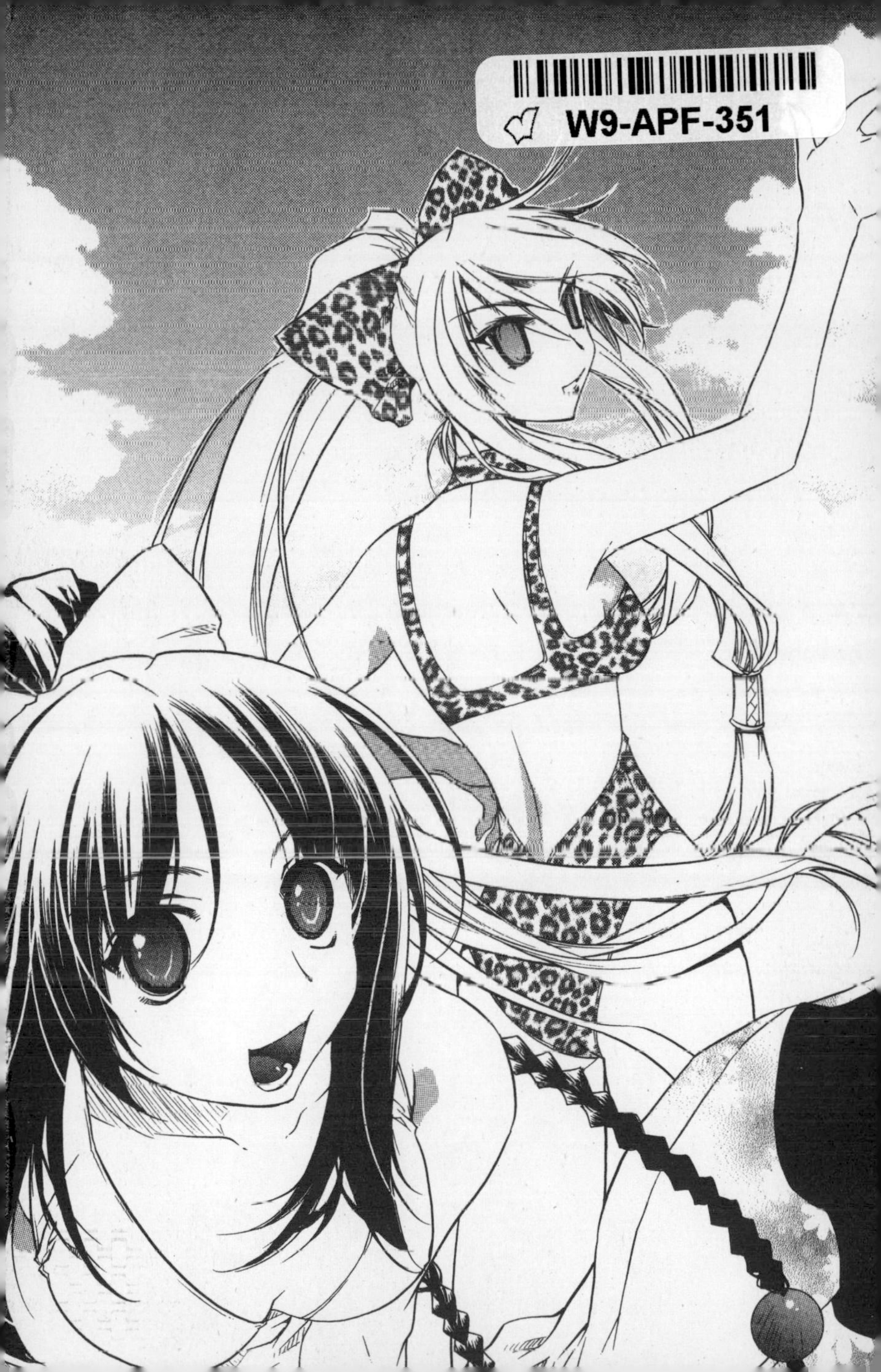

CHRONICLES OF THE CURSED SWORD

Volume 10

Story by
YEO BEOP-RYONG
Art by
PARK HUI-JIN

HAMBURG // LONDON // LOS ANGELES // TOKYO

Chronicles of the Cursed Sword Vol. 10
written by Yeo Beop-Ryong
illustrated by Park Hui-Jin

Translation - Yongju Ryu
English Adaptation - Matt Varosky
Copy Editor - Peter Ahlstrom
Retouch and Lettering - Jason Milligan
Production Artist - James Lee
Cover Design - Gary Shum

Editor - Aaron Suhr
Digital Imaging Manager - Chris Buford
Pre-Press Manager - Antonio DePietro
Production Managers - Jennifer Miller and Mutsumi Miyazaki
Art Director - Matt Alford
Managing Editor - Jill Freshney
VP of Production - Ron Klamert
Editor-in-Chief - Mike Kiley
President and C.O.O. - John Parker
Publisher and C.E.O. - Stuart Levy

A **TOKYOPOP**® Manga

TOKYOPOP Inc.
5900 Wilshire Blvd. Suite 2000
Los Angeles, CA 90036

E-mail: info@TOKYOPOP.com
Come visit us online at www.TOKYOPOP.com

ISBN: 1-59532-387-2

First TOKYOPOP printing: January 2005
10 9 8 7 6 5 4 3 2 1
Printed in the USA or Canada

Chronicles

CHRONICLES OF THE CURSED SWORD

the cast of characters

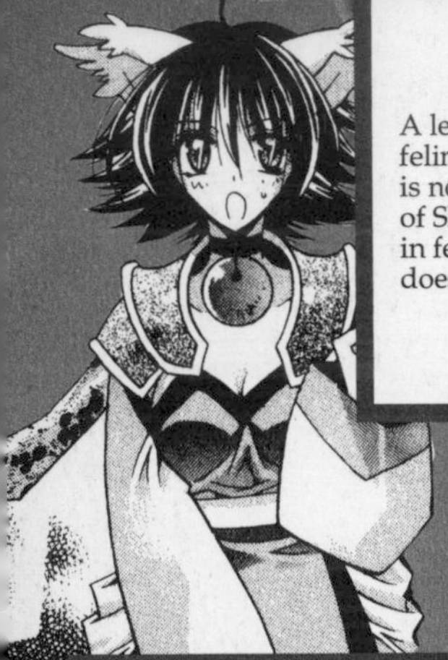

MINGLING

A lesser demon with feline qualities, Mingling is now the loyal follower of Shyao Lin. She lives in fear of Rey, who still doesn't trust her.

THE PASA SWORD

A living sword that hungers for demon blood. It grants its user incredible power, but at a great cost—it can take over the user's body and, in time, his soul.

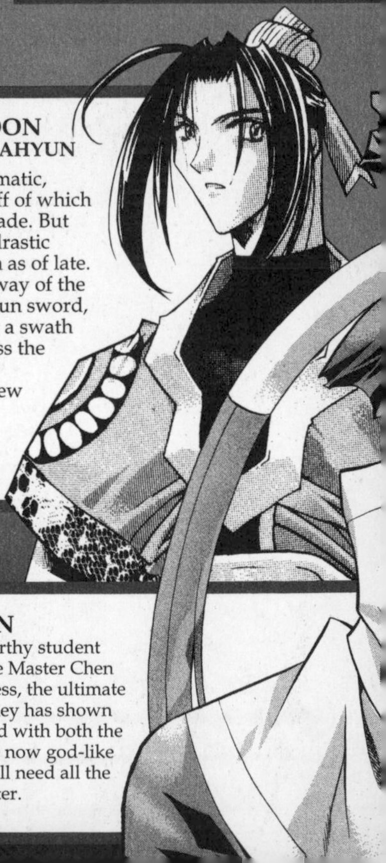

JARYOON
KING OF HAHYUN

Noble and charismatic, Jaryoon is the stuff of which great kings are made. But there has been a drastic change in Jaryoon as of late. Now under the sway of the spirit of the PaChun sword, Jaryoon is cutting a swath of humanity across the countryside as he searches for his new prey...Rey.

SHYAO LIN

A sorceress, previously Rey's traveling companion and greatest ally. Shyao has recently discovered that she is, in fact, one of the Eight Sages of the Azure Pavilion, sent to gather information in the Human Realm. Much to her dismay, she has been told that she must now kill Rey Yan.

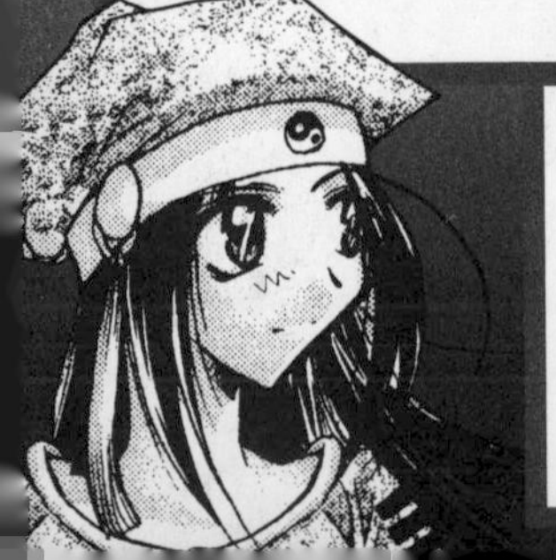

REY YAN

Rey has proven to be a worthy student of the wise and diminutive Master Chen Kaihu. At the Mujin Fortress, the ultimate warrior testing grounds, Rey has shown his martial arts mettle. And with both the possessed Jaryoon and the now god-like Shyao after his blood—he'll need all the survival skills he can muster.

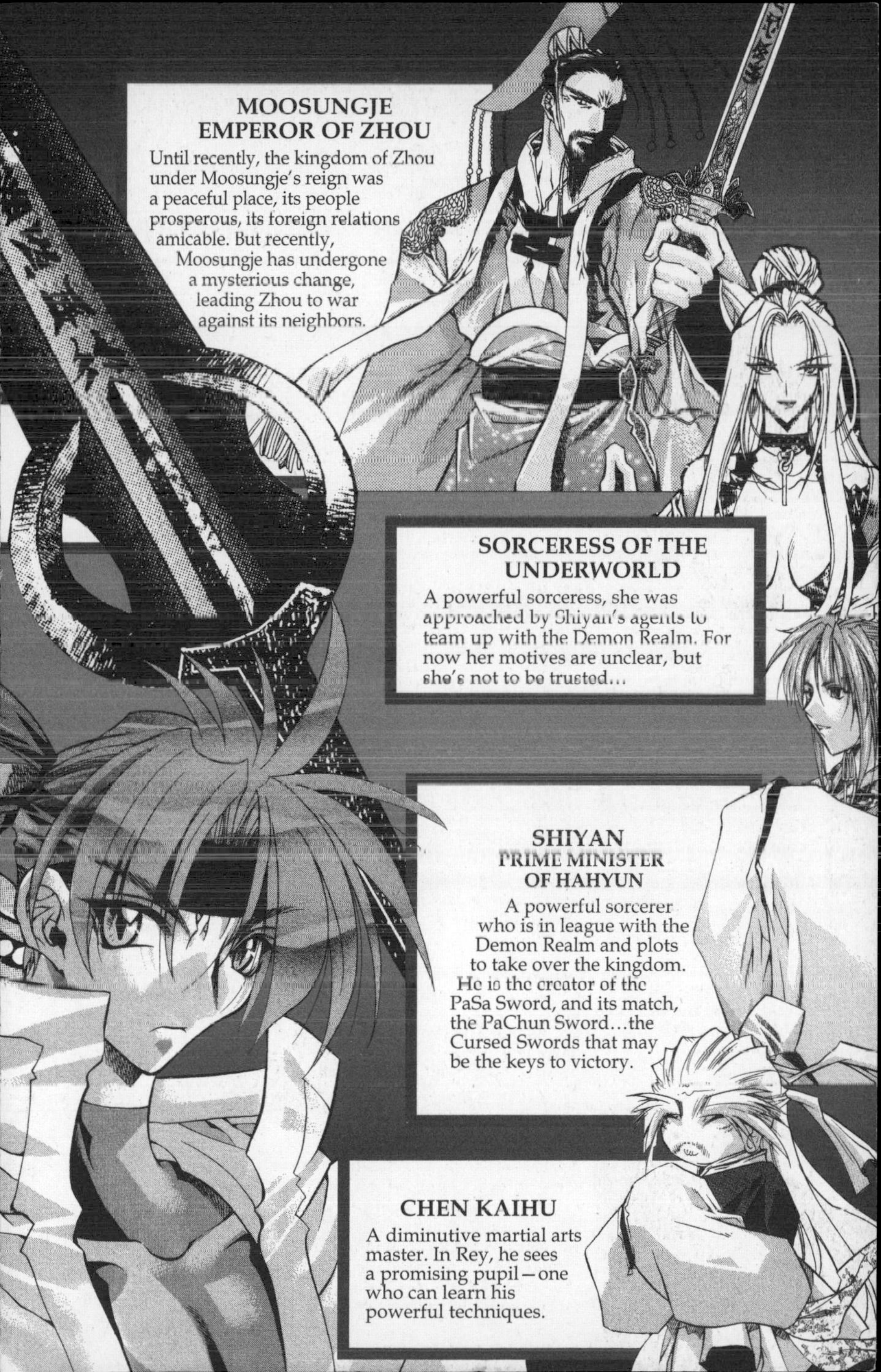
MOOSUNGJE
EMPEROR OF ZHOU
Until recently, the kingdom of Zhou under Moosungje's reign was a peaceful place, its people prosperous, its foreign relations amicable. But recently, Moosungje has undergone a mysterious change, leading Zhou to war against its neighbors.
SORCERESS OF THE UNDERWORLD
A powerful sorceress, she was approached by Shiyan's agents to team up with the Demon Realm. For now her motives are unclear, but she's not to be trusted...
SHIYAN
PRIME MINISTER OF HAHYUN
A powerful sorcerer who is in league with the Demon Realm and plots to take over the kingdom. He is the creator of the PaSa Sword, and its match, the PaChun Sword...the Cursed Swords that may be the keys to victory.
CHEN KAIHU
A diminutive martial arts master. In Rey, he sees a promising pupil—one who can learn his powerful techniques.

CHRONICLES OF THE CURSED SWORD

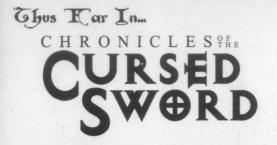

It is told that in eons past, the Emperor of the Heavenly Realm banished his only heir to the Demon Realm. This was the beginning of a centuries-long struggle between the Heavenly Realm and the Demon Emperor — an epic war that would shake the Earth and spill the blood of countless humans and demons alike.

Two mystical swords are the keys that keep the Demon Emperor at bay — the PaSa sword, which feeds upon the blood of slain demons, and its dark mate, the PaChun sword, which thirsts for human blood.

A young warrior, Rey Yan, has been possessed by the spirit of the PaSa sword, while the once-noble King Jaryoon has fallen under the influence of the PaChun. Pitted against each other by unseen forces and hunted by both enemies and former allies, the two unsuspecting pawns are now all that stand between the world of men and a hell on earth…

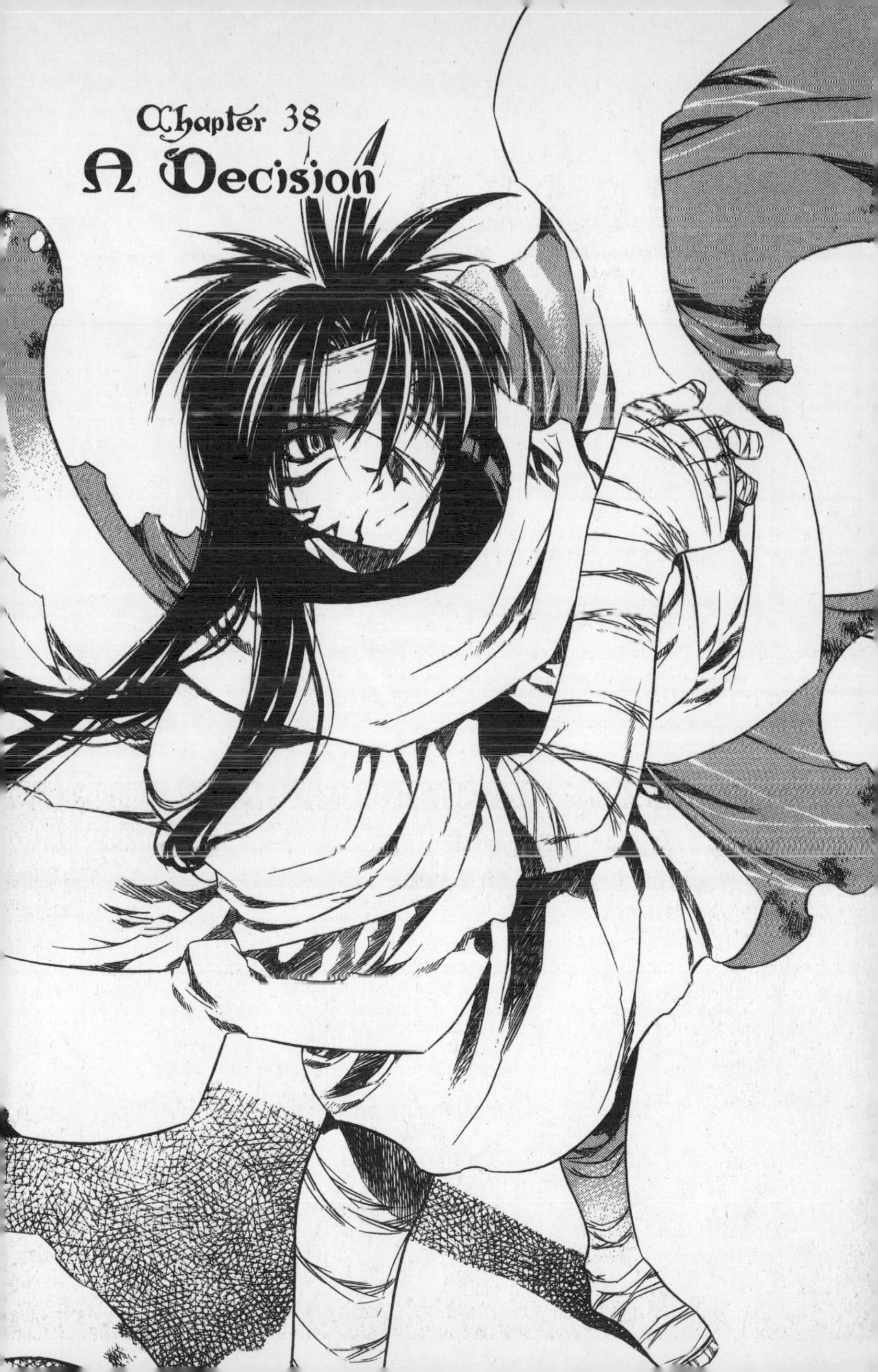
Chapter 38
A Decision

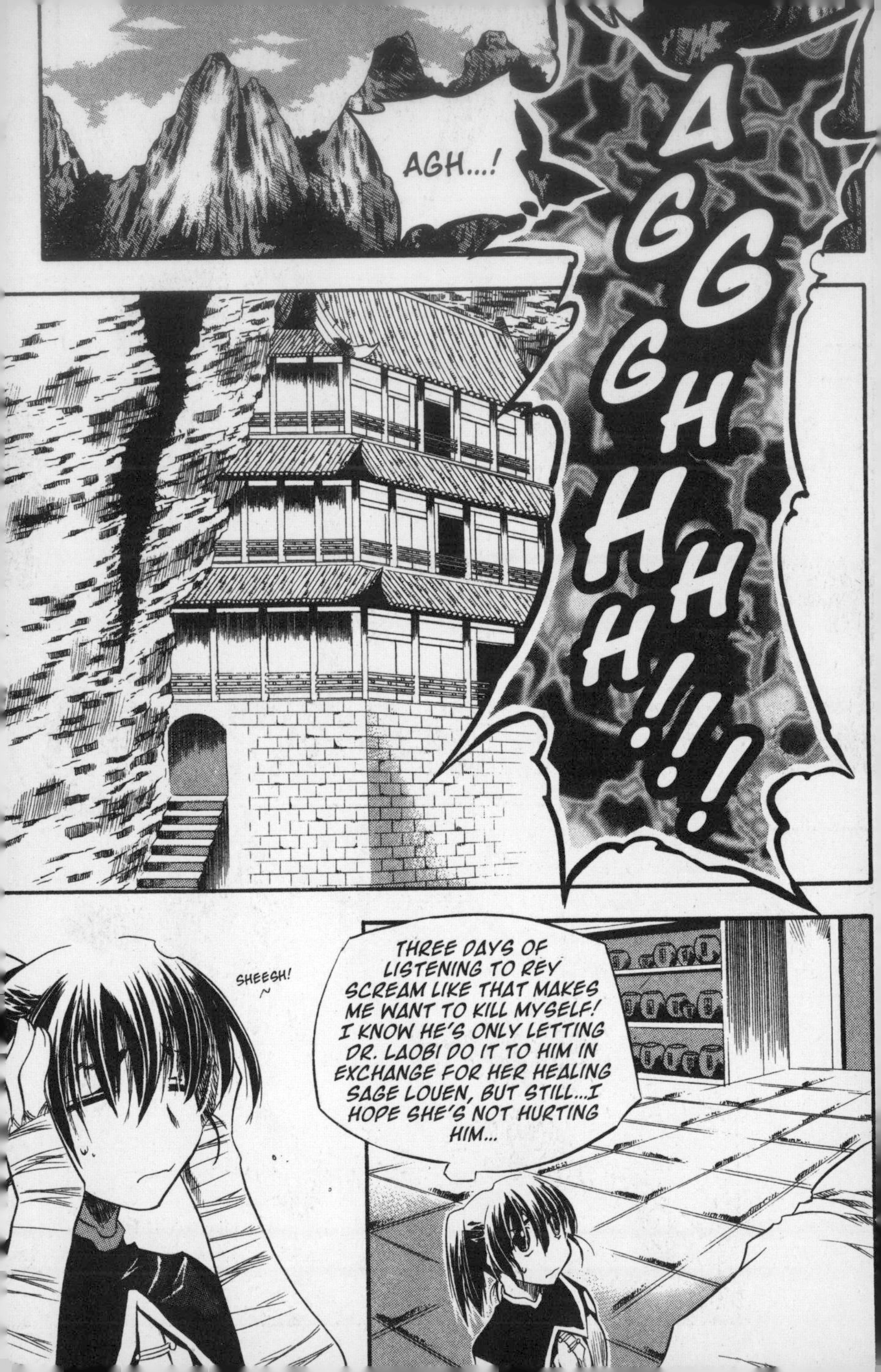
AGH...!
AGGGHHHHH!!!!
SHEESH!
THREE DAYS OF LISTENING TO REY SCREAM LIKE THAT MAKES ME WANT TO KILL MYSELF! I KNOW HE'S ONLY LETTING DR. LAOBI DO IT TO HIM IN EXCHANGE FOR HER HEALING SAGE LOUEN, BUT STILL...I HOPE SHE'S NOT HURTING HIM...

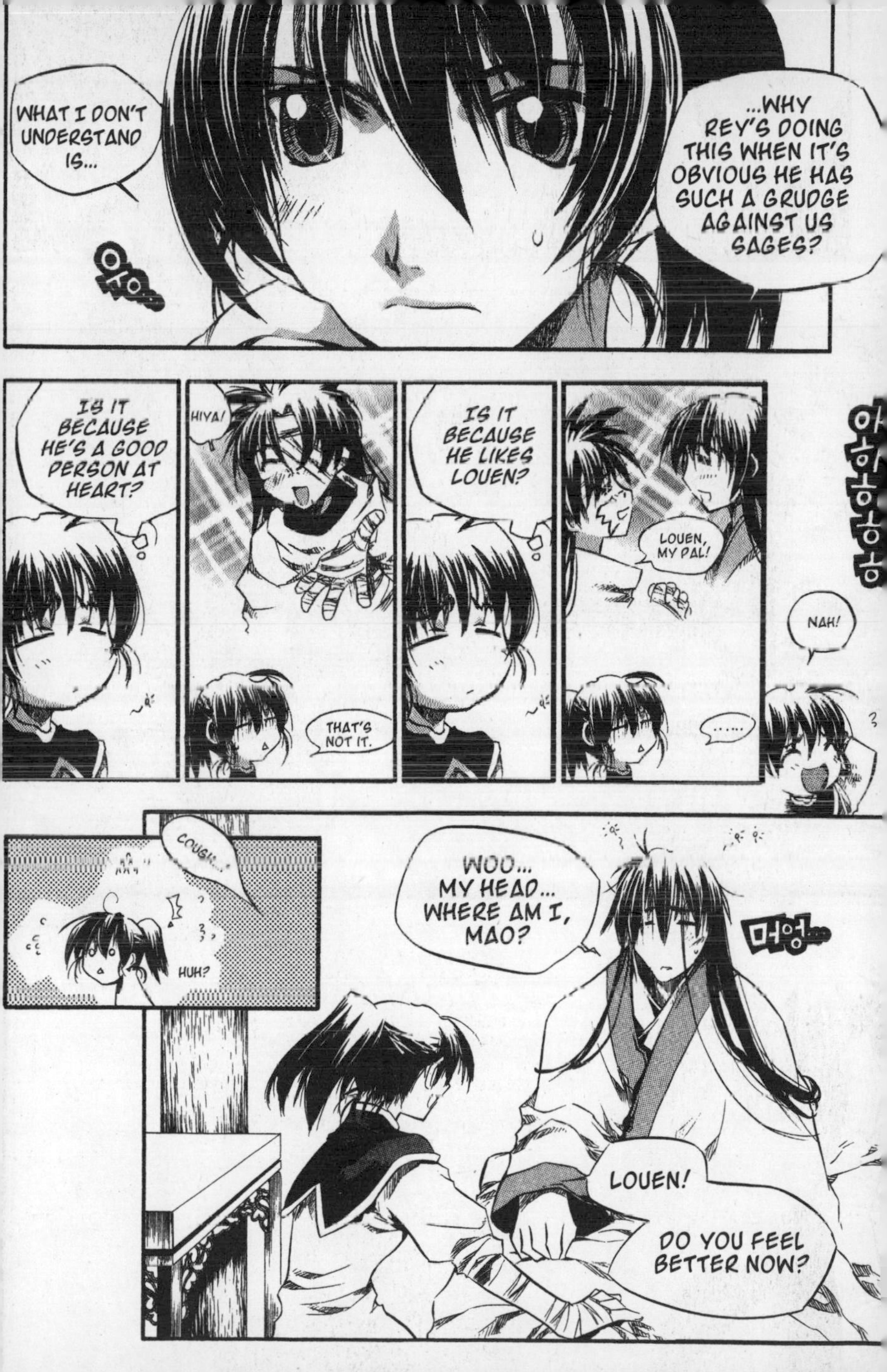

WHAT I DON'T UNDERSTAND IS...
오오...
...WHY REY'S DOING THIS WHEN IT'S OBVIOUS HE HAS SUCH A GRUDGE AGAINST US SAGES?
IS IT BECAUSE HE'S A GOOD PERSON AT HEART?
HIYA!
THAT'S NOT IT.
IS IT BECAUSE HE LIKES LOUEN?
LOUEN, MY PAL!
......
NAH!
아하하하하
COUGH...
HUH?
WOO... MY HEAD... WHERE AM I, MAO?
머엉...
LOUEN!
DO YOU FEEL BETTER NOW?

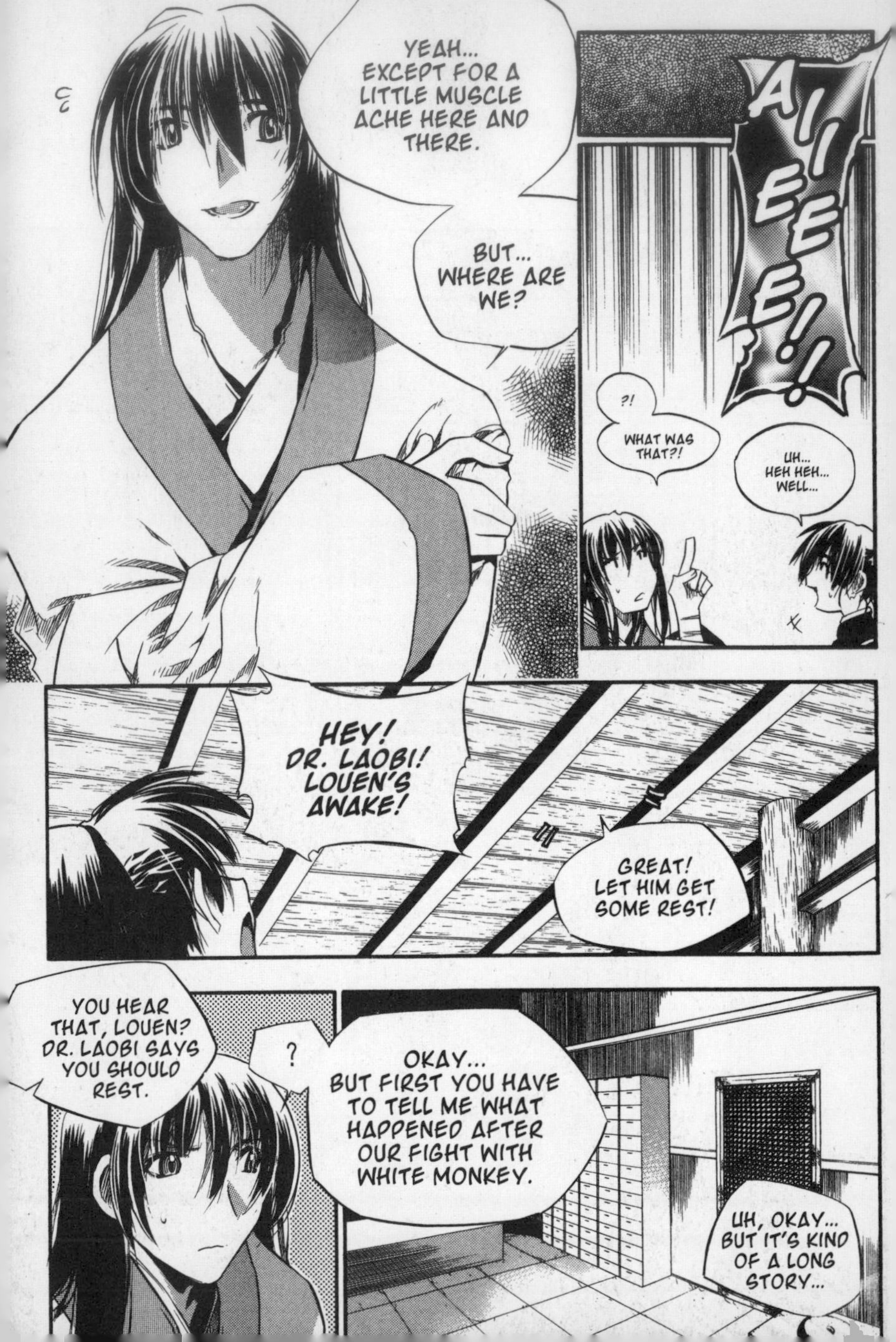
YEAH... EXCEPT FOR A LITTLE MUSCLE ACHE HERE AND THERE.
BUT... WHERE ARE WE?
AIIEEEE!!
?!
WHAT WAS THAT?!
UH... HEH HEH... WELL...
HEY! DR. LAOBI! LOUEN'S AWAKE!
GREAT! LET HIM GET SOME REST!
YOU HEAR THAT, LOUEN? DR. LAOBI SAYS YOU SHOULD REST.
?
OKAY... BUT FIRST YOU HAVE TO TELL ME WHAT HAPPENED AFTER OUR FIGHT WITH WHITE MONKEY.
UH, OKAY... BUT IT'S KIND OF A LONG STORY...

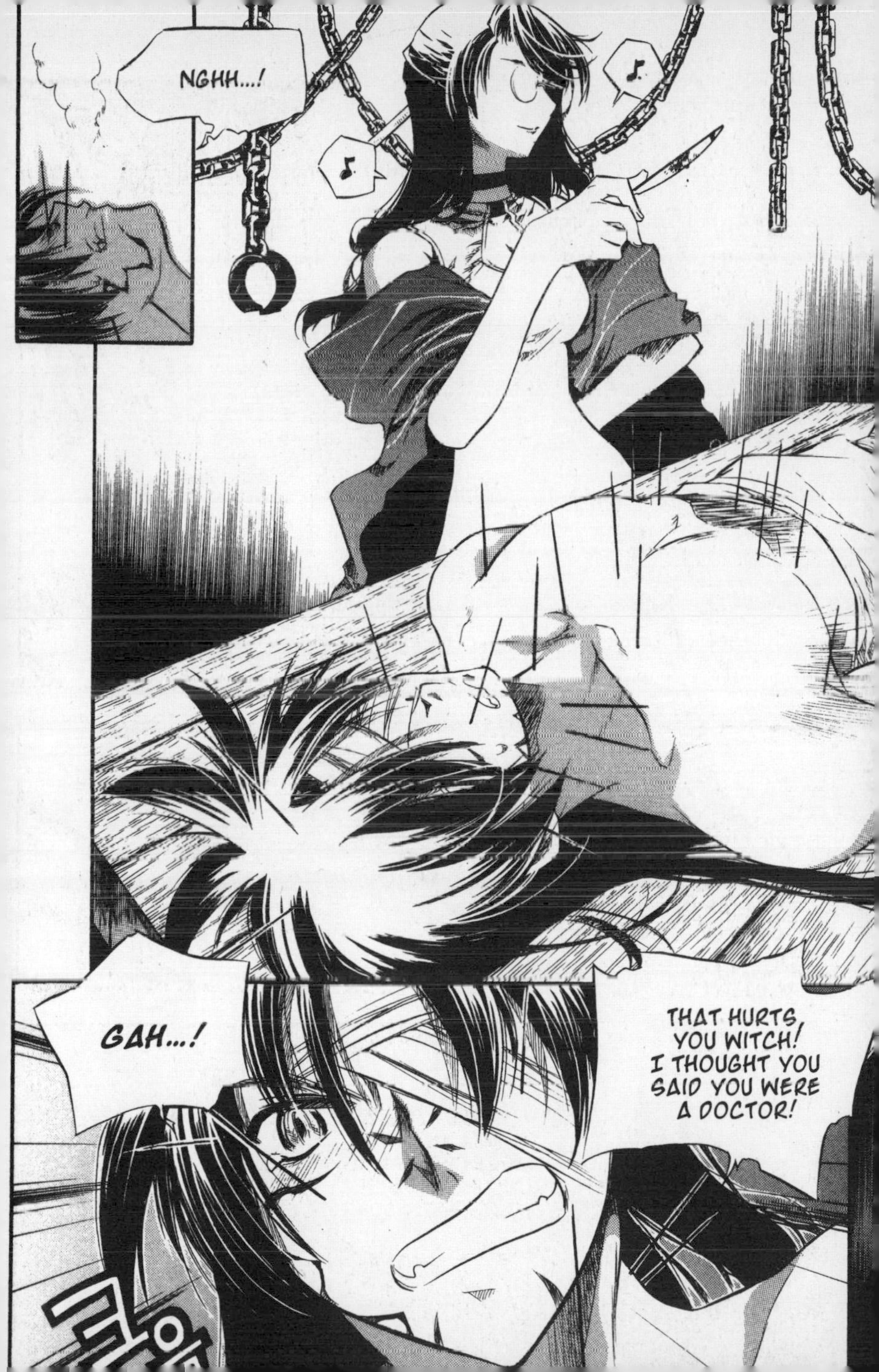
NGHH...!
♪
♪
GAH...!
THAT HURTS, YOU WITCH! I THOUGHT YOU SAID YOU WERE A DOCTOR!

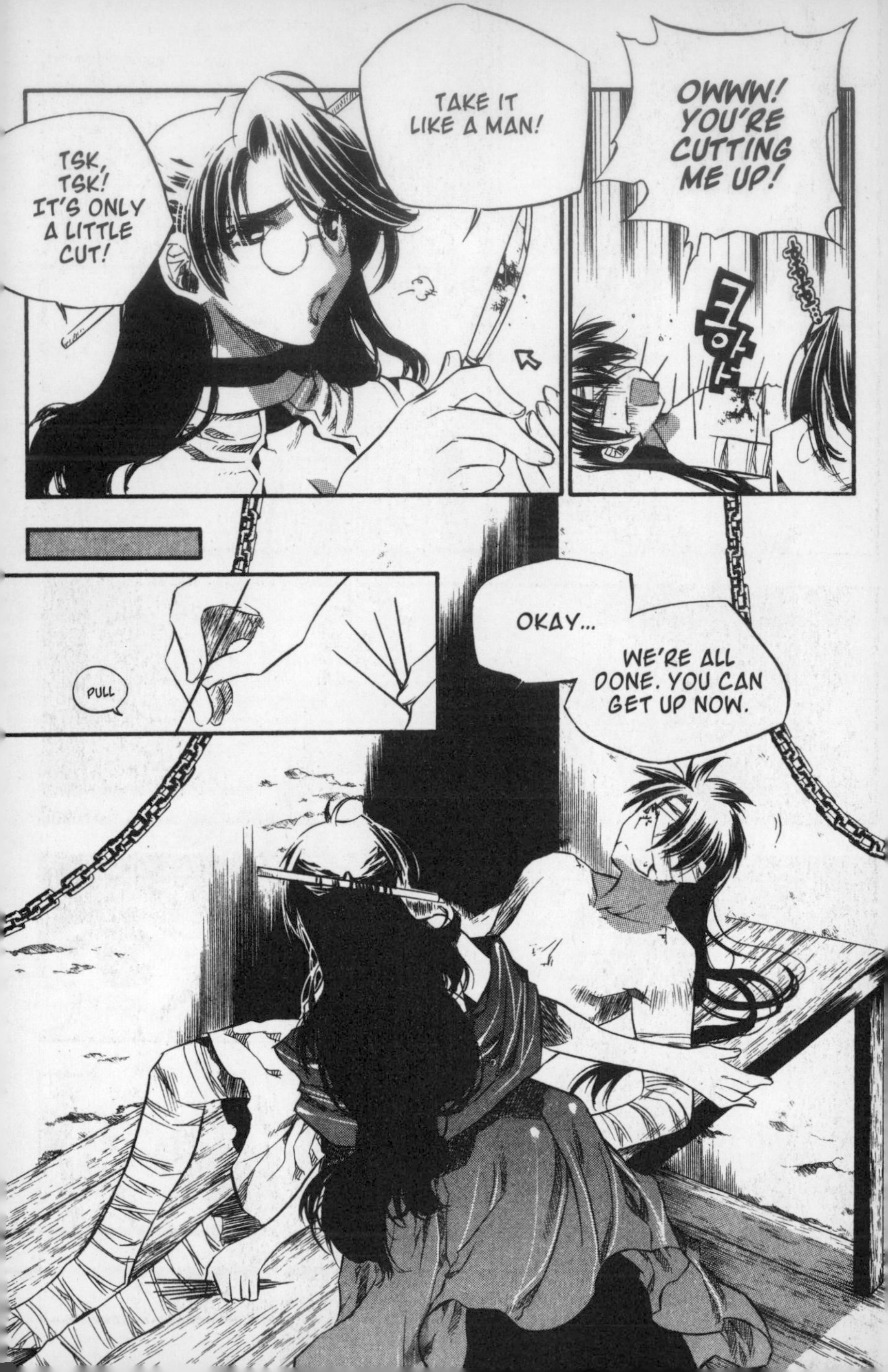
TSK, TSK! IT'S ONLY A LITTLE CUT!
TAKE IT LIKE A MAN!
OWWW! YOU'RE CUTTING ME UP!
PULL
OKAY...
WE'RE ALL DONE. YOU CAN GET UP NOW.

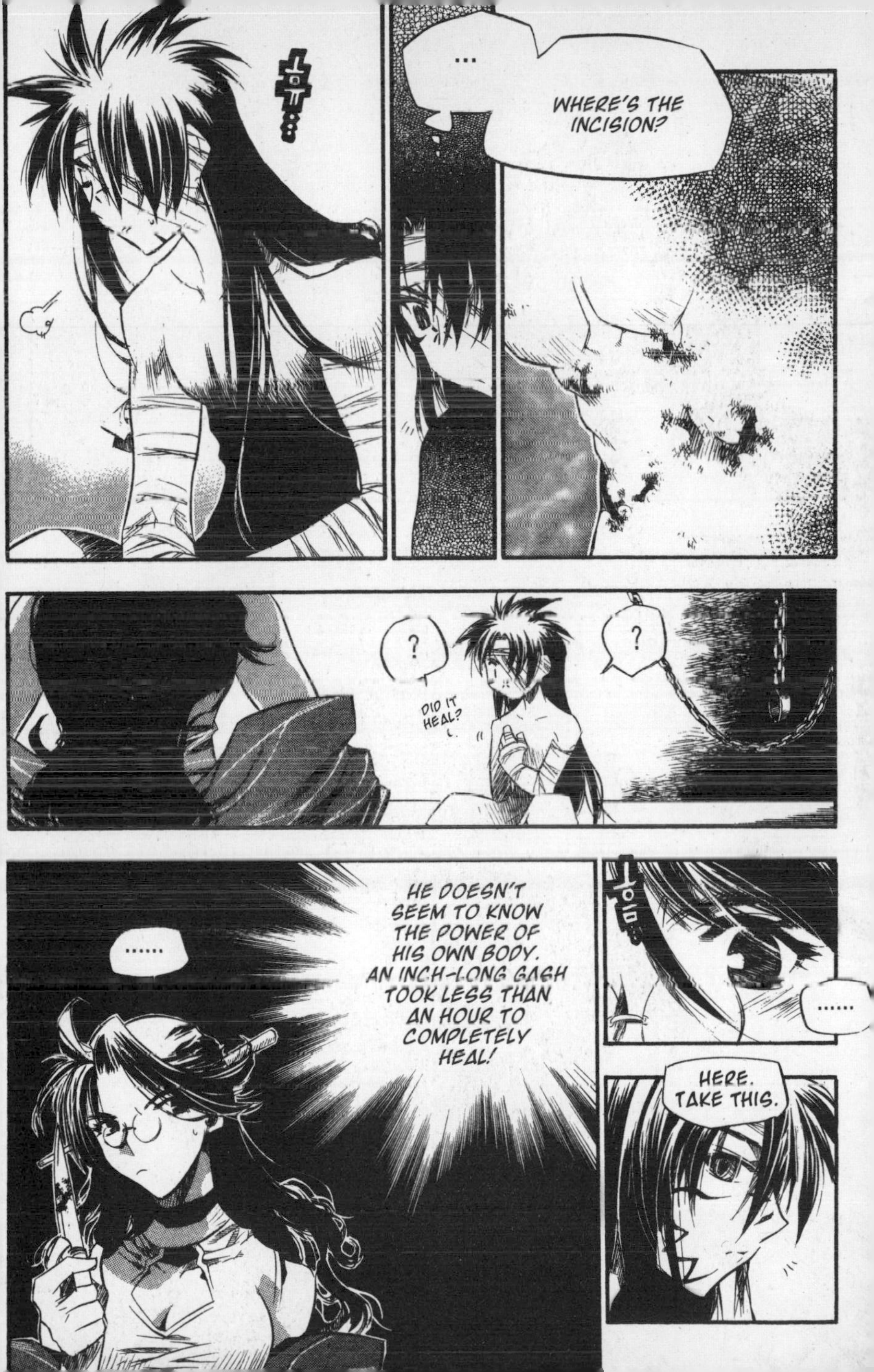
...
WHERE'S THE INCISION?
?
DID IT HEAL?
?
......
HE DOESN'T SEEM TO KNOW THE POWER OF HIS OWN BODY. AN INCH-LONG GASH TOOK LESS THAN AN HOUR TO COMPLETELY HEAL!
......
HERE. TAKE THIS.

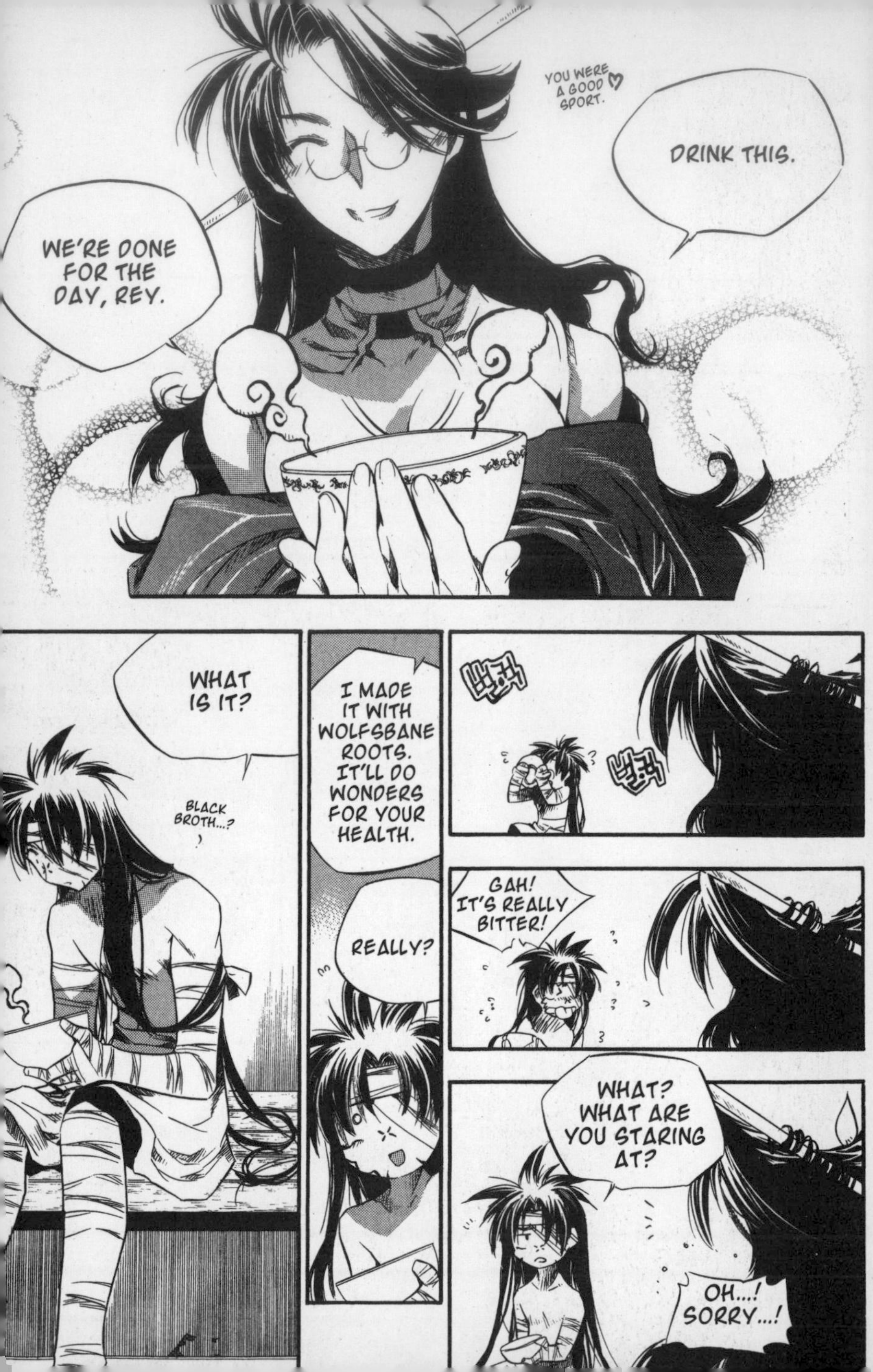
WE'RE DONE FOR THE DAY, REY.
YOU WERE A GOOD SPORT.
DRINK THIS.
WHAT IS IT?
BLACK BROTH...?
I MADE IT WITH WOLFSBANE ROOTS. IT'LL DO WONDERS FOR YOUR HEALTH.
REALLY?
GAH! IT'S REALLY BITTER!
WHAT? WHAT ARE YOU STARING AT?
OH...! SORRY...!

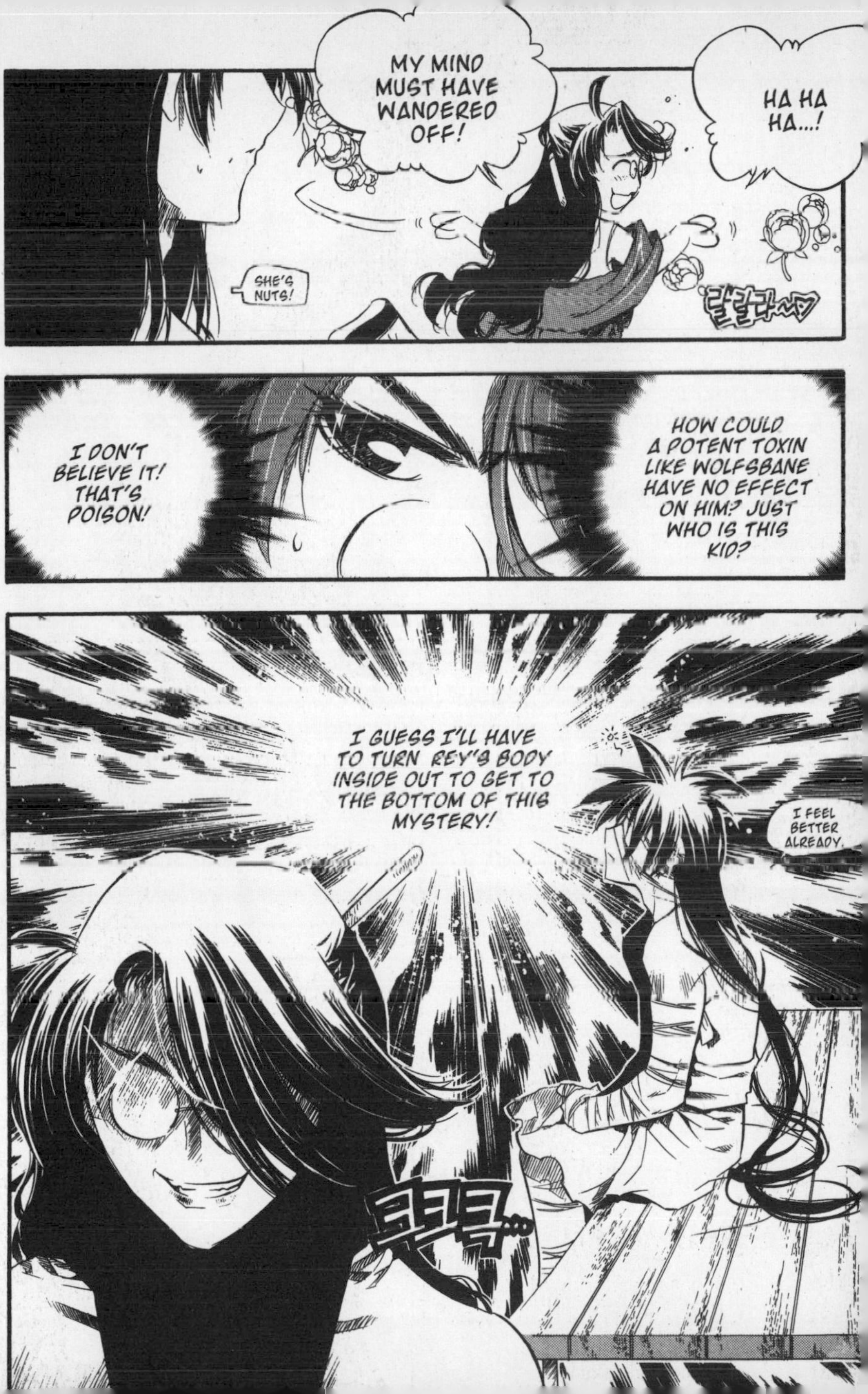
MY MIND MUST HAVE WANDERED OFF!
HA HA HA...!
SHE'S NUTS!
랄랄라~♡
I DON'T BELIEVE IT! THAT'S POISON!
HOW COULD A POTENT TOXIN LIKE WOLFSBANE HAVE NO EFFECT ON HIM? JUST WHO IS THIS KID?
I GUESS I'LL HAVE TO TURN REY'S BODY INSIDE OUT TO GET TO THE BOTTOM OF THIS MYSTERY!
I FEEL BETTER ALREADY.

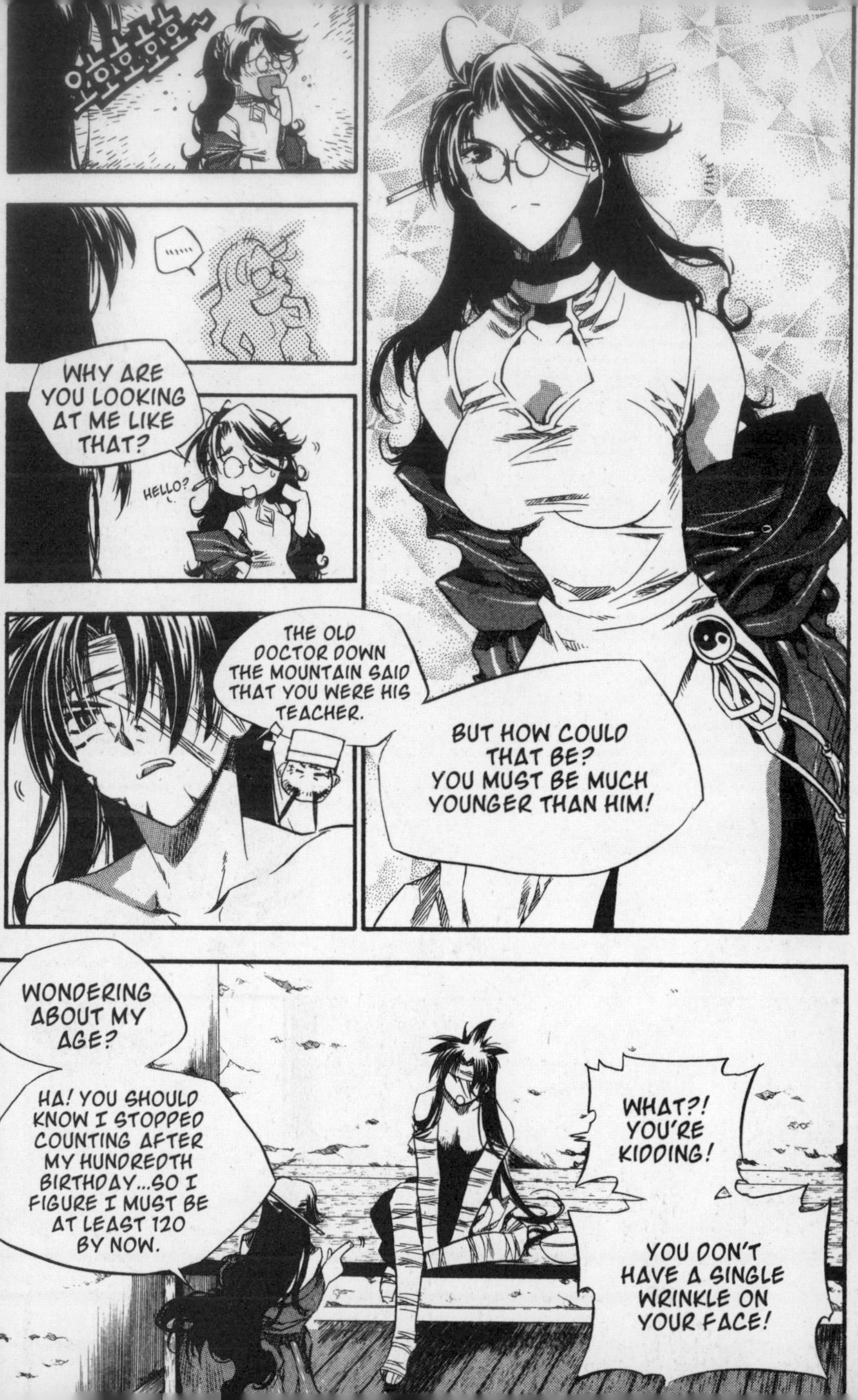
......
WHY ARE YOU LOOKING AT ME LIKE THAT?
HELLO?
THE OLD DOCTOR DOWN THE MOUNTAIN SAID THAT YOU WERE HIS TEACHER.
BUT HOW COULD THAT BE? YOU MUST BE MUCH YOUNGER THAN HIM!
WONDERING ABOUT MY AGE?
HA! YOU SHOULD KNOW I STOPPED COUNTING AFTER MY HUNDREDTH BIRTHDAY...SO I FIGURE I MUST BE AT LEAST 120 BY NOW.
WHAT?! YOU'RE KIDDING!
YOU DON'T HAVE A SINGLE WRINKLE ON YOUR FACE!

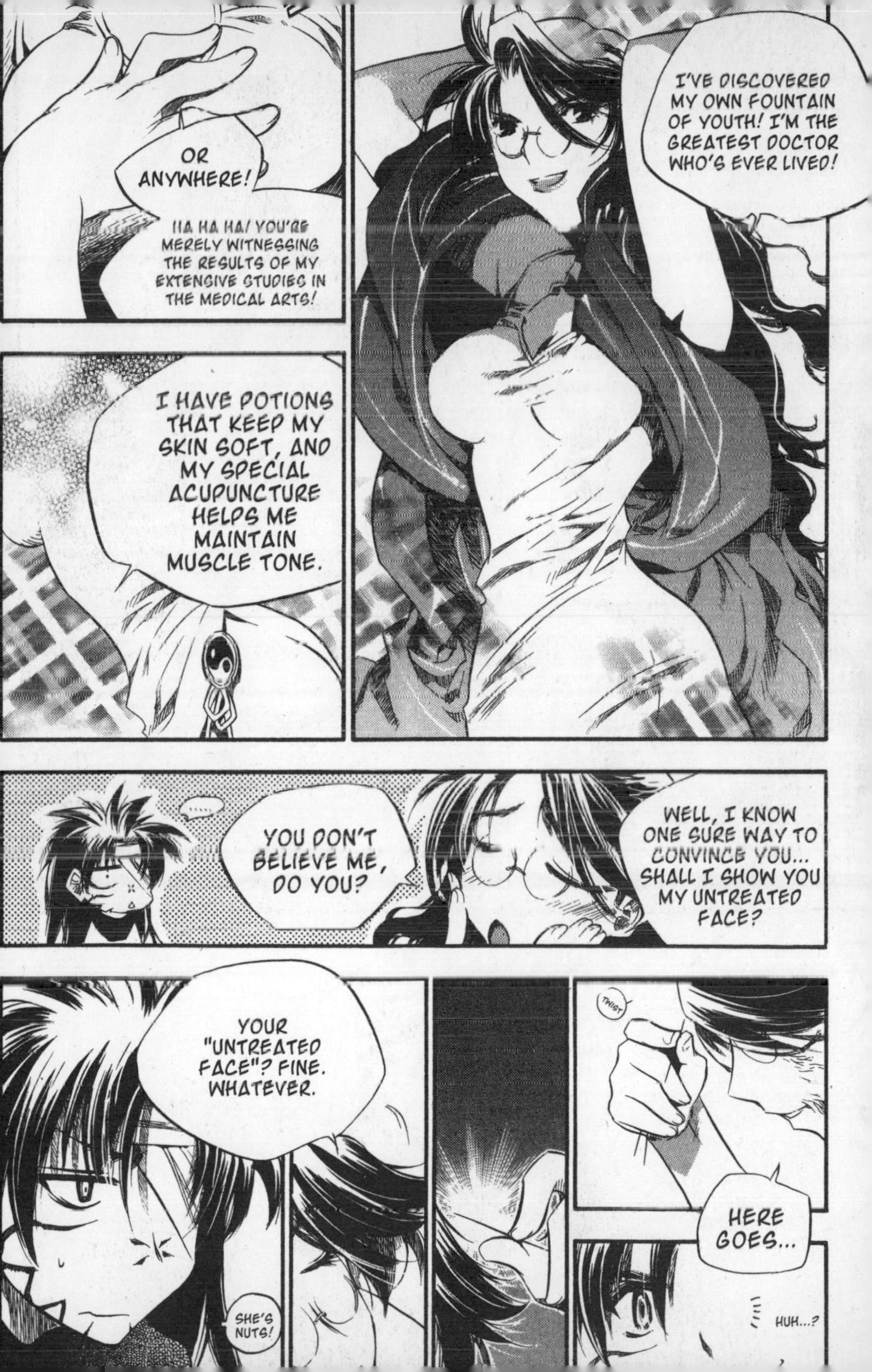
OR ANYWHERE!
HA HA HA! YOU'RE MERELY WITNESSING THE RESULTS OF MY EXTENSIVE STUDIES IN THE MEDICAL ARTS!
I HAVE POTIONS THAT KEEP MY SKIN SOFT, AND MY SPECIAL ACUPUNCTURE HELPS ME MAINTAIN MUSCLE TONE.
I'VE DISCOVERED MY OWN FOUNTAIN OF YOUTH! I'M THE GREATEST DOCTOR WHO'S EVER LIVED!
......
YOU DON'T BELIEVE ME, DO YOU?
WELL, I KNOW ONE SURE WAY TO CONVINCE YOU... SHALL I SHOW YOU MY UNTREATED FACE?
YOUR "UNTREATED FACE"? FINE. WHATEVER.
SHE'S NUTS!
TWIST
HERE GOES...
HUH...?

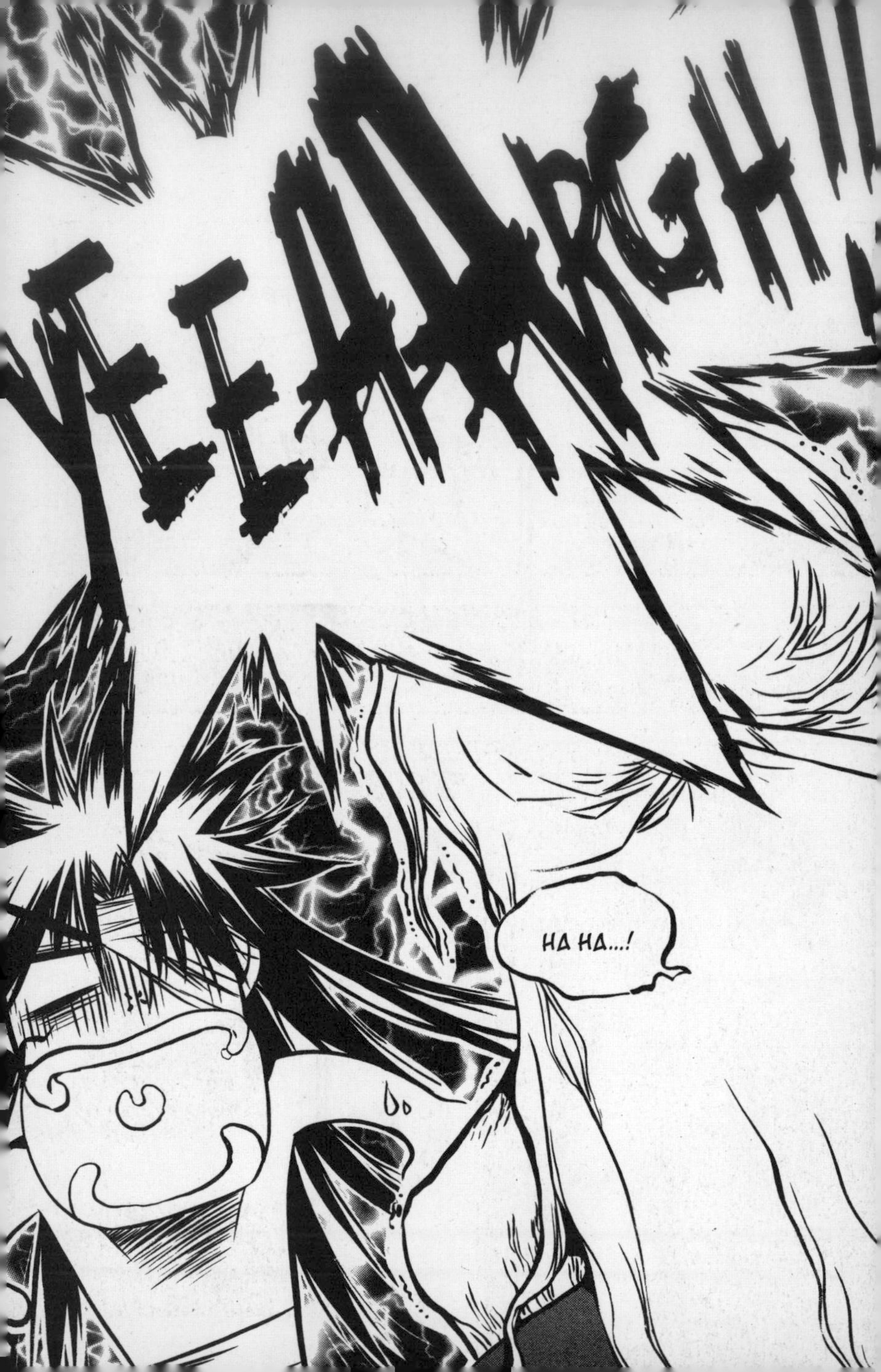
YEEAAARGH!!!
HA HA...!

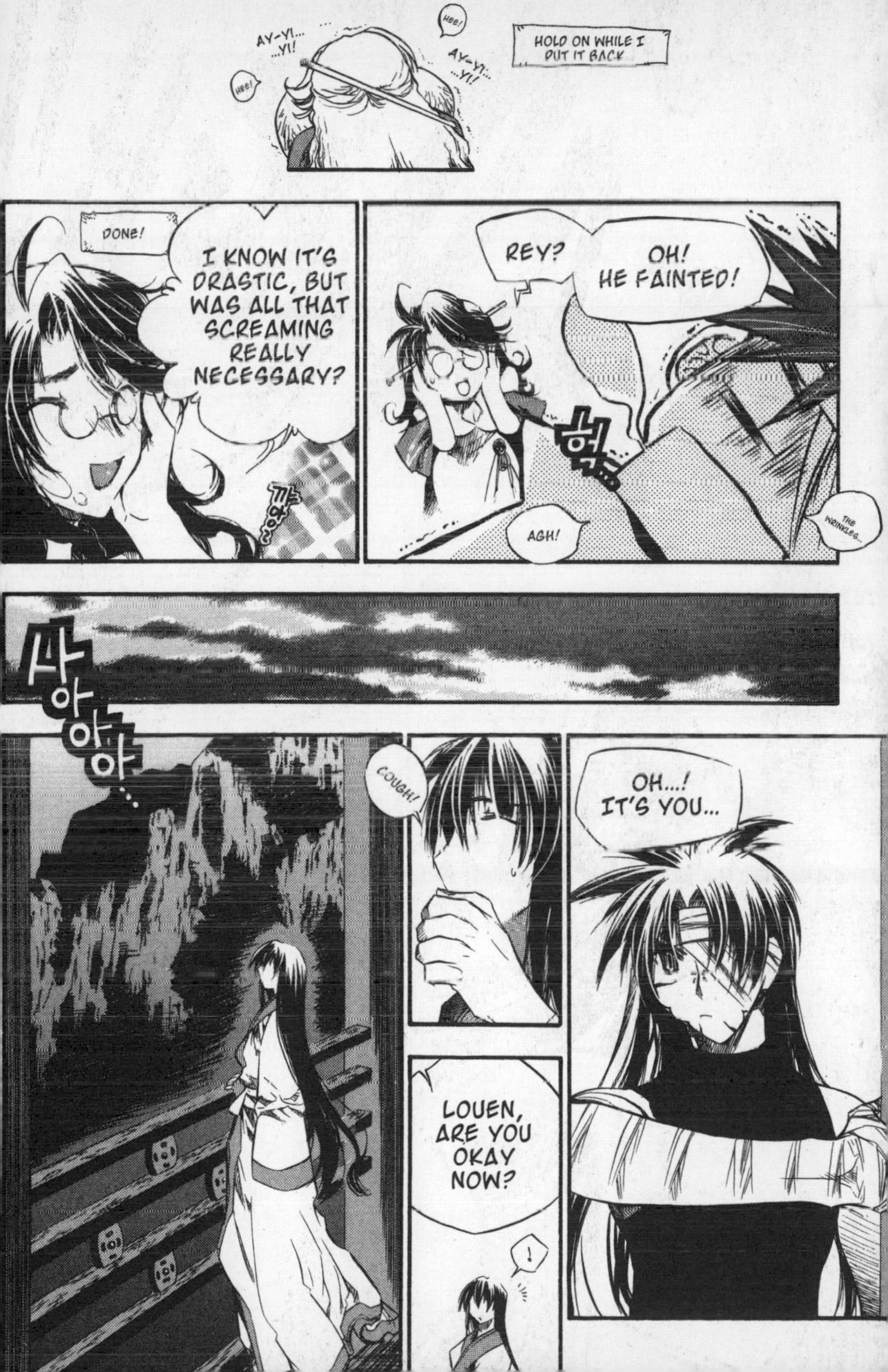
AY-YI...
...YI!
HEE!
HEE!
AY-YI...
...YI!
HOLD ON WHILE I PUT IT BACK
DONE!
I KNOW IT'S DRASTIC, BUT WAS ALL THAT SCREAMING REALLY NECESSARY?
REY?
OH! HE FAINTED!
헉...
AGH!
THE WRINKLES...
사아아아...
COUGH!
OH...! IT'S YOU...
LOUEN, ARE YOU OKAY NOW?
!

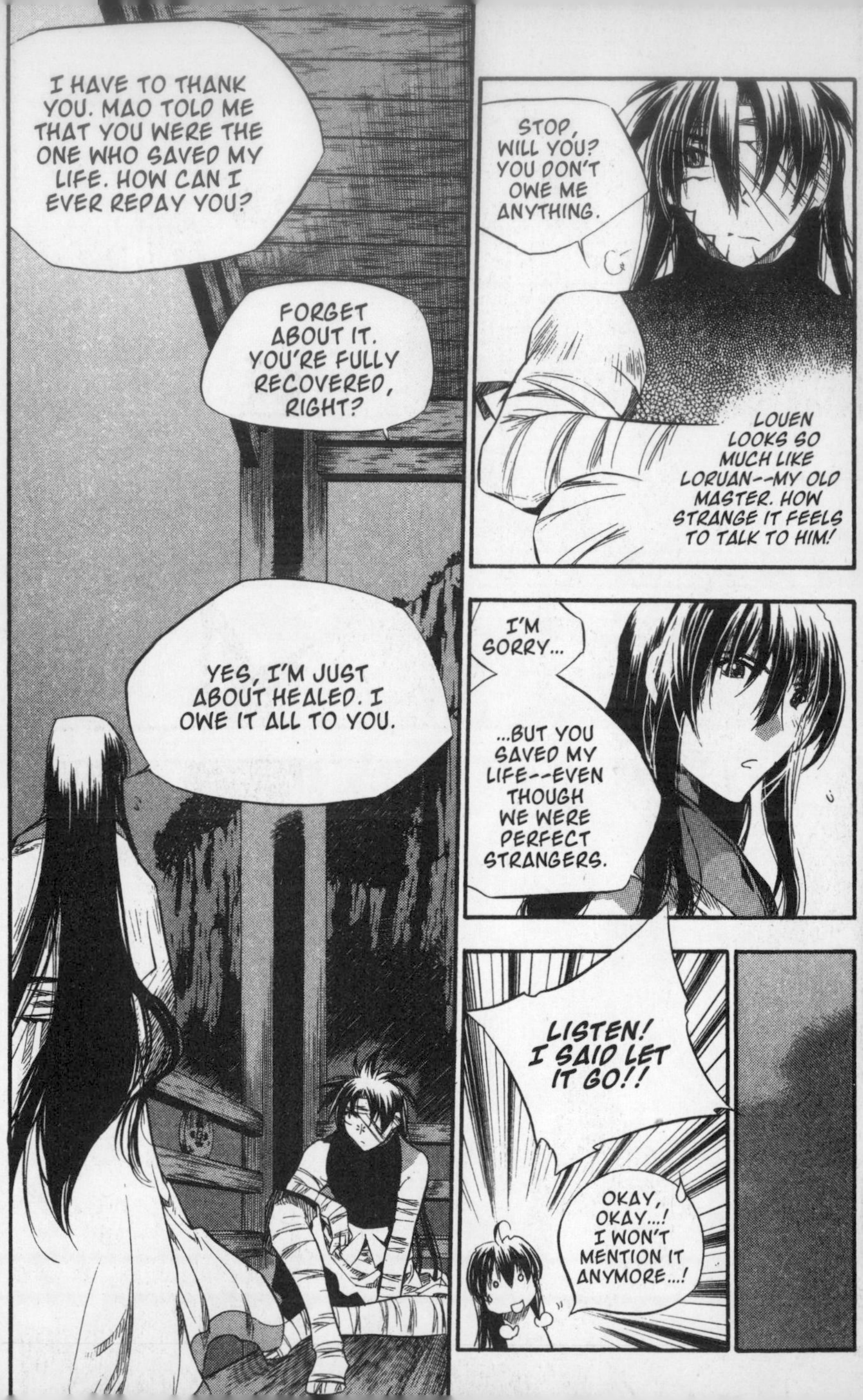

I HAVE TO THANK YOU. MAO TOLD ME THAT YOU WERE THE ONE WHO SAVED MY LIFE. HOW CAN I EVER REPAY YOU?
FORGET ABOUT IT. YOU'RE FULLY RECOVERED, RIGHT?
YES, I'M JUST ABOUT HEALED. I OWE IT ALL TO YOU.
STOP, WILL YOU? YOU DON'T OWE ME ANYTHING.
LOUEN LOOKS SO MUCH LIKE LORUAN--MY OLD MASTER. HOW STRANGE IT FEELS TO TALK TO HIM!
I'M SORRY...
...BUT YOU SAVED MY LIFE--EVEN THOUGH WE WERE PERFECT STRANGERS.
LISTEN! I SAID LET IT GO!!
OKAY, OKAY...! I WON'T MENTION IT ANYMORE...!

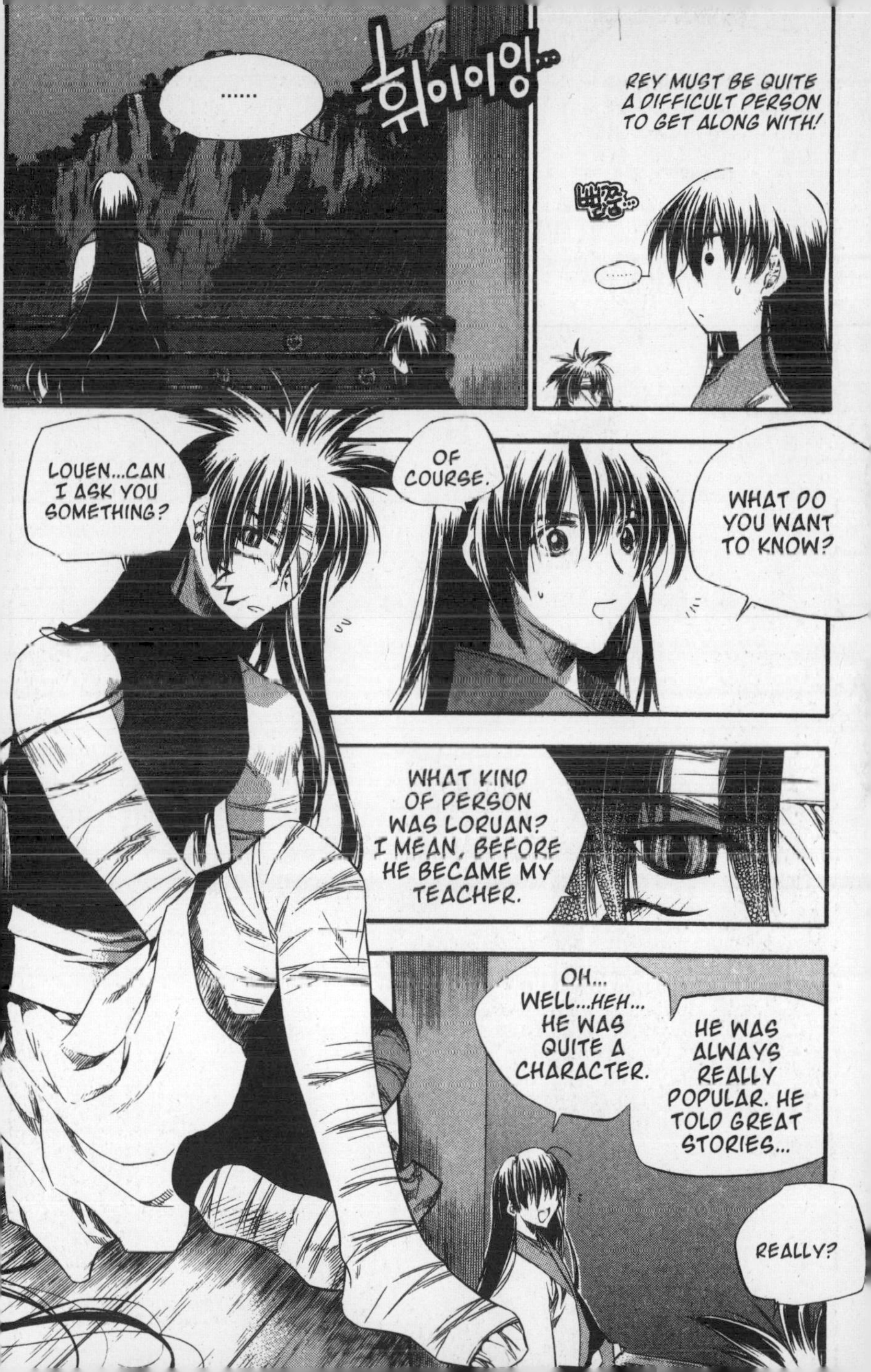
......
휘이이잉...
REY MUST BE QUITE A DIFFICULT PERSON TO GET ALONG WITH!
뻘쭘...
......
LOUEN...CAN I ASK YOU SOMETHING?
OF COURSE.
WHAT DO YOU WANT TO KNOW?
WHAT KIND OF PERSON WAS LORUAN? I MEAN, BEFORE HE BECAME MY TEACHER.
OH... WELL...HEH... HE WAS QUITE A CHARACTER.
HE WAS ALWAYS REALLY POPULAR. HE TOLD GREAT STORIES...
REALLY?

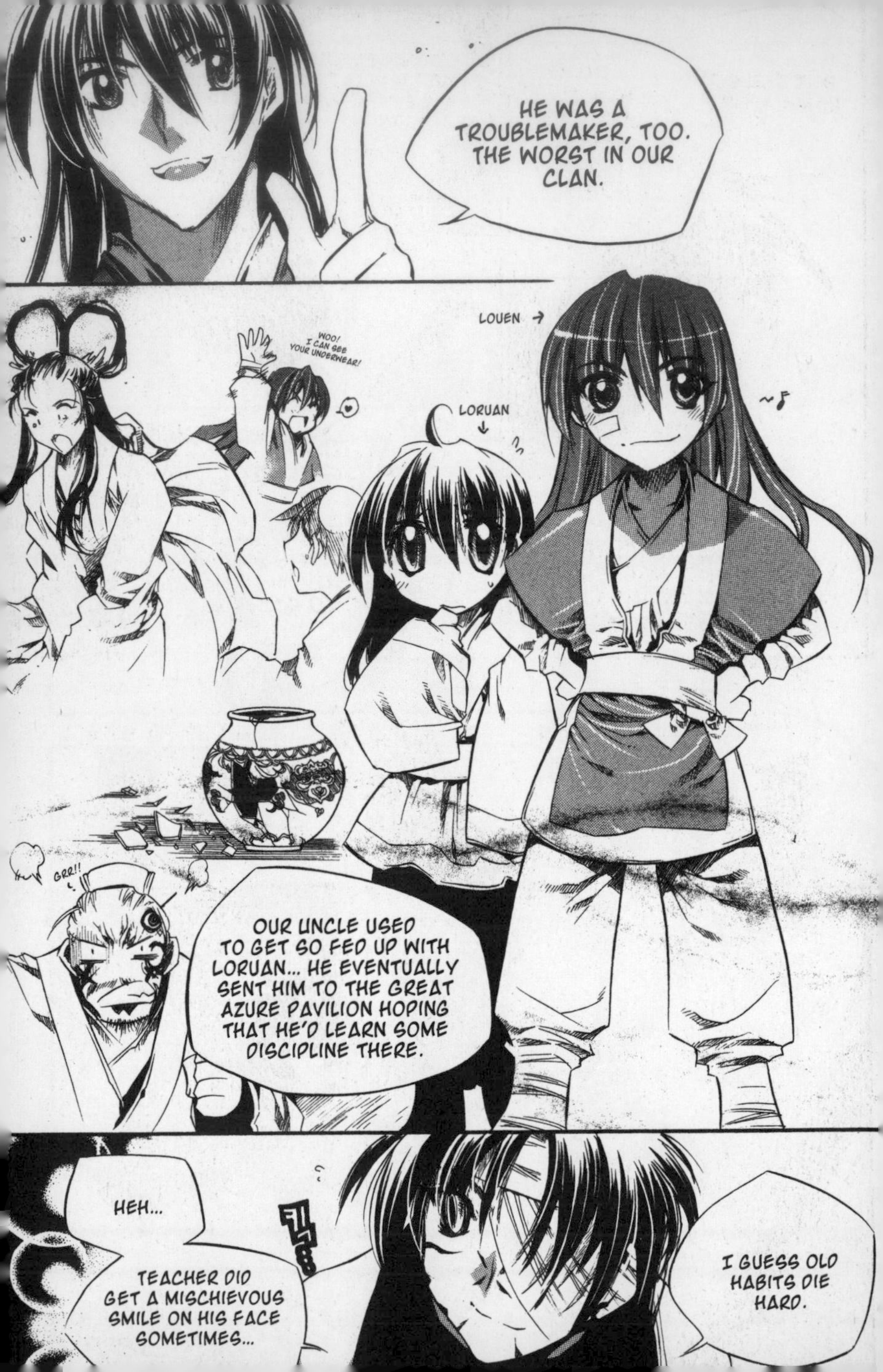
HE WAS A TROUBLEMAKER, TOO. THE WORST IN OUR CLAN.
WOO! I CAN SEE YOUR UNDERWEAR!
LOUEN →
LORUAN ↓
GRR!!
OUR UNCLE USED TO GET SO FED UP WITH LORUAN... HE EVENTUALLY SENT HIM TO THE GREAT AZURE PAVILION HOPING THAT HE'D LEARN SOME DISCIPLINE THERE.
HEH...
TEACHER DID GET A MISCHIEVOUS SMILE ON HIS FACE SOMETIMES...
I GUESS OLD HABITS DIE HARD.

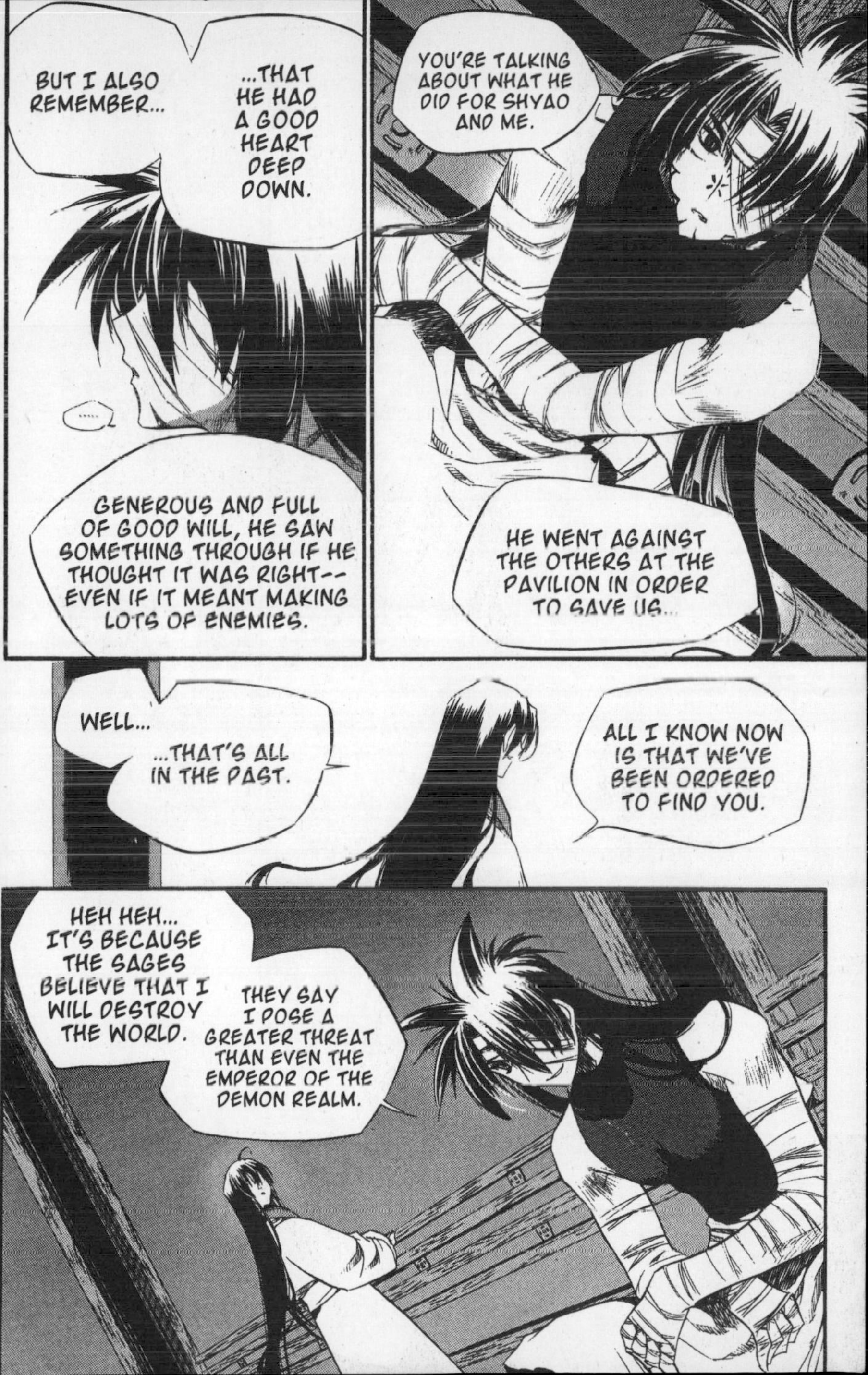
BUT I ALSO REMEMBER...
...THAT HE HAD A GOOD HEART DEEP DOWN.
......
GENEROUS AND FULL OF GOOD WILL, HE SAW SOMETHING THROUGH IF HE THOUGHT IT WAS RIGHT-- EVEN IF IT MEANT MAKING LOTS OF ENEMIES.
YOU'RE TALKING ABOUT WHAT HE DID FOR SHYAO AND ME.
HE WENT AGAINST THE OTHERS AT THE PAVILION IN ORDER TO SAVE US...
WELL...
...THAT'S ALL IN THE PAST.
ALL I KNOW NOW IS THAT WE'VE BEEN ORDERED TO FIND YOU.
HEH HEH... IT'S BECAUSE THE SAGES BELIEVE THAT I WILL DESTROY THE WORLD.
THEY SAY I POSE A GREATER THREAT THAN EVEN THE EMPEROR OF THE DEMON REALM.

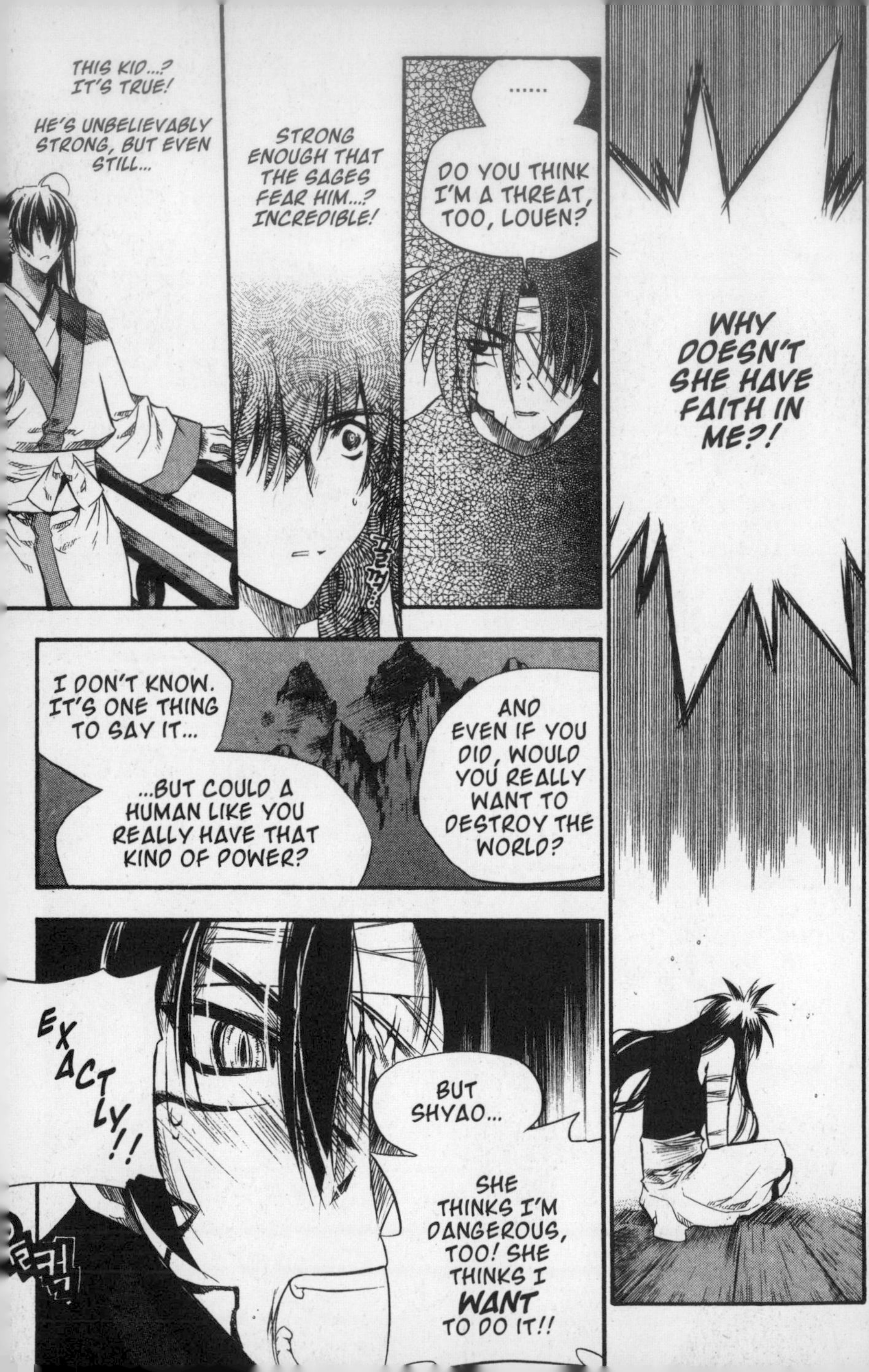
THIS KID...? IT'S TRUE!
HE'S UNBELIEVABLY STRONG, BUT EVEN STILL...
STRONG ENOUGH THAT THE SAGES FEAR HIM...? INCREDIBLE!
......
DO YOU THINK I'M A THREAT, TOO, LOUEN?
I DON'T KNOW. IT'S ONE THING TO SAY IT...
...BUT COULD A HUMAN LIKE YOU REALLY HAVE THAT KIND OF POWER?
AND EVEN IF YOU DID, WOULD YOU REALLY WANT TO DESTROY THE WORLD?
EXACTLY!!
BUT SHYAO...
SHE THINKS I'M DANGEROUS, TOO! SHE THINKS I WANT TO DO IT!!
WHY DOESN'T SHE HAVE FAITH IN ME?!

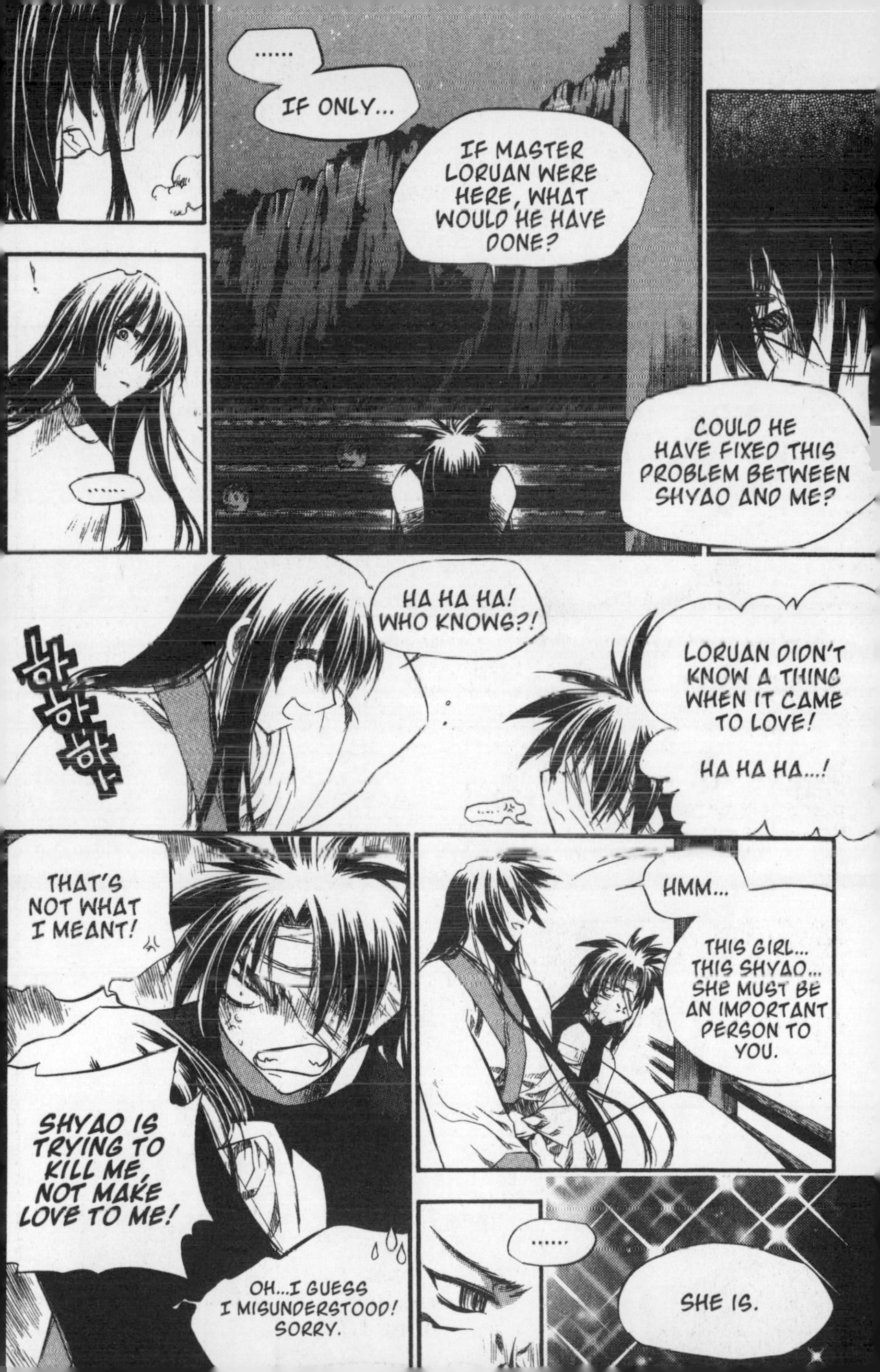
!
......
......
IF ONLY...
IF MASTER LORUAN WERE HERE, WHAT WOULD HE HAVE DONE?
COULD HE HAVE FIXED THIS PROBLEM BETWEEN SHYAO AND ME?
하하하
HA HA HA! WHO KNOWS?!
LORUAN DIDN'T KNOW A THING WHEN IT CAME TO LOVE!
HA HA HA...!
.....
THAT'S NOT WHAT I MEANT!
SHYAO IS TRYING TO KILL ME, NOT MAKE LOVE TO ME!
OH...I GUESS I MISUNDERSTOOD! SORRY.
HMM...
THIS GIRL... THIS SHYAO... SHE MUST BE AN IMPORTANT PERSON TO YOU.
......
SHE IS.

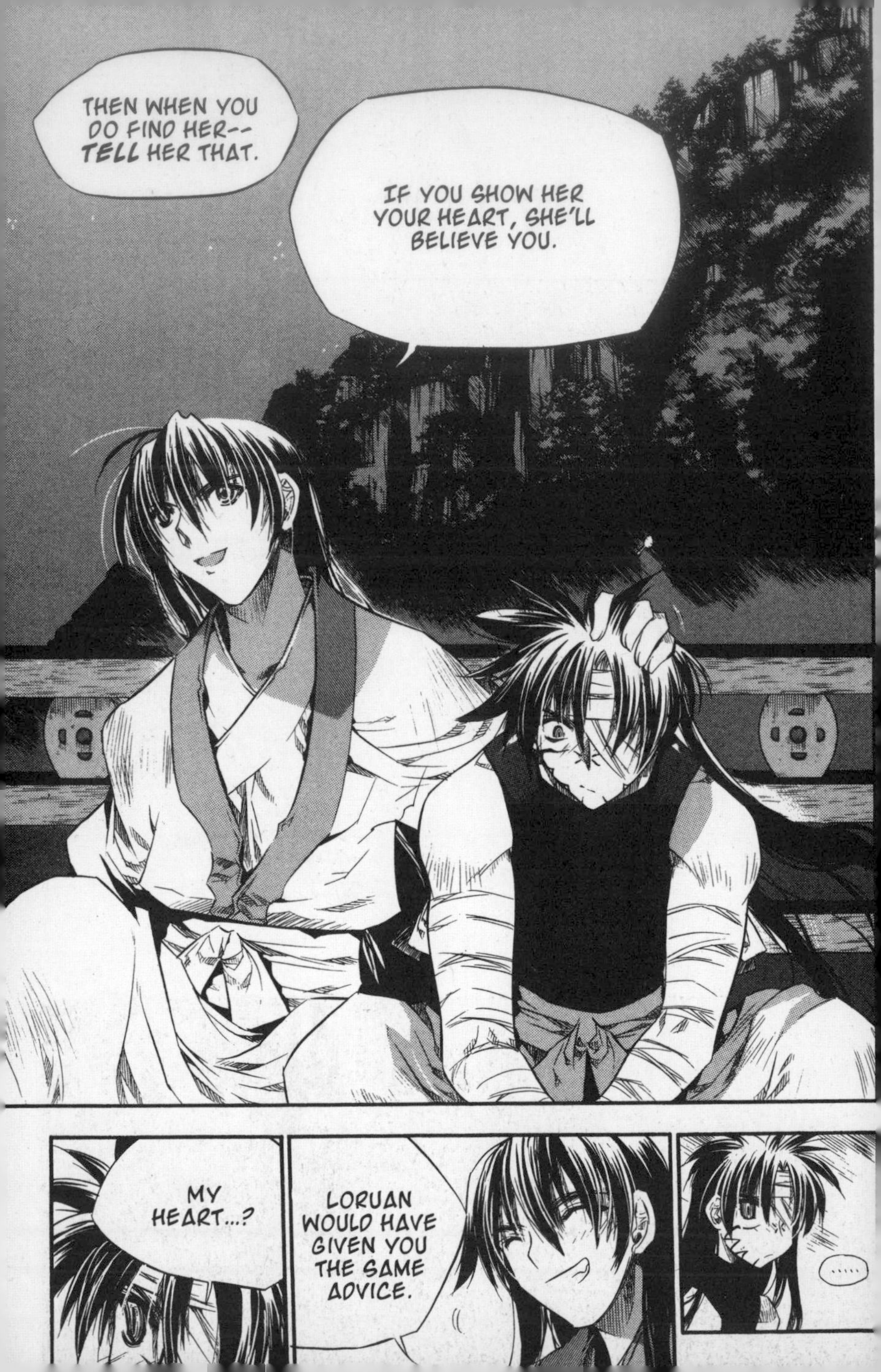
THEN WHEN YOU DO FIND HER-- TELL HER THAT.
IF YOU SHOW HER YOUR HEART, SHE'LL BELIEVE YOU.
MY HEART...?
LORUAN WOULD HAVE GIVEN YOU THE SAME ADVICE.
.....

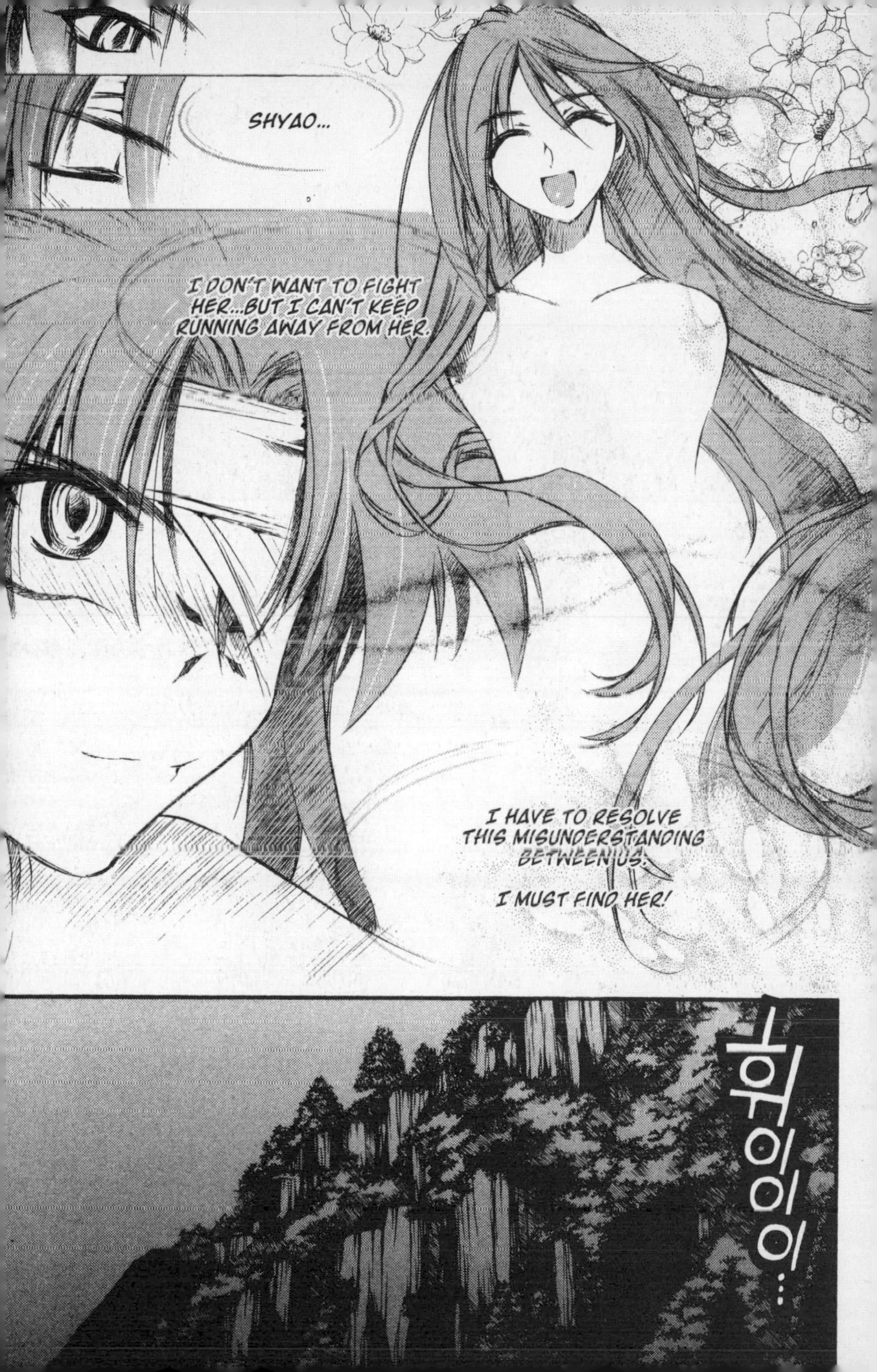
SHYAO...
I DON'T WANT TO FIGHT HER...BUT I CAN'T KEEP RUNNING AWAY FROM HER.
I HAVE TO RESOLVE THIS MISUNDERSTANDING BETWEEN US.
I MUST FIND HER!
훠이이이...

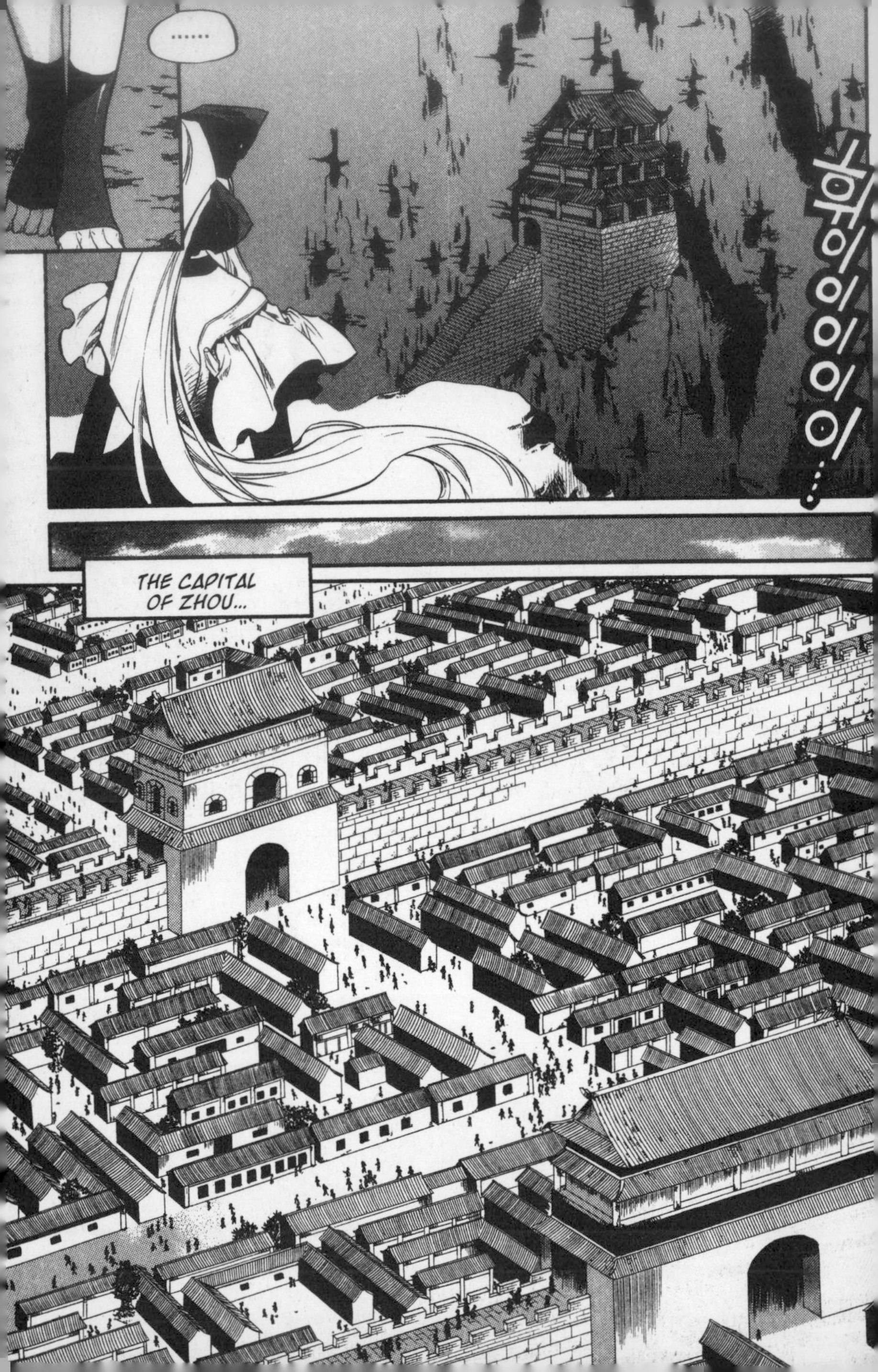
......
화아아아아아...
THE CAPITAL OF ZHOU...

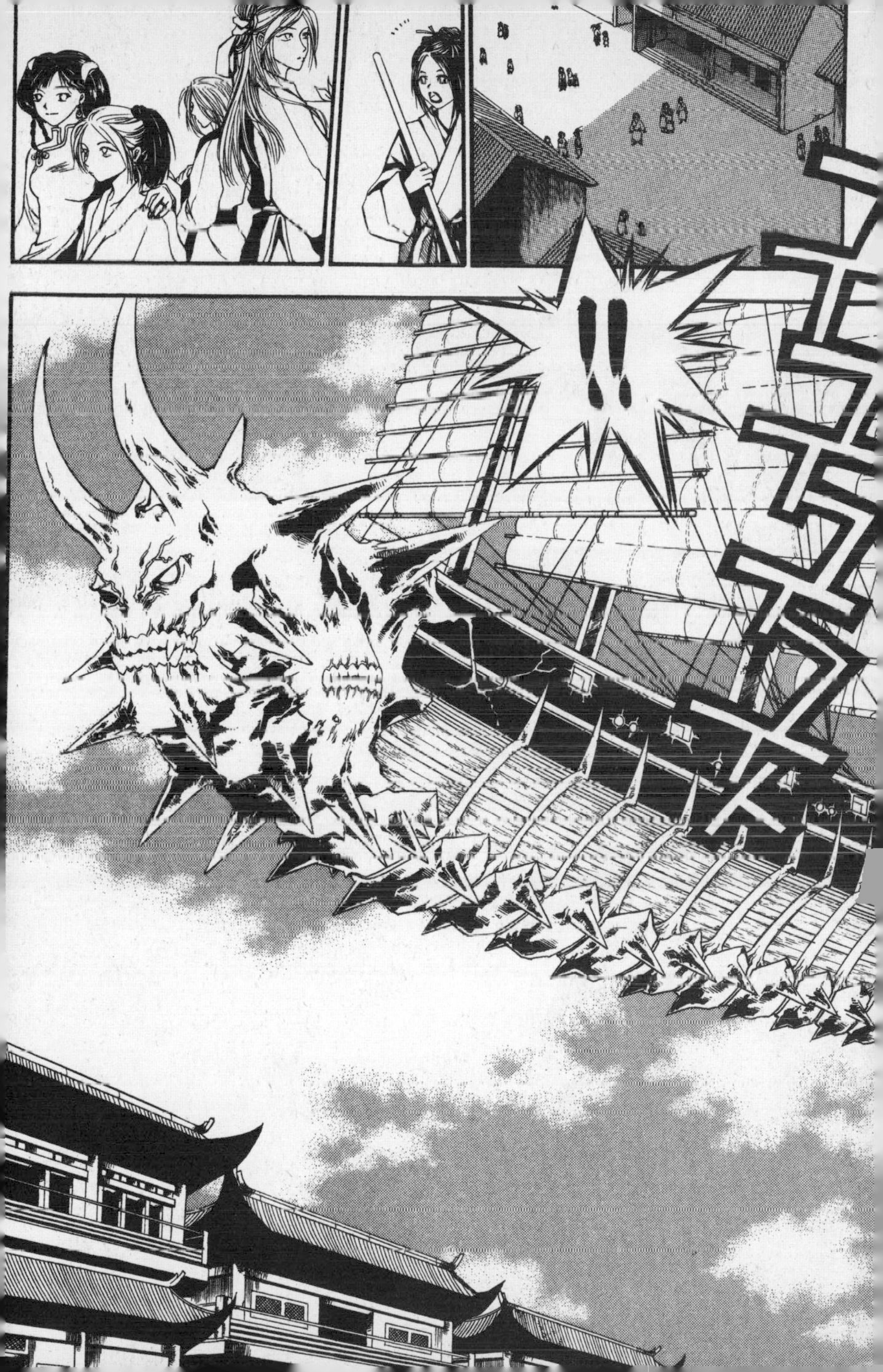
!!

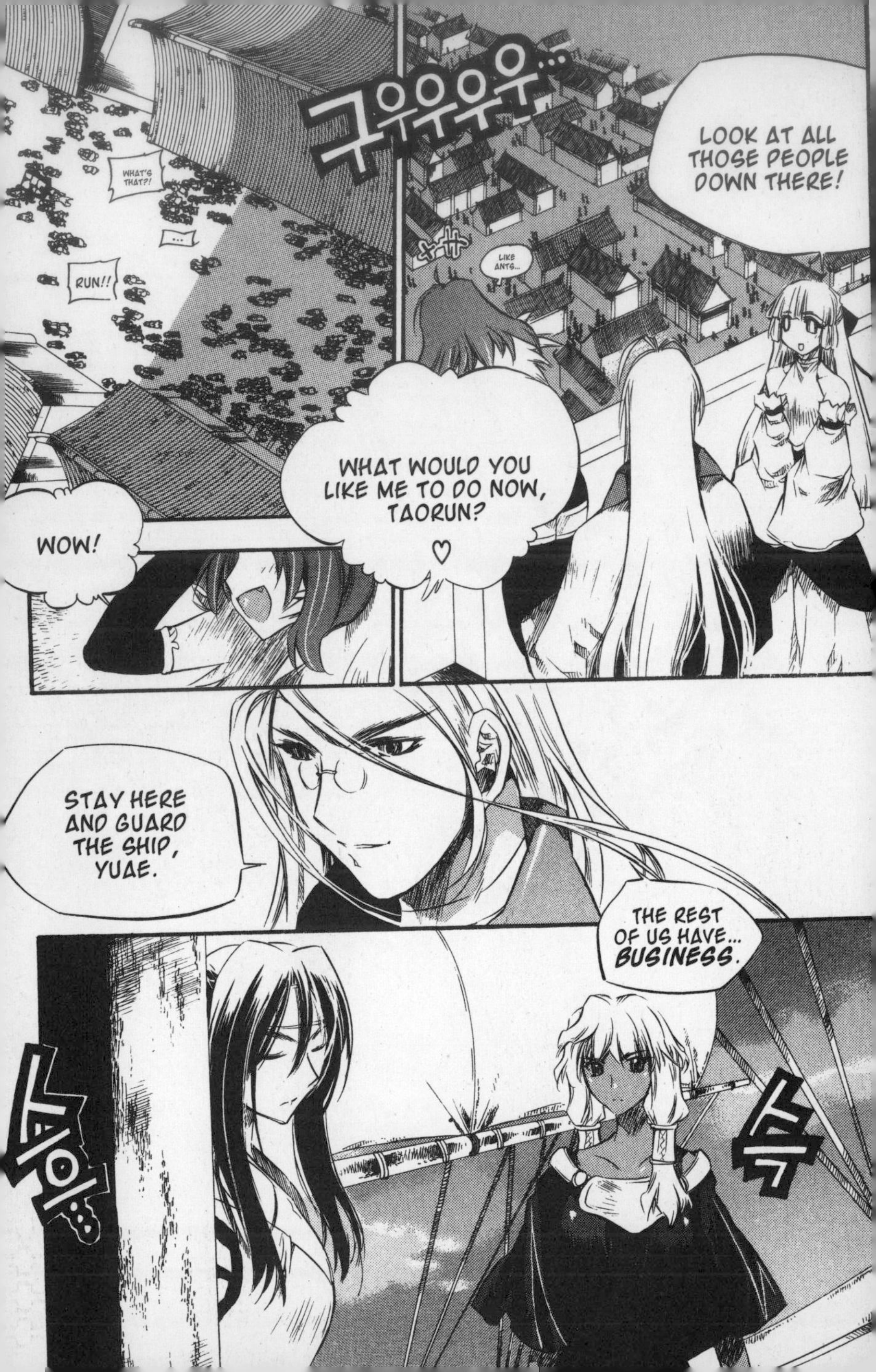
WHAT'S THAT?!
...
RUN!!
구우우우우...
LOOK AT ALL THOSE PEOPLE DOWN THERE!
LIKE ANTS...
WOW!
WHAT WOULD YOU LIKE ME TO DO NOW, TAORUN? ♡
STAY HERE AND GUARD THE SHIP, YUAE.
THE REST OF US HAVE... **BUSINESS**.
쉬이...

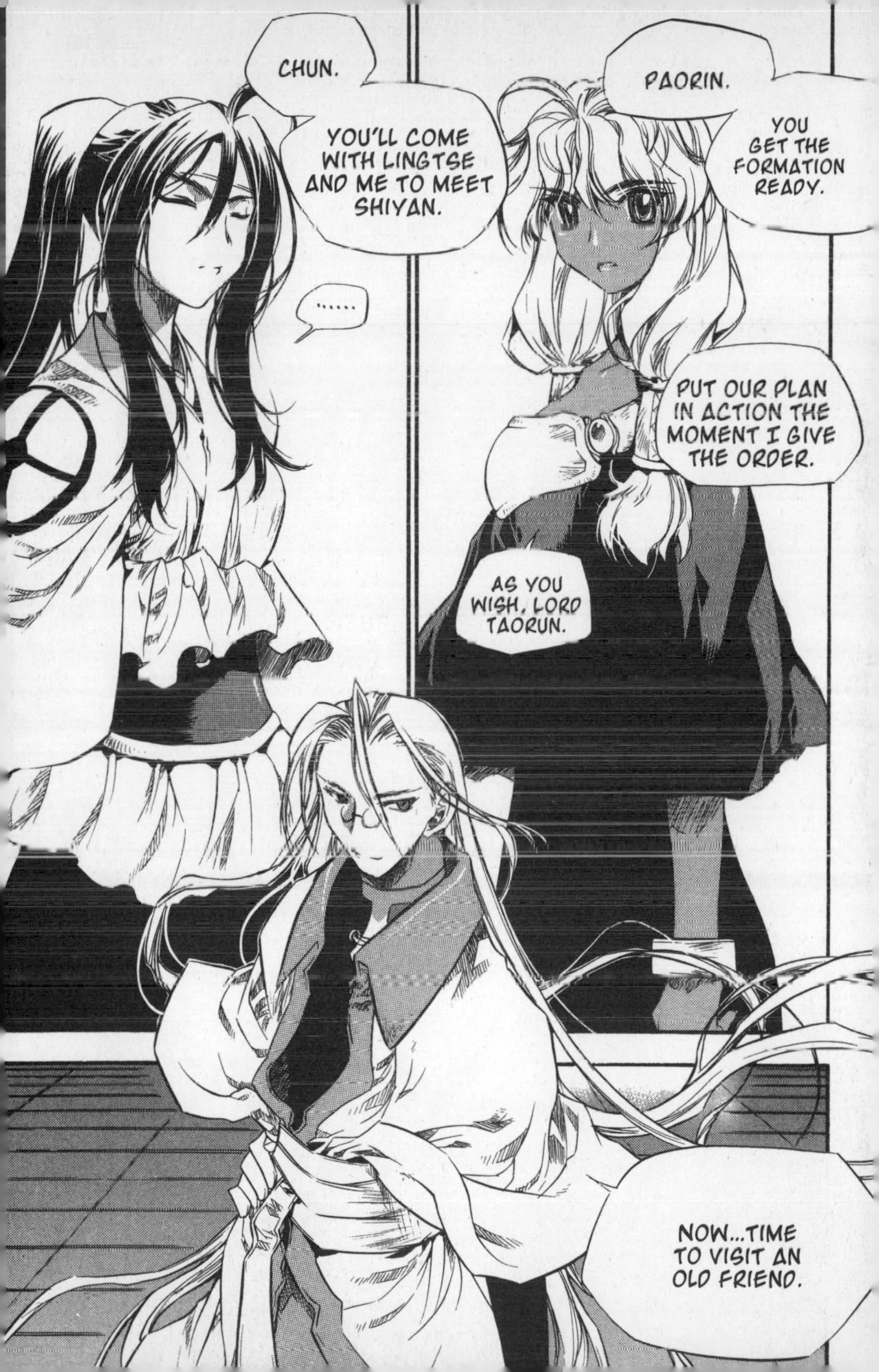
CHUN.
YOU'LL COME WITH LINGTSE AND ME TO MEET SHIYAN.
......
PAORIN.
YOU GET THE FORMATION READY.
PUT OUR PLAN IN ACTION THE MOMENT I GIVE THE ORDER.
AS YOU WISH, LORD TAORUN.
NOW...TIME TO VISIT AN OLD FRIEND.

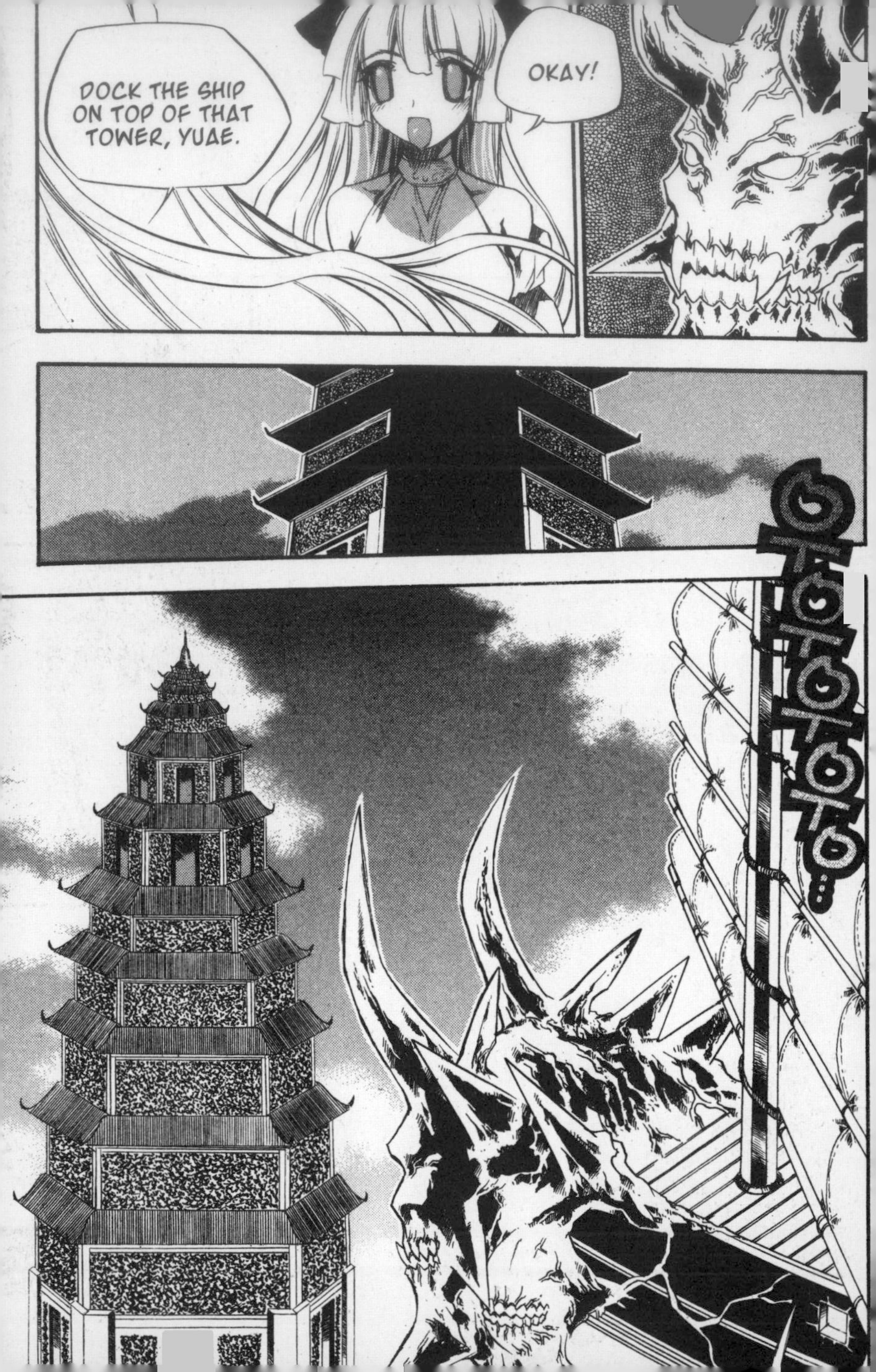
DOCK THE SHIP ON TOP OF THAT TOWER, YUAE.
OKAY!
우우우웅...

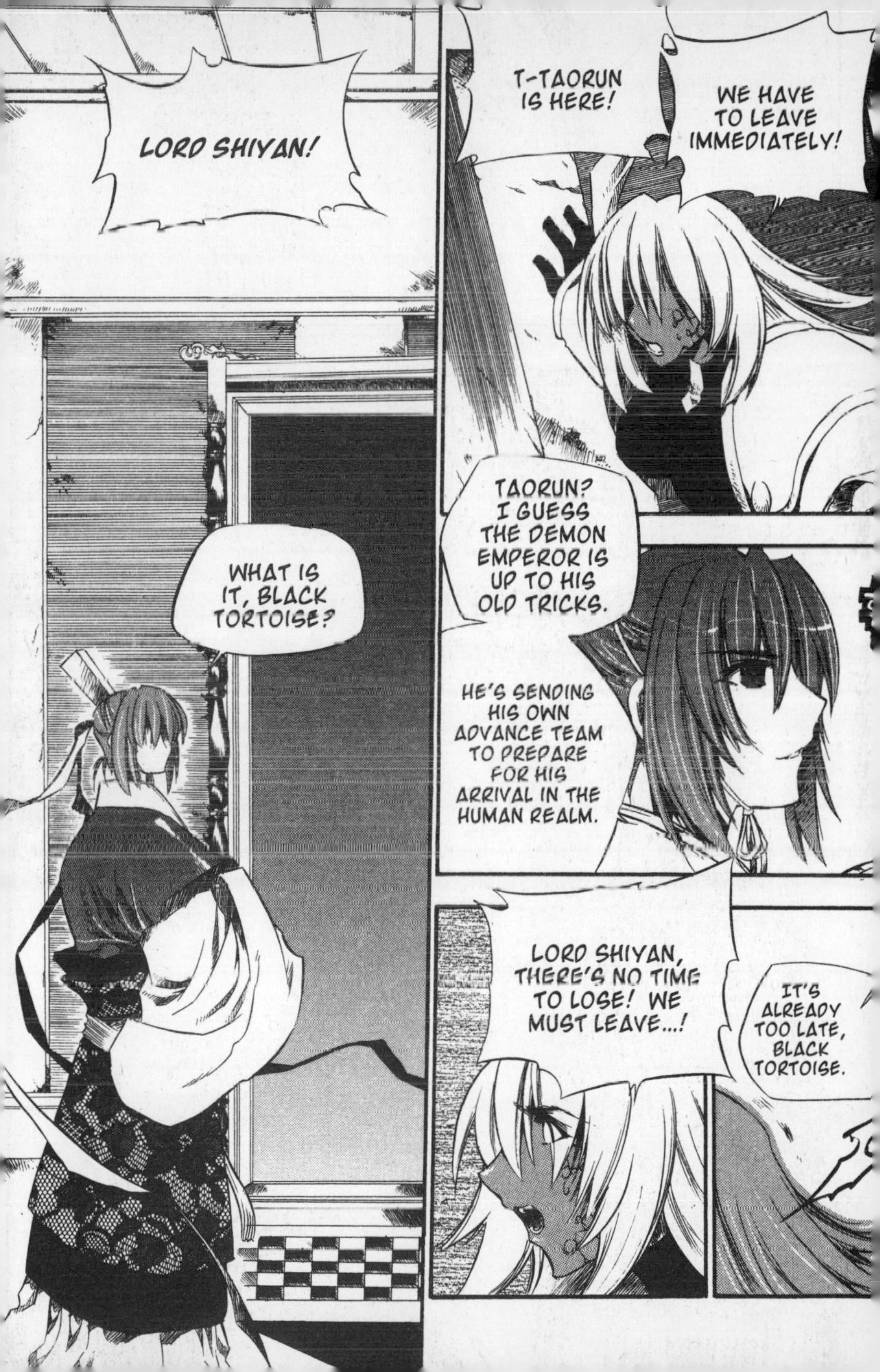
LORD SHIYAN!
WHAT IS IT, BLACK TORTOISE?
T-TAORUN IS HERE!
WE HAVE TO LEAVE IMMEDIATELY!
TAORUN? I GUESS THE DEMON EMPEROR IS UP TO HIS OLD TRICKS.
HE'S SENDING HIS OWN ADVANCE TEAM TO PREPARE FOR HIS ARRIVAL IN THE HUMAN REALM.
LORD SHIYAN, THERE'S NO TIME TO LOSE! WE MUST LEAVE...!
IT'S ALREADY TOO LATE, BLACK TORTOISE.

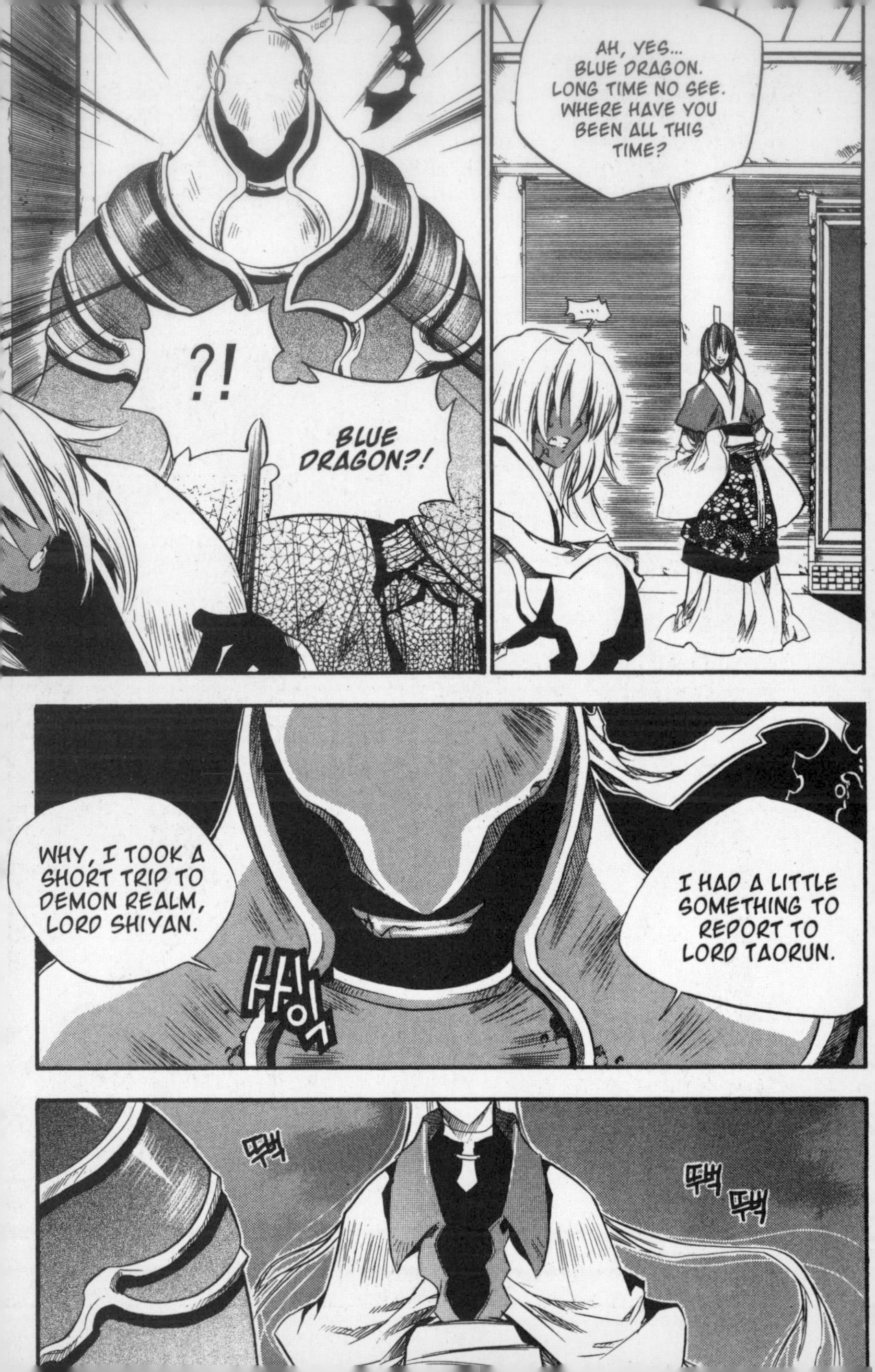
?!
BLUE DRAGON?!
AH, YES... BLUE DRAGON. LONG TIME NO SEE. WHERE HAVE YOU BEEN ALL THIS TIME?
WHY, I TOOK A SHORT TRIP TO DEMON REALM, LORD SHIYAN.
I HAD A LITTLE SOMETHING TO REPORT TO LORD TAORUN.
뚜벅
뚜벅
뚜벅

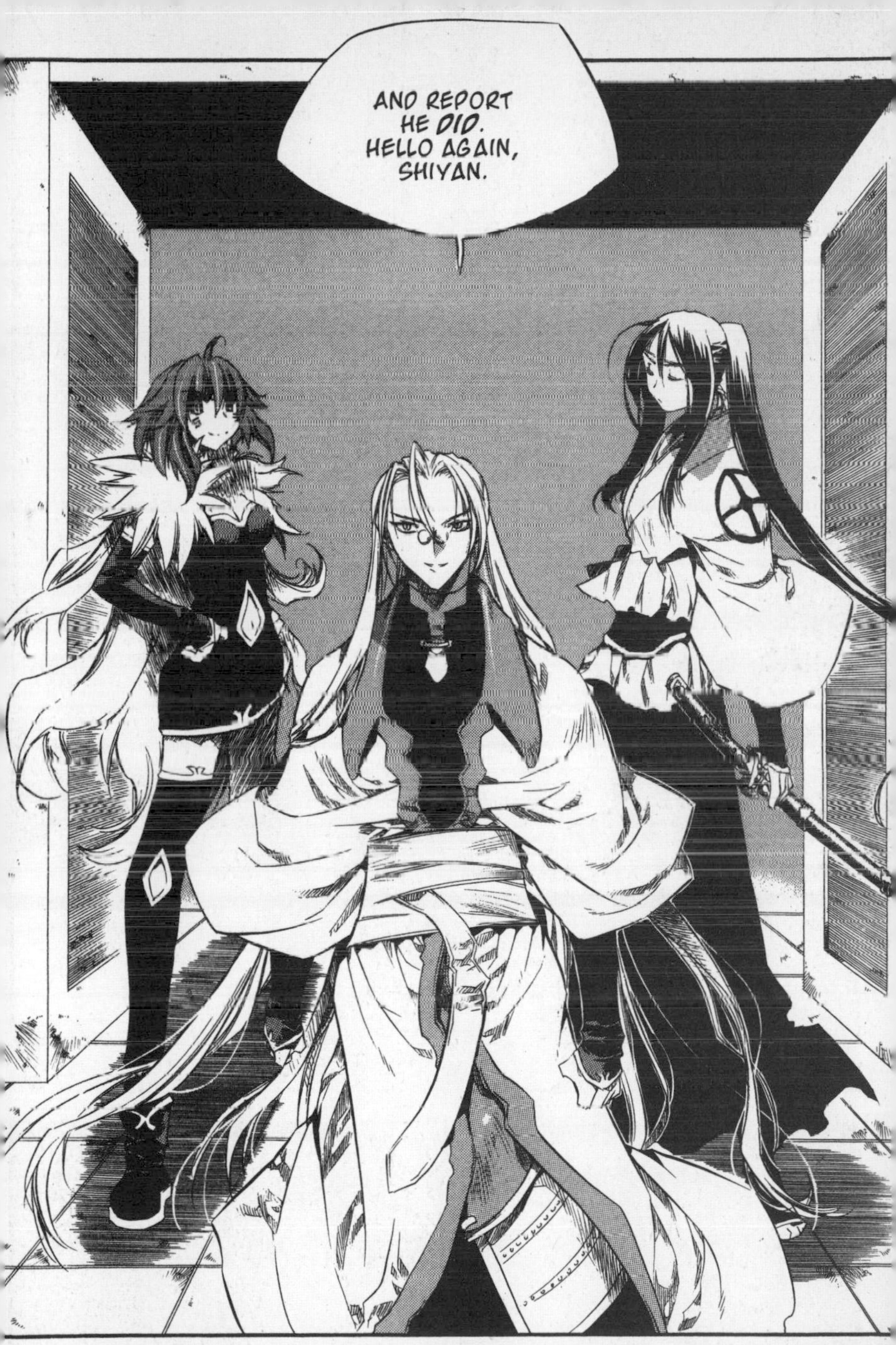
AND REPORT HE *DID*. HELLO AGAIN, SHIYAN.

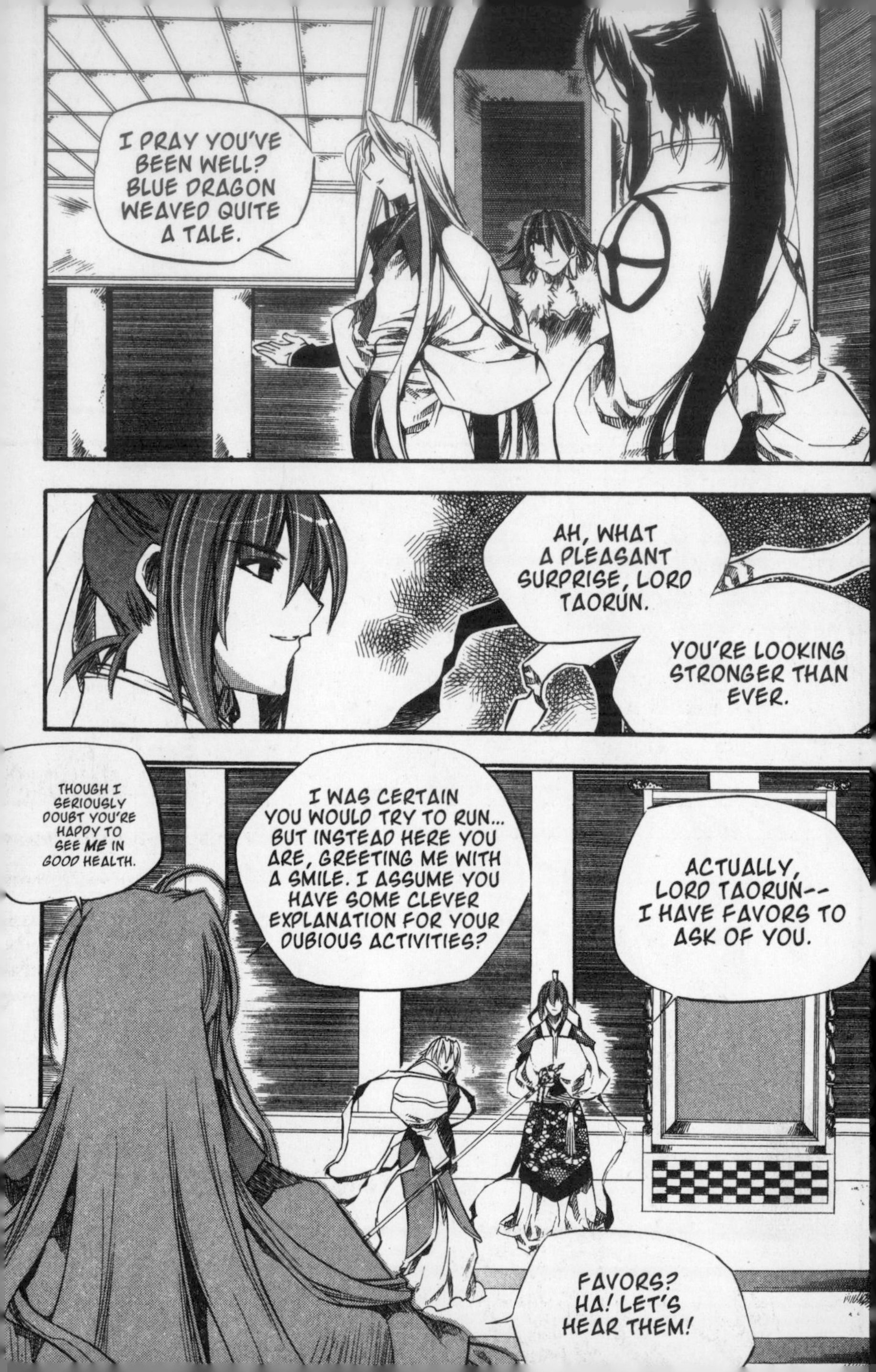
I PRAY YOU'VE BEEN WELL? BLUE DRAGON WEAVED QUITE A TALE.
AH, WHAT A PLEASANT SURPRISE, LORD TAORÚN.
YOU'RE LOOKING STRONGER THAN EVER.
THOUGH I SERIOUSLY DOUBT YOU'RE HAPPY TO SEE ME IN GOOD HEALTH.
I WAS CERTAIN YOU WOULD TRY TO RUN... BUT INSTEAD HERE YOU ARE, GREETING ME WITH A SMILE. I ASSUME YOU HAVE SOME CLEVER EXPLANATION FOR YOUR DUBIOUS ACTIVITIES?
ACTUALLY, LORD TAORÚN-- I HAVE FAVORS TO ASK OF YOU.
FAVORS? HA! LET'S HEAR THEM!

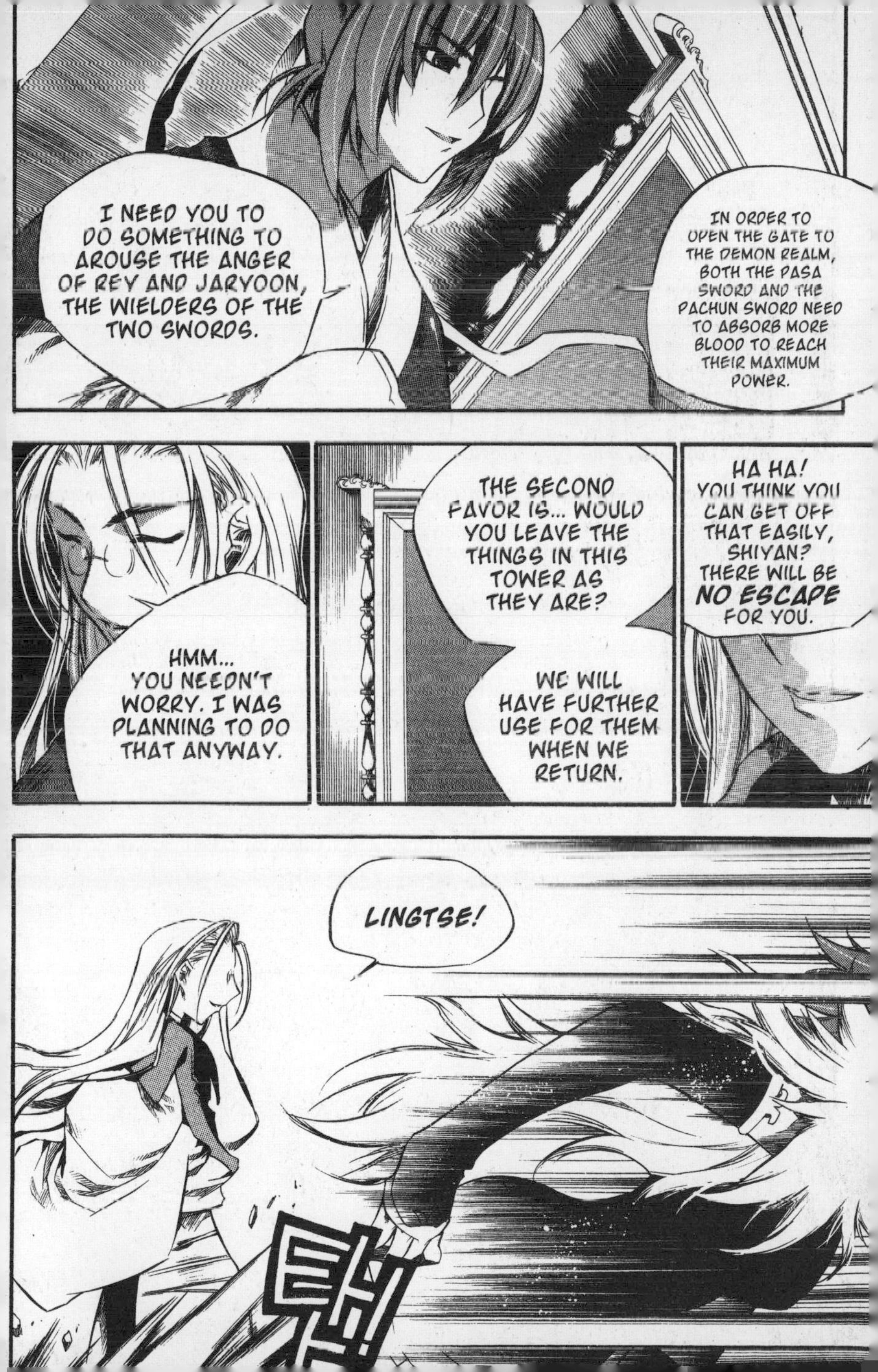
I NEED YOU TO DO SOMETHING TO AROUSE THE ANGER OF REY AND JARYOON, THE WIELDERS OF THE TWO SWORDS.
IN ORDER TO OPEN THE GATE TO THE DEMON REALM, BOTH THE PASA SWORD AND THE PACHUN SWORD NEED TO ABSORB MORE BLOOD TO REACH THEIR MAXIMUM POWER.
HMM... YOU NEEDN'T WORRY. I WAS PLANNING TO DO THAT ANYWAY.
THE SECOND FAVOR IS... WOULD YOU LEAVE THE THINGS IN THIS TOWER AS THEY ARE?
WE WILL HAVE FURTHER USE FOR THEM WHEN WE RETURN.
HA HA! YOU THINK YOU CAN GET OFF THAT EASILY, SHIYAN? THERE WILL BE **NO ESCAPE** FOR YOU.
LINGTSE!

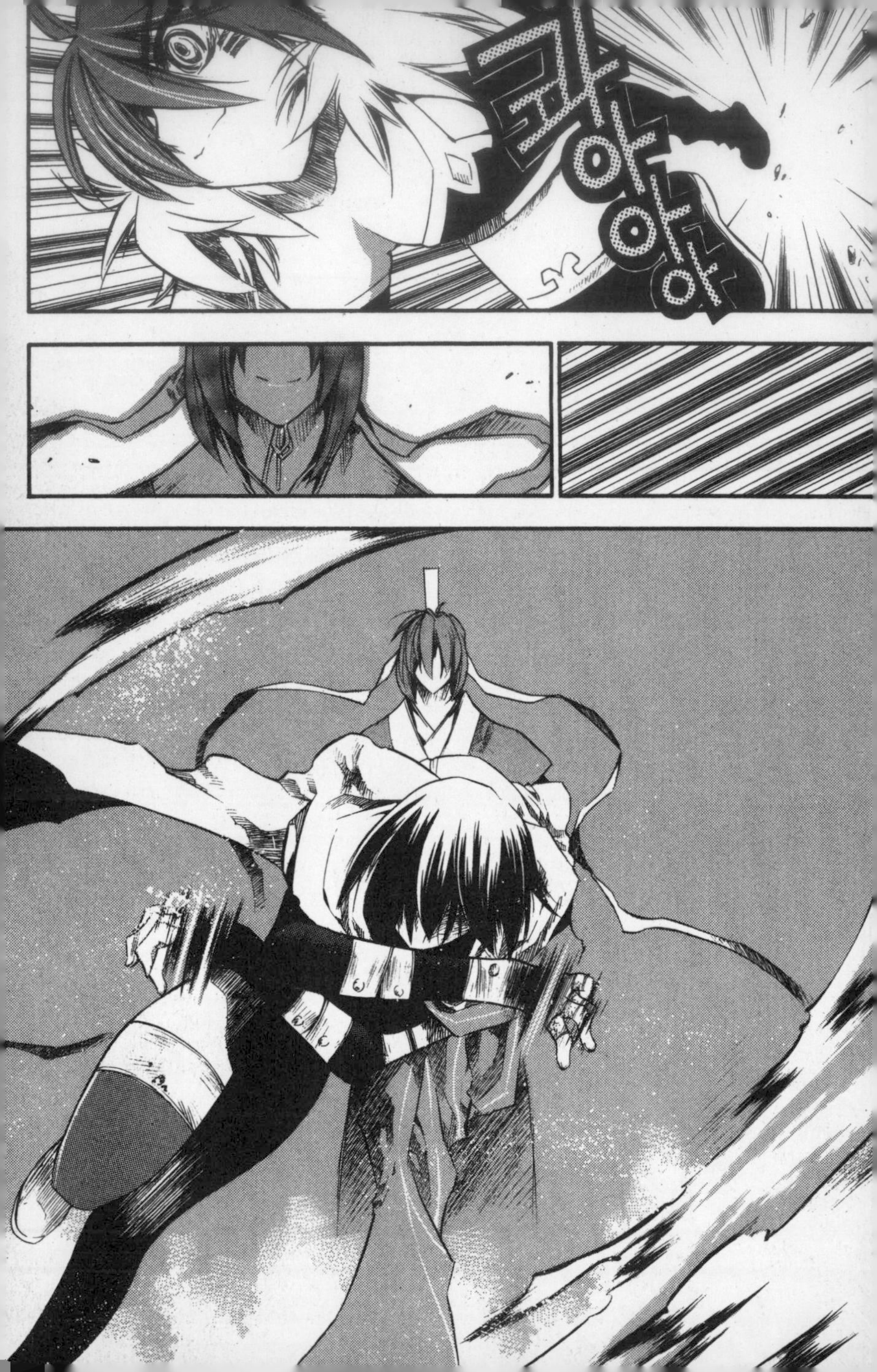

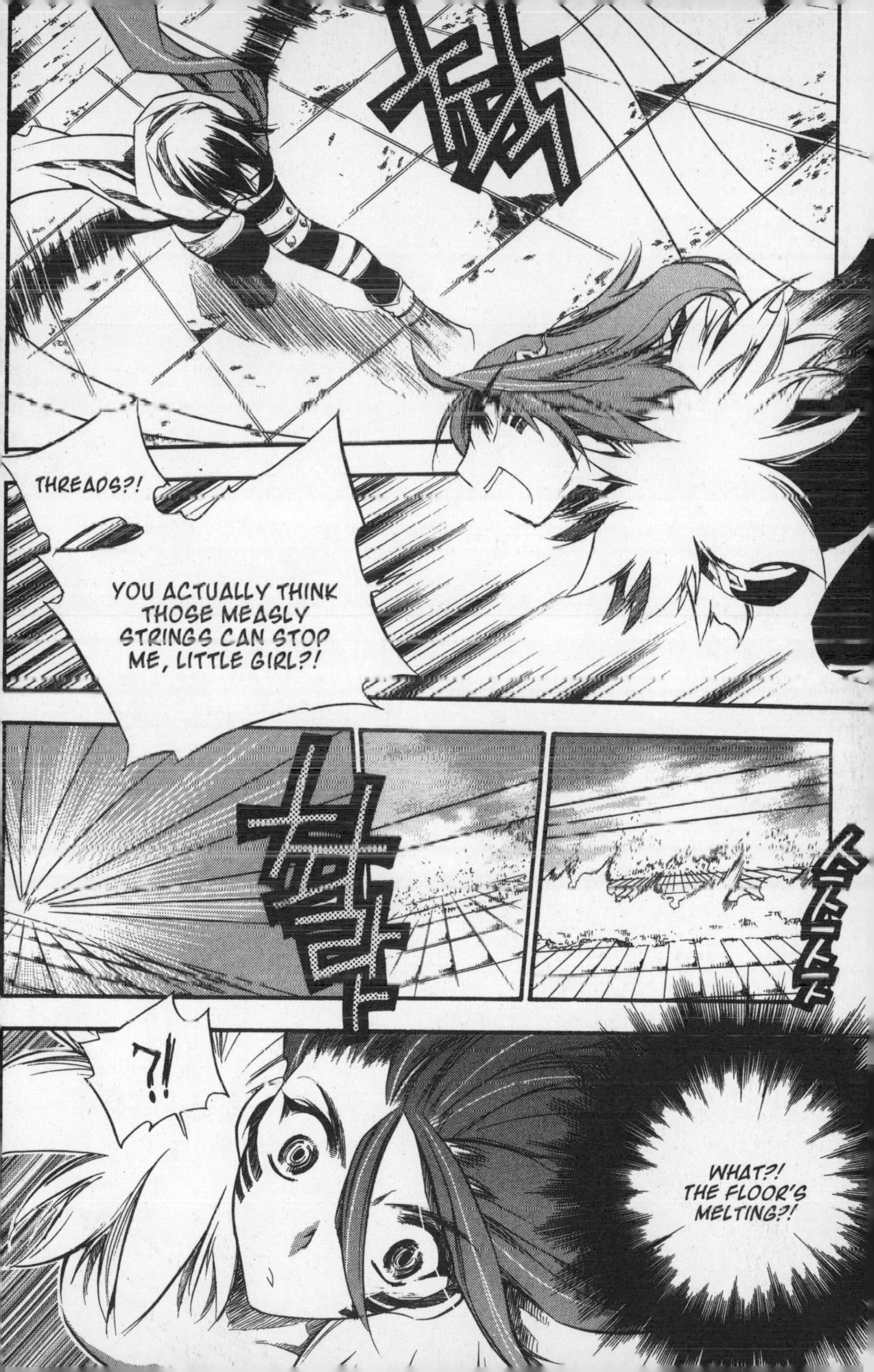
THREADS?!
YOU ACTUALLY THINK THOSE MEASLY STRINGS CAN STOP ME, LITTLE GIRL?!
?!
WHAT?! THE FLOOR'S MELTING?!

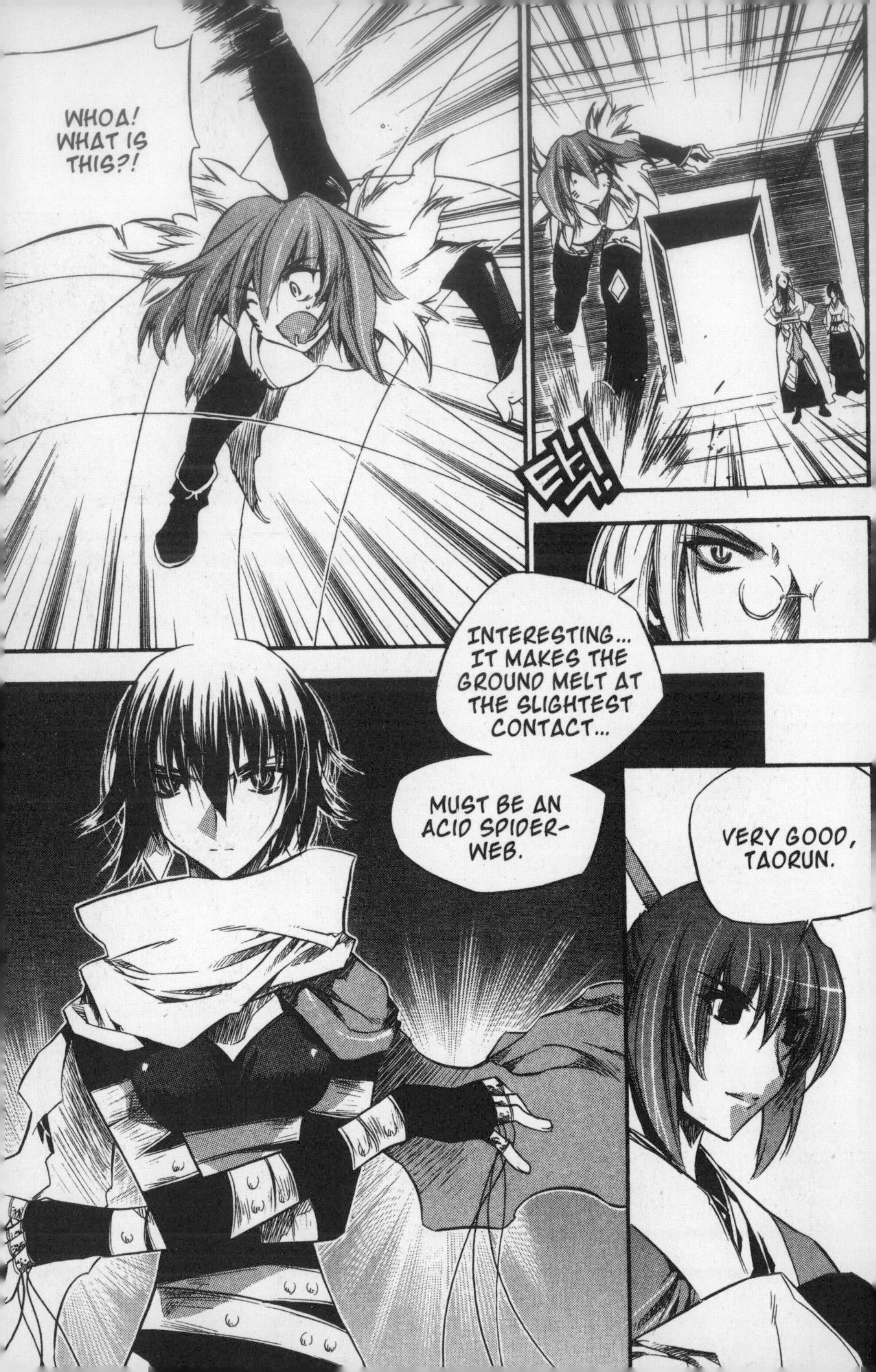
WHOA! WHAT IS THIS?!
INTERESTING... IT MAKES THE GROUND MELT AT THE SLIGHTEST CONTACT...
MUST BE AN ACID SPIDER-WEB.
VERY GOOD, TAORUN.

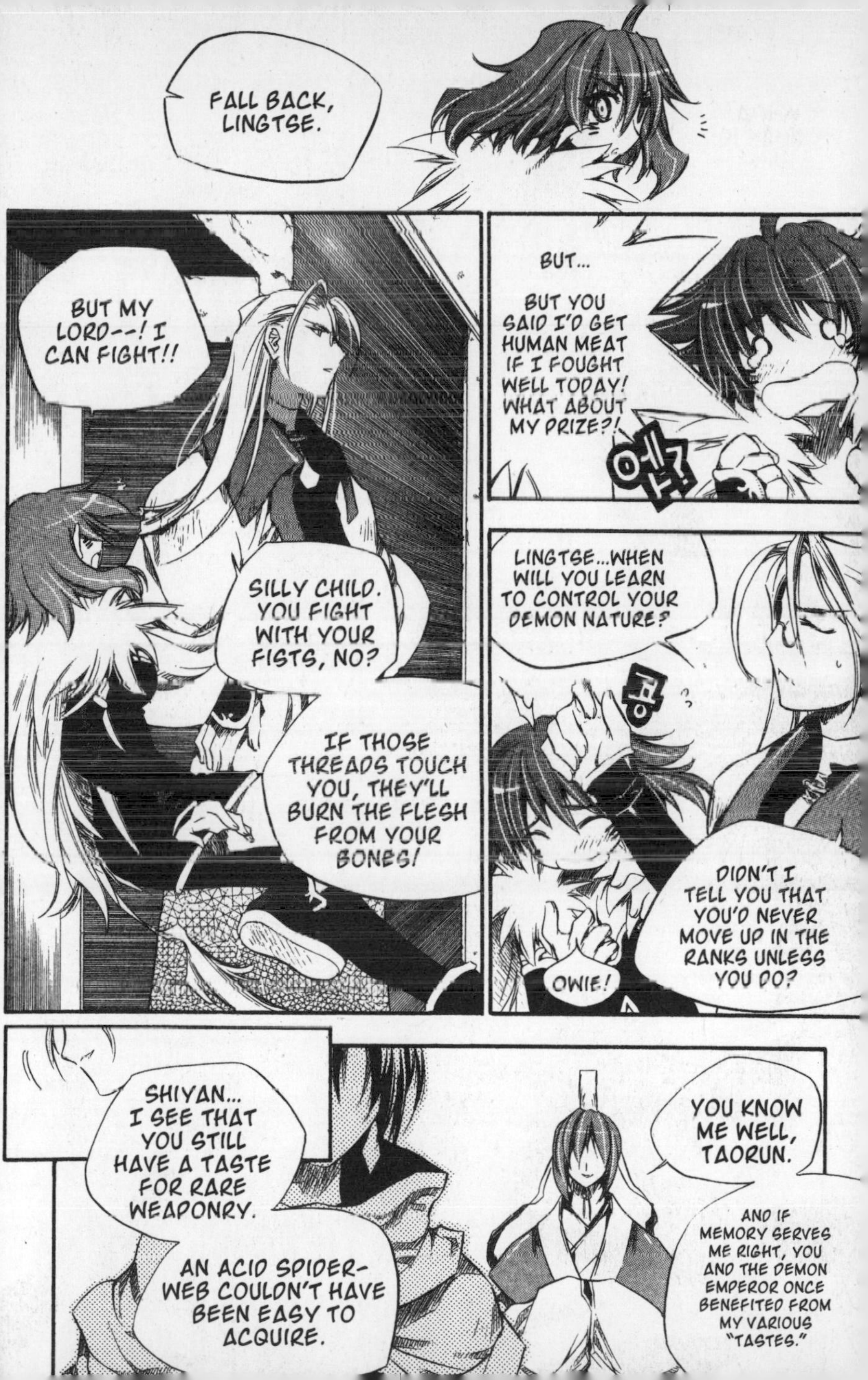
FALL BACK, LINGTSE.
BUT MY LORD--! I CAN FIGHT!!
SILLY CHILD. YOU FIGHT WITH YOUR FISTS, NO?
IF THOSE THREADS TOUCH YOU, THEY'LL BURN THE FLESH FROM YOUR BONES!
BUT...
BUT YOU SAID I'D GET HUMAN MEAT IF I FOUGHT WELL TODAY! WHAT ABOUT MY PRIZE?!
LINGTSE...WHEN WILL YOU LEARN TO CONTROL YOUR DEMON NATURE?
DIDN'T I TELL YOU THAT YOU'D NEVER MOVE UP IN THE RANKS UNLESS YOU DO?
OWIE!
SHIYAN... I SEE THAT YOU STILL HAVE A TASTE FOR RARE WEAPONRY.
AN ACID SPIDER-WEB COULDN'T HAVE BEEN EASY TO ACQUIRE.
YOU KNOW ME WELL, TAORUN.
AND IF MEMORY SERVES ME RIGHT, YOU AND THE DEMON EMPEROR ONCE BENEFITED FROM MY VARIOUS "TASTES."

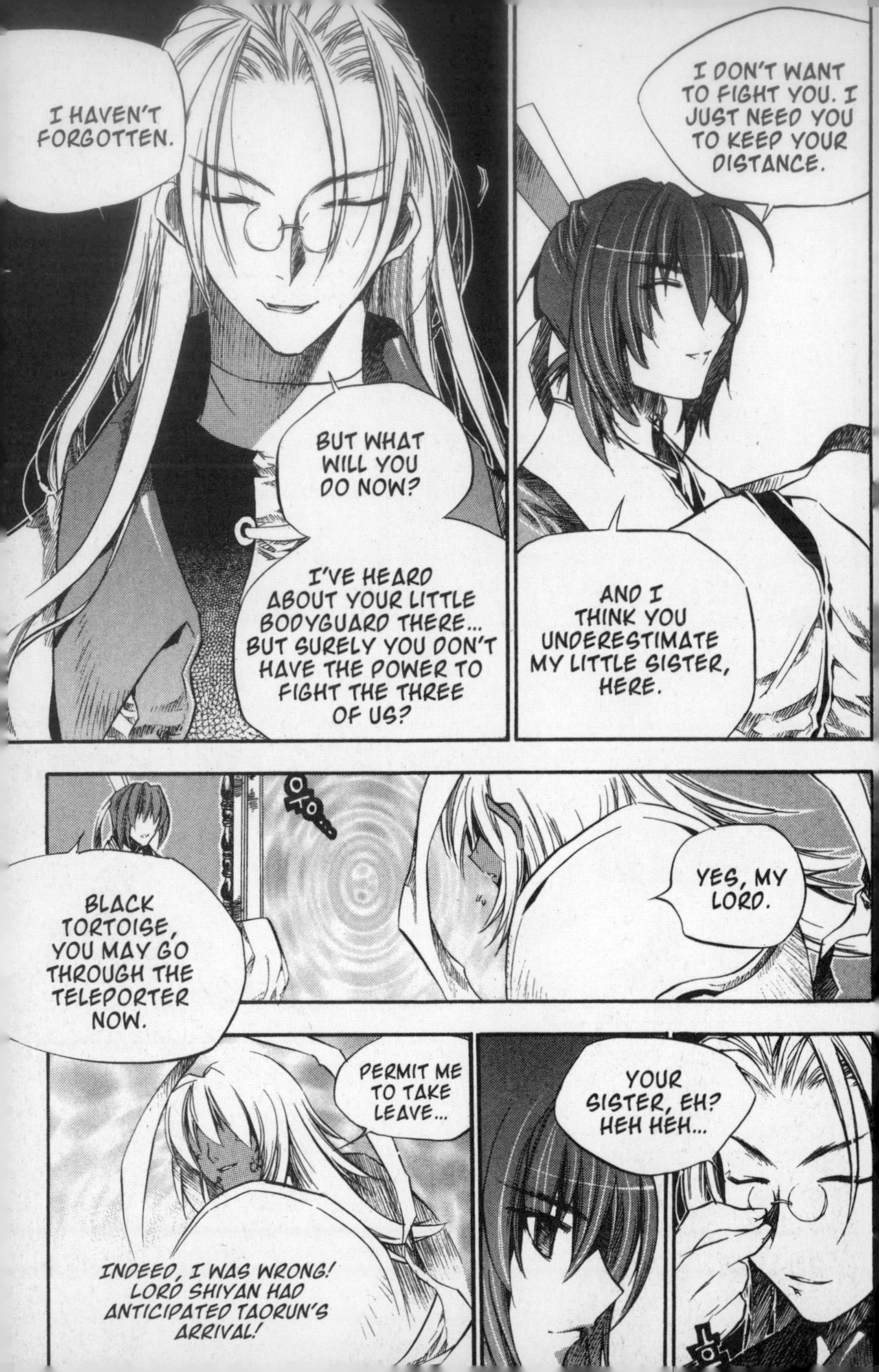
I HAVEN'T FORGOTTEN.
BUT WHAT WILL YOU DO NOW?
I'VE HEARD ABOUT YOUR LITTLE BODYGUARD THERE... BUT SURELY YOU DON'T HAVE THE POWER TO FIGHT THE THREE OF US?
I DON'T WANT TO FIGHT YOU. I JUST NEED YOU TO KEEP YOUR DISTANCE.
AND I THINK YOU UNDERESTIMATE MY LITTLE SISTER, HERE.
BLACK TORTOISE, YOU MAY GO THROUGH THE TELEPORTER NOW.
YES, MY LORD.
PERMIT ME TO TAKE LEAVE...
INDEED, I WAS WRONG! LORD SHIYAN HAD ANTICIPATED TAORUN'S ARRIVAL!
YOUR SISTER, EH? HEH HEH...

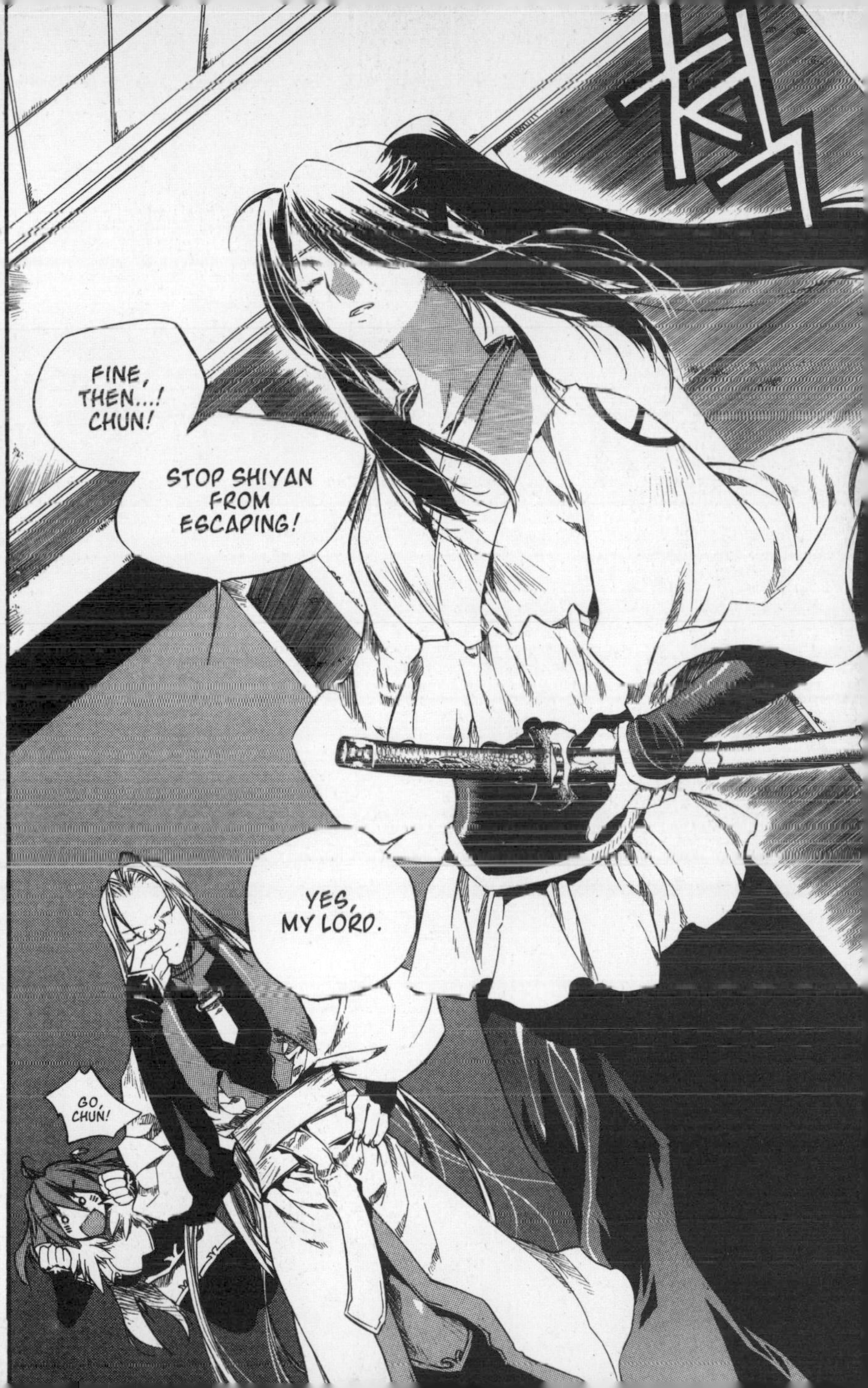
FINE, THEN...! CHUN!
STOP SHIYAN FROM ESCAPING!
YES, MY LORD.
GO, CHUN!

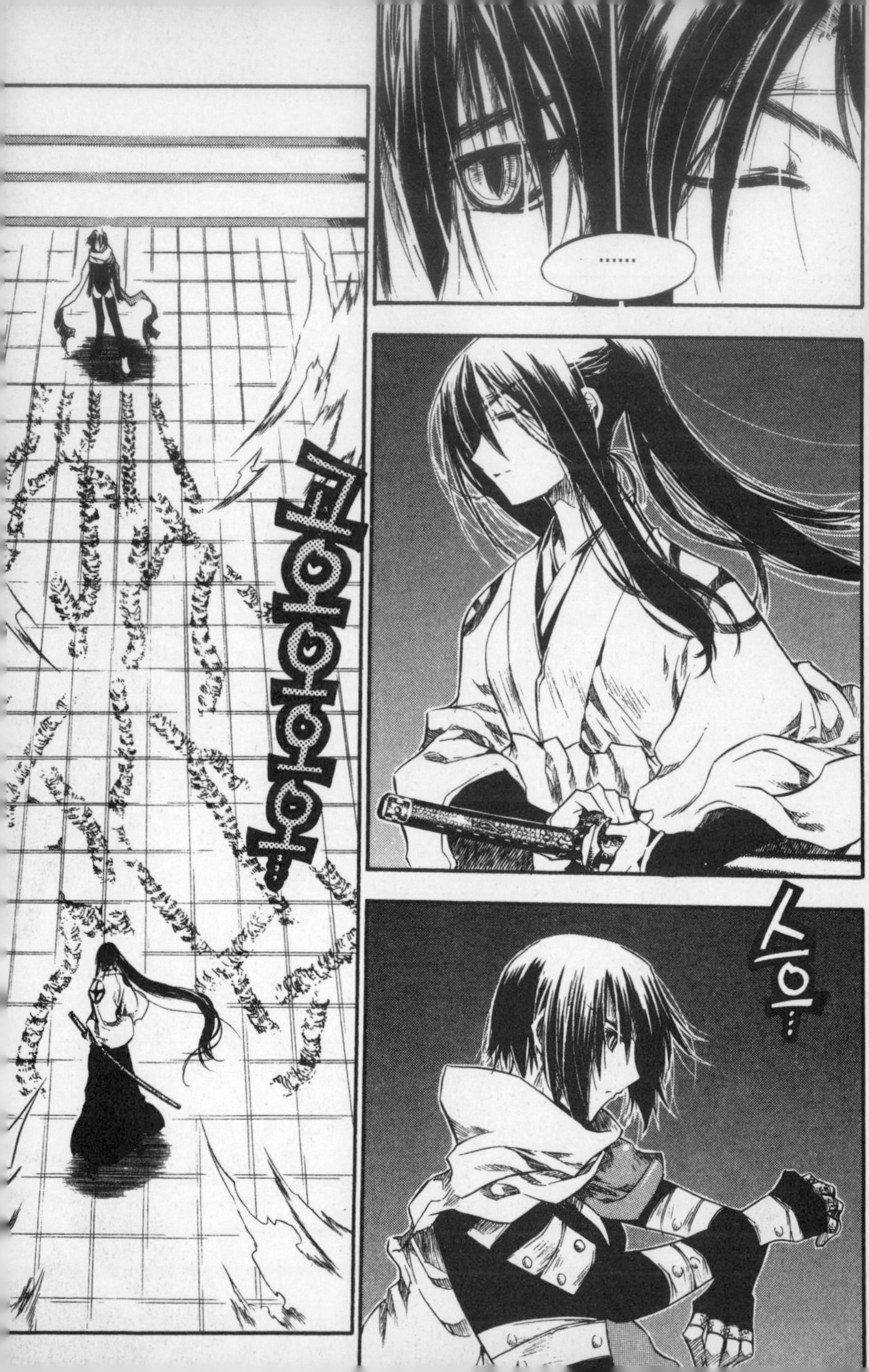
크으으으으...
......
스으...

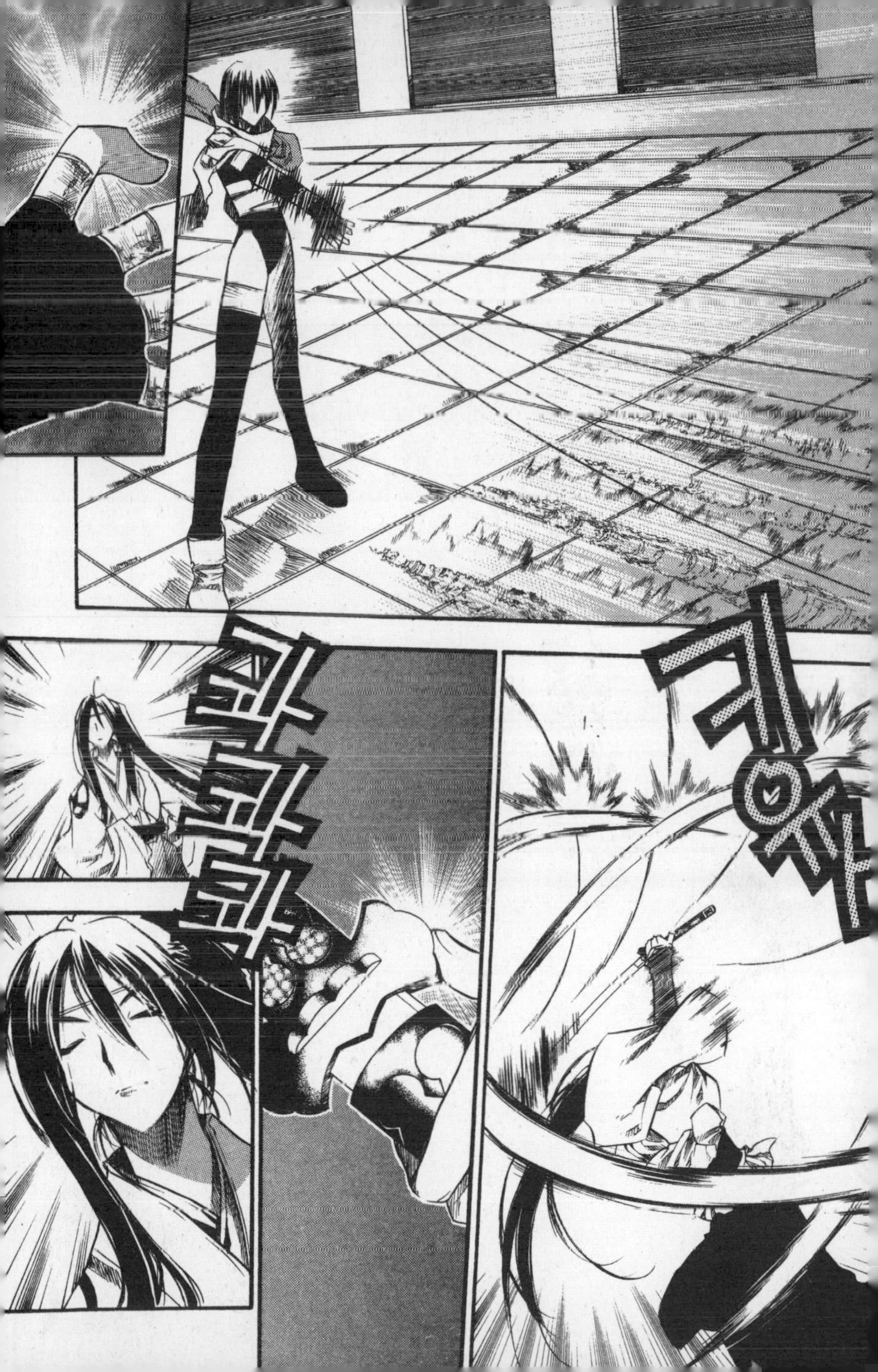
콰콰콰
키야

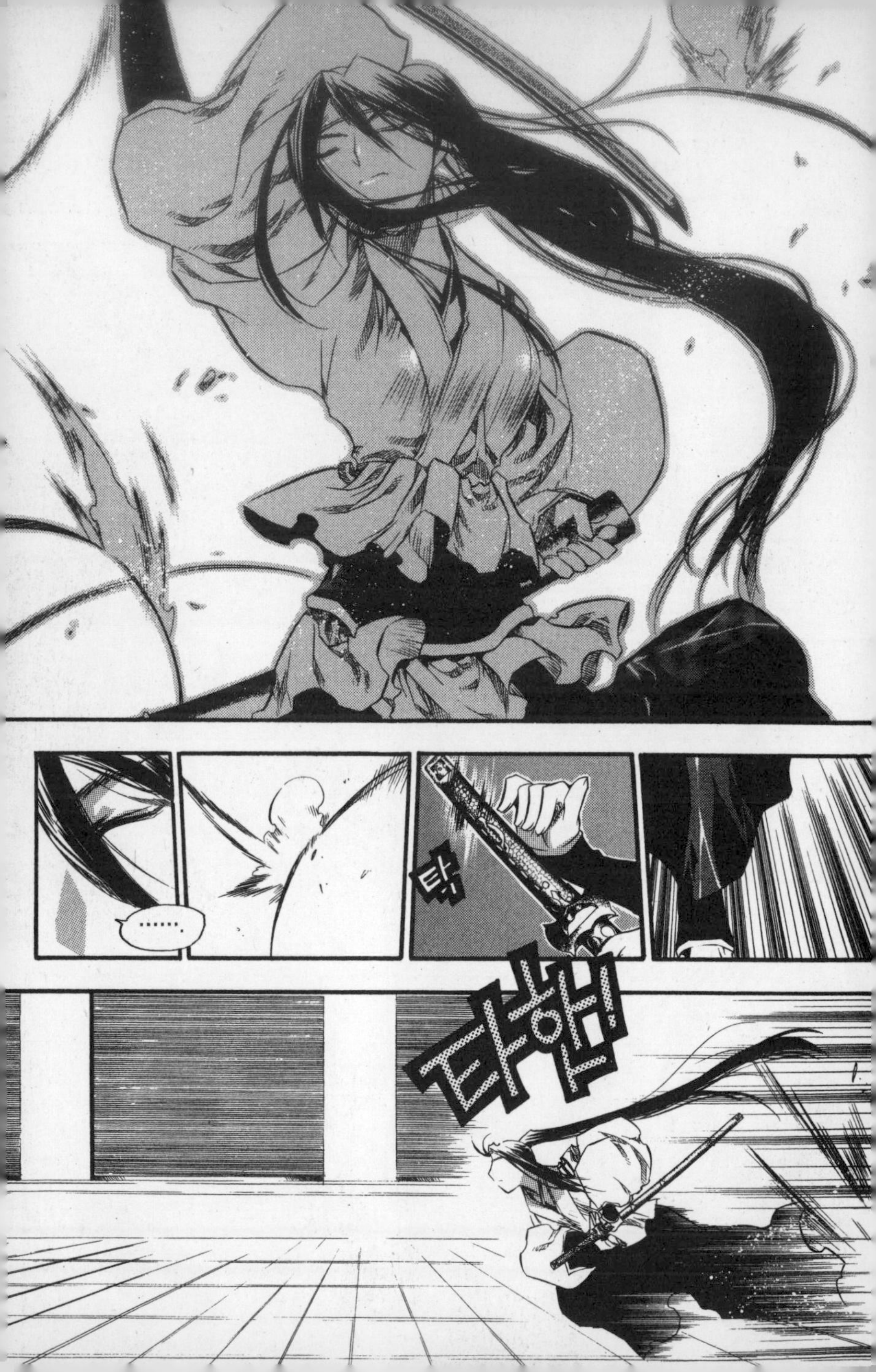

......
탁
파앗!

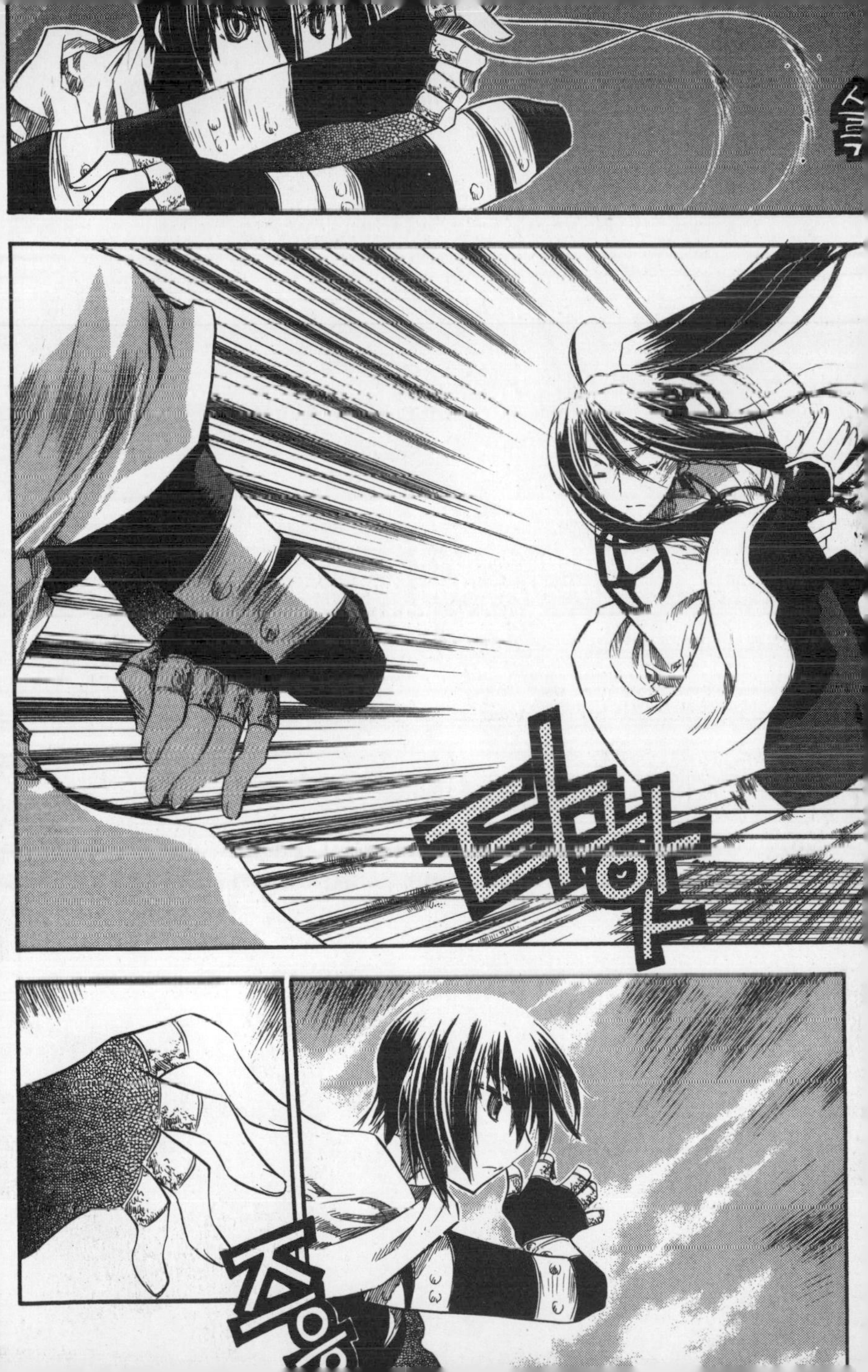

스륵

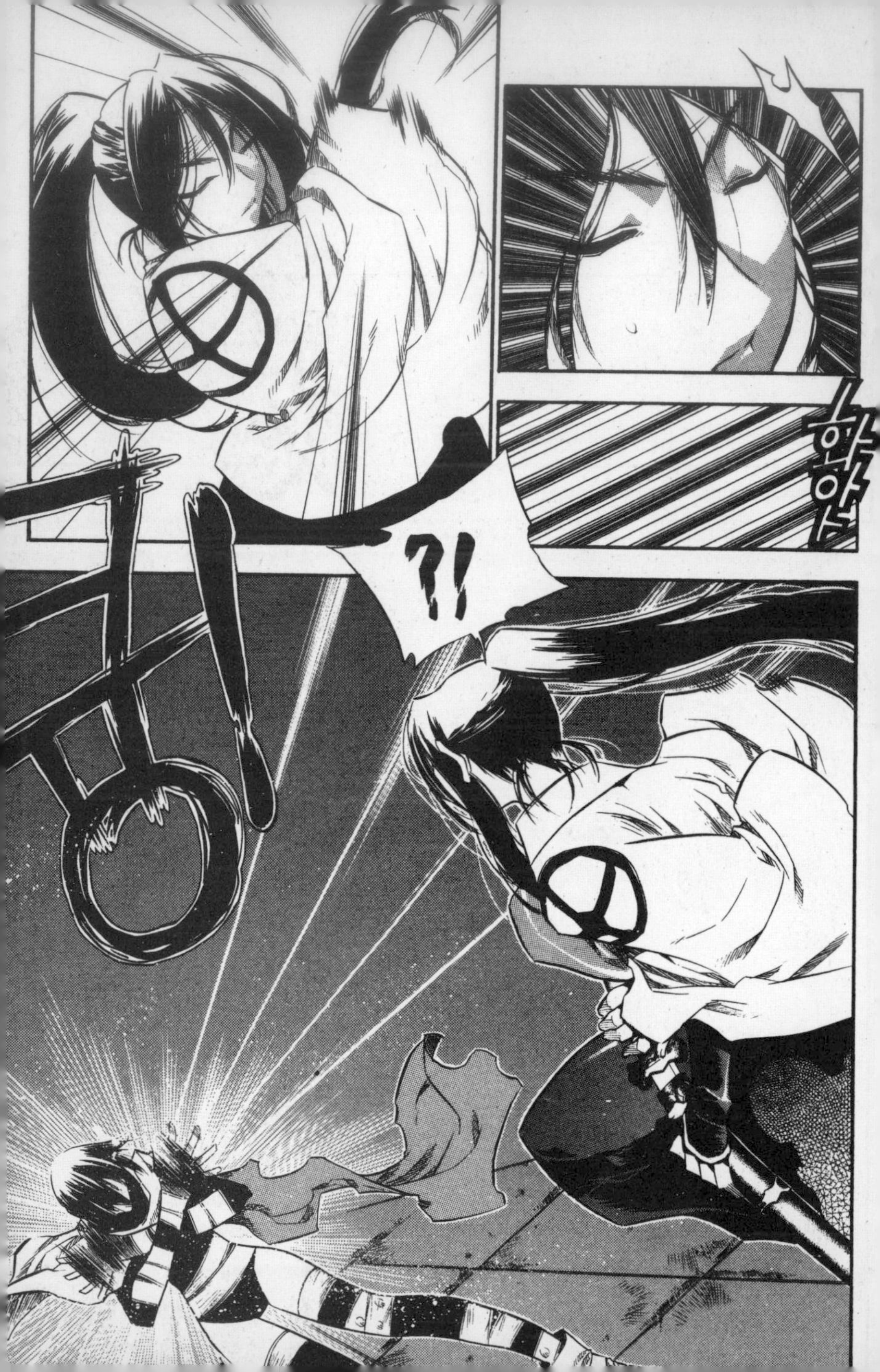
하앗
?!

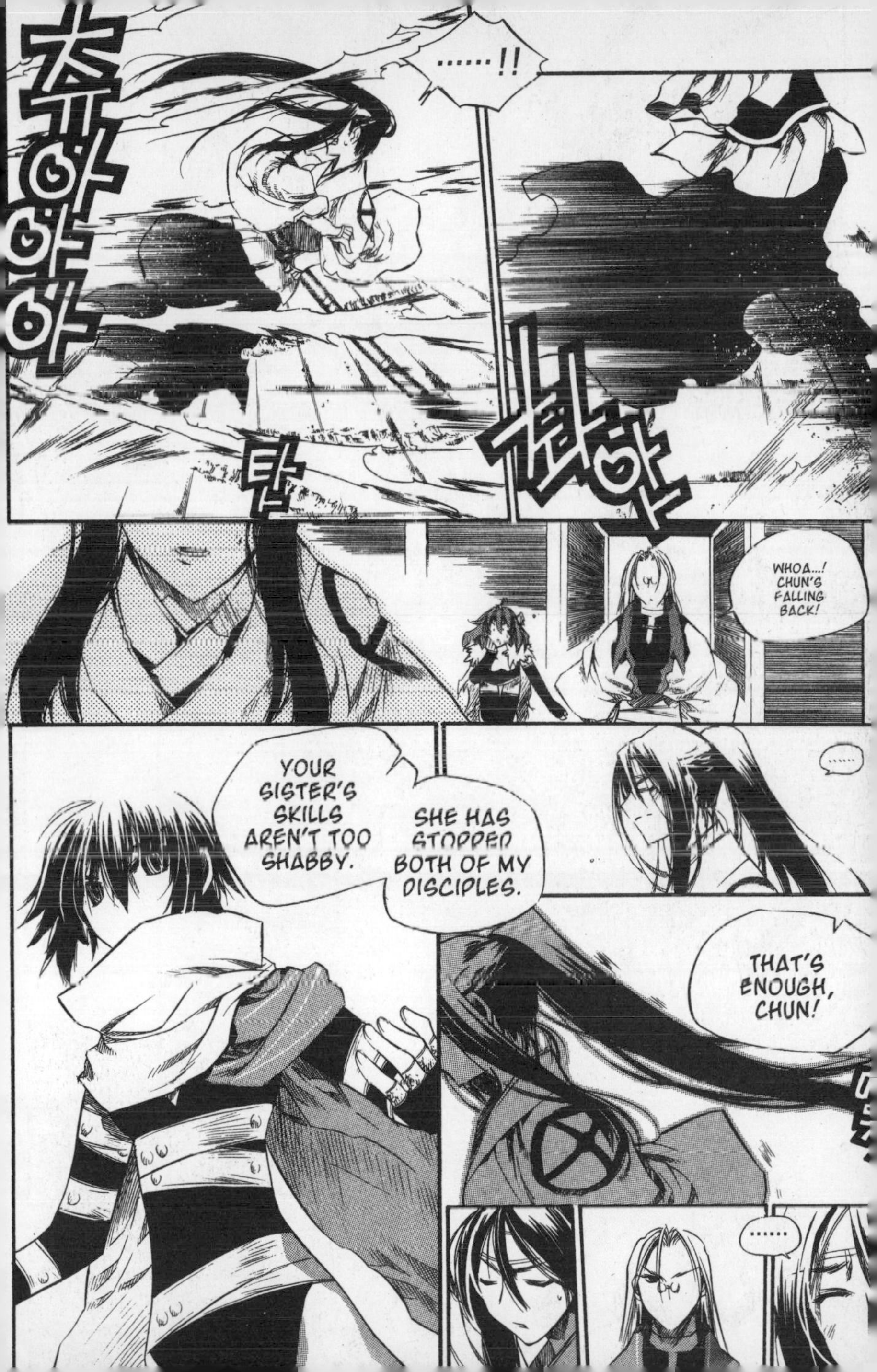
......!!
WHOA...! CHUN'S FALLING BACK!
YOUR SISTER'S SKILLS AREN'T TOO SHABBY.
SHE HAS STOPPED BOTH OF MY DISCIPLES.
......
THAT'S ENOUGH, CHUN!
......

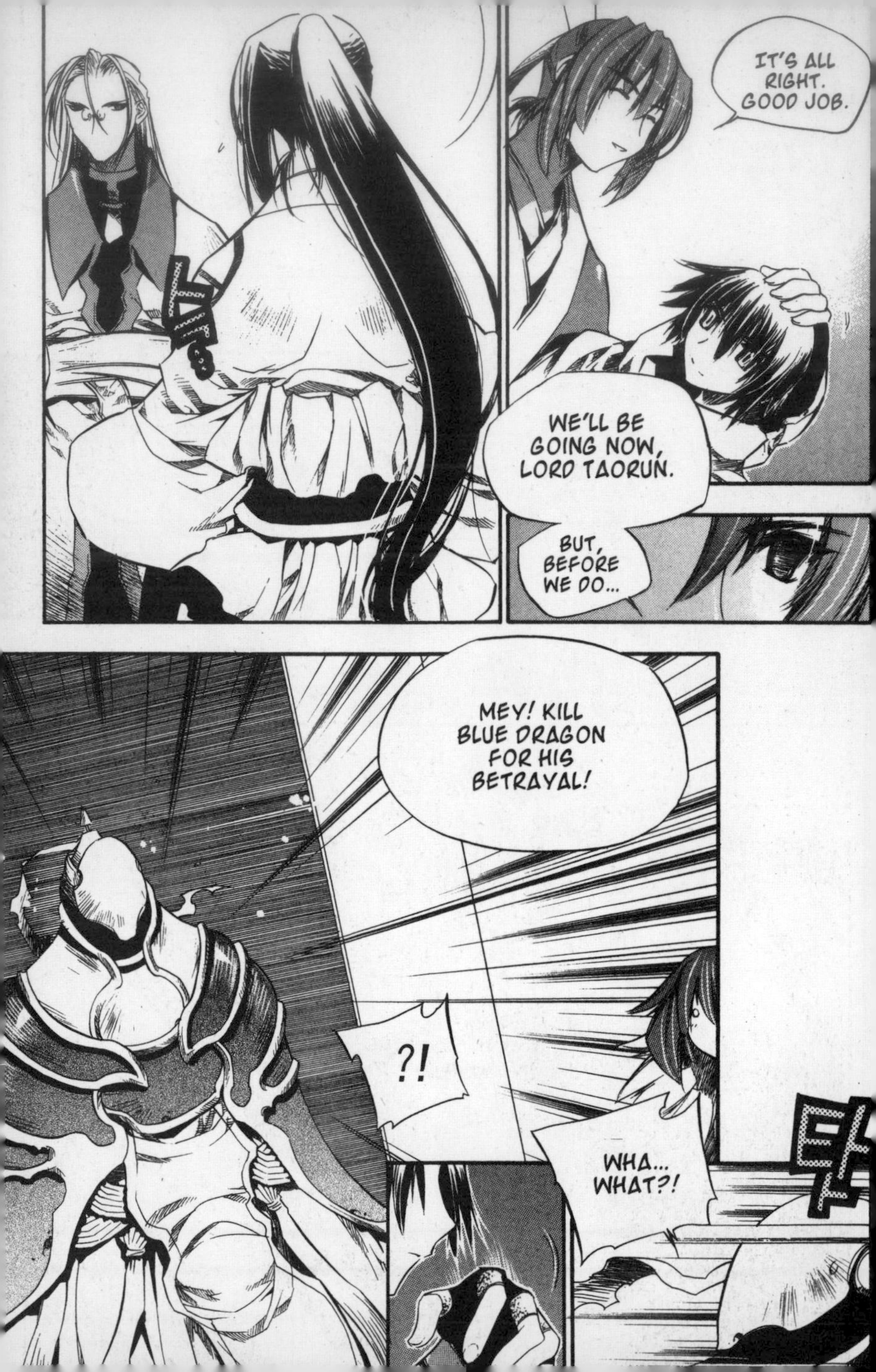
IT'S ALL RIGHT. GOOD JOB.
WE'LL BE GOING NOW, LORD TAORUN.
BUT, BEFORE WE DO...
MEY! KILL BLUE DRAGON FOR HIS BETRAYAL!
?!
WHA... WHAT?!

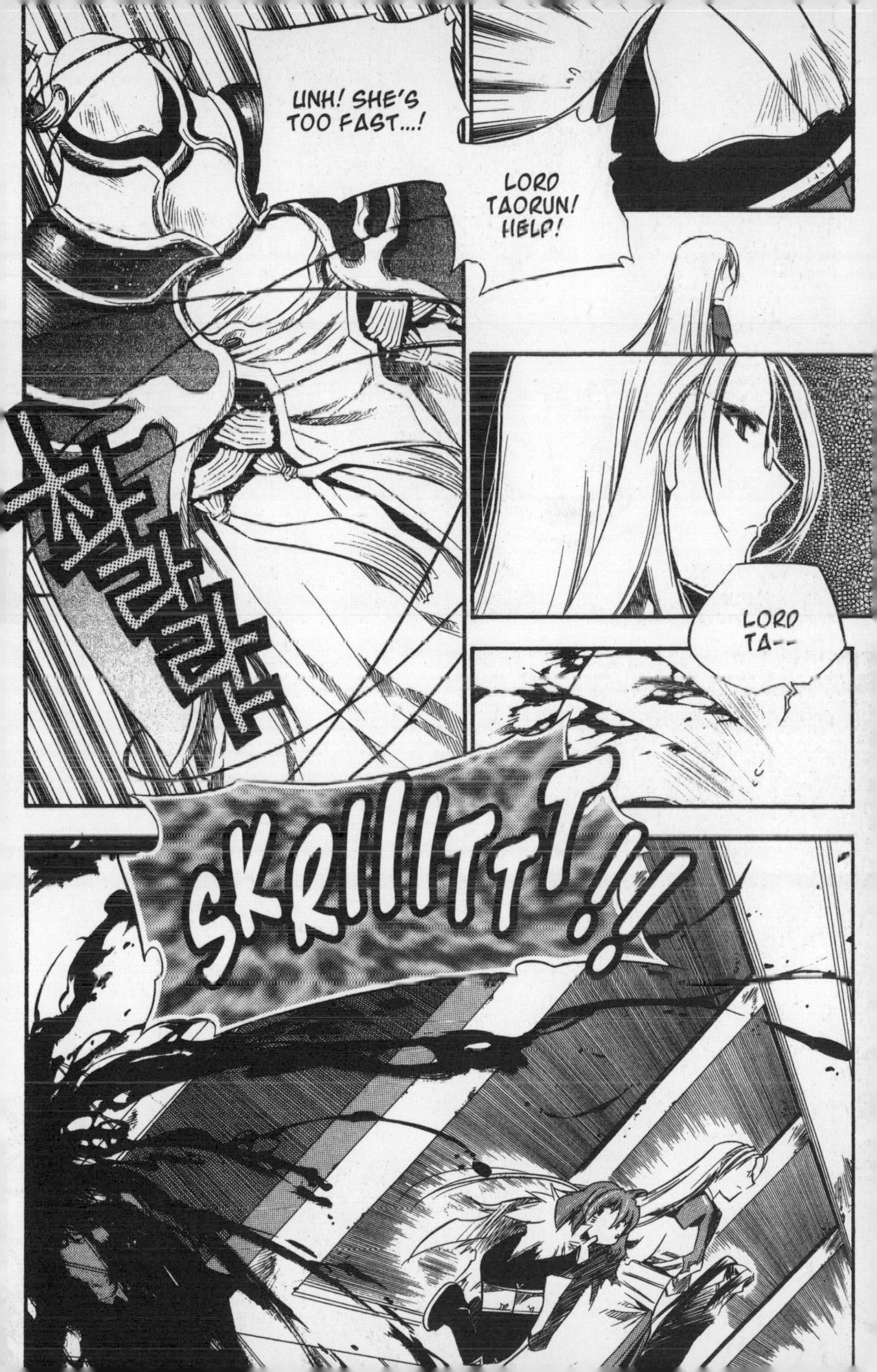
UNH! SHE'S TOO FAST...!
LORD TAORUN! HELP!
LORD TA--
SKRIIITTT!!

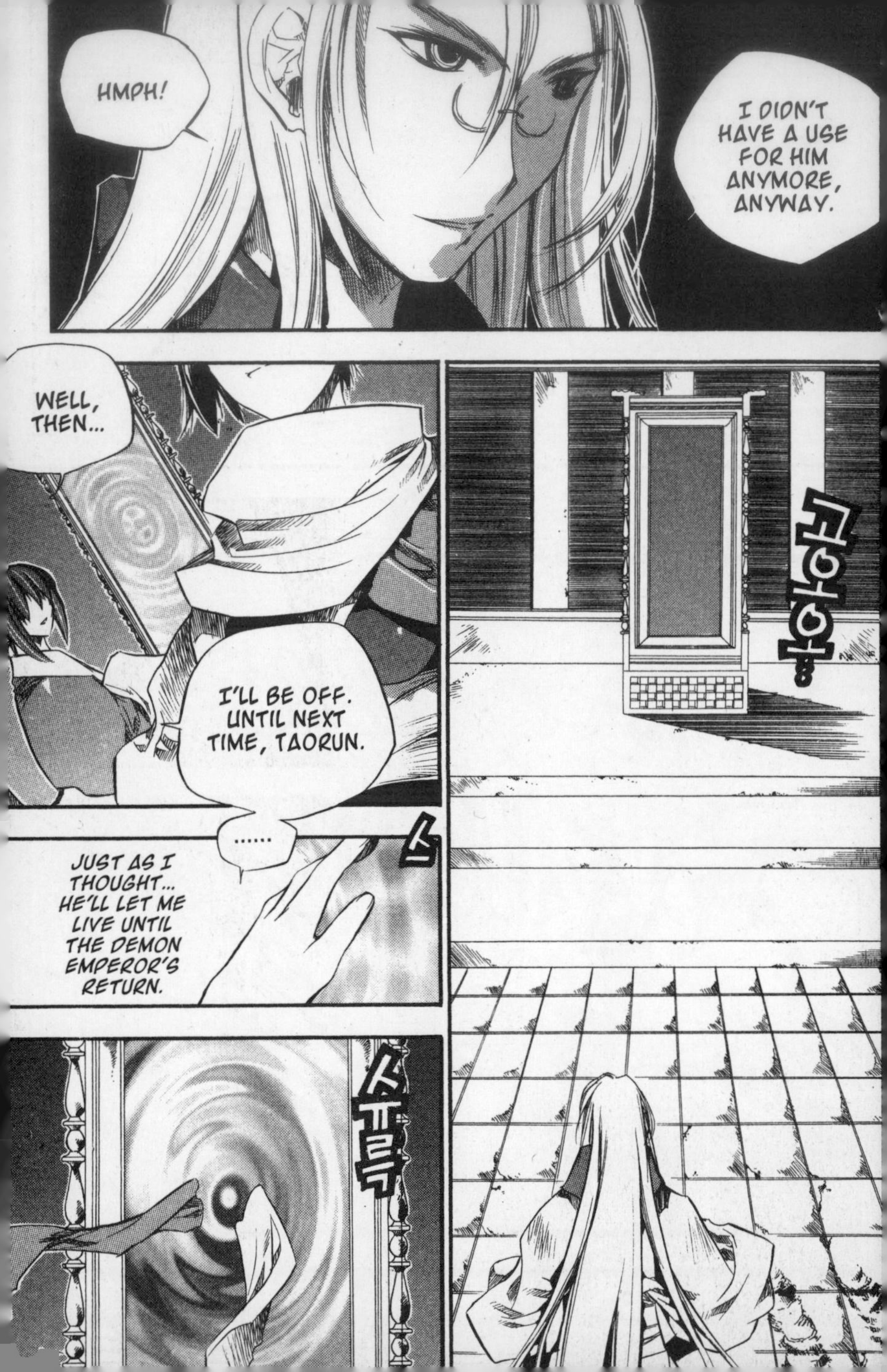
HMPH!
I DIDN'T HAVE A USE FOR HIM ANYMORE, ANYWAY.
WELL, THEN...
I'LL BE OFF. UNTIL NEXT TIME, TAORUN.
......
스-
JUST AS I THOUGHT... HE'LL LET ME LIVE UNTIL THE DEMON EMPEROR'S RETURN.

ENJOY YOUR VICTORY, SHIYAN. BUT REALIZE IT'S ONLY BECAUSE THE DEMON EMPEROR KNOWS YOUR EVERY MOVE THAT HE FEELS NO NEED TO ELIMINATE YOU JUST YET!

LET'S GO, GIRLS.

PARTY'S OVER. WE HAVE WORK TO DO.

PAORIN! OPEN THE DEMON CURTAINS AND SECURE OUR PASSAGE TO THE OTHER WORLD!

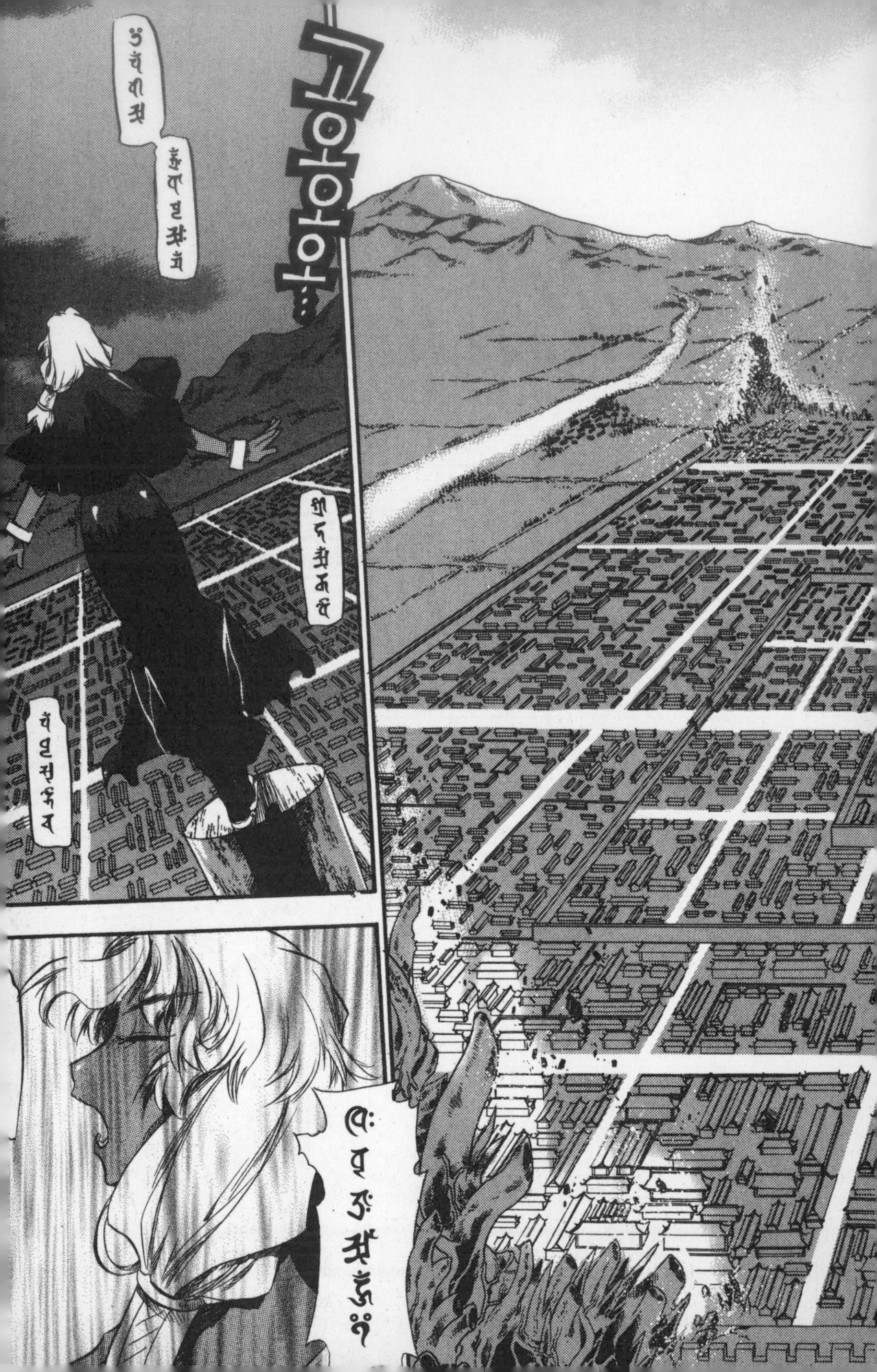
고오오오오…

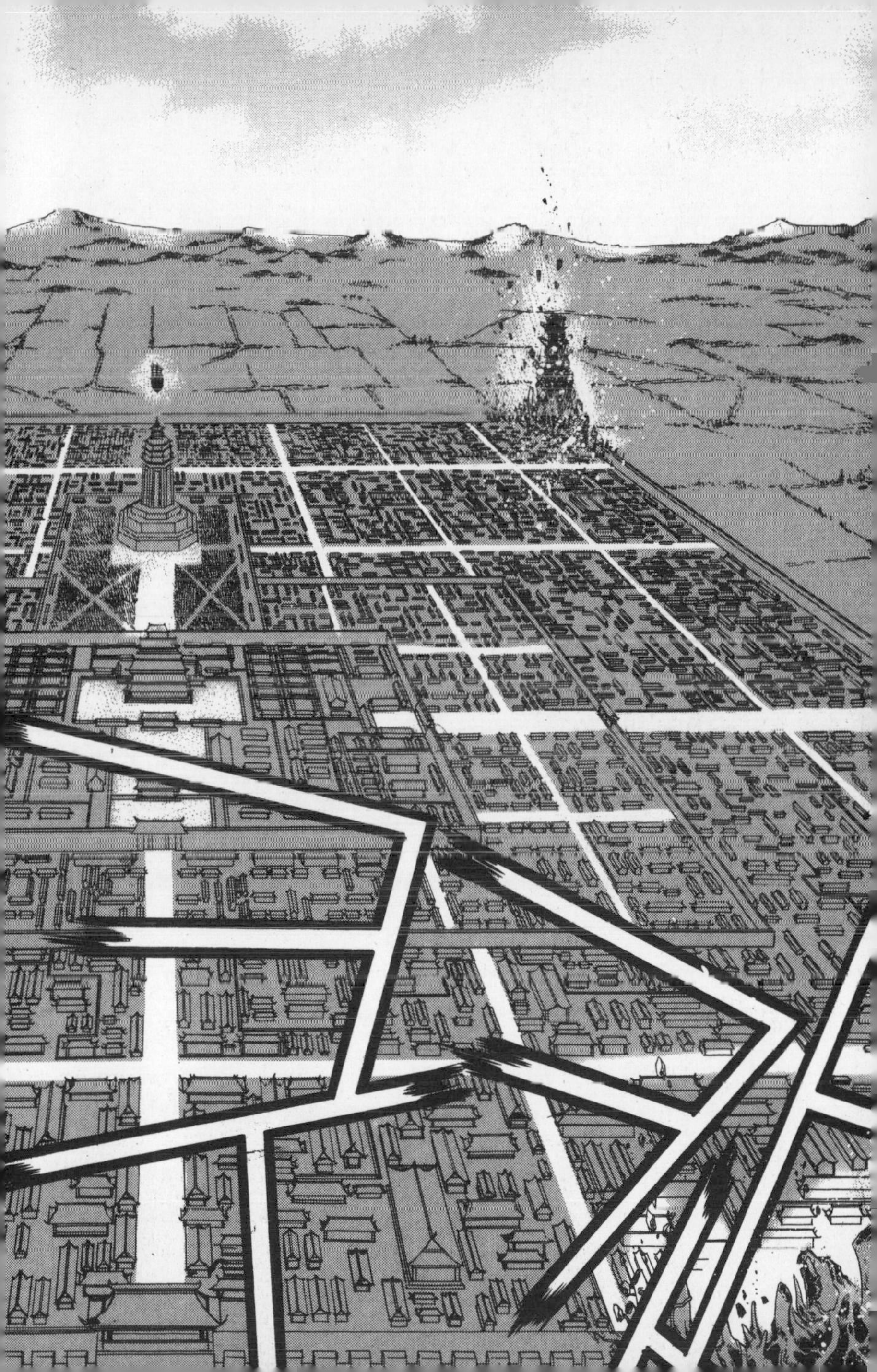

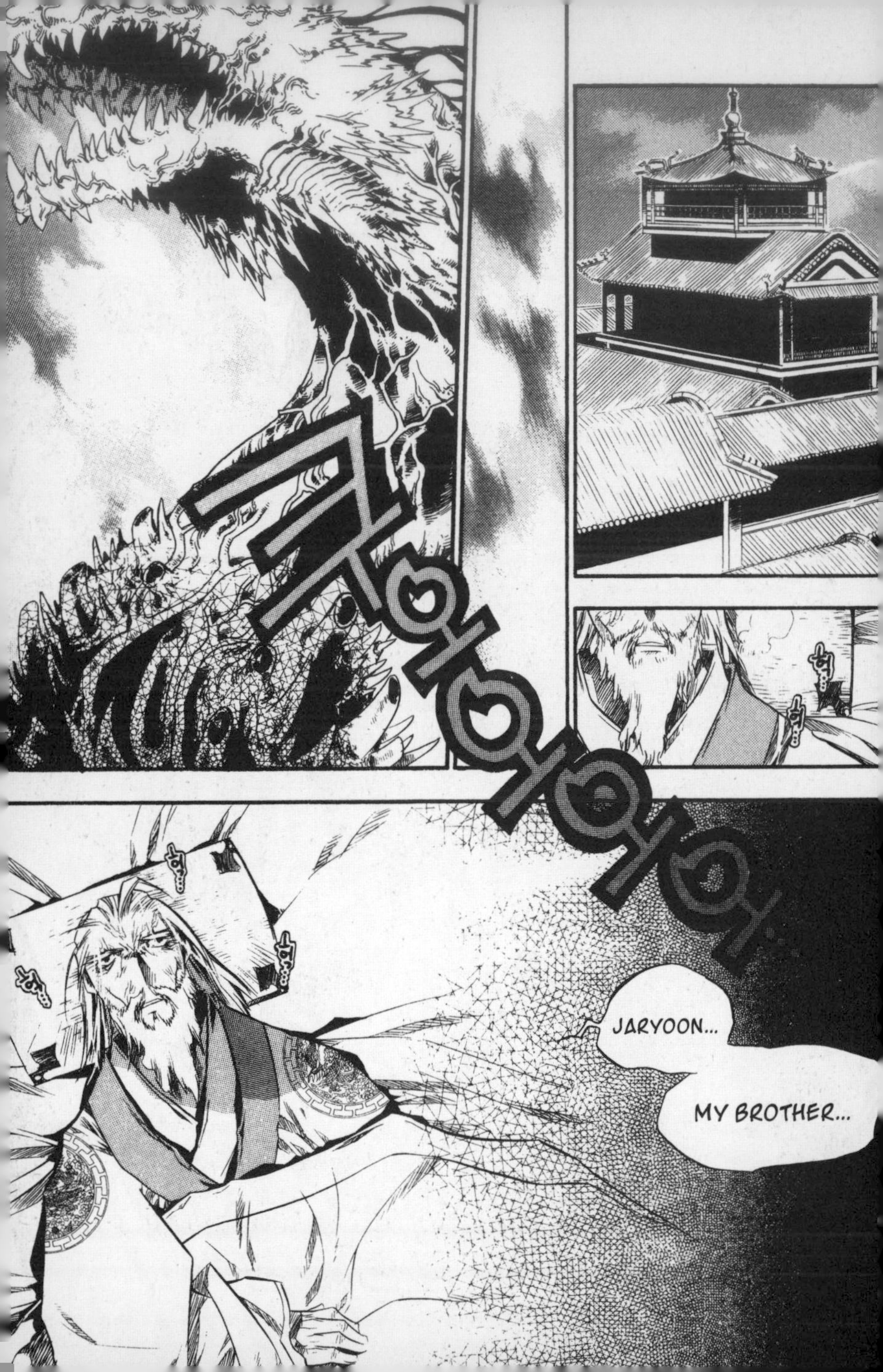
JARYOON...
MY BROTHER...

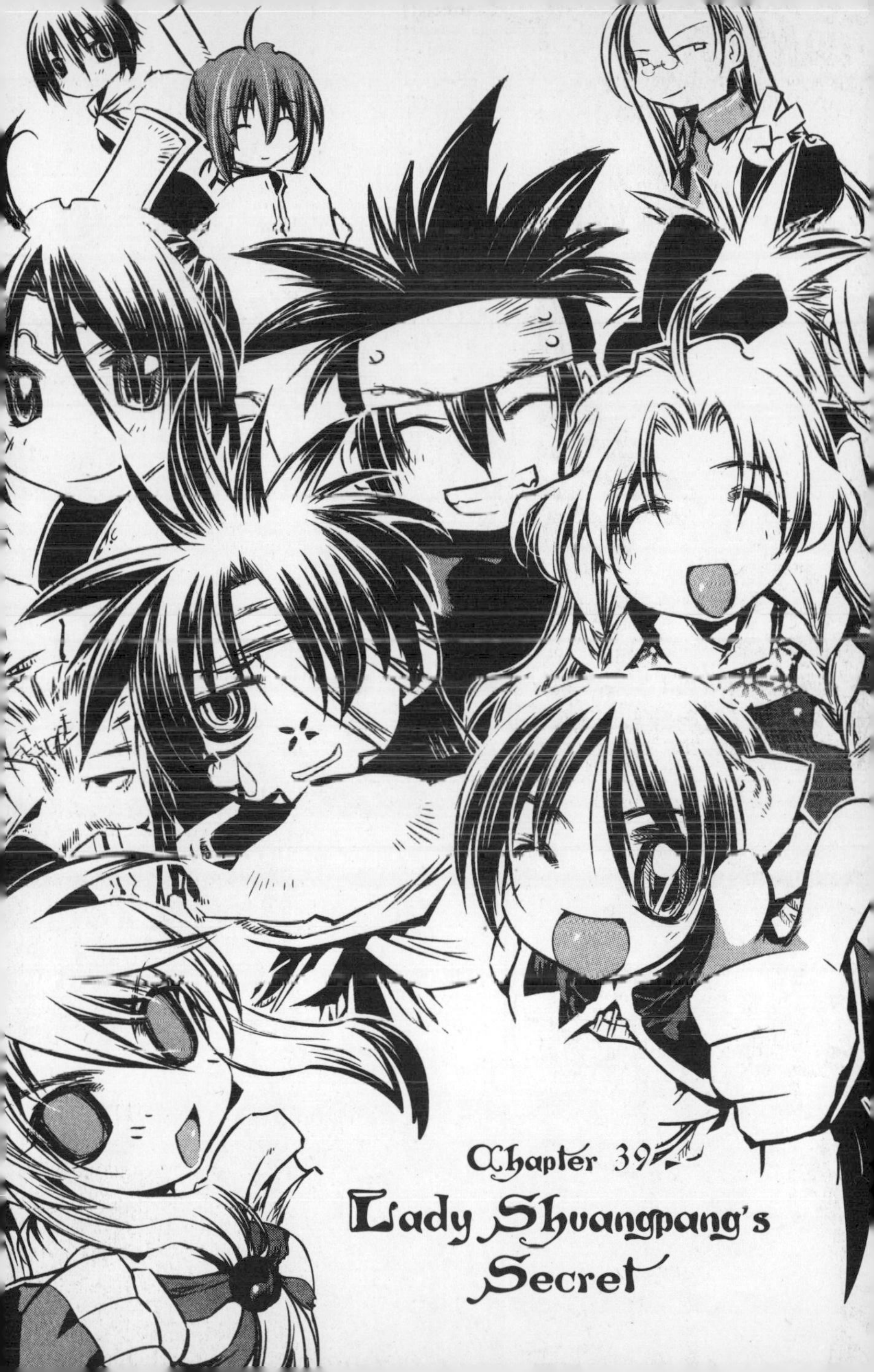

Chapter 39

Lady Shuangpang's Secret

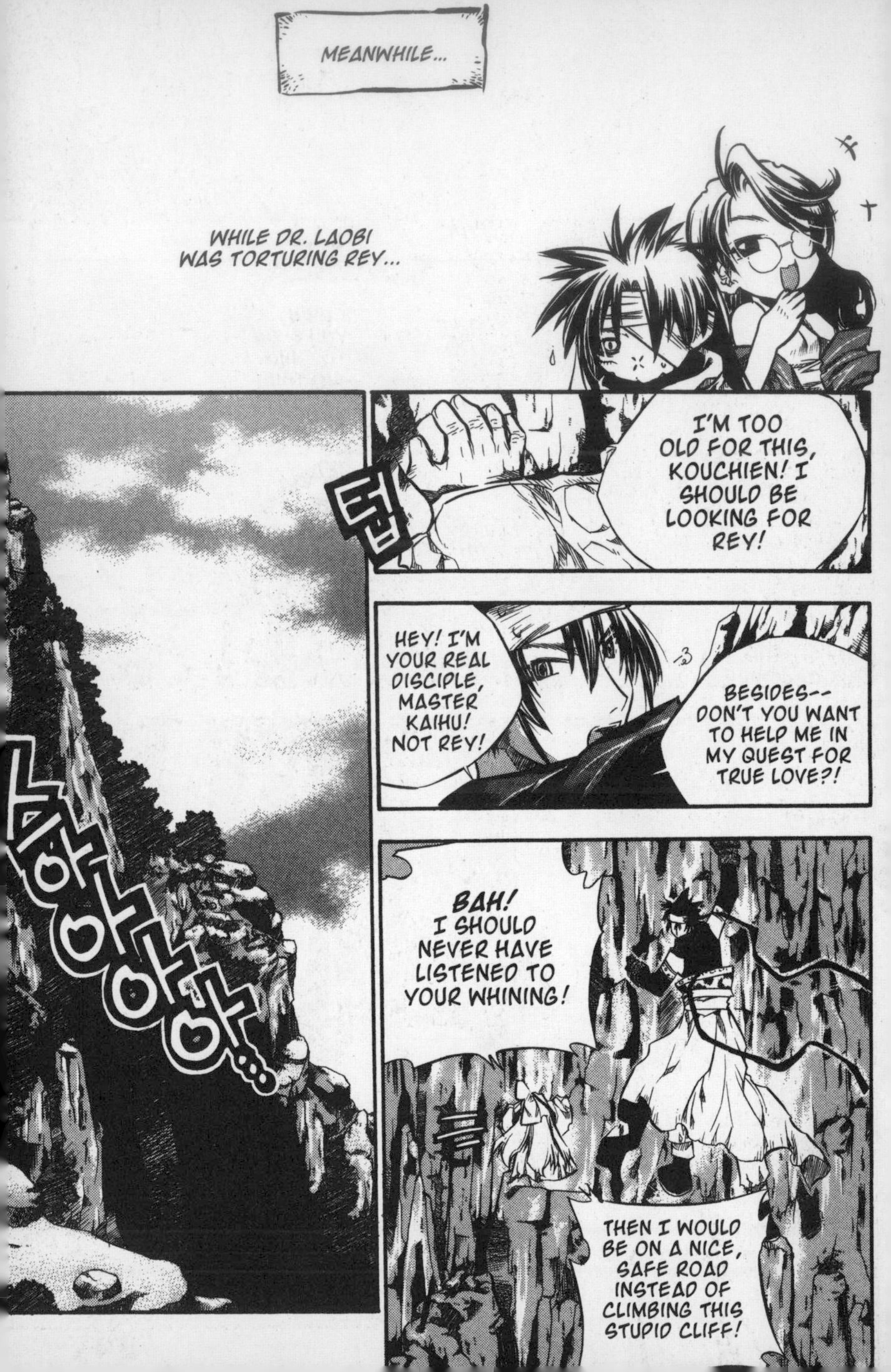
MEANWHILE...
WHILE DR. LAOBI WAS TORTURING REY...
I'M TOO OLD FOR THIS, KOUCHIEN! I SHOULD BE LOOKING FOR REY!
HEY! I'M YOUR REAL DISCIPLE, MASTER KAIHU! NOT REY!
BESIDES-- DON'T YOU WANT TO HELP ME IN MY QUEST FOR TRUE LOVE?!
BAH! I SHOULD NEVER HAVE LISTENED TO YOUR WHINING!
THEN I WOULD BE ON A NICE, SAFE ROAD INSTEAD OF CLIMBING THIS STUPID CLIFF!

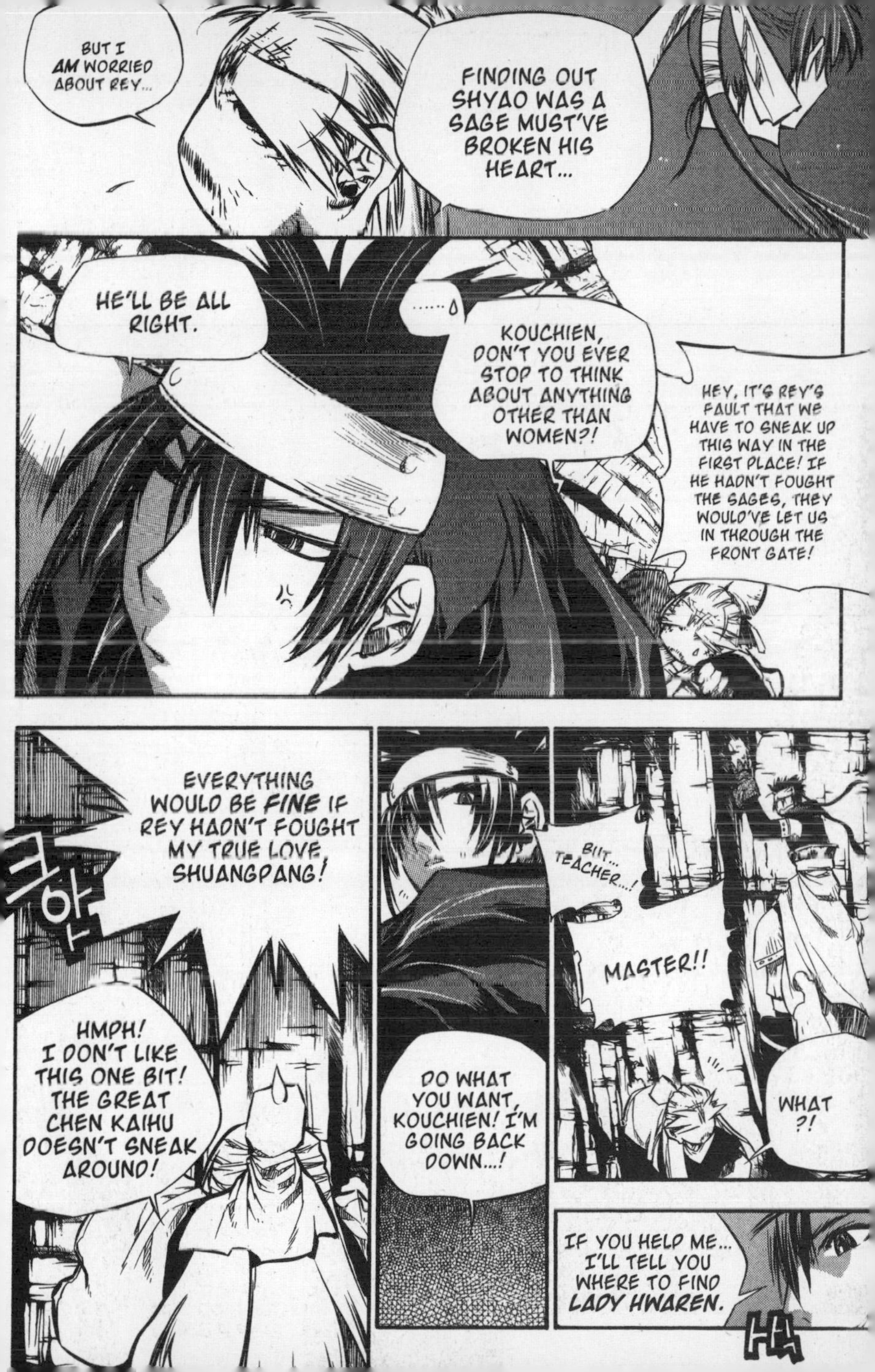
BUT I AM WORRIED ABOUT REY...
FINDING OUT SHYAO WAS A SAGE MUST'VE BROKEN HIS HEART...
HE'LL BE ALL RIGHT.
......
KOUCHIEN, DON'T YOU EVER STOP TO THINK ABOUT ANYTHING OTHER THAN WOMEN?!
HEY, IT'S REY'S FAULT THAT WE HAVE TO SNEAK UP THIS WAY IN THE FIRST PLACE! IF HE HADN'T FOUGHT THE SAGES, THEY WOULD'VE LET US IN THROUGH THE FRONT GATE!
EVERYTHING WOULD BE FINE IF REY HADN'T FOUGHT MY TRUE LOVE, SHUANGPANG!
HMPH! I DON'T LIKE THIS ONE BIT! THE GREAT CHEN KAIHU DOESN'T SNEAK AROUND!
DO WHAT YOU WANT, KOUCHIEN! I'M GOING BACK DOWN...!
BUT... TEACHER...!
MASTER!!
WHAT?!
IF YOU HELP ME... I'LL TELL YOU WHERE TO FIND LADY HWAREN.

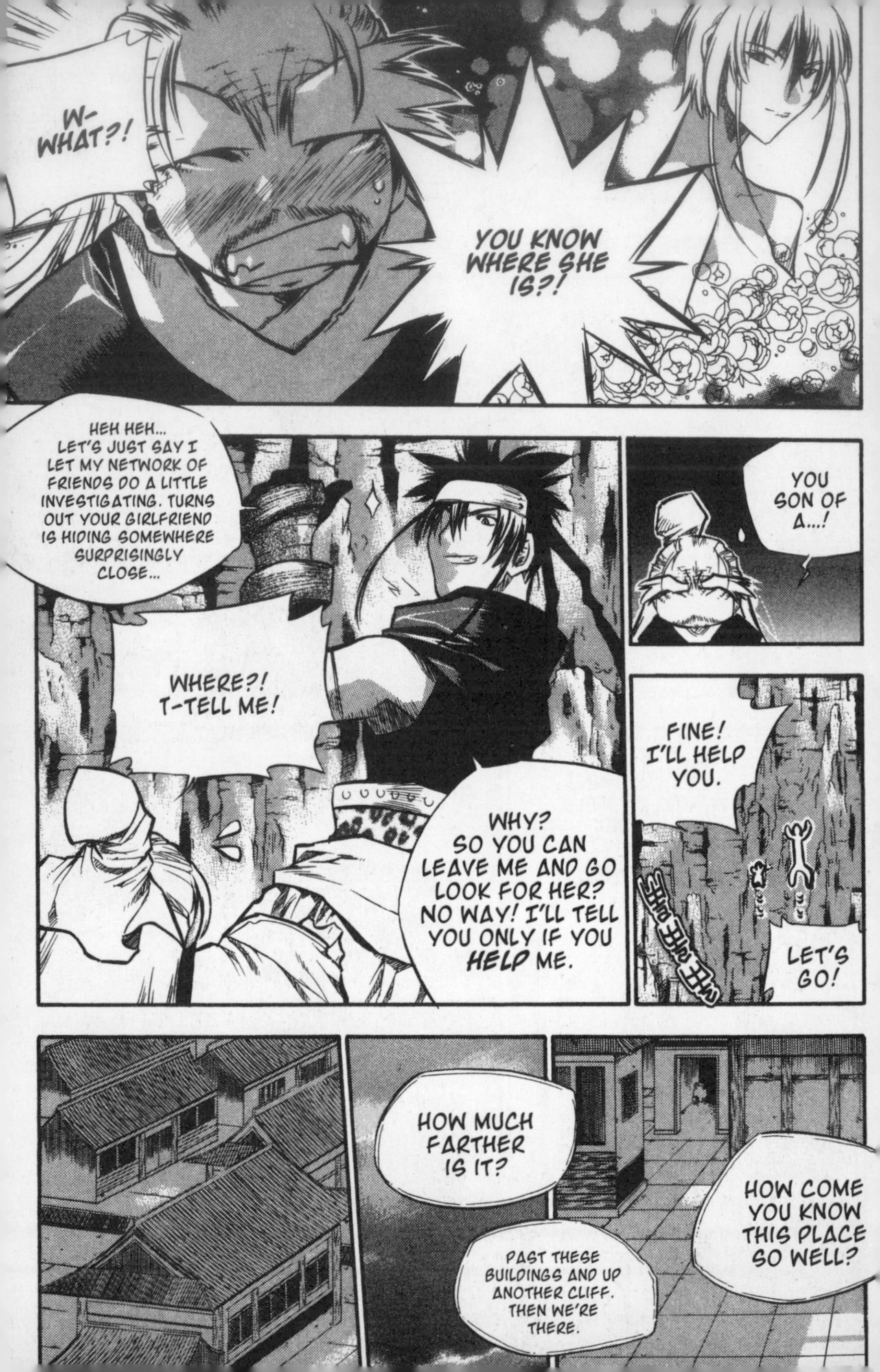
W-WHAT?!
YOU KNOW WHERE SHE IS?!
HEH HEH... LET'S JUST SAY I LET MY NETWORK OF FRIENDS DO A LITTLE INVESTIGATING. TURNS OUT YOUR GIRLFRIEND IS HIDING SOMEWHERE SURPRISINGLY CLOSE...
WHERE?! T-TELL ME!
WHY? SO YOU CAN LEAVE ME AND GO LOOK FOR HER? NO WAY! I'LL TELL YOU ONLY IF YOU HELP ME.
YOU SON OF A...!
FINE! I'LL HELP YOU.
LET'S GO!
HOW MUCH FARTHER IS IT?
PAST THESE BUILDINGS AND UP ANOTHER CLIFF. THEN WE'RE THERE.
HOW COME YOU KNOW THIS PLACE SO WELL?

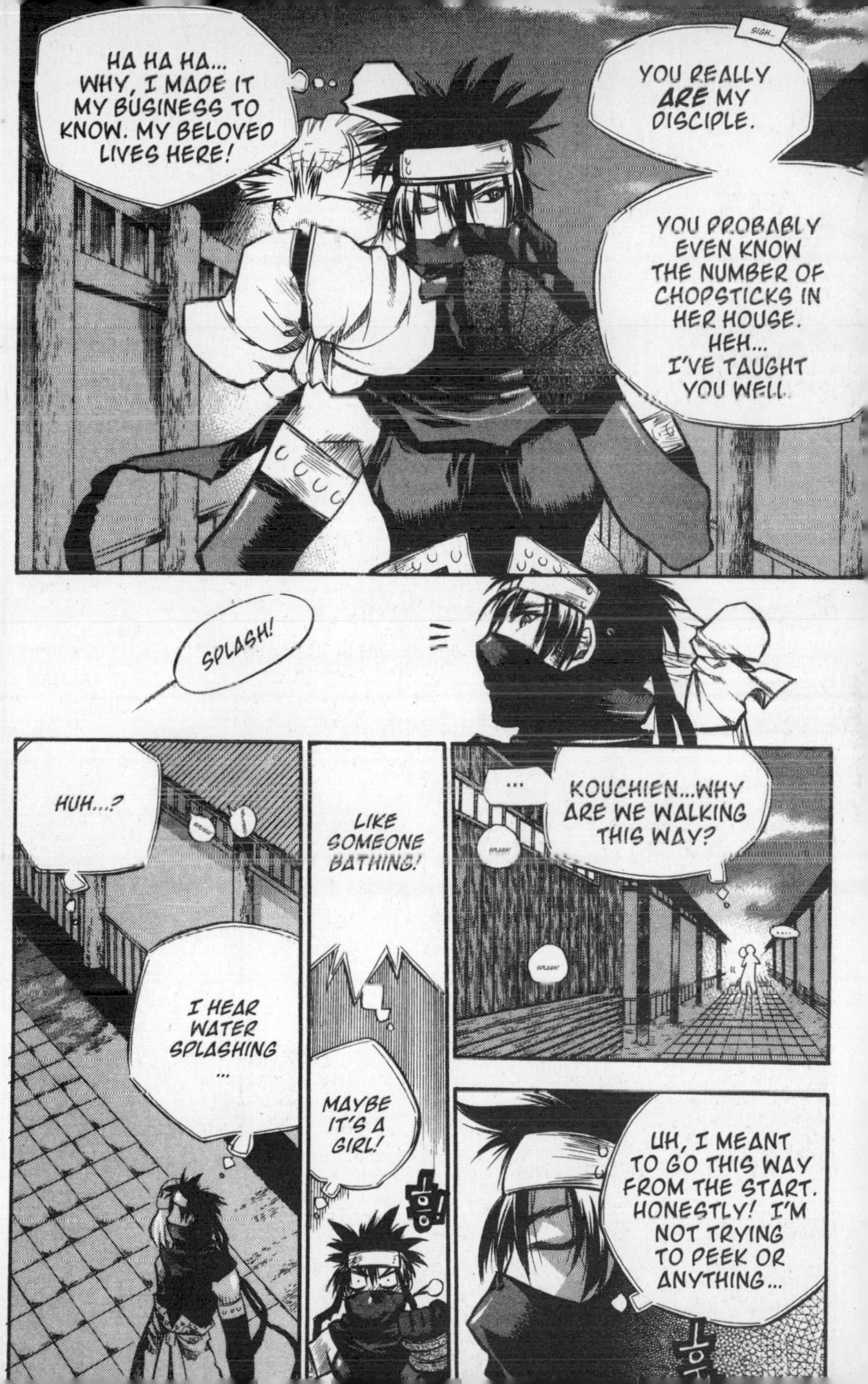
HA HA HA... WHY, I MADE IT MY BUSINESS TO KNOW. MY BELOVED LIVES HERE!
SIGH...
YOU REALLY **ARE** MY DISCIPLE.
YOU PROBABLY EVEN KNOW THE NUMBER OF CHOPSTICKS IN HER HOUSE. HEH... I'VE TAUGHT YOU WELL.
SPLASH!
HUH...?
I HEAR WATER SPLASHING ...
LIKE SOMEONE BATHING!
MAYBE IT'S A GIRL!
...
KOUCHIEN...WHY ARE WE WALKING THIS WAY?
UH, I MEANT TO GO THIS WAY FROM THE START. HONESTLY! I'M NOT TRYING TO PEEK OR ANYTHING...

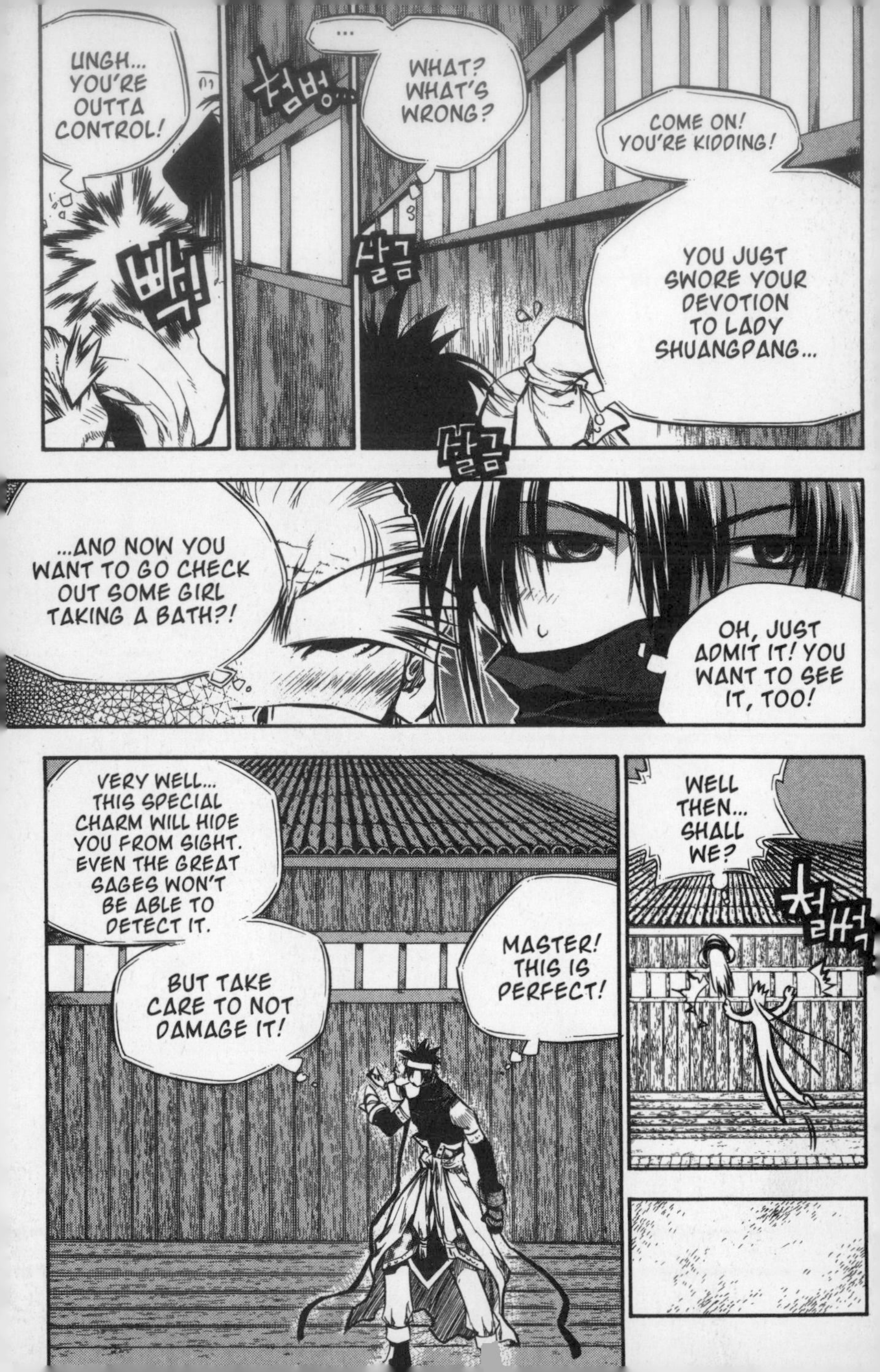
UNGH... YOU'RE OUTTA CONTROL!
빡
...
첨벙...
WHAT? WHAT'S WRONG?
COME ON! YOU'RE KIDDING!
살금
YOU JUST SWORE YOUR DEVOTION TO LADY SHUANGPANG...
살금
...AND NOW YOU WANT TO GO CHECK OUT SOME GIRL TAKING A BATH?!
OH, JUST ADMIT IT! YOU WANT TO SEE IT, TOO!
VERY WELL... THIS SPECIAL CHARM WILL HIDE YOU FROM SIGHT. EVEN THE GREAT SAGES WON'T BE ABLE TO DETECT IT.
BUT TAKE CARE TO NOT DAMAGE IT!
MASTER! THIS IS PERFECT!
WELL THEN... SHALL WE?

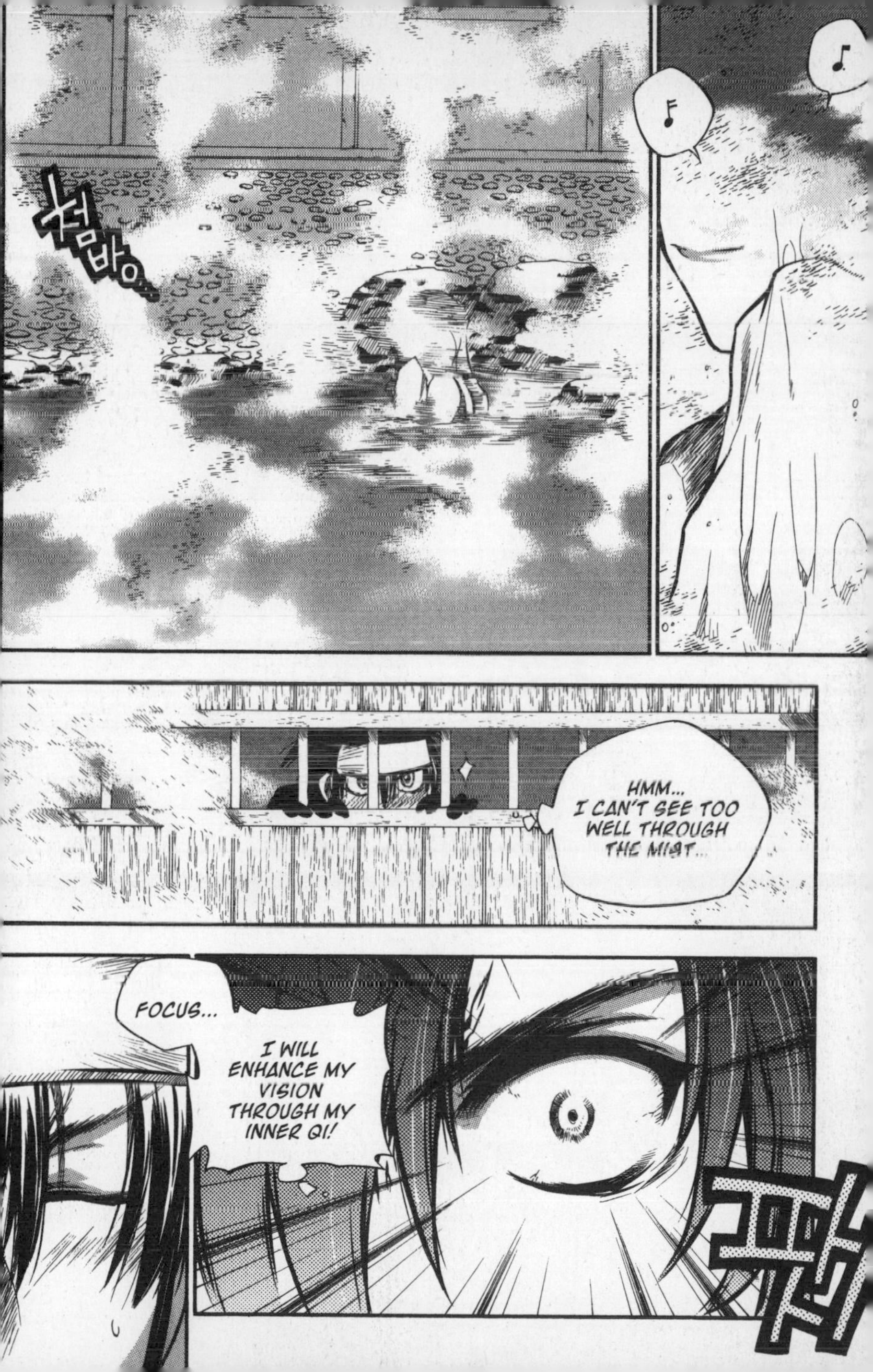
첨바아...
HMM... I CAN'T SEE TOO WELL THROUGH THE MIST...
FOCUS...
I WILL ENHANCE MY VISION THROUGH MY INNER QI!

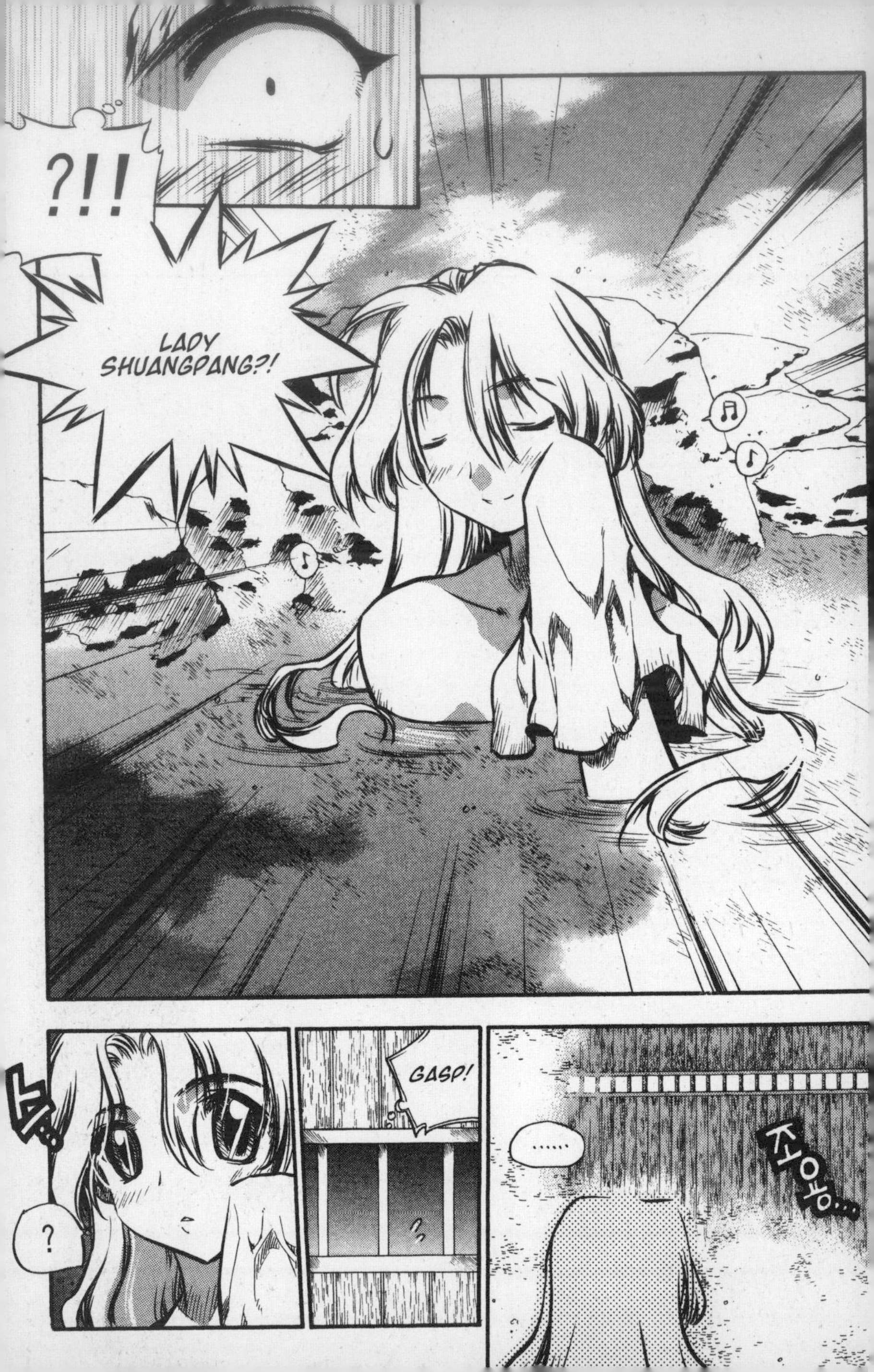
?!!
LADY SHUANGPANG?!
......
GASP!
?

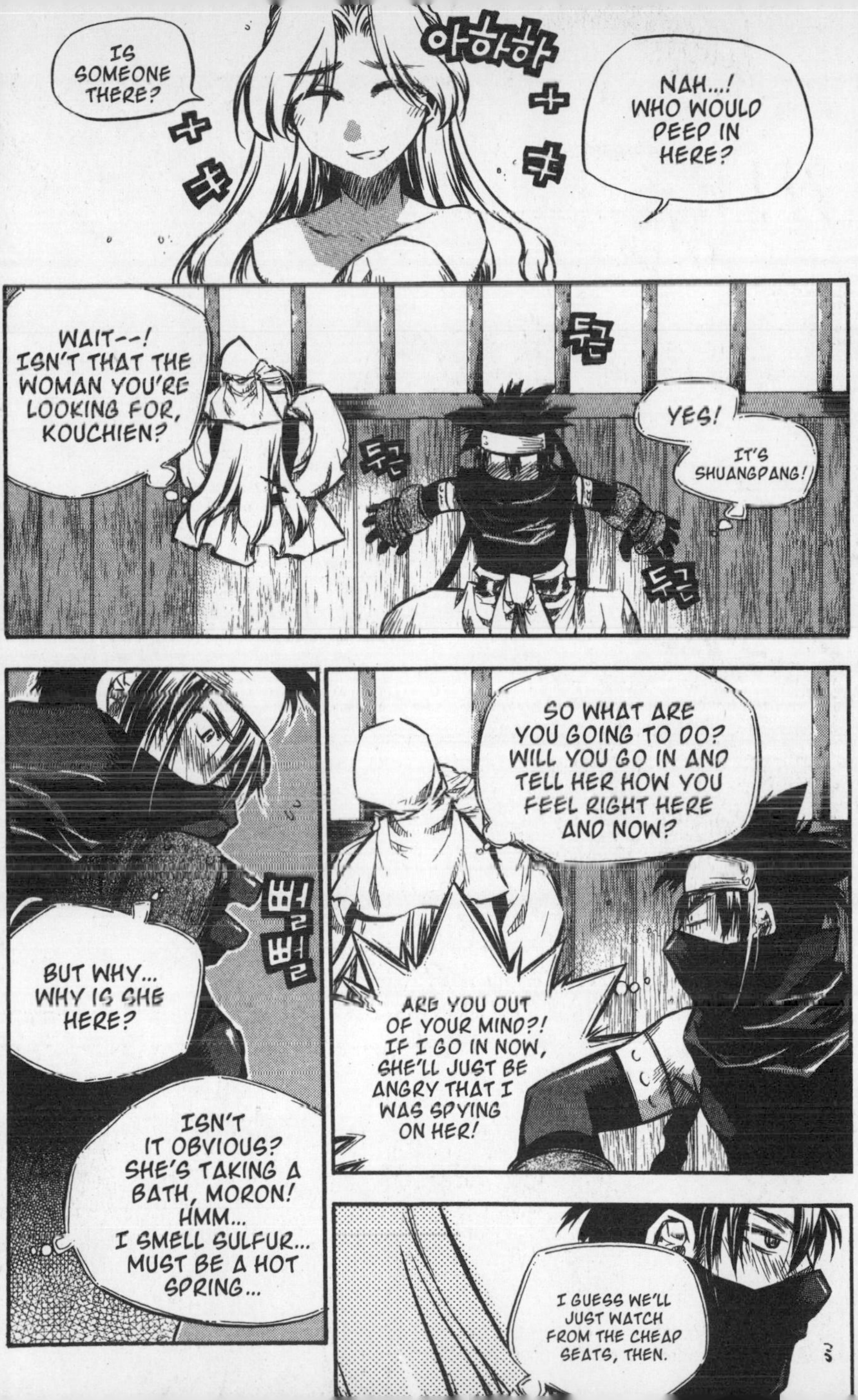
IS SOMEONE THERE?
아하하
NAH...! WHO WOULD PEEP IN HERE?
WAIT--! ISN'T THAT THE WOMAN YOU'RE LOOKING FOR, KOUCHIEN?
두근
두근
YES!
IT'S SHUANGPANG!
두근
삐질 삐질
BUT WHY... WHY IS SHE HERE?
ISN'T IT OBVIOUS? SHE'S TAKING A BATH, MORON! HMM... I SMELL SULFUR... MUST BE A HOT SPRING...
SO WHAT ARE YOU GOING TO DO? WILL YOU GO IN AND TELL HER HOW YOU FEEL RIGHT HERE AND NOW?
ARE YOU OUT OF YOUR MIND?! IF I GO IN NOW, SHE'LL JUST BE ANGRY THAT I WAS SPYING ON HER!
I GUESS WE'LL JUST WATCH FROM THE CHEAP SEATS, THEN.

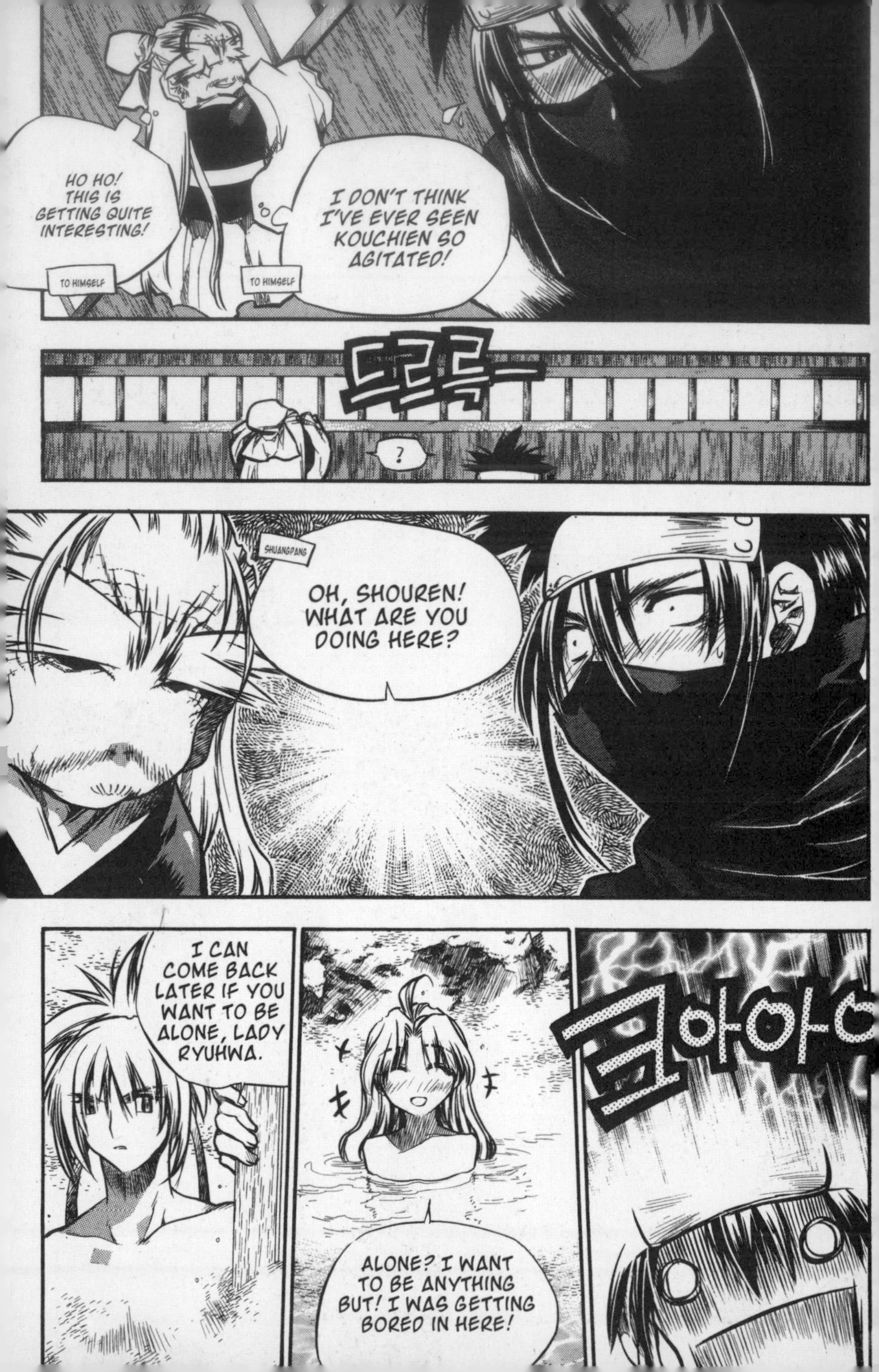
HO HO! THIS IS GETTING QUITE INTERESTING!
TO HIMSELF
I DON'T THINK I'VE EVER SEEN KOUCHIEN SO AGITATED!
TO HIMSELF
드르륵-
?
SHUANGPANG
OH, SHOUREN! WHAT ARE YOU DOING HERE?
I CAN COME BACK LATER IF YOU WANT TO BE ALONE, LADY RYUHWA.
ALONE? I WANT TO BE ANYTHING BUT! I WAS GETTING BORED IN HERE!

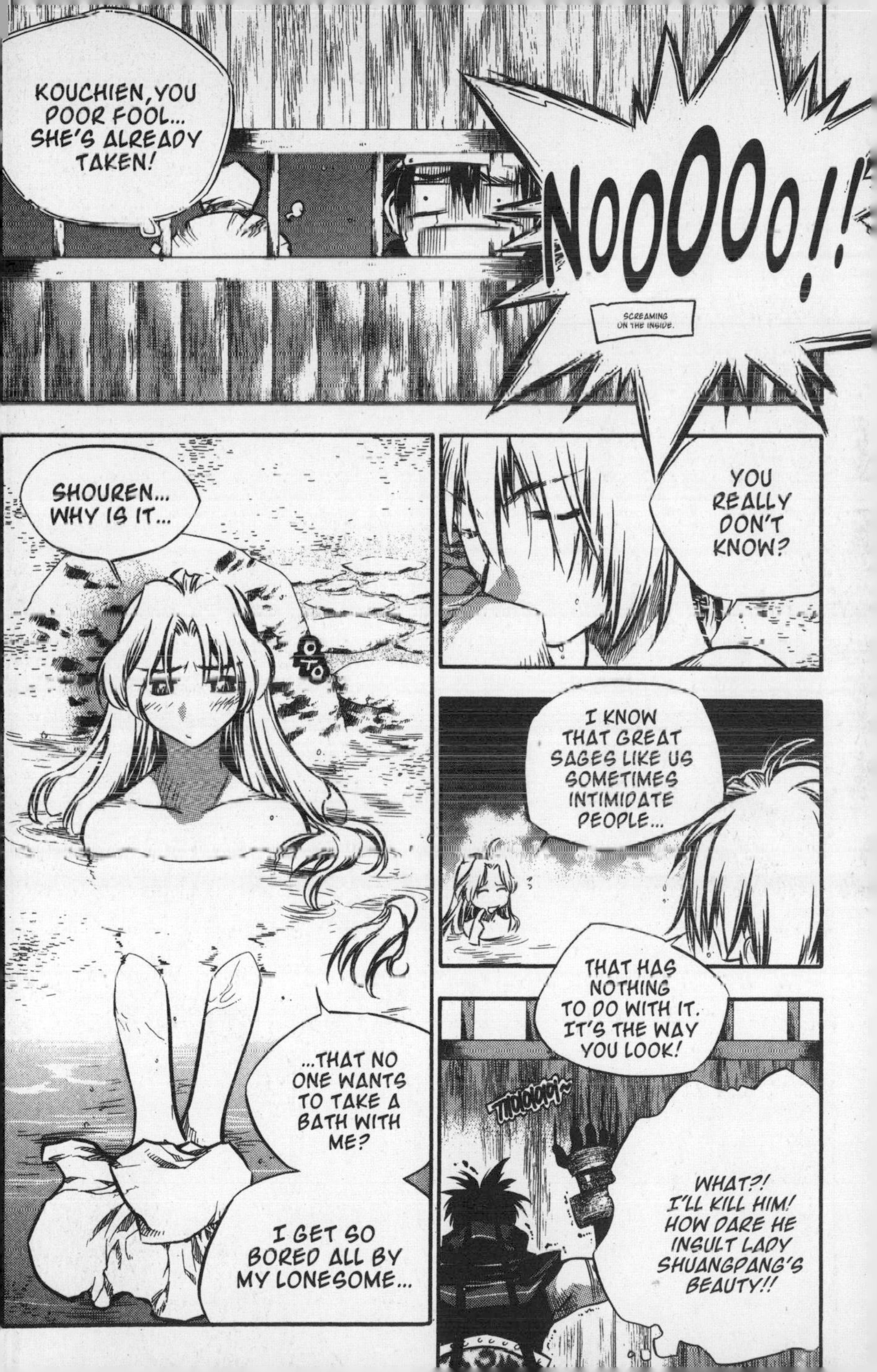
KOUCHIEN, YOU POOR FOOL... SHE'S ALREADY TAKEN!
NOOOOo!!
SCREAMING ON THE INSIDE.
SHOUREN... WHY IS IT...
...THAT NO ONE WANTS TO TAKE A BATH WITH ME?
I GET SO BORED ALL BY MY LONESOME...
YOU REALLY DON'T KNOW?
I KNOW THAT GREAT SAGES LIKE US SOMETIMES INTIMIDATE PEOPLE...
THAT HAS NOTHING TO DO WITH IT. IT'S THE WAY YOU LOOK!
WHAT?! I'LL KILL HIM! HOW DARE HE INSULT LADY SHUANGPANG'S BEAUTY!!

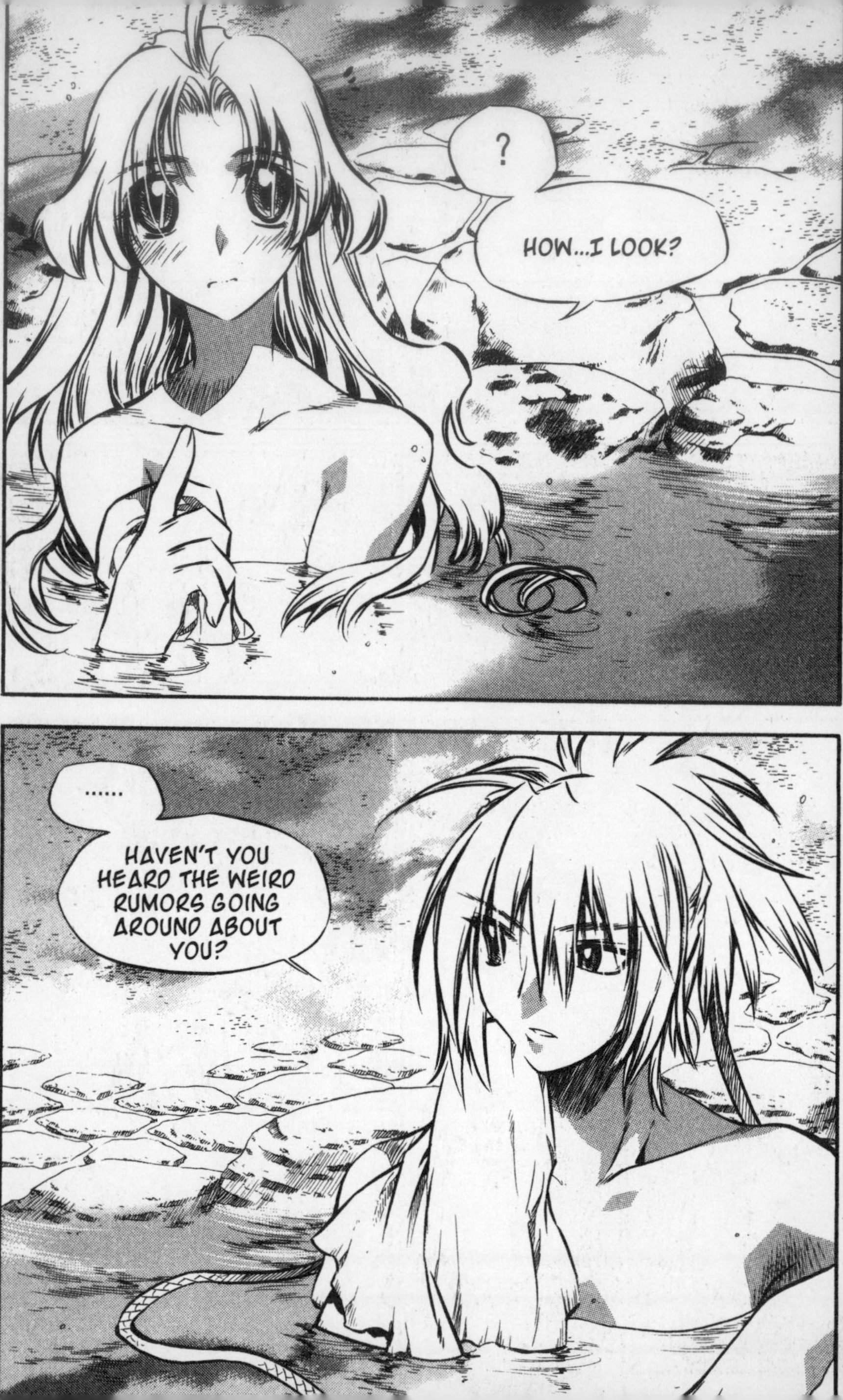
?
HOW...I LOOK?
......
HAVEN'T YOU HEARD THE WEIRD RUMORS GOING AROUND ABOUT YOU?

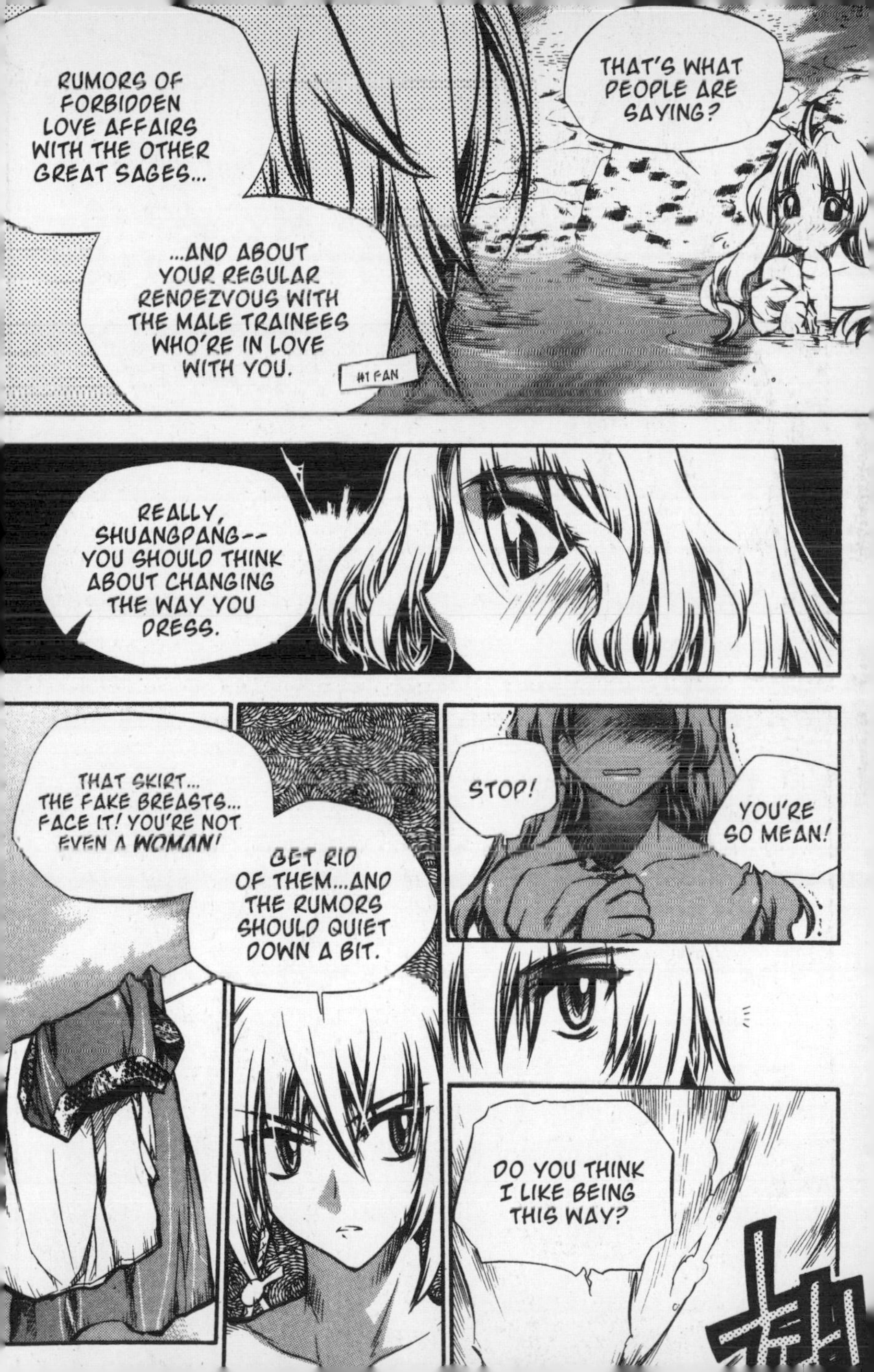
RUMORS OF FORBIDDEN LOVE AFFAIRS WITH THE OTHER GREAT SAGES...
...AND ABOUT YOUR REGULAR RENDEZVOUS WITH THE MALE TRAINEES WHO'RE IN LOVE WITH YOU.
#1 FAN
THAT'S WHAT PEOPLE ARE SAYING?
REALLY, SHUANGPANG-- YOU SHOULD THINK ABOUT CHANGING THE WAY YOU DRESS.
THAT SKIRT... THE FAKE BREASTS... FACE IT! YOU'RE NOT EVEN A *WOMAN*!
GET RID OF THEM...AND THE RUMORS SHOULD QUIET DOWN A BIT.
STOP!
YOU'RE SO MEAN!
DO YOU THINK I LIKE BEING THIS WAY?

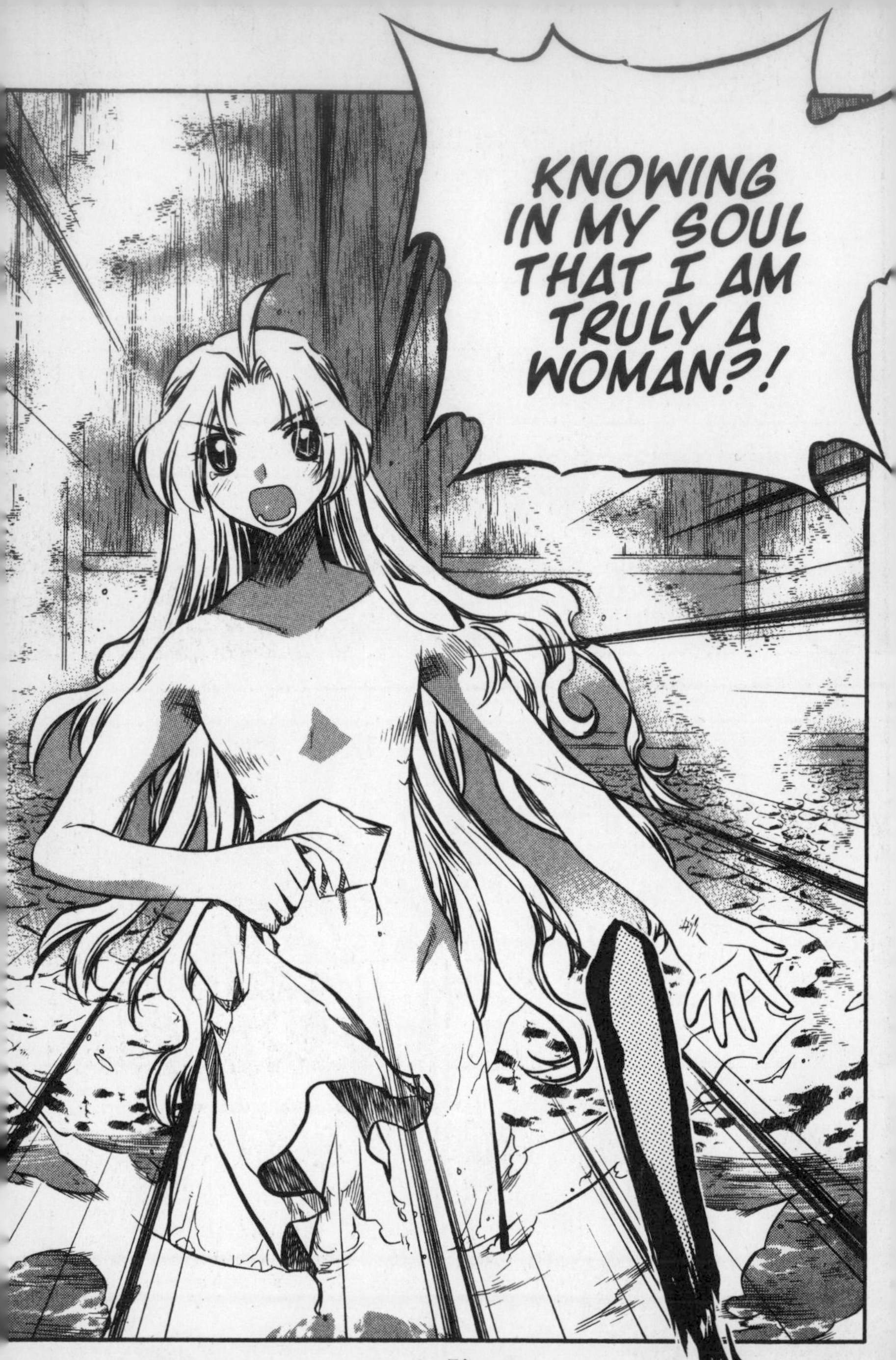
KNOWING IN MY SOUL THAT I AM TRULY A WOMAN?!

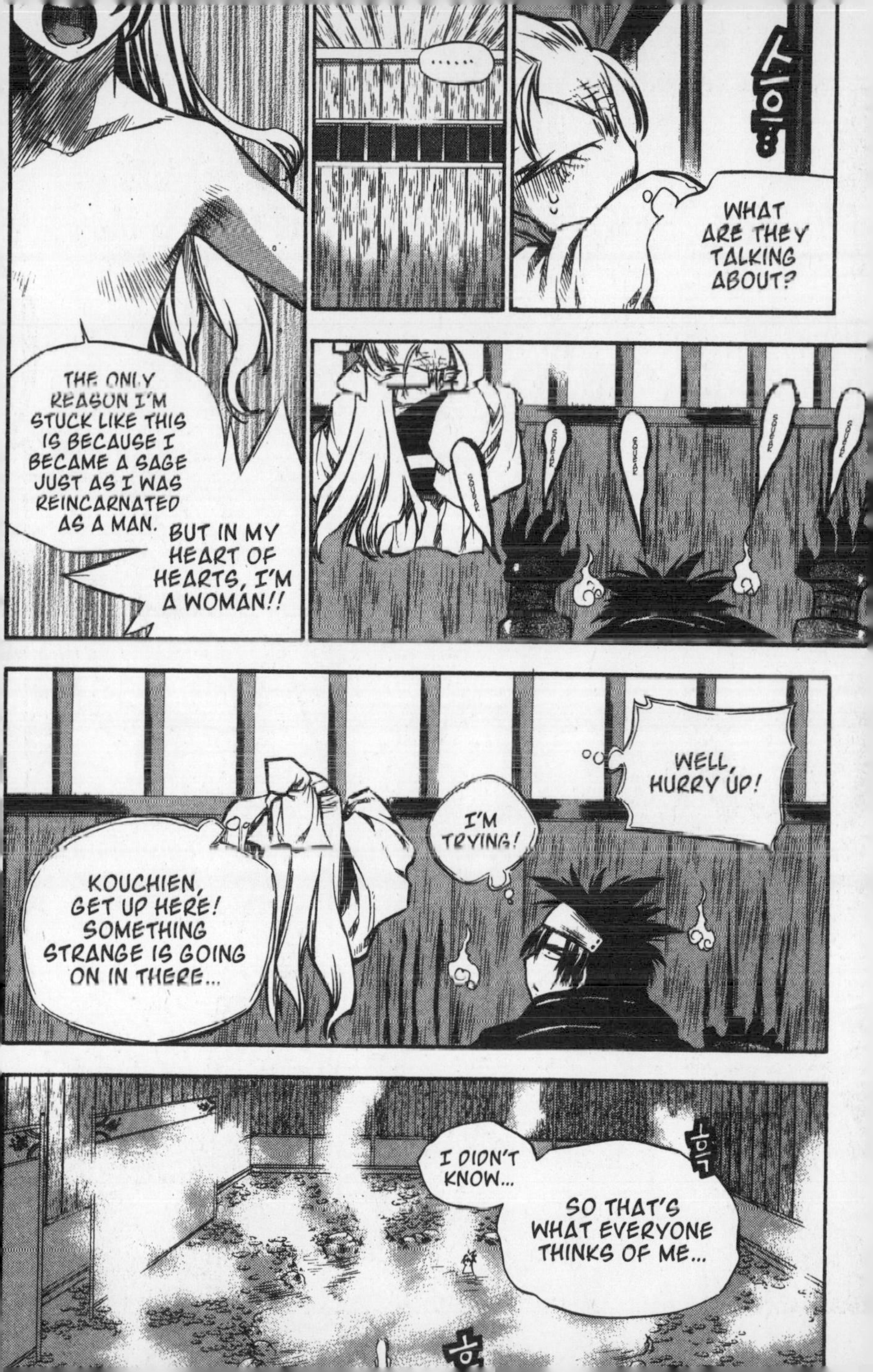
THE ONLY REASON I'M STUCK LIKE THIS IS BECAUSE I BECAME A SAGE JUST AS I WAS REINCARNATED AS A MAN.
BUT IN MY HEART OF HEARTS, I'M A WOMAN!!
......
WHAT ARE THEY TALKING ABOUT?
SQUEAK
SQUEAK
SQUEAK
SQUEAK
SQUEAK
KOUCHIEN, GET UP HERE! SOMETHING STRANGE IS GOING ON IN THERE...
I'M TRYING!
WELL, HURRY UP!
I DIDN'T KNOW...
SO THAT'S WHAT EVERYONE THINKS OF ME...

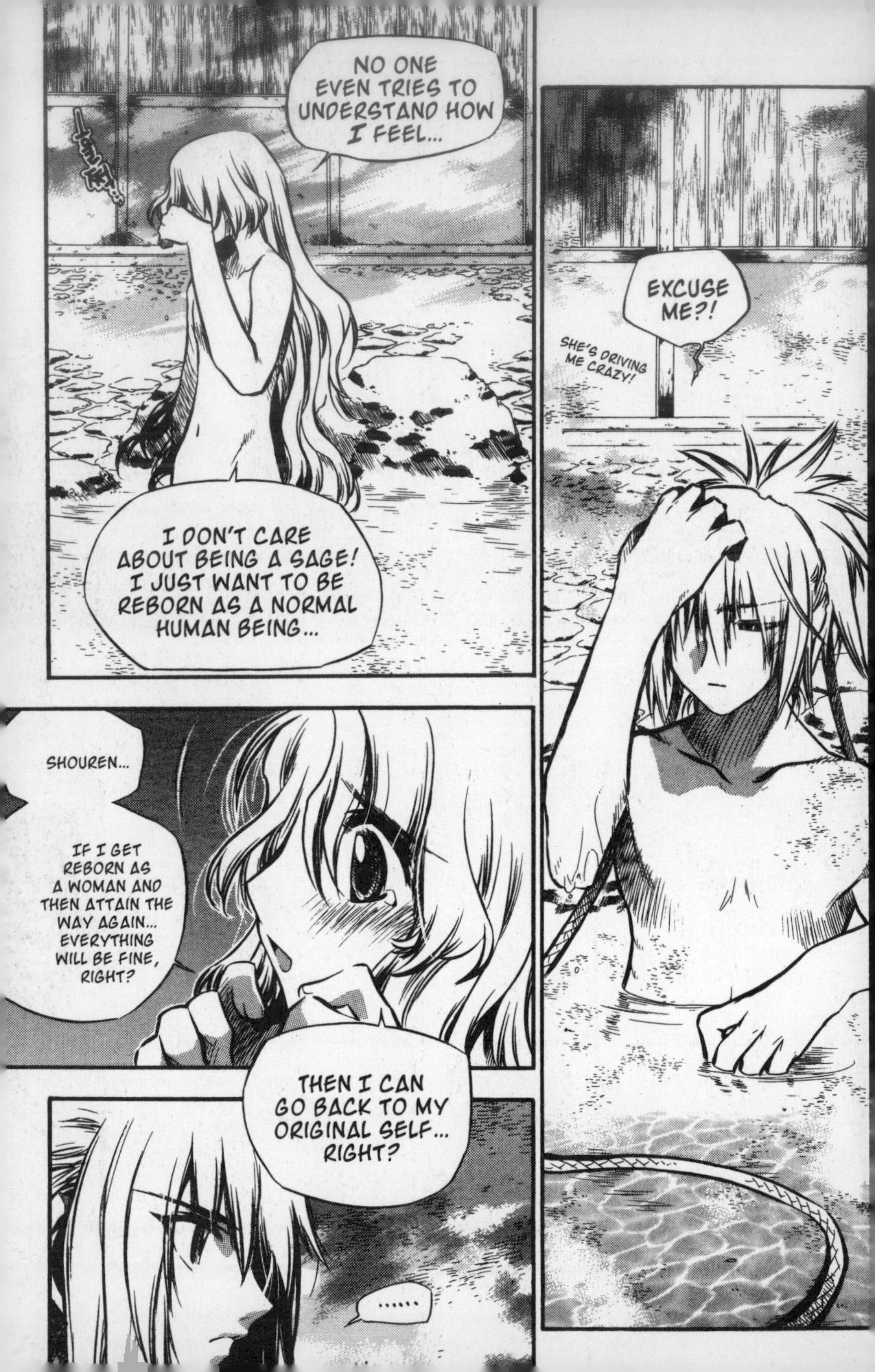
NO ONE EVEN TRIES TO UNDERSTAND HOW I FEEL...
I DON'T CARE ABOUT BEING A SAGE! I JUST WANT TO BE REBORN AS A NORMAL HUMAN BEING...
SHOUREN...
IF I GET REBORN AS A WOMAN AND THEN ATTAIN THE WAY AGAIN... EVERYTHING WILL BE FINE, RIGHT?
THEN I CAN GO BACK TO MY ORIGINAL SELF... RIGHT?
......
EXCUSE ME?!
SHE'S DRIVING ME CRAZY!

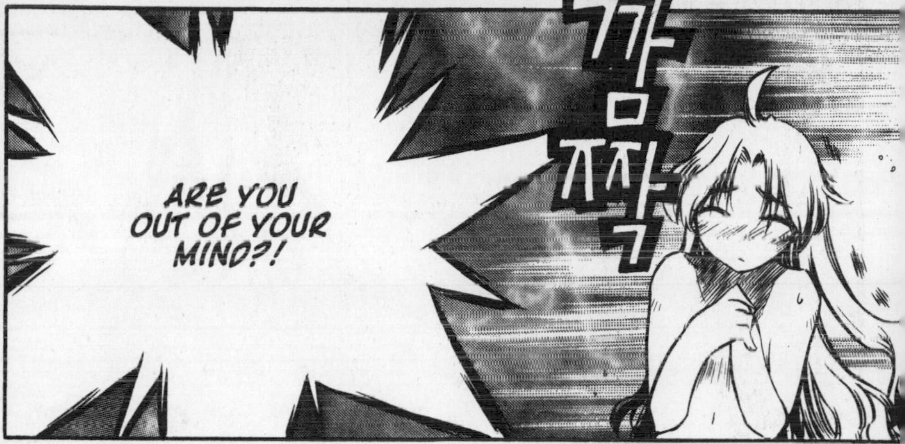
ARE YOU OUT OF YOUR MIND?!
깜짝

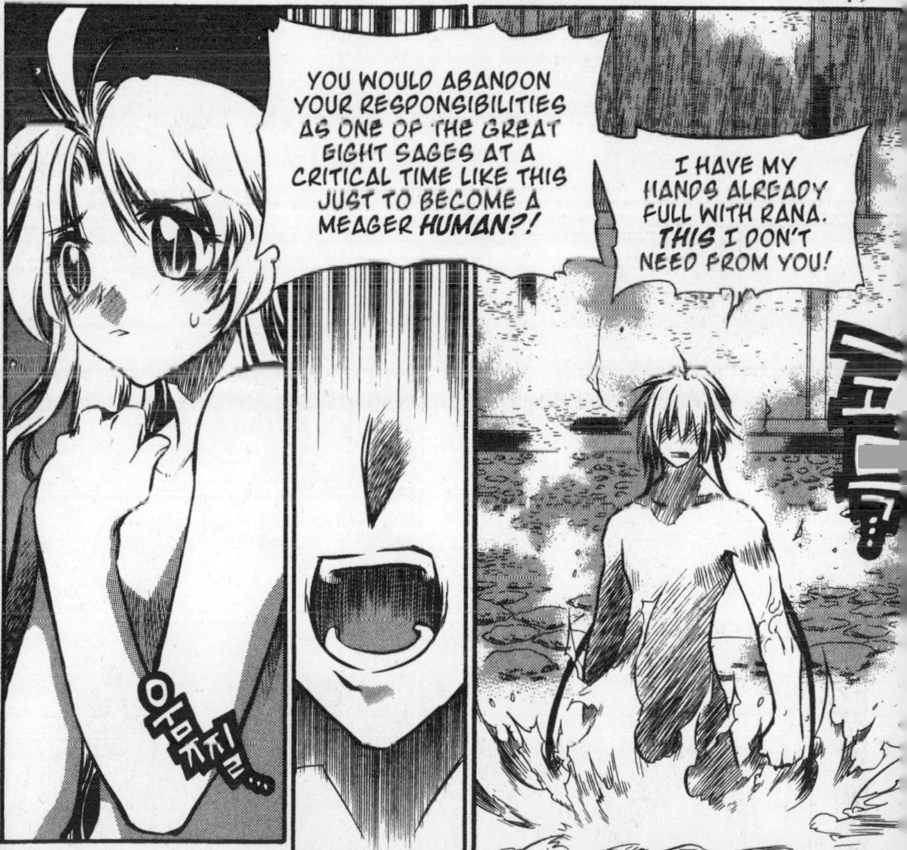
YOU WOULD ABANDON YOUR RESPONSIBILITIES AS ONE OF THE GREAT EIGHT SAGES AT A CRITICAL TIME LIKE THIS JUST TO BECOME A MEAGER HUMAN?!
I HAVE MY HANDS ALREADY FULL WITH RANA. THIS I DON'T NEED FROM YOU!

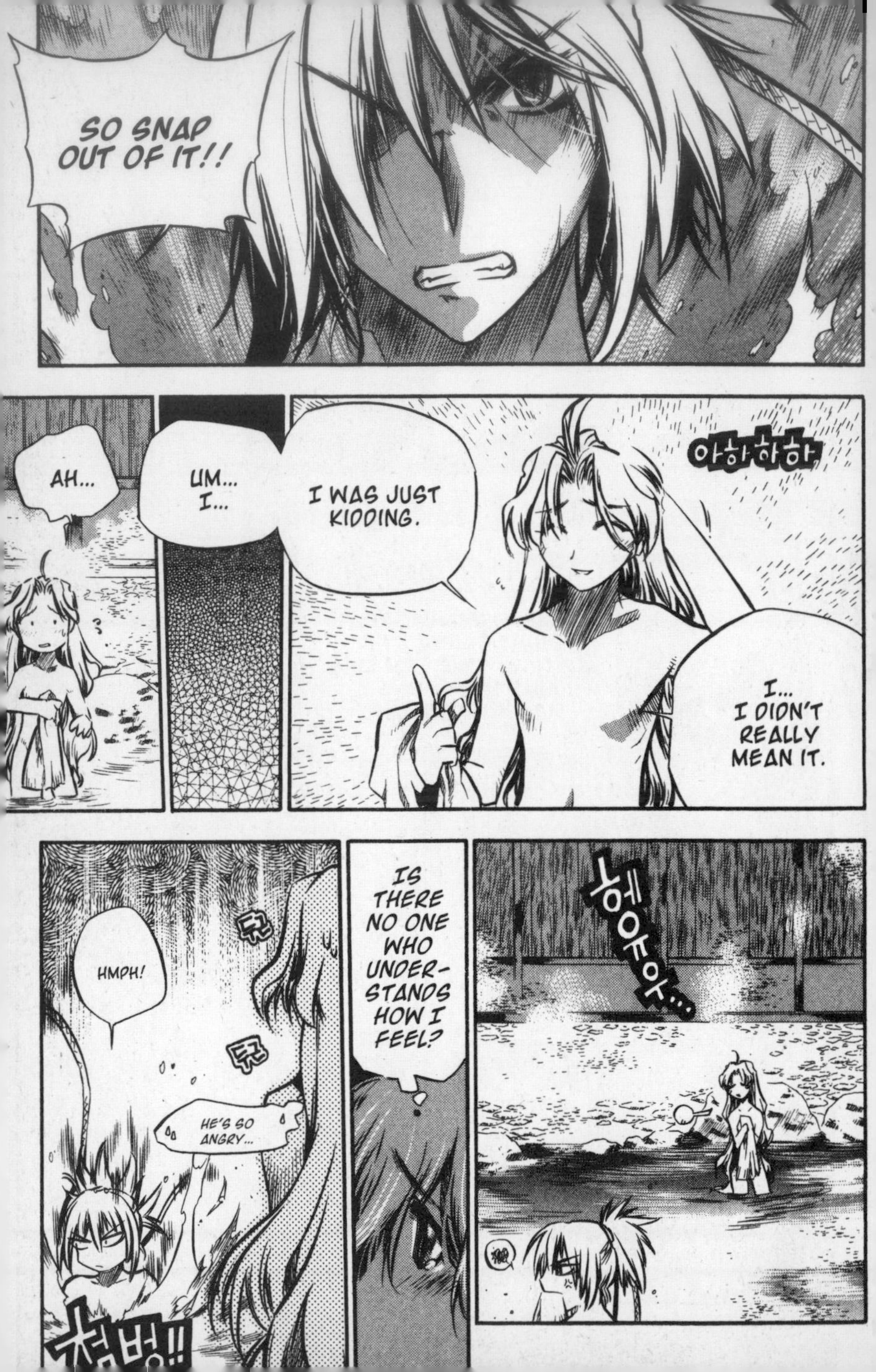
SO SNAP OUT OF IT!!
AH...
UM... I...
I WAS JUST KIDDING.
아하하하
I... I DIDN'T REALLY MEAN IT.
HMPH!
HE'S SO ANGRY...
IS THERE NO ONE WHO UNDER-STANDS HOW I FEEL?

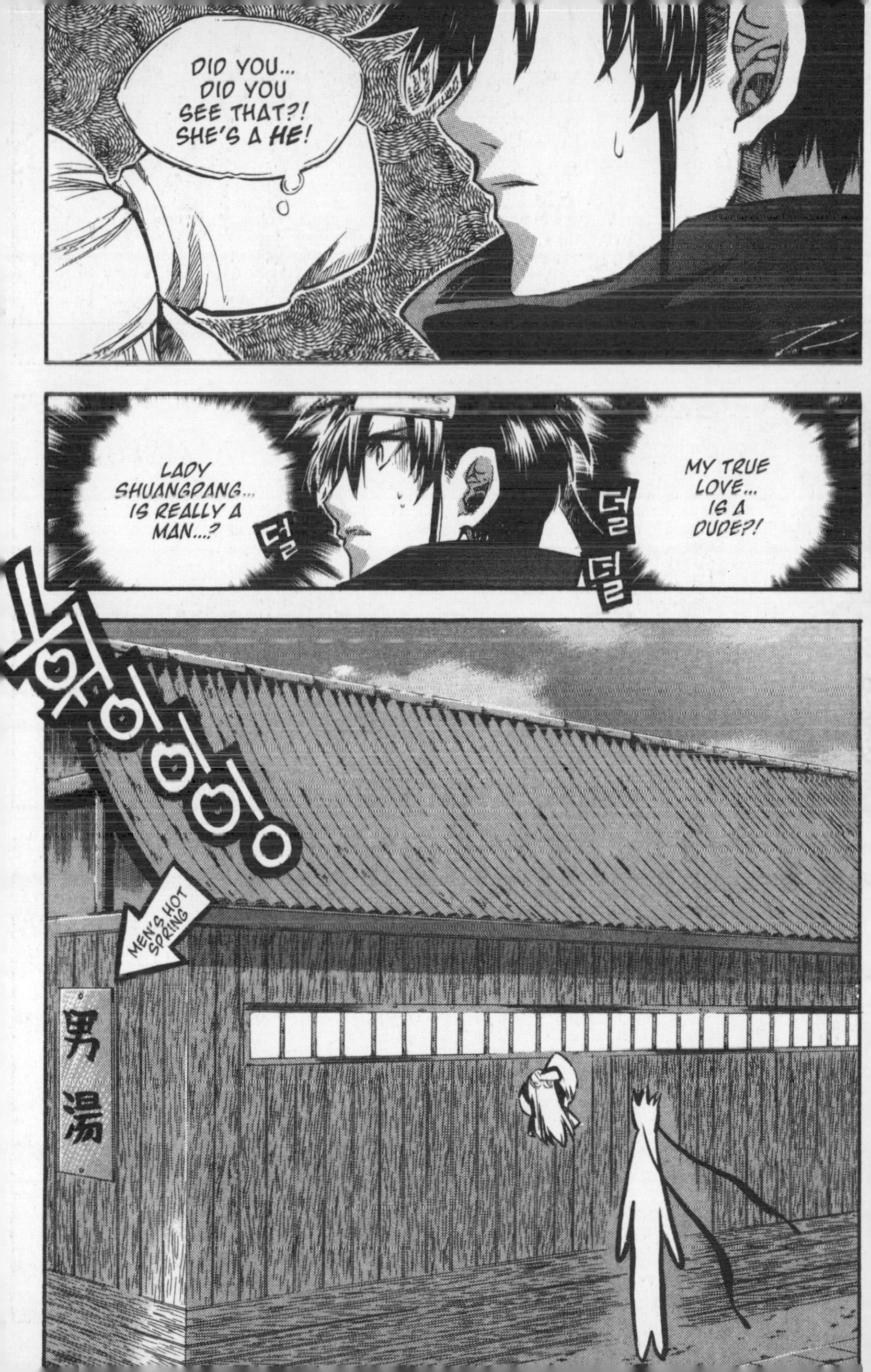
DID YOU... DID YOU SEE THAT?! SHE'S A HE!
LADY SHUANGPANG... IS REALLY A MAN...?
덜
덜 덜
MY TRUE LOVE... IS A DUDE?!
휘이이이잉
MEN'S HOT SPRING
男湯

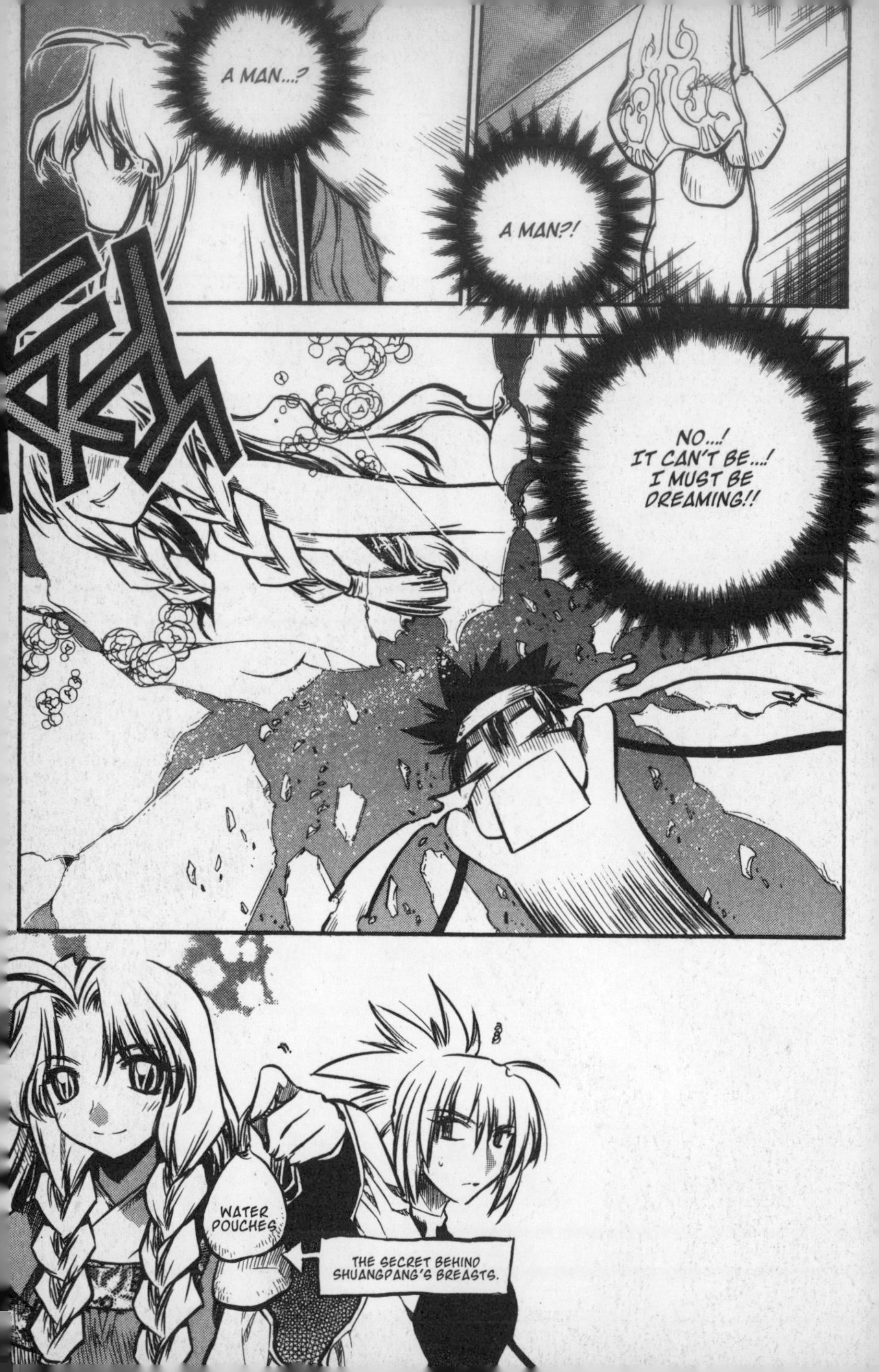

A MAN...?
A MAN?!
NO...! IT CAN'T BE...! I MUST BE DREAMING!!
WATER POUCHES
THE SECRET BEHIND SHUANGPANG'S BREASTS.

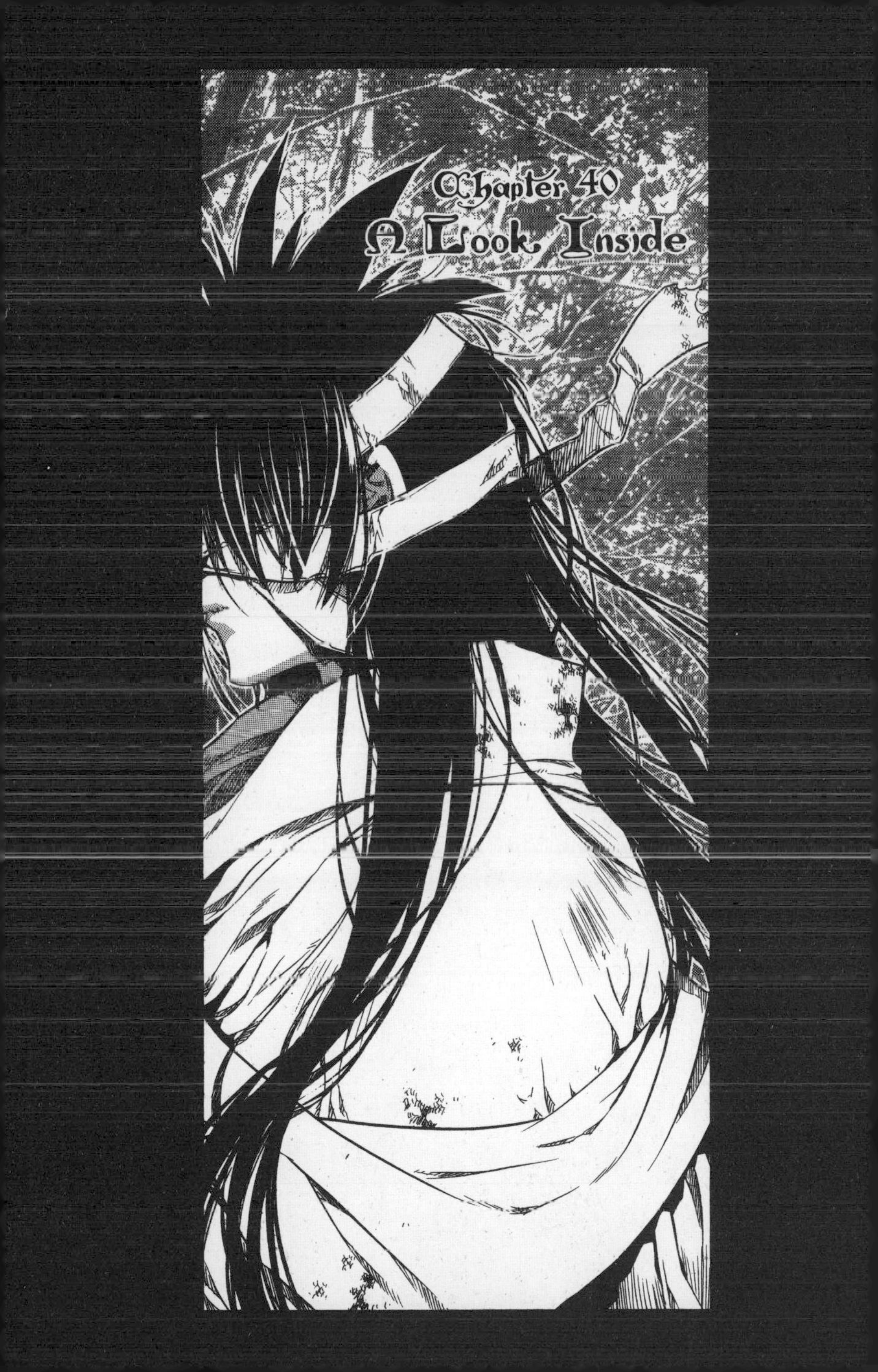
Chapter 40
A Look Inside

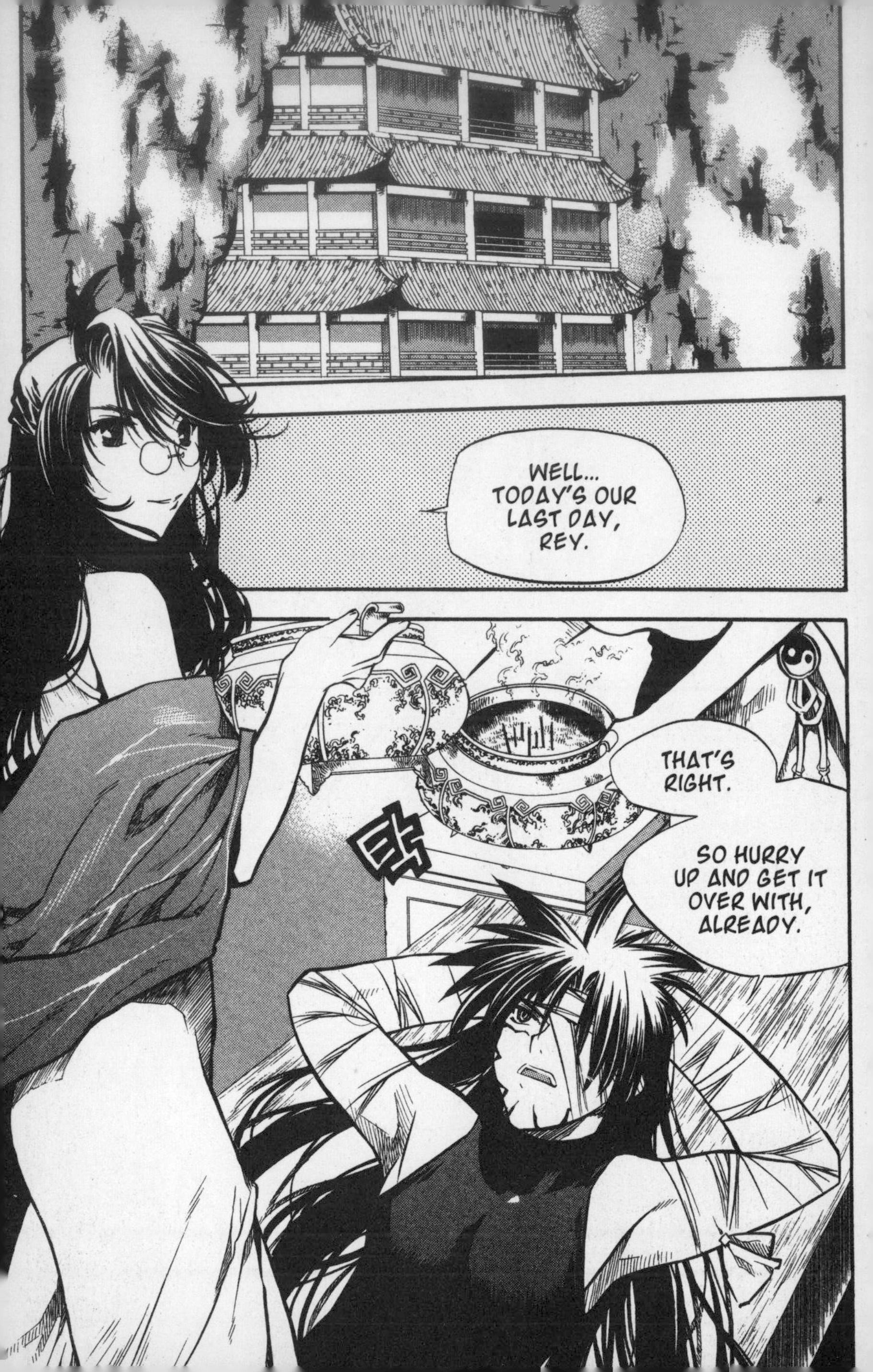
WELL... TODAY'S OUR LAST DAY, REY.
THAT'S RIGHT.
SO HURRY UP AND GET IT OVER WITH, ALREADY.

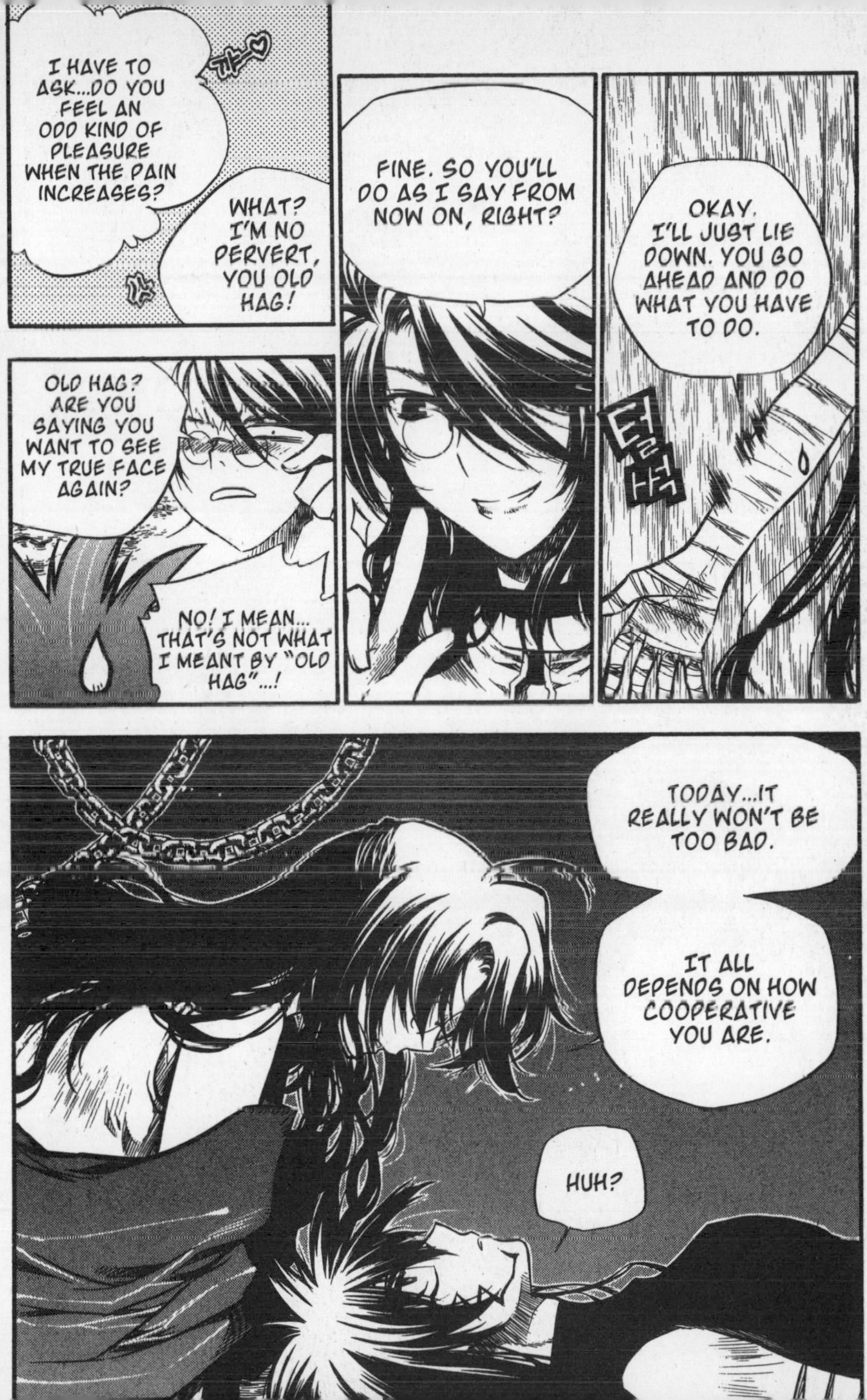
I HAVE TO ASK...DO YOU FEEL AN ODD KIND OF PLEASURE WHEN THE PAIN INCREASES?
WHAT? I'M NO PERVERT, YOU OLD HAG!
OLD HAG? ARE YOU SAYING YOU WANT TO SEE MY TRUE FACE AGAIN?
NO! I MEAN... THAT'S NOT WHAT I MEANT BY "OLD HAG"...!
FINE. SO YOU'LL DO AS I SAY FROM NOW ON, RIGHT?
OKAY. I'LL JUST LIE DOWN. YOU GO AHEAD AND DO WHAT YOU HAVE TO DO.
TODAY...IT REALLY WON'T BE TOO BAD.
IT ALL DEPENDS ON HOW COOPERATIVE YOU ARE.
HUH?

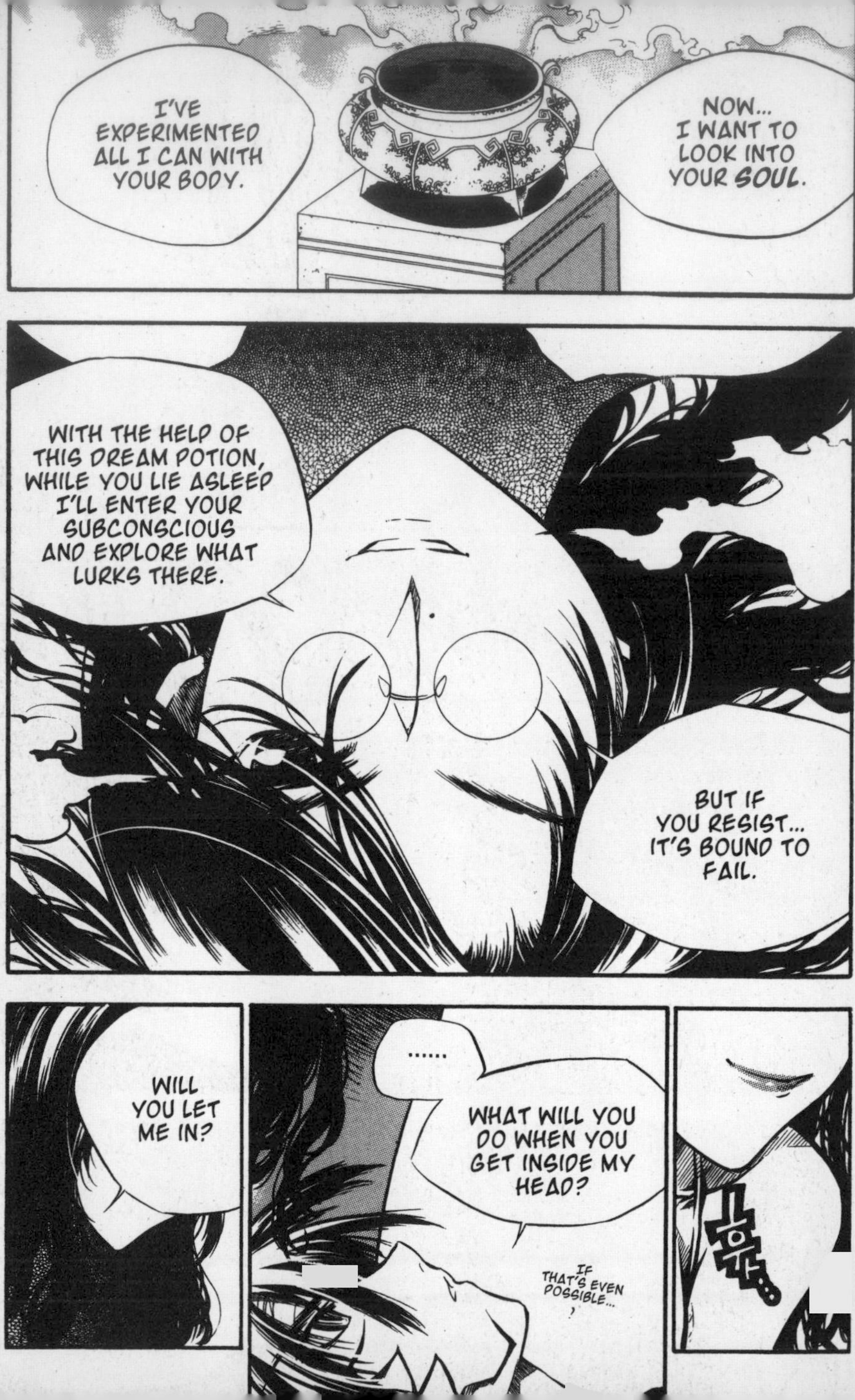
I'VE EXPERIMENTED ALL I CAN WITH YOUR BODY.
NOW... I WANT TO LOOK INTO YOUR **SOUL**.
WITH THE HELP OF THIS DREAM POTION, WHILE YOU LIE ASLEEP I'LL ENTER YOUR SUBCONSCIOUS AND EXPLORE WHAT LURKS THERE.
BUT IF YOU RESIST... IT'S BOUND TO FAIL.
WILL YOU LET ME IN?
......
WHAT WILL YOU DO WHEN YOU GET INSIDE MY HEAD?
IF THAT'S EVEN POSSIBLE...

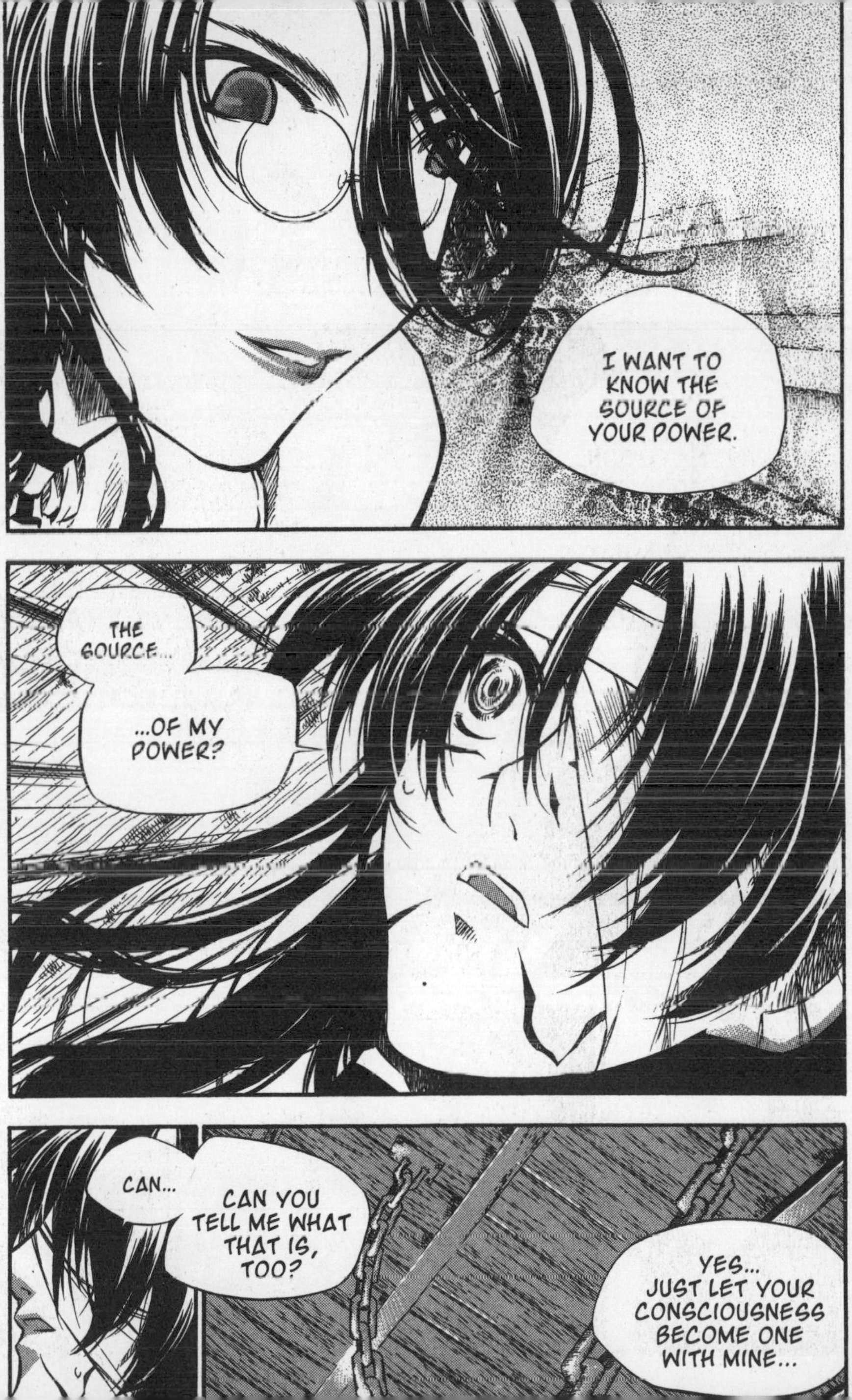
I WANT TO KNOW THE SOURCE OF YOUR POWER.
THE SOURCE...
...OF MY POWER?
CAN...
CAN YOU TELL ME WHAT THAT IS, TOO?
YES... JUST LET YOUR CONSCIOUSNESS BECOME ONE WITH MINE...

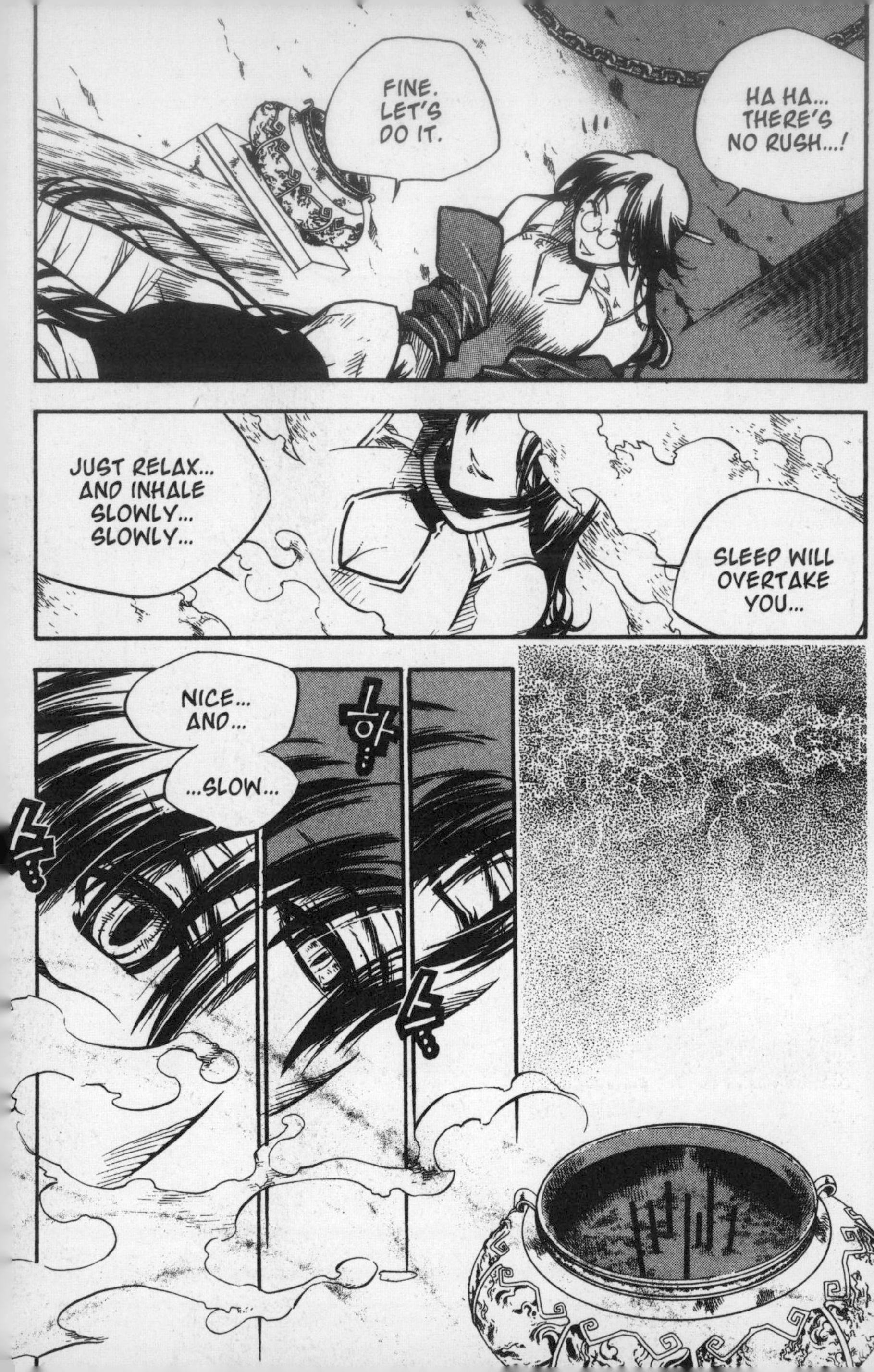
FINE. LET'S DO IT.
HA HA... THERE'S NO RUSH...!
JUST RELAX... AND INHALE SLOWLY... SLOWLY...
SLEEP WILL OVERTAKE YOU...
NICE... AND...
...SLOW...

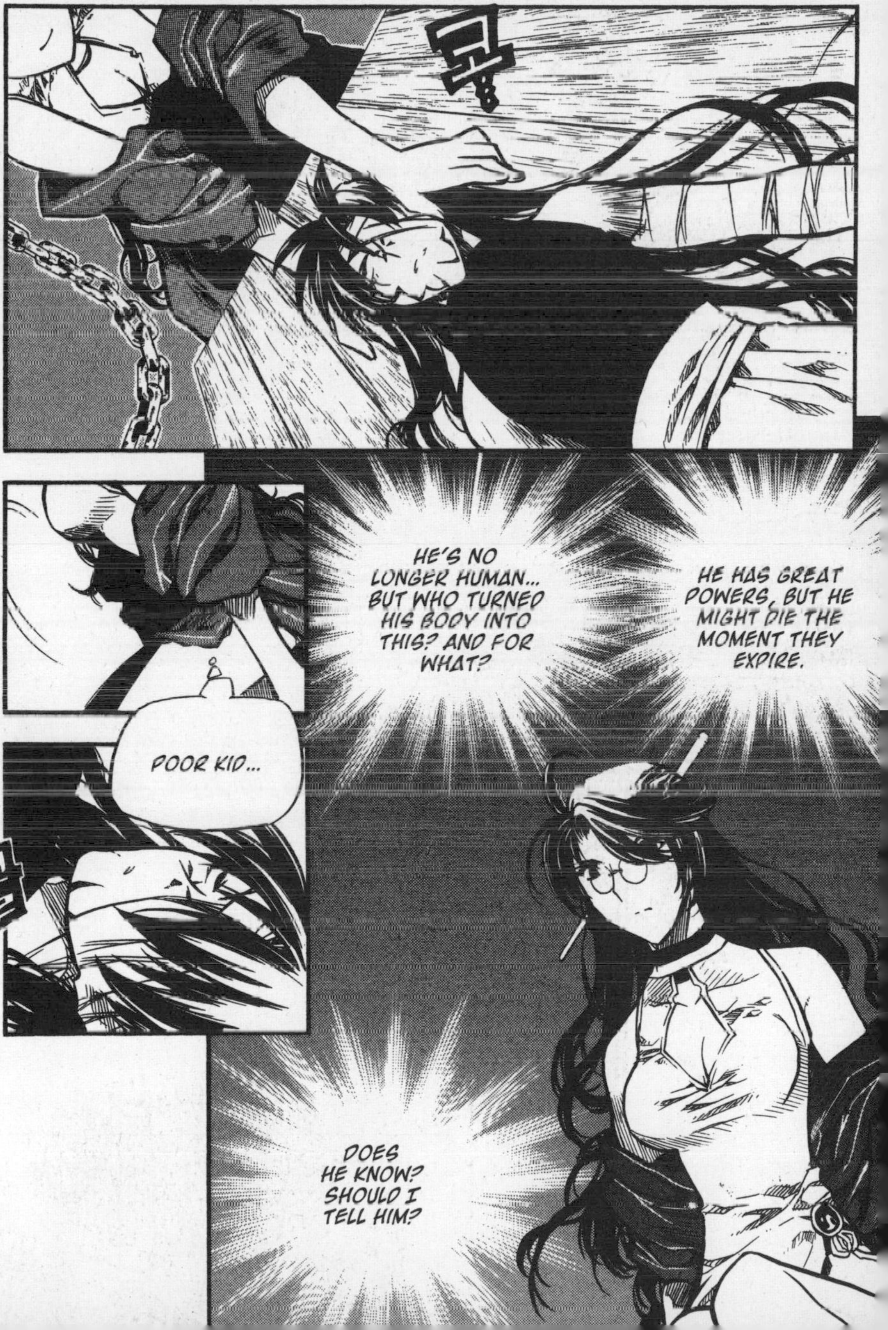
HE'S NO LONGER HUMAN... BUT WHO TURNED HIS BODY INTO THIS? AND FOR WHAT?
HE HAS GREAT POWERS, BUT HE MIGHT DIE THE MOMENT THEY EXPIRE.
POOR KID...
DOES HE KNOW? SHOULD I TELL HIM?

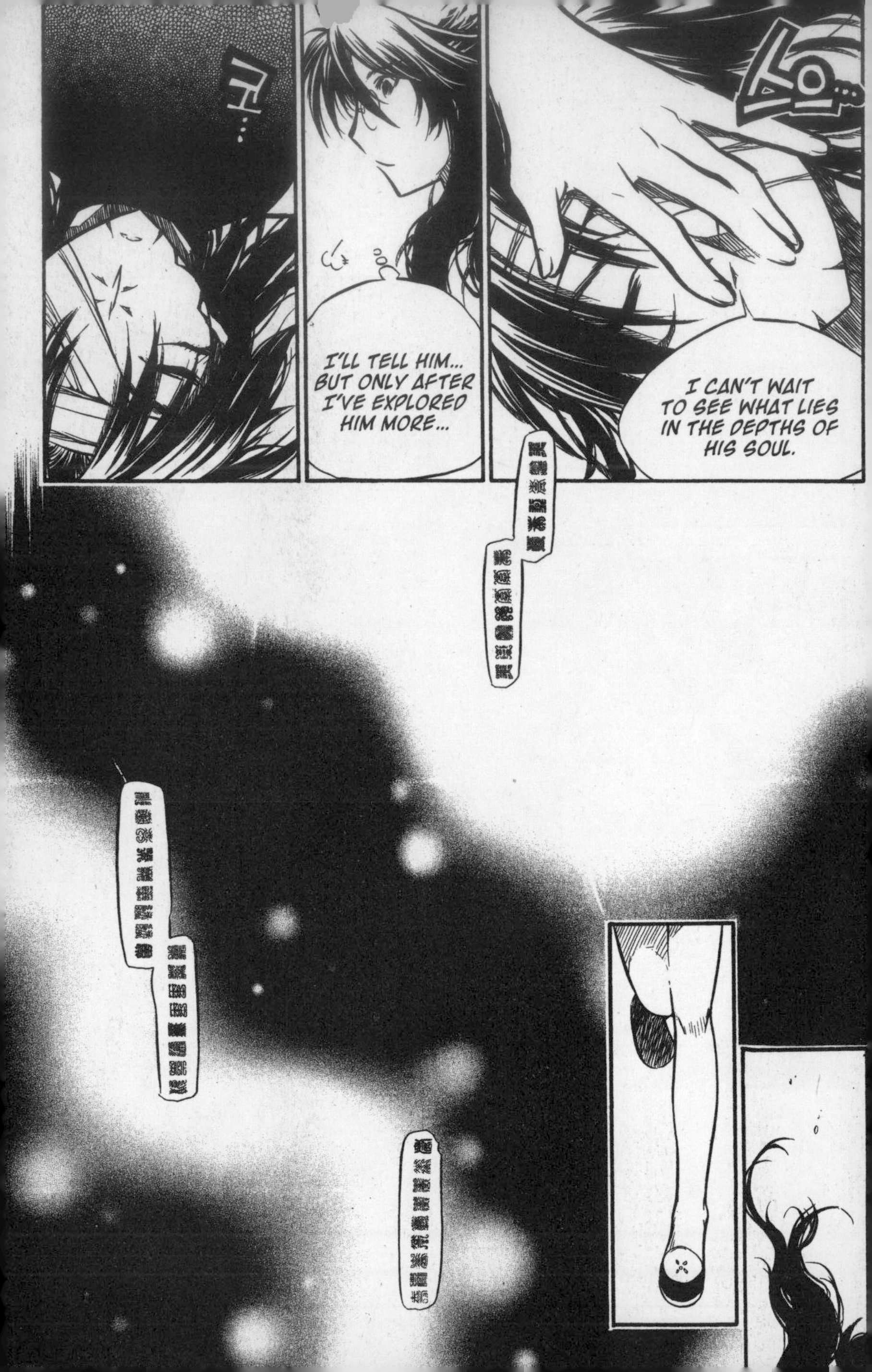
I'LL TELL HIM... BUT ONLY AFTER I'VE EXPLORED HIM MORE...
I CAN'T WAIT TO SEE WHAT LIES IN THE DEPTHS OF HIS SOUL.

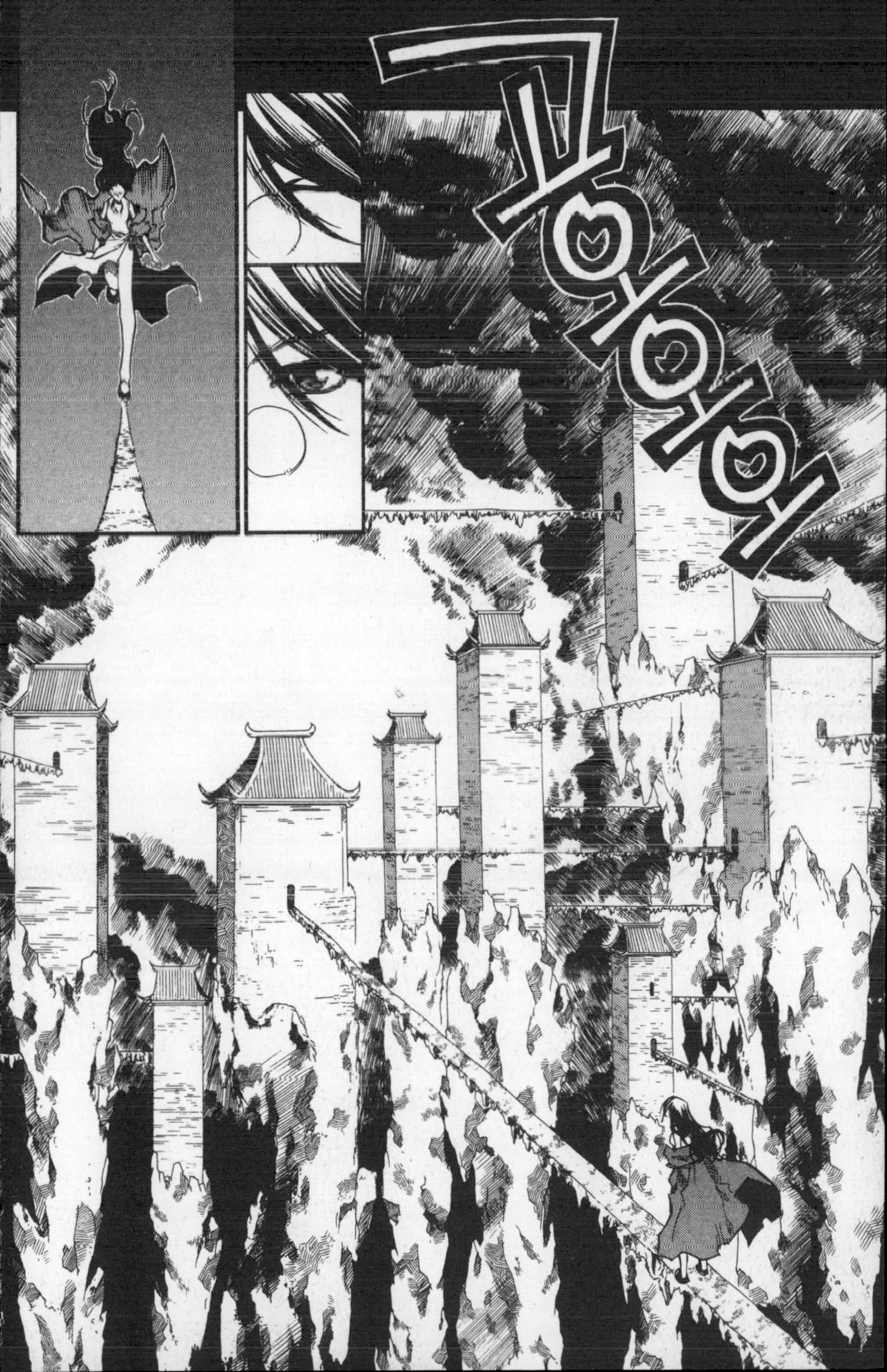

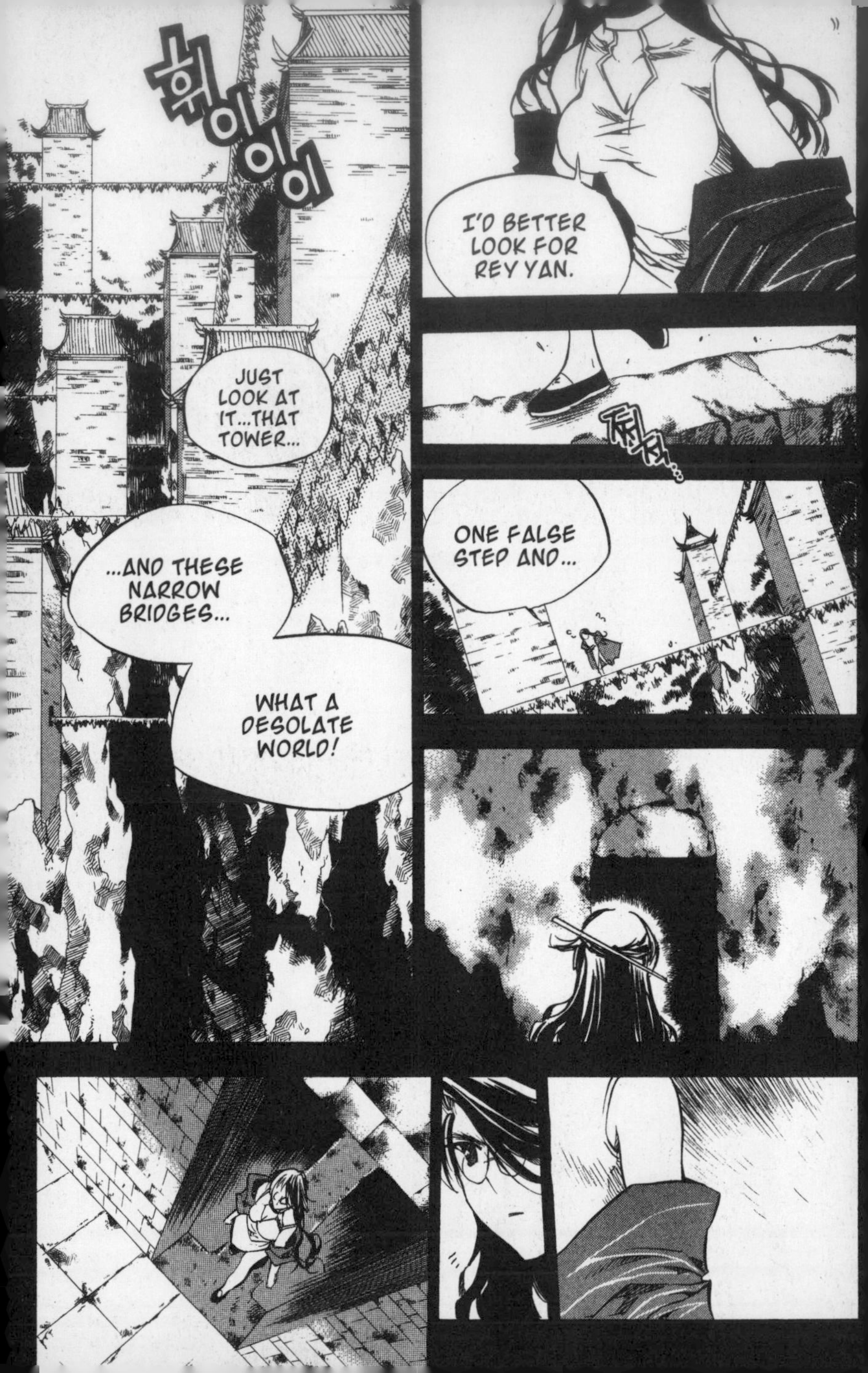
휘이이이
JUST LOOK AT IT...THAT TOWER...
...AND THESE NARROW BRIDGES...
WHAT A DESOLATE WORLD!
I'D BETTER LOOK FOR REY YAN.
ONE FALSE STEP AND...

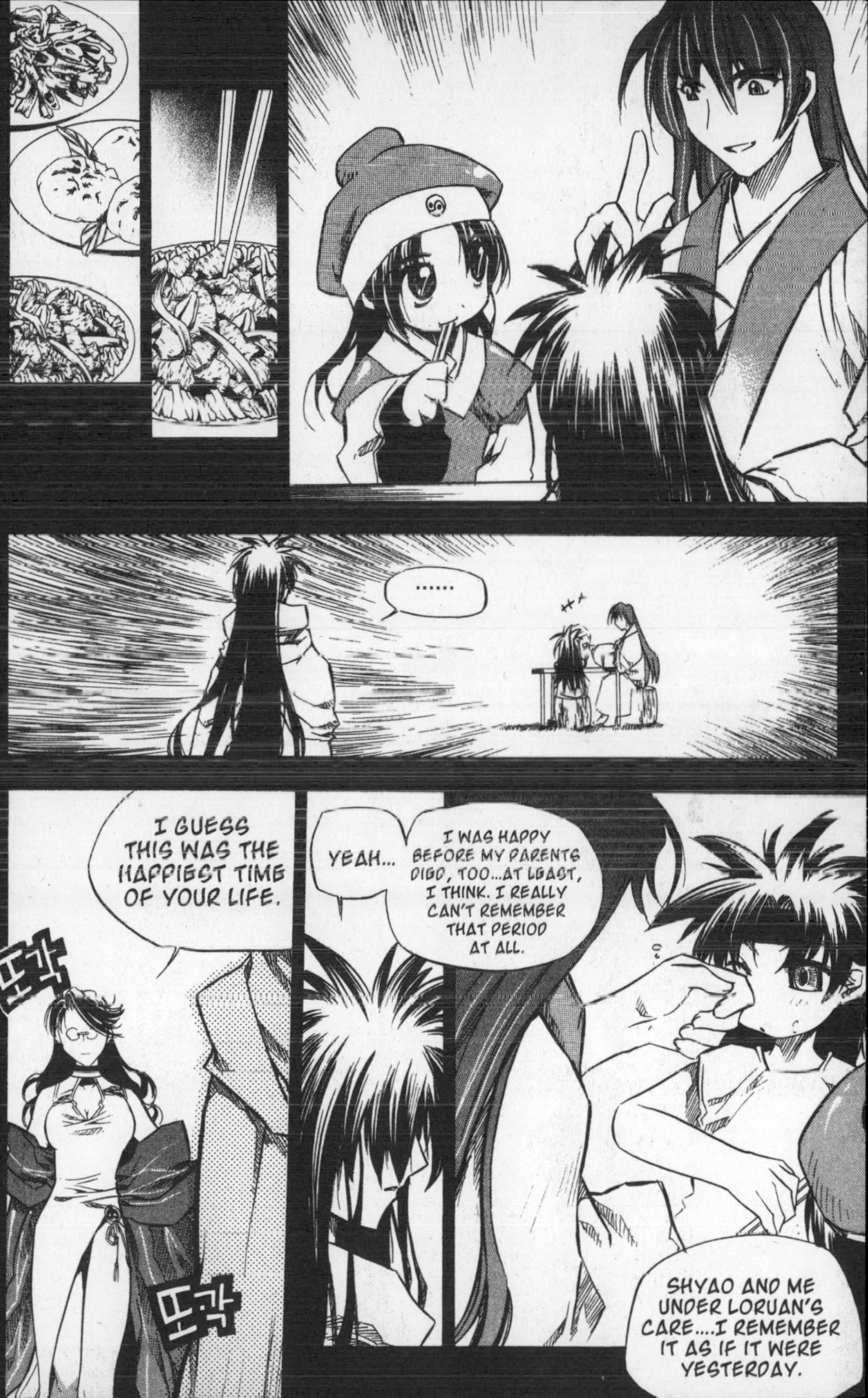
......
I GUESS THIS WAS THE HAPPIEST TIME OF YOUR LIFE.
또각
또각
YEAH...
I WAS HAPPY BEFORE MY PARENTS DIED, TOO...AT LEAST, I THINK. I REALLY CAN'T REMEMBER THAT PERIOD AT ALL.
SHYAO AND ME UNDER LORUAN'S CARE....I REMEMBER IT AS IF IT WERE YESTERDAY.

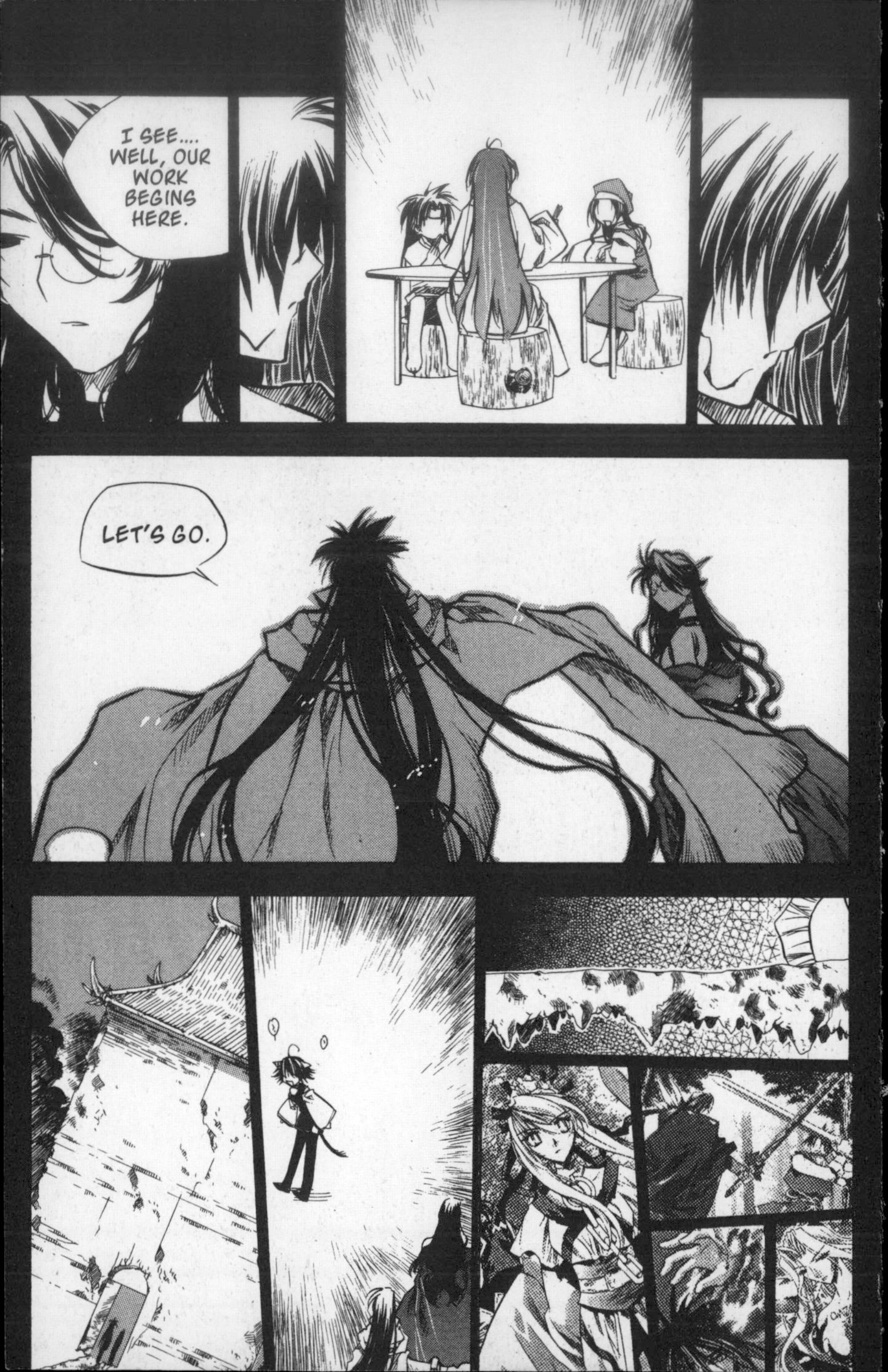
I SEE.... WELL, OUR WORK BEGINS HERE.
LET'S GO.

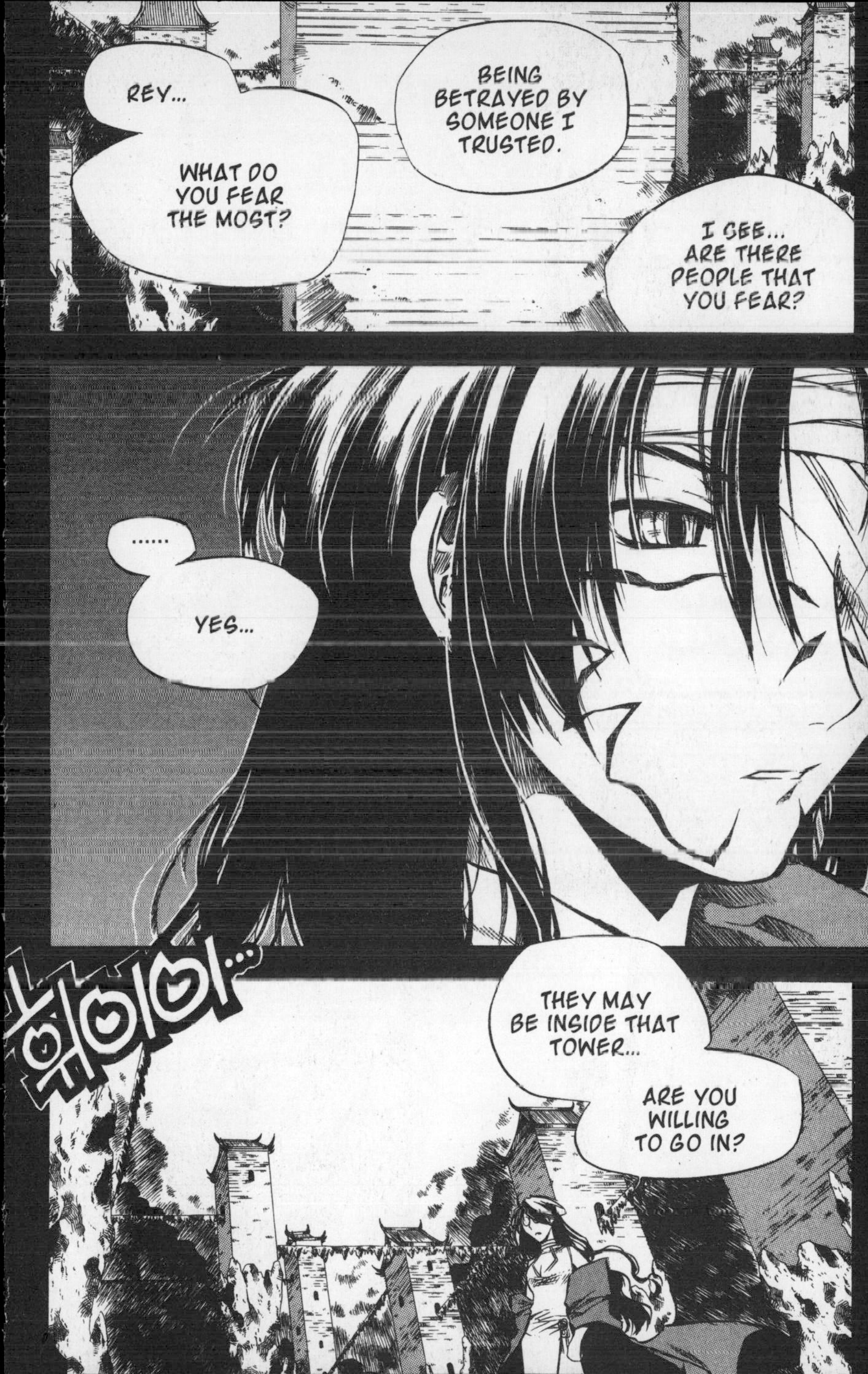
REY...
WHAT DO YOU FEAR THE MOST?
BEING BETRAYED BY SOMEONE I TRUSTED.
I SEE... ARE THERE PEOPLE THAT YOU FEAR?
......
YES...
휘이이이…
THEY MAY BE INSIDE THAT TOWER...
ARE YOU WILLING TO GO IN?

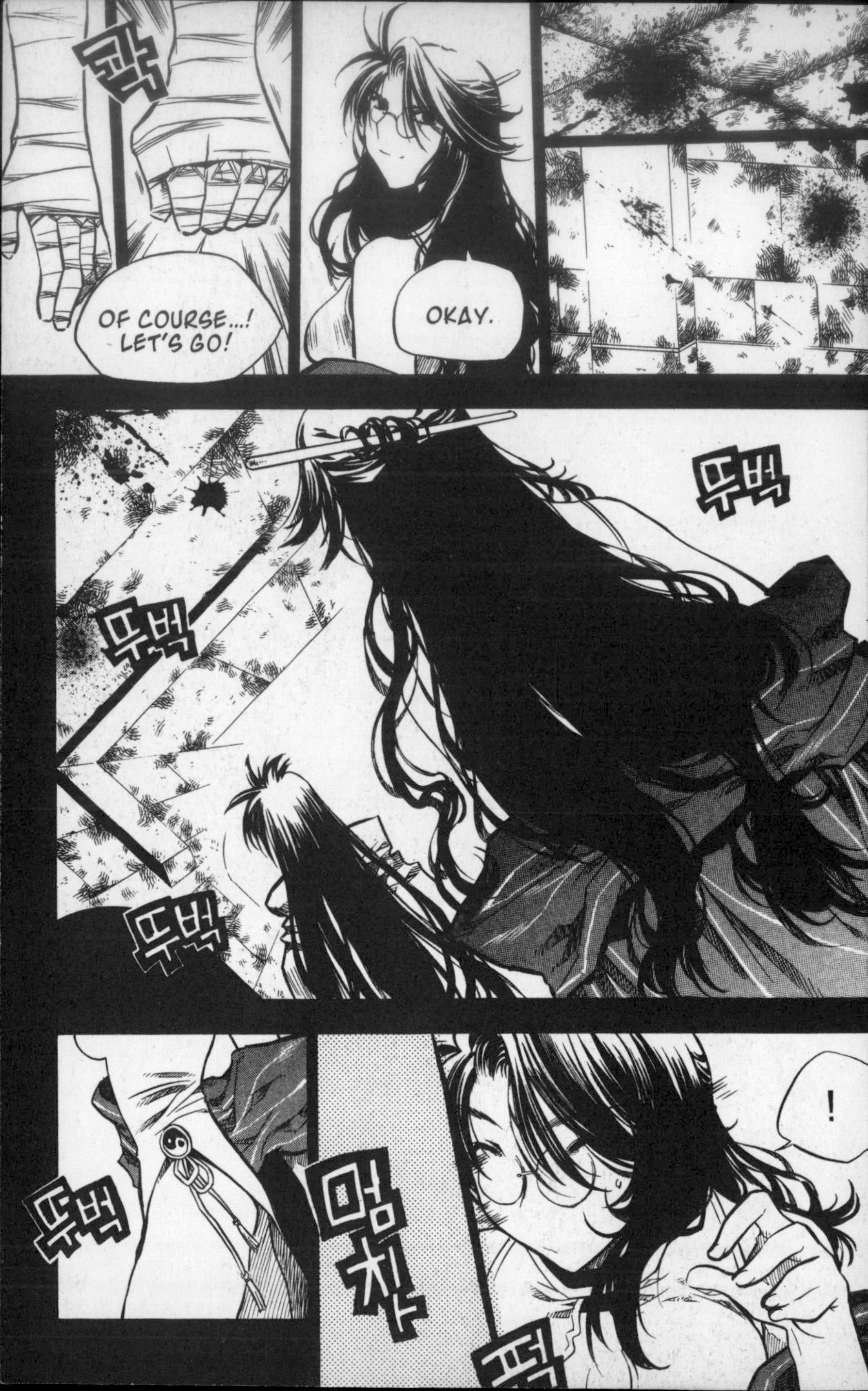
콱
OF COURSE...! LET'S GO!
OKAY.
뚜벅
뚜벅
뚜벅
뚜벅
멈칫
!

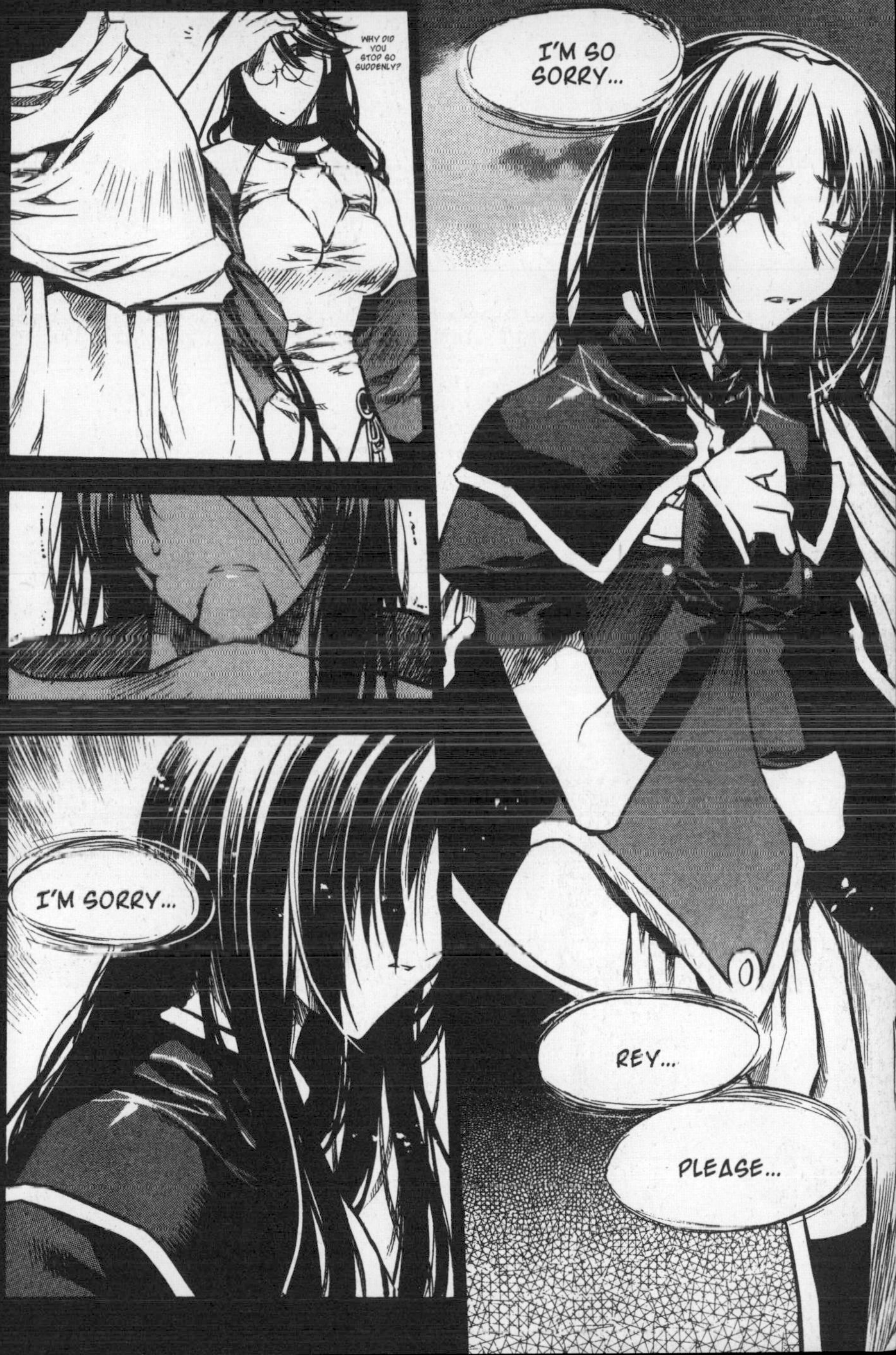
WHY DID YOU STOP SO SUDDENLY?
I'M SORRY...
I'M SO SORRY...
REY...
PLEASE...

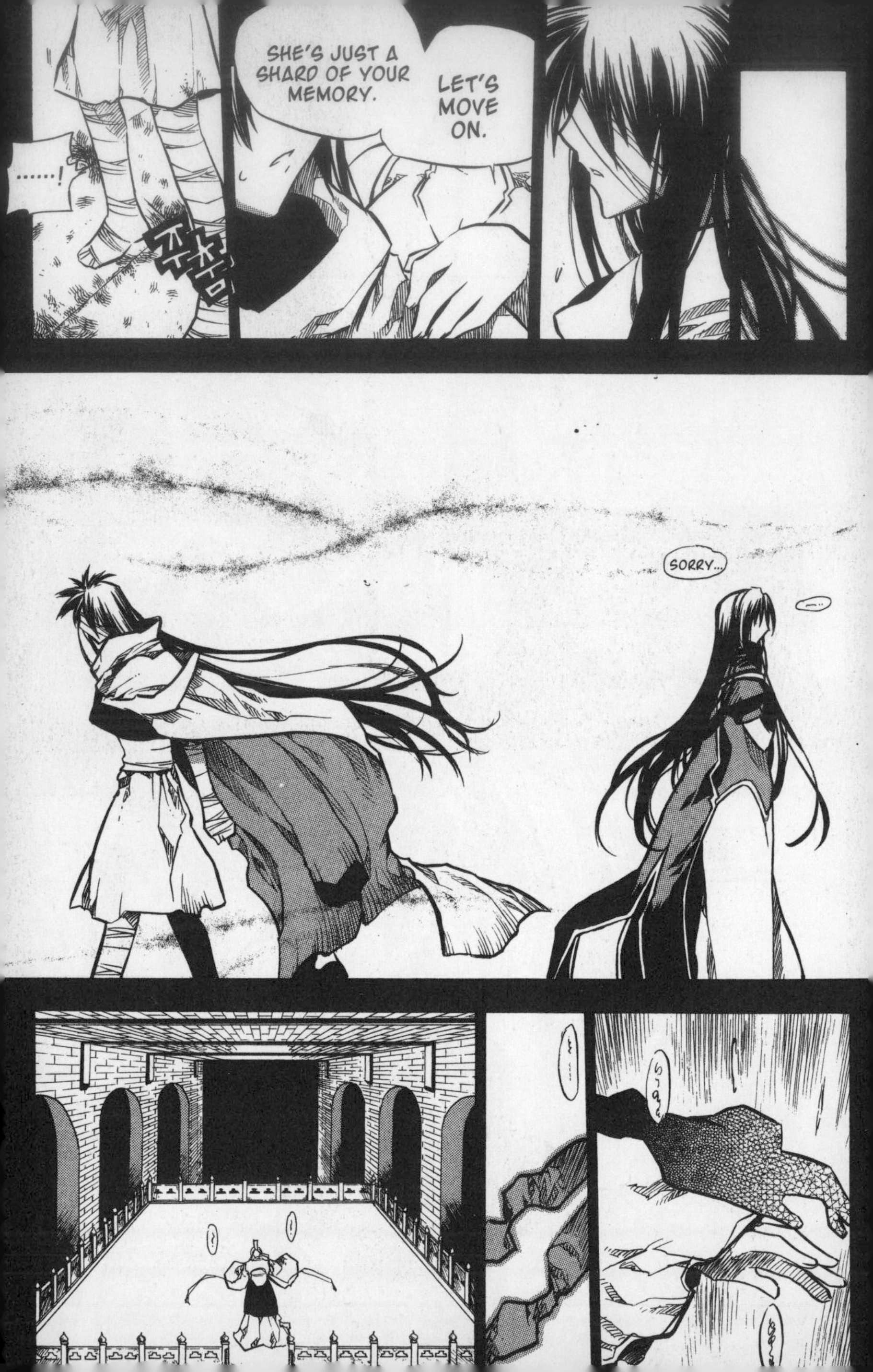

......!
SHE'S JUST A SHARD OF YOUR MEMORY.
LET'S MOVE ON.
SORRY...
—...

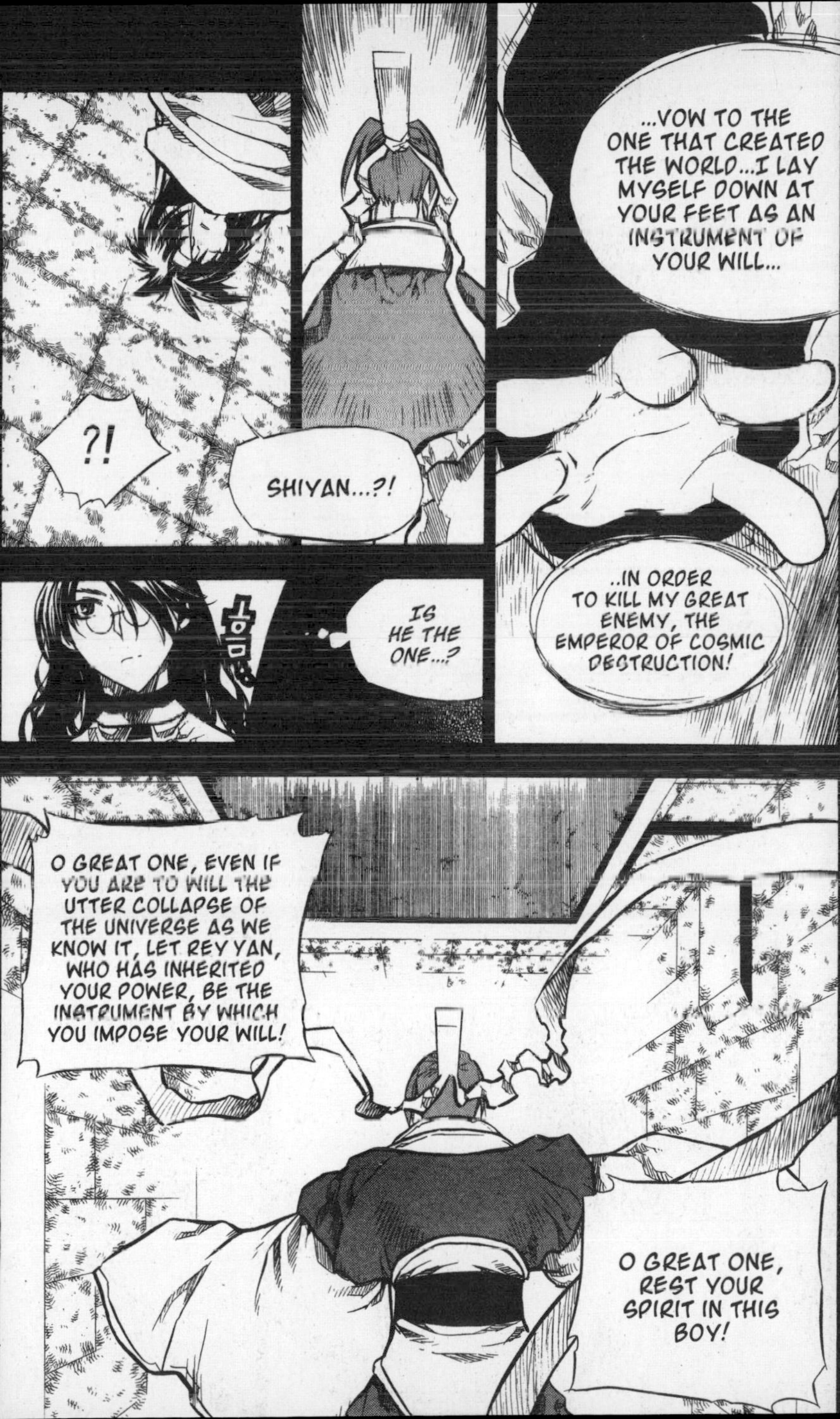
?!
SHIYAN...?!
IS HE THE ONE...?
...VOW TO THE ONE THAT CREATED THE WORLD...I LAY MYSELF DOWN AT YOUR FEET AS AN INSTRUMENT OF YOUR WILL...
..IN ORDER TO KILL MY GREAT ENEMY, THE EMPEROR OF COSMIC DESTRUCTION!
O GREAT ONE, EVEN IF YOU ARE TO WILL THE UTTER COLLAPSE OF THE UNIVERSE AS WE KNOW IT, LET REY YAN, WHO HAS INHERITED YOUR POWER, BE THE INSTRUMENT BY WHICH YOU IMPOSE YOUR WILL!
O GREAT ONE, REST YOUR SPIRIT IN THIS BOY!

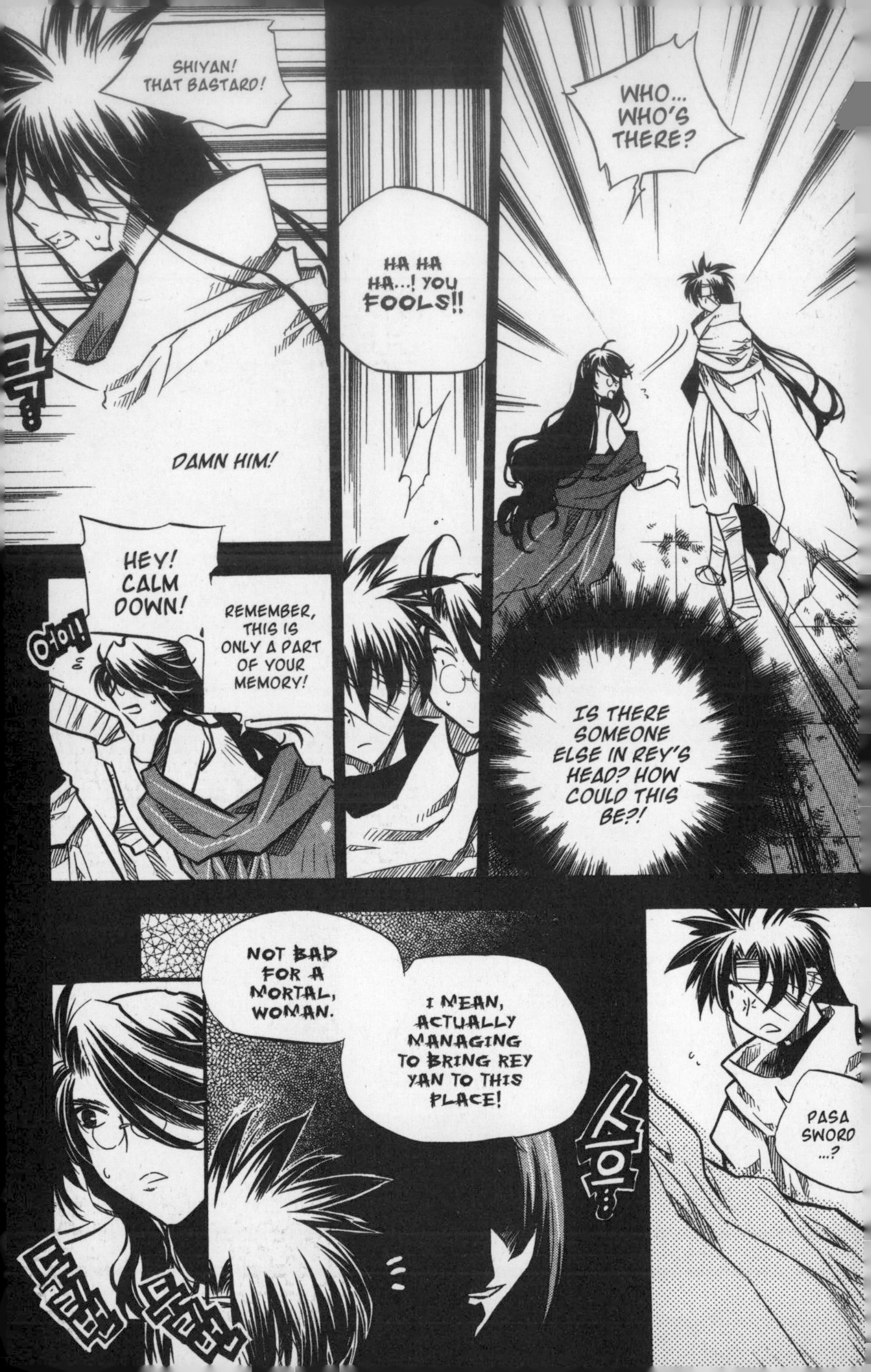
SHIYAN! THAT BASTARD!
DAMN HIM!
HA HA HA...! YOU FOOLS!!
WHO... WHO'S THERE?
HEY! CALM DOWN!
REMEMBER, THIS IS ONLY A PART OF YOUR MEMORY!
IS THERE SOMEONE ELSE IN REY'S HEAD? HOW COULD THIS BE?!
NOT BAD FOR A MORTAL, WOMAN.
I MEAN, ACTUALLY MANAGING TO BRING REY YAN TO THIS PLACE!
PASA SWORD ...?

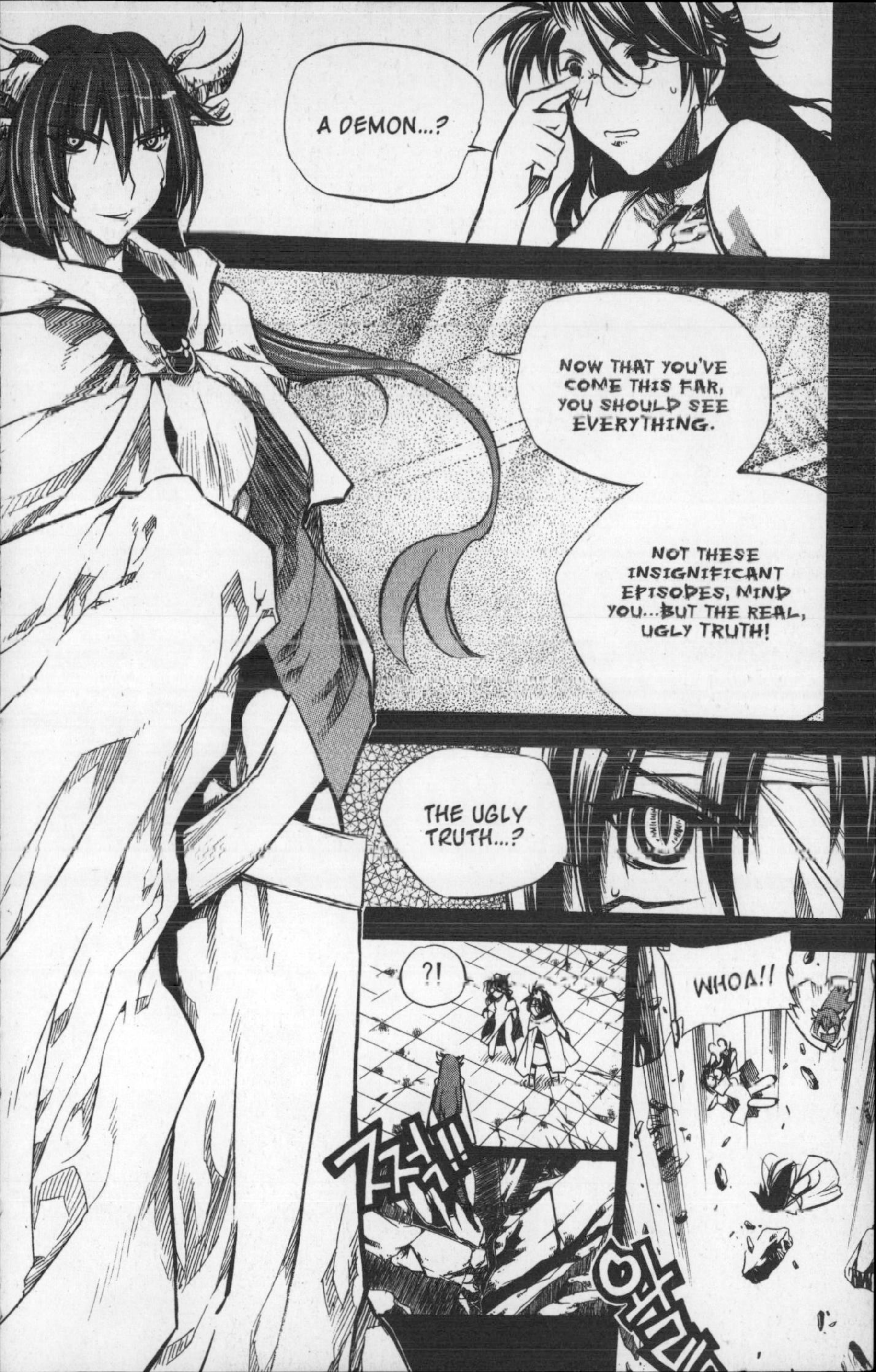
A DEMON...?
NOW THAT YOU'VE COME THIS FAR, YOU SHOULD SEE EVERYTHING.
NOT THESE INSIGNIFICANT EPISODES, MIND YOU...BUT THE REAL, UGLY TRUTH!
THE UGLY TRUTH...?
?!
WHOA!!

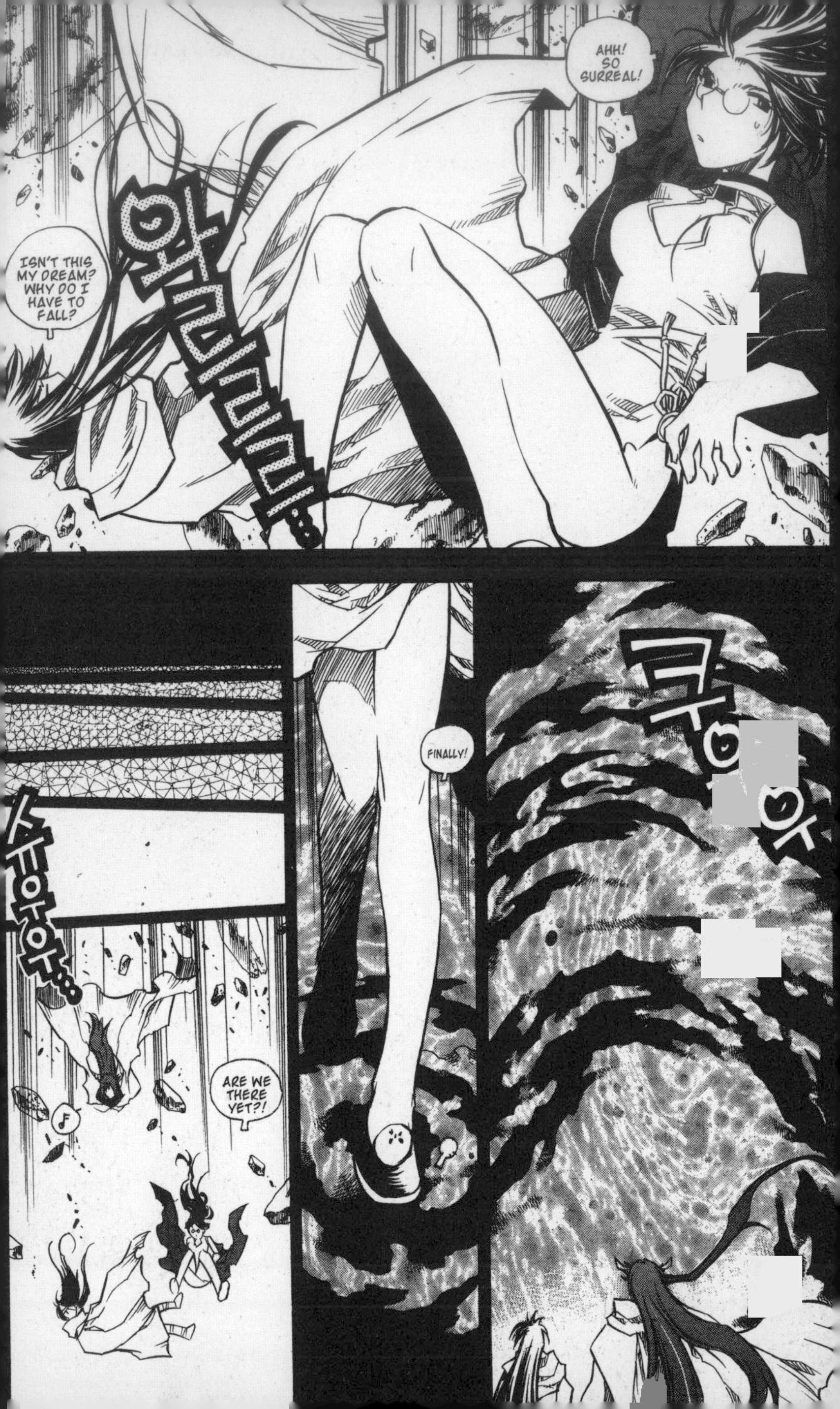
ISN'T THIS MY DREAM? WHY DO I HAVE TO FALL?
AHH! SO SURREAL!
ARE WE THERE YET?!
FINALLY!

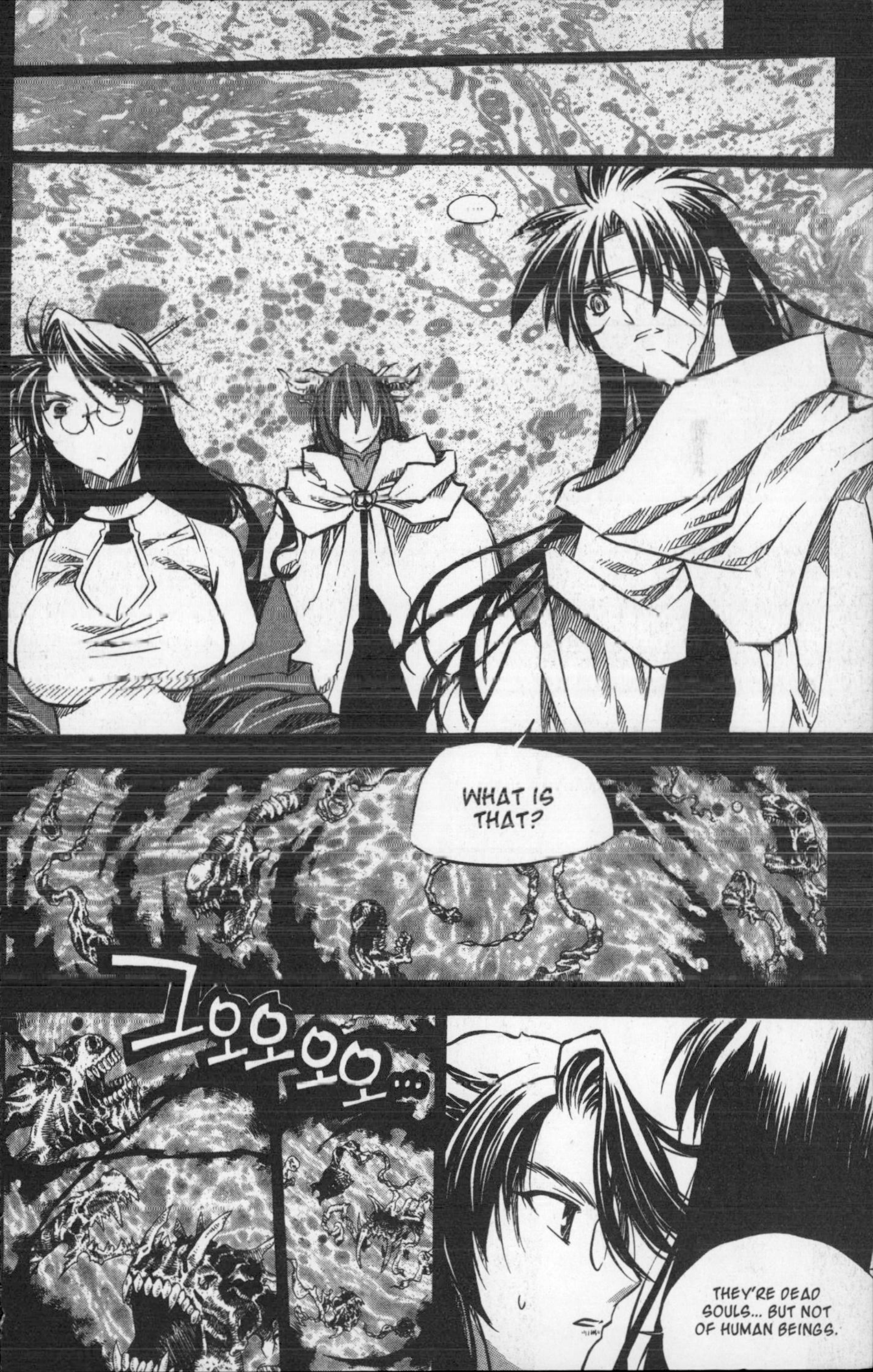
...
WHAT IS THAT?
그오오오오오...
THEY'RE DEAD SOULS... BUT NOT OF HUMAN BEINGS.

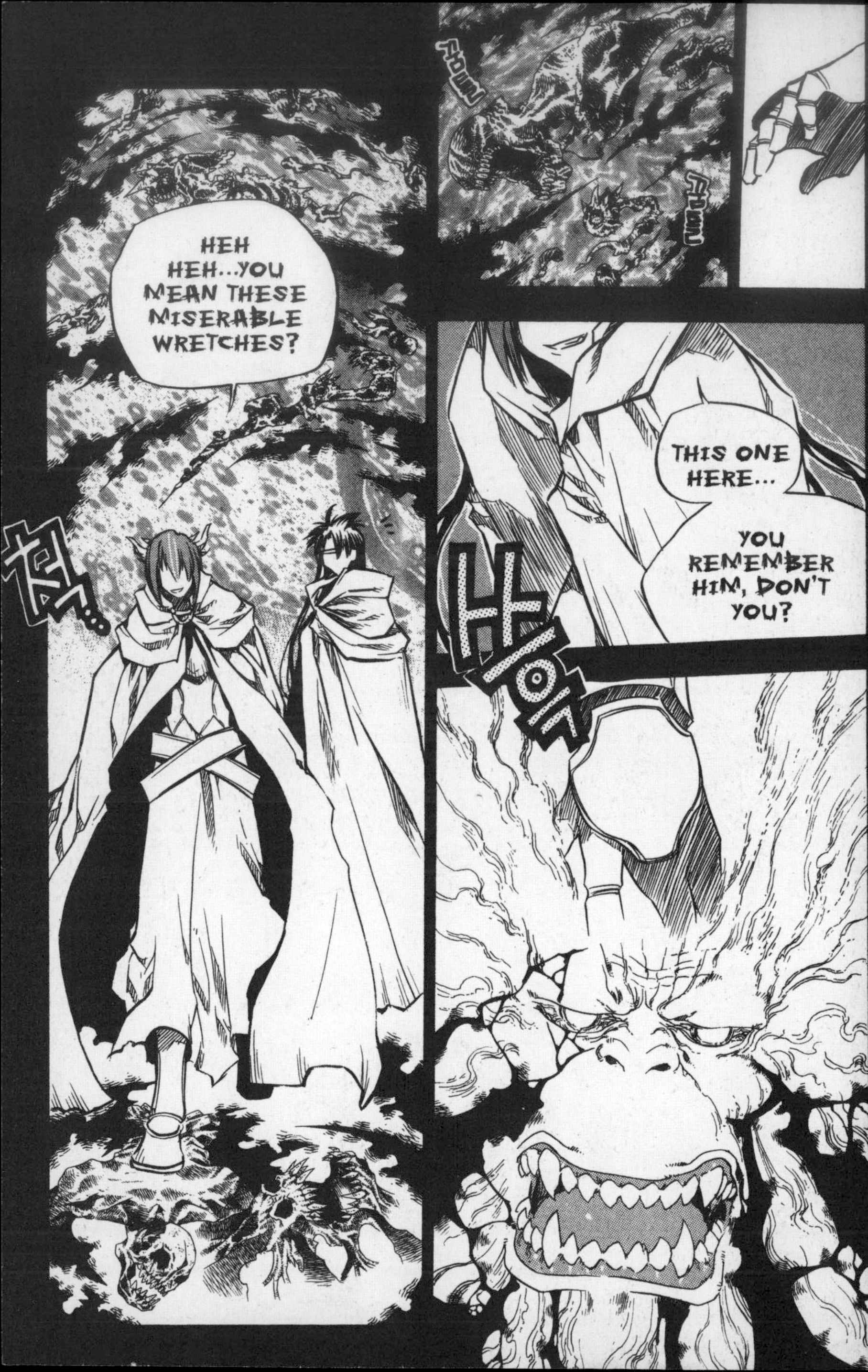
HEH HEH...YOU MEAN THESE MISERABLE WRETCHES?
THIS ONE HERE...
YOU REMEMBER HIM, DON'T YOU?

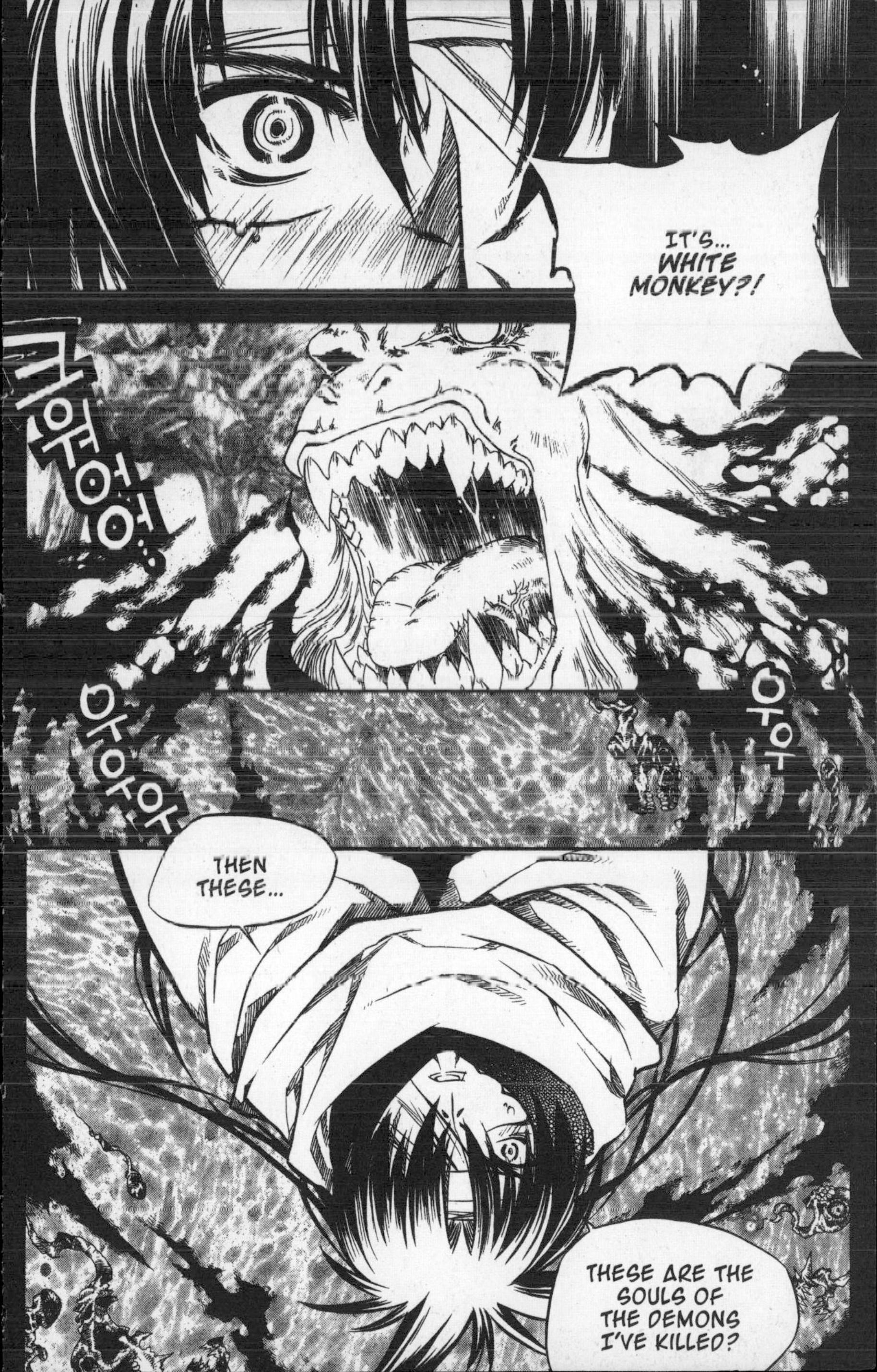
IT'S... WHITE MONKEY?!
크아아아...
아아아
아아
THEN THESE...
THESE ARE THE SOULS OF THE DEMONS I'VE KILLED?

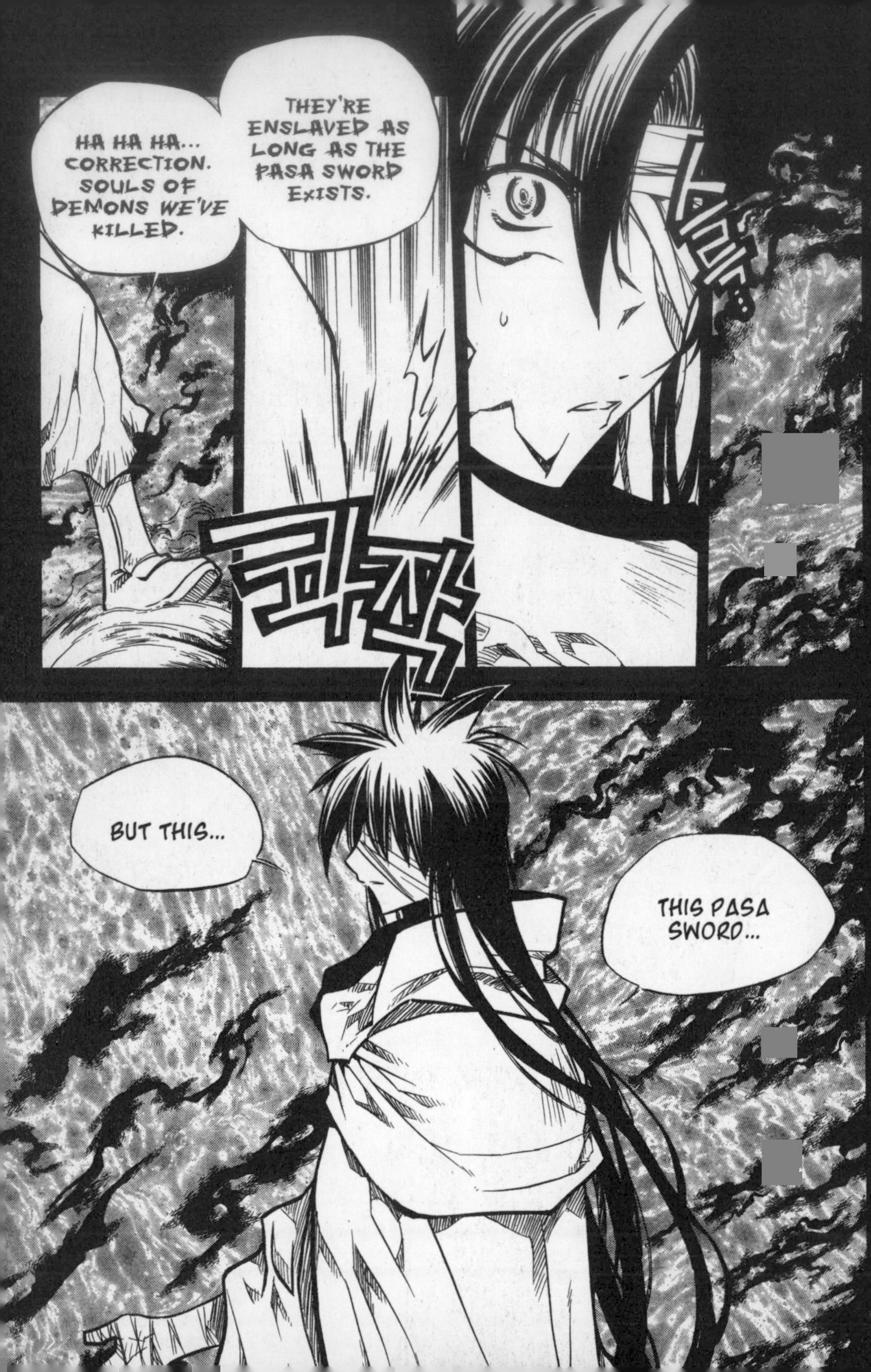
HA HA HA... CORRECTION. SOULS OF DEMONS WE'VE KILLED.
THEY'RE ENSLAVED AS LONG AS THE PASA SWORD EXISTS.
BUT THIS...
THIS PASA SWORD...

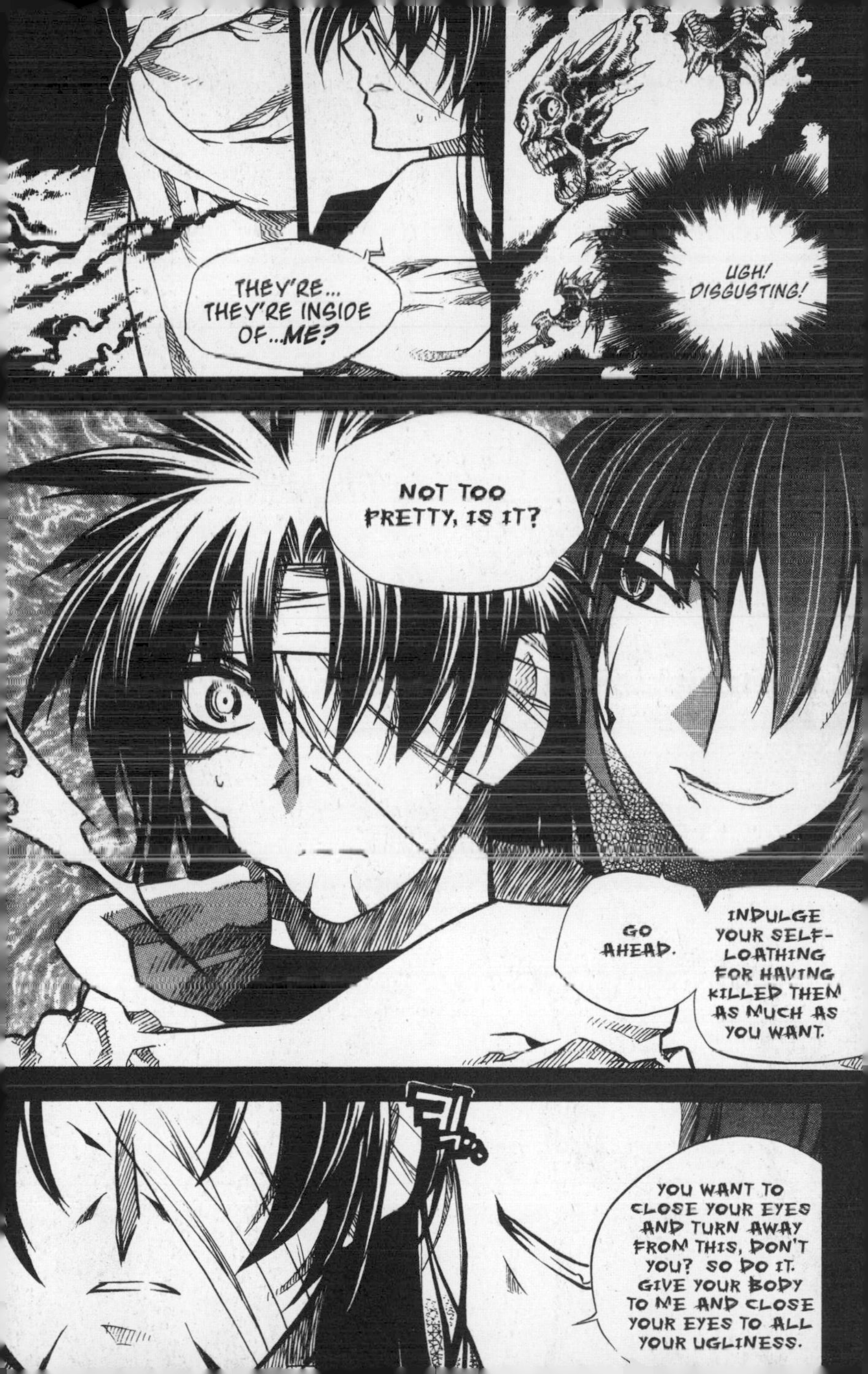
THEY'RE... THEY'RE INSIDE OF...ME?
UGH! DISGUSTING!
NOT TOO PRETTY, IS IT?
GO AHEAD.
INDULGE YOUR SELF-LOATHING FOR HAVING KILLED THEM AS MUCH AS YOU WANT.
YOU WANT TO CLOSE YOUR EYES AND TURN AWAY FROM THIS, DON'T YOU? SO DO IT. GIVE YOUR BODY TO ME AND CLOSE YOUR EYES TO ALL YOUR UGLINESS.

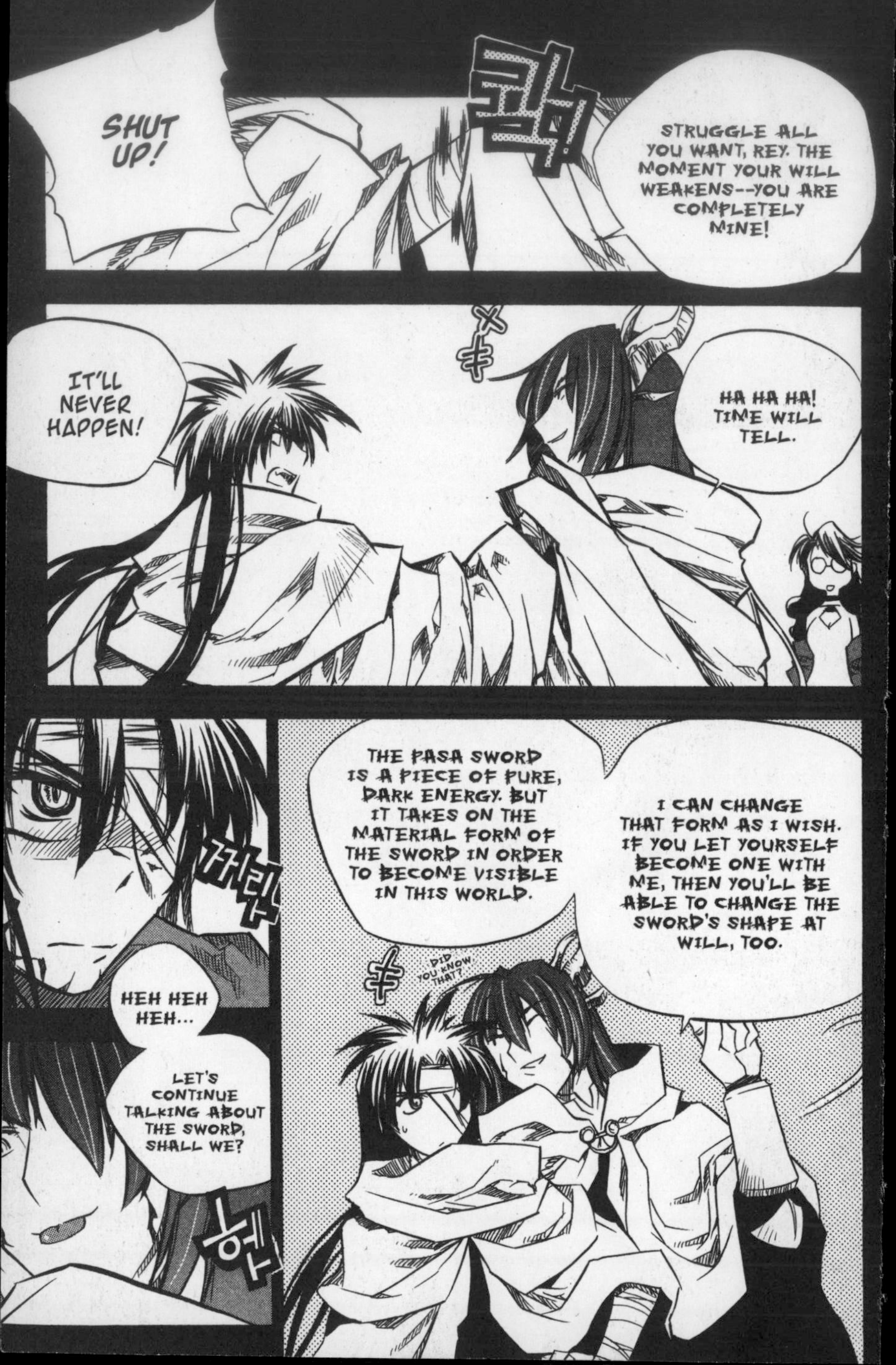
SHUT UP!
STRUGGLE ALL YOU WANT, REY. THE MOMENT YOUR WILL WEAKENS--YOU ARE COMPLETELY MINE!
IT'LL NEVER HAPPEN!
HA HA HA! TIME WILL TELL.
HEH HEH HEH...
LET'S CONTINUE TALKING ABOUT THE SWORD, SHALL WE?
THE PASA SWORD IS A PIECE OF PURE, DARK ENERGY. BUT IT TAKES ON THE MATERIAL FORM OF THE SWORD IN ORDER TO BECOME VISIBLE IN THIS WORLD.
I CAN CHANGE THAT FORM AS I WISH. IF YOU LET YOURSELF BECOME ONE WITH ME, THEN YOU'LL BE ABLE TO CHANGE THE SWORD'S SHAPE AT WILL, TOO.
DID YOU KNOW THAT?

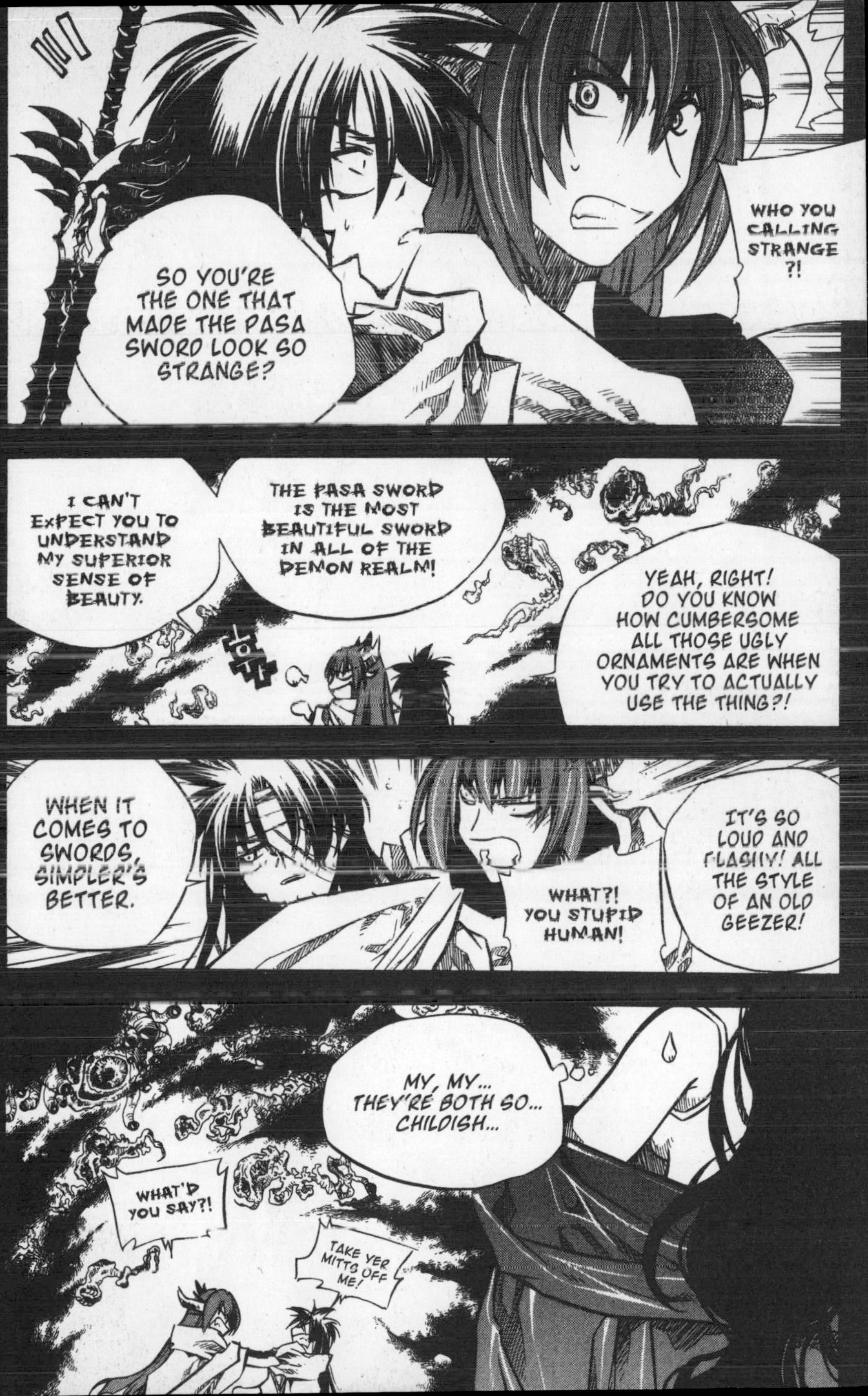
SO YOU'RE THE ONE THAT MADE THE PASA SWORD LOOK SO STRANGE?
WHO YOU CALLING STRANGE ?!
I CAN'T EXPECT YOU TO UNDERSTAND MY SUPERIOR SENSE OF BEAUTY.
THE PASA SWORD IS THE MOST BEAUTIFUL SWORD IN ALL OF THE DEMON REALM!
YEAH, RIGHT! DO YOU KNOW HOW CUMBERSOME ALL THOSE UGLY ORNAMENTS ARE WHEN YOU TRY TO ACTUALLY USE THE THING?!
WHEN IT COMES TO SWORDS, SIMPLER'S BETTER.
WHAT?! YOU STUPID HUMAN!
IT'S SO LOUD AND FLASHY! ALL THE STYLE OF AN OLD GEEZER!
MY, MY... THEY'RE BOTH SO... CHILDISH...
WHAT'D YOU SAY?!
TAKE YER MITTS OFF ME!

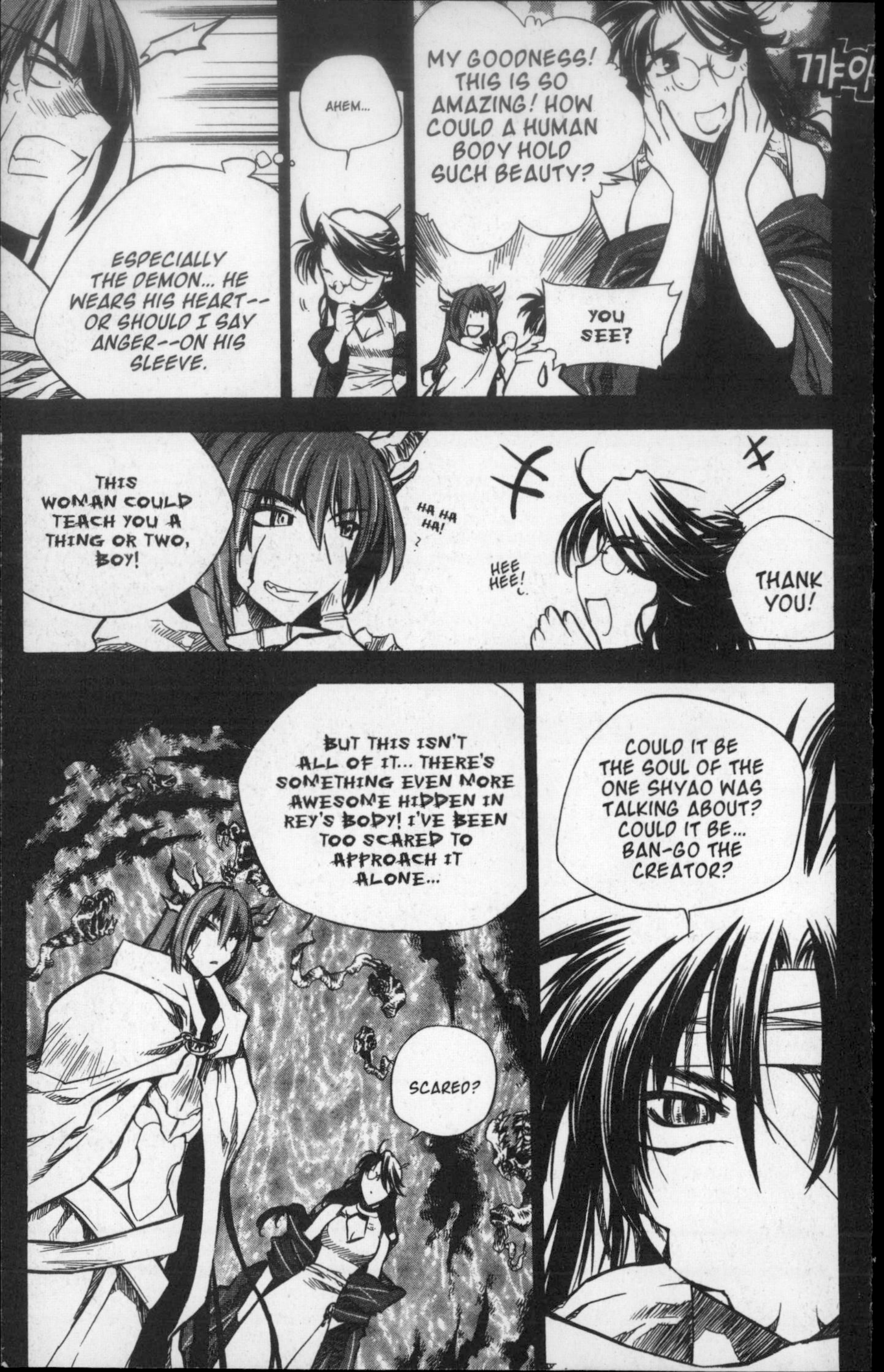
ESPECIALLY THE DEMON... HE WEARS HIS HEART--OR SHOULD I SAY ANGER--ON HIS SLEEVE.
AHEM...
MY GOODNESS! THIS IS SO AMAZING! HOW COULD A HUMAN BODY HOLD SUCH BEAUTY?
YOU SEE?
THIS WOMAN COULD TEACH YOU A THING OR TWO, BOY!
HA HA HA!
HEE HEE!
THANK YOU!
BUT THIS ISN'T ALL OF IT... THERE'S SOMETHING EVEN MORE AWESOME HIDDEN IN REY'S BODY! I'VE BEEN TOO SCARED TO APPROACH IT ALONE...
SCARED?
COULD IT BE THE SOUL OF THE ONE SHYAO WAS TALKING ABOUT? COULD IT BE... BAN-GO THE CREATOR?

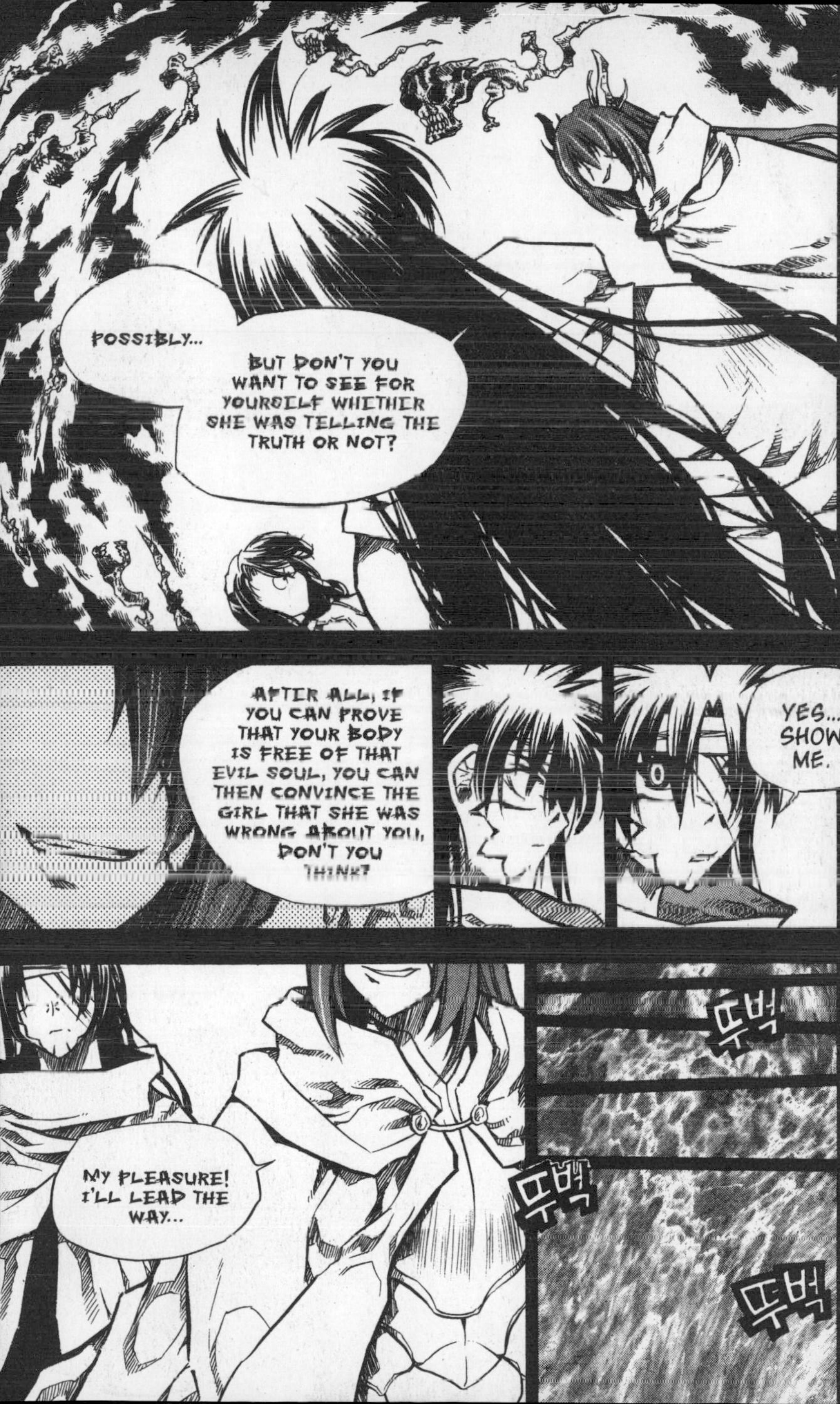
POSSIBLY...
BUT DON'T YOU WANT TO SEE FOR YOURSELF WHETHER SHE WAS TELLING THE TRUTH OR NOT?
AFTER ALL, IF YOU CAN PROVE THAT YOUR BODY IS FREE OF THAT EVIL SOUL, YOU CAN THEN CONVINCE THE GIRL THAT SHE WAS WRONG ABOUT YOU, DON'T YOU THINK?
YES... SHOW ME.
MY PLEASURE! I'LL LEAD THE WAY...
뚜벅
뚜벅
뚜벅

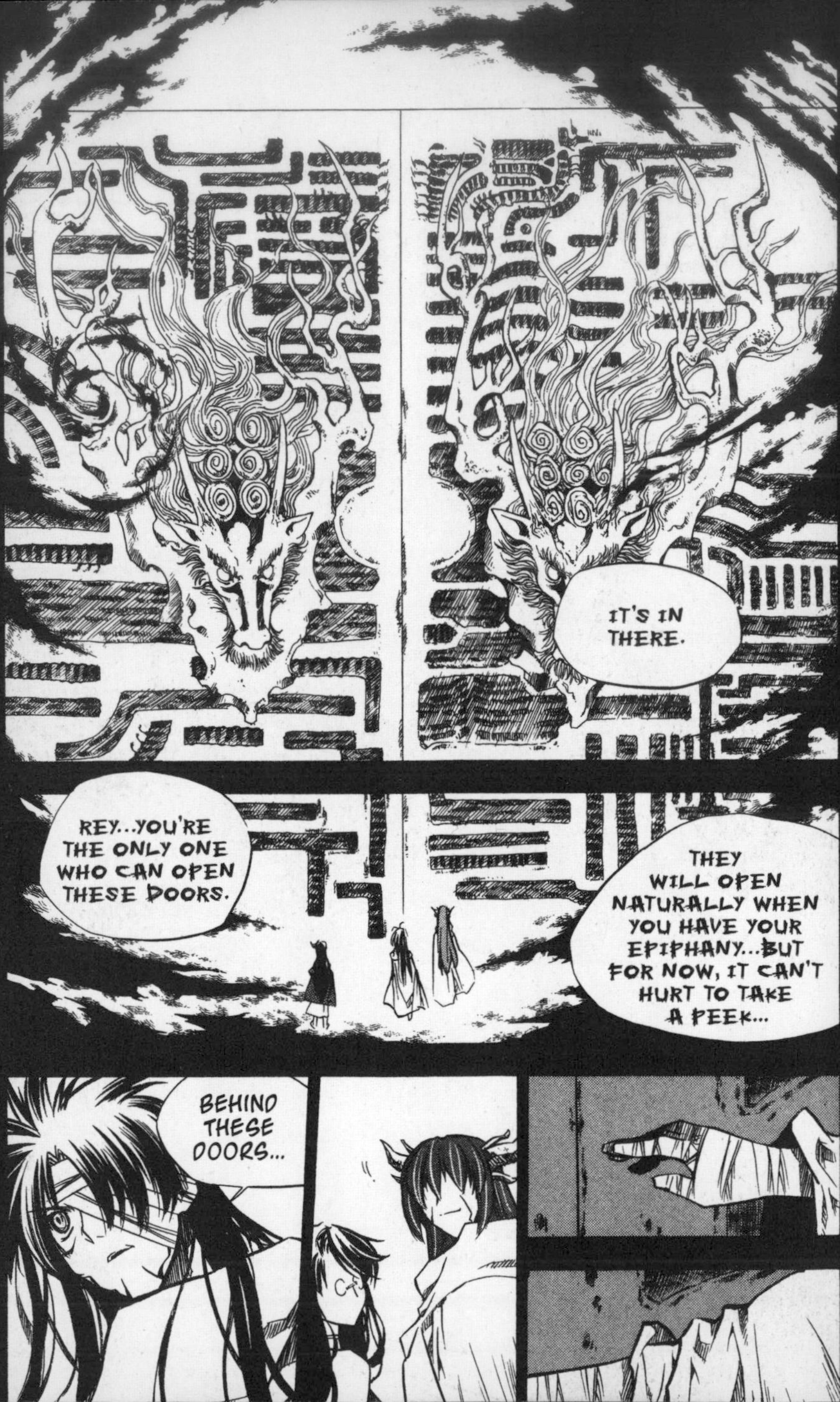
IT'S IN THERE.
REY...YOU'RE THE ONLY ONE WHO CAN OPEN THESE DOORS.
THEY WILL OPEN NATURALLY WHEN YOU HAVE YOUR EPIPHANY...BUT FOR NOW, IT CAN'T HURT TO TAKE A PEEK...
BEHIND THESE DOORS...

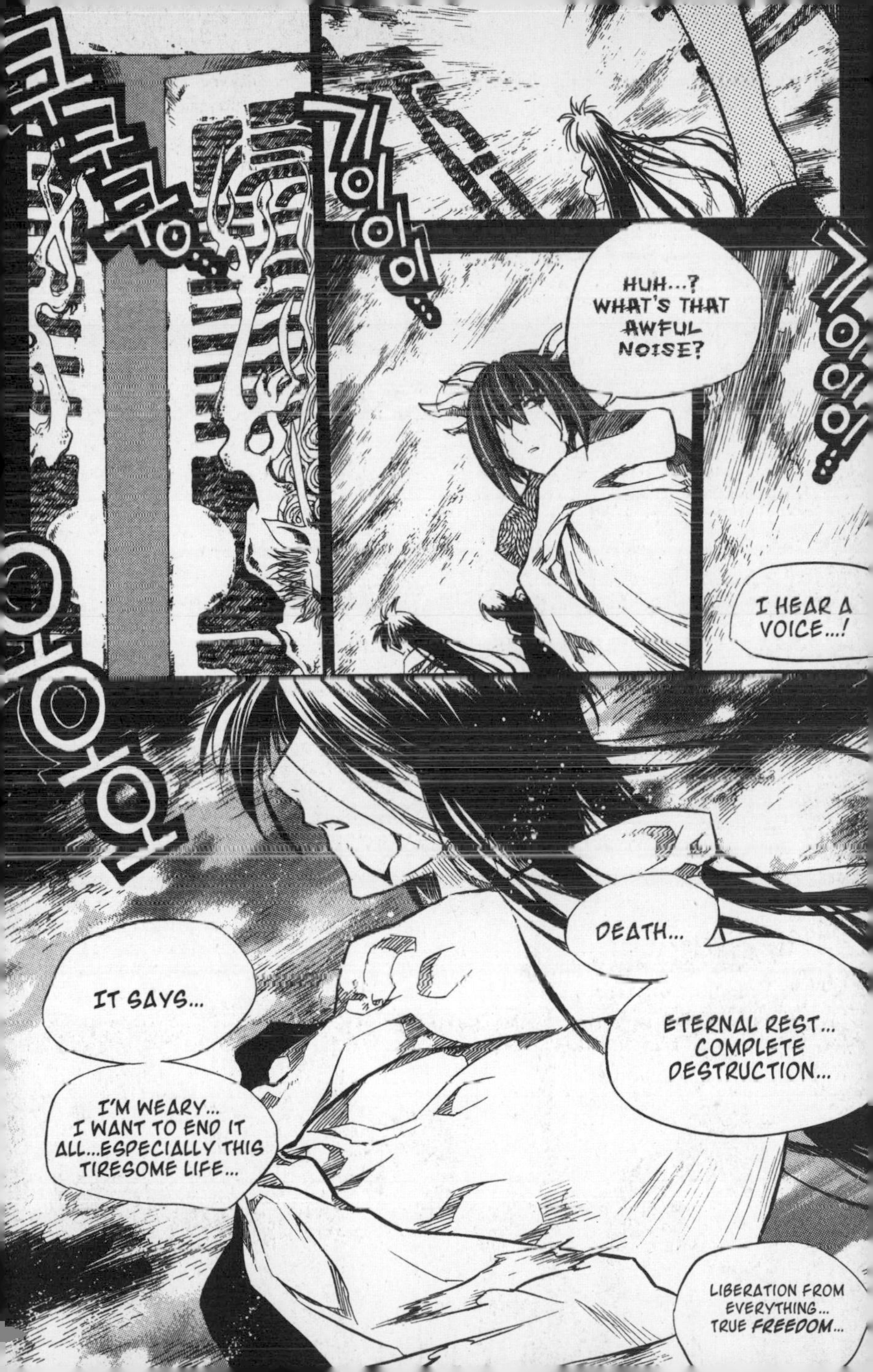
HUH...? WHAT'S THAT AWFUL NOISE?
I HEAR A VOICE...!
IT SAYS...
DEATH...
ETERNAL REST... COMPLETE DESTRUCTION...
I'M WEARY... I WANT TO END IT ALL...ESPECIALLY THIS TIRESOME LIFE...
LIBERATION FROM EVERYTHING... TRUE *FREEDOM*...

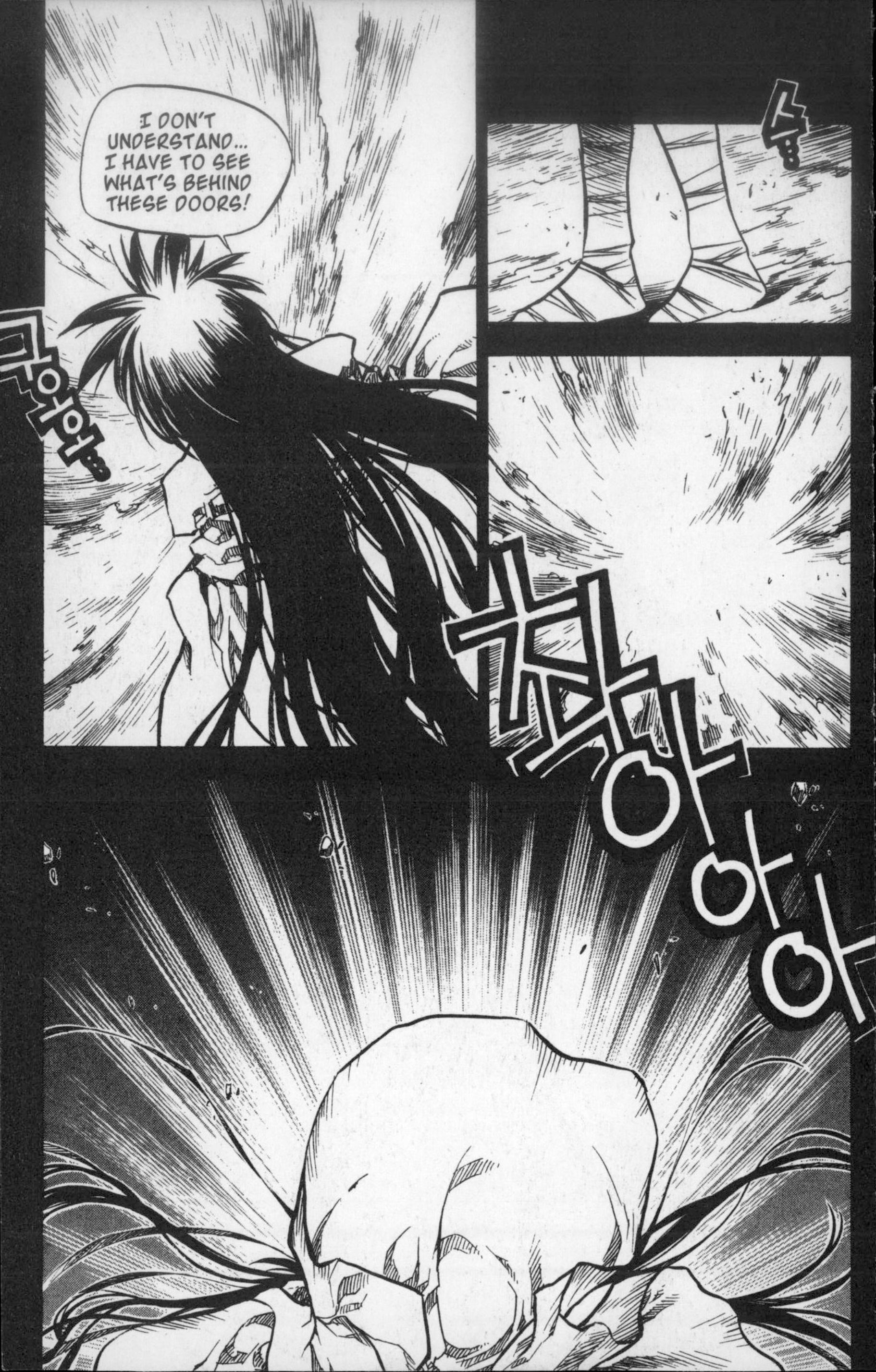
I DON'T UNDERSTAND... I HAVE TO SEE WHAT'S BEHIND THESE DOORS!

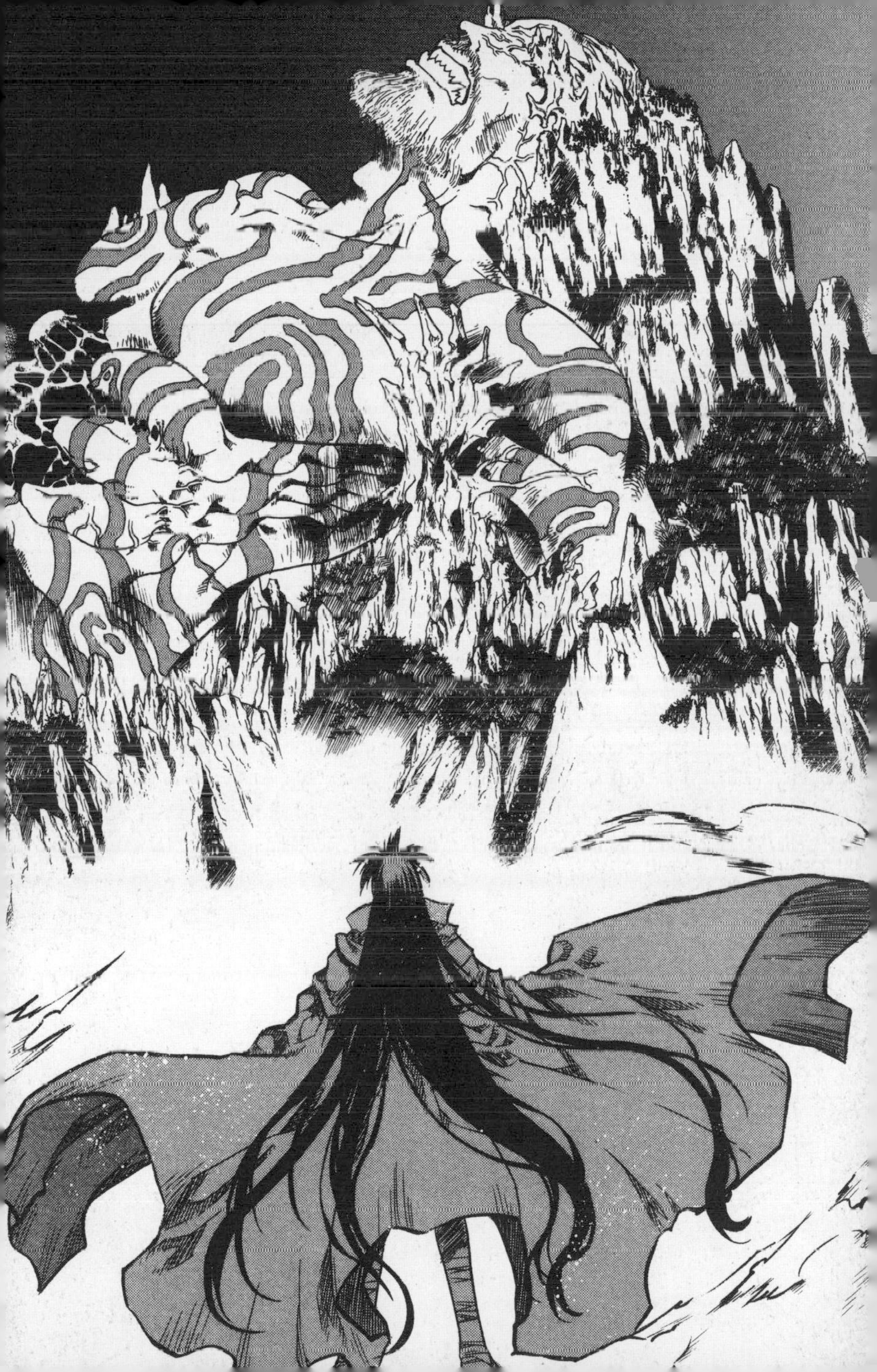

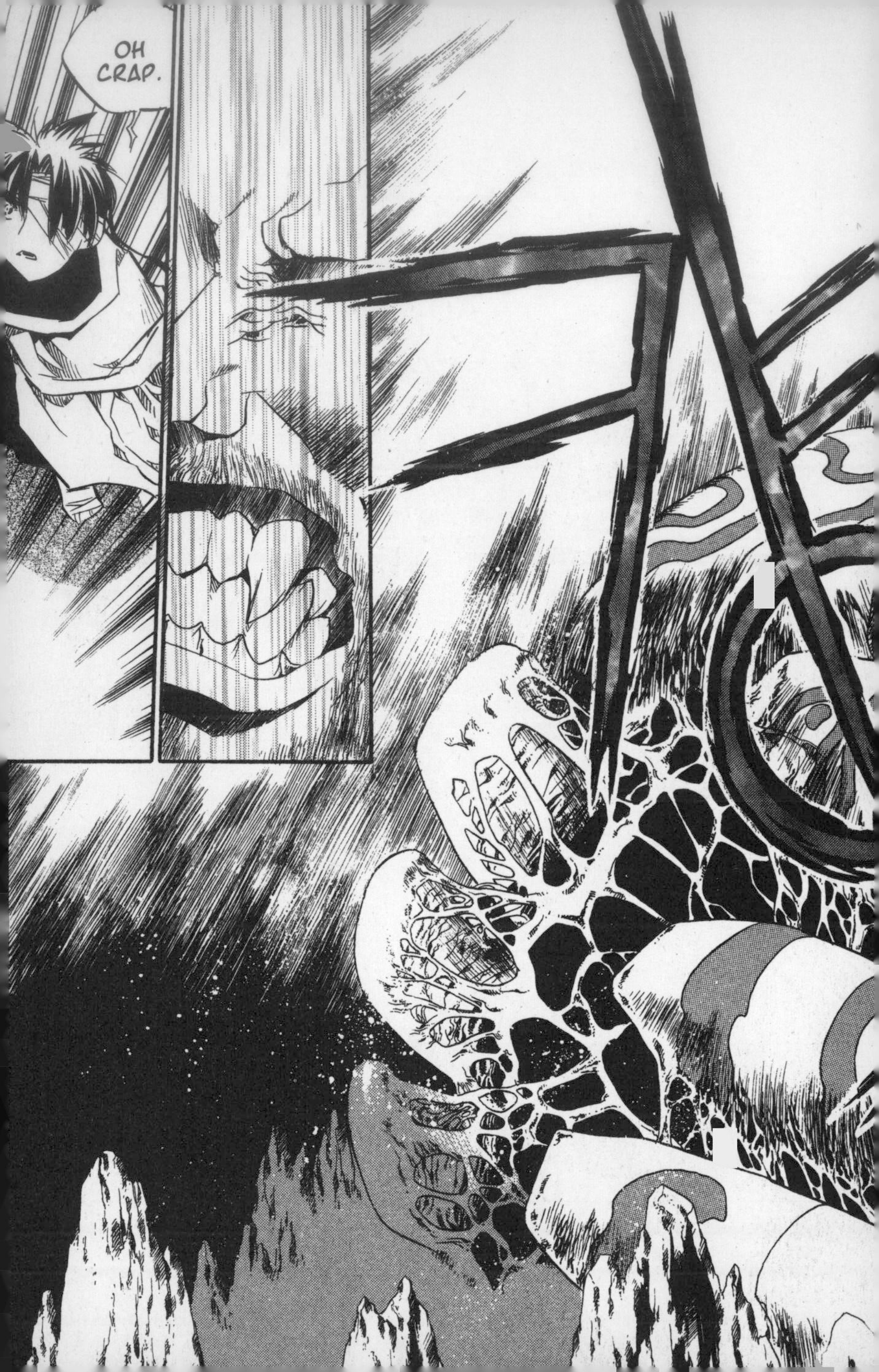
OH CRAP.

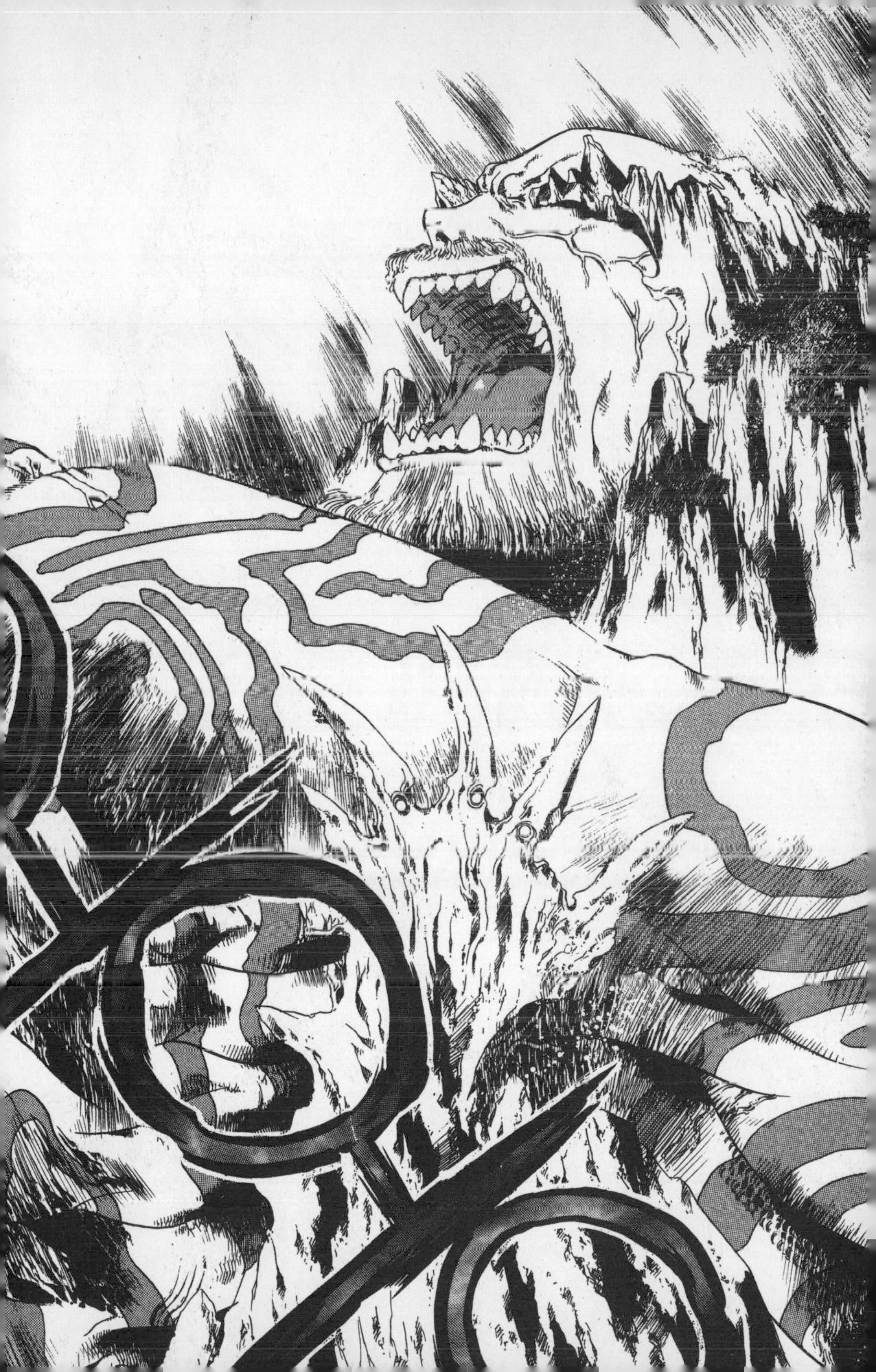

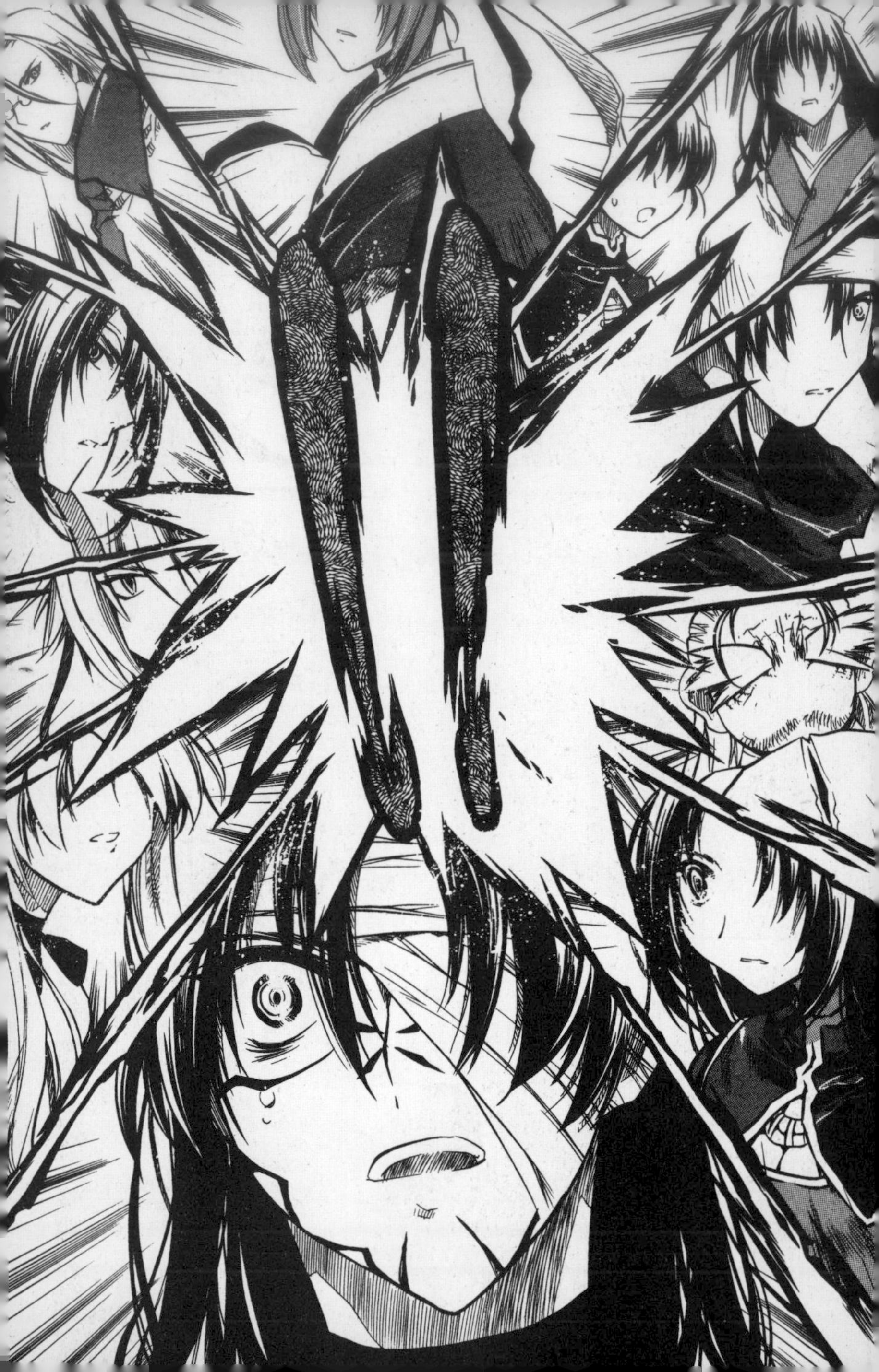

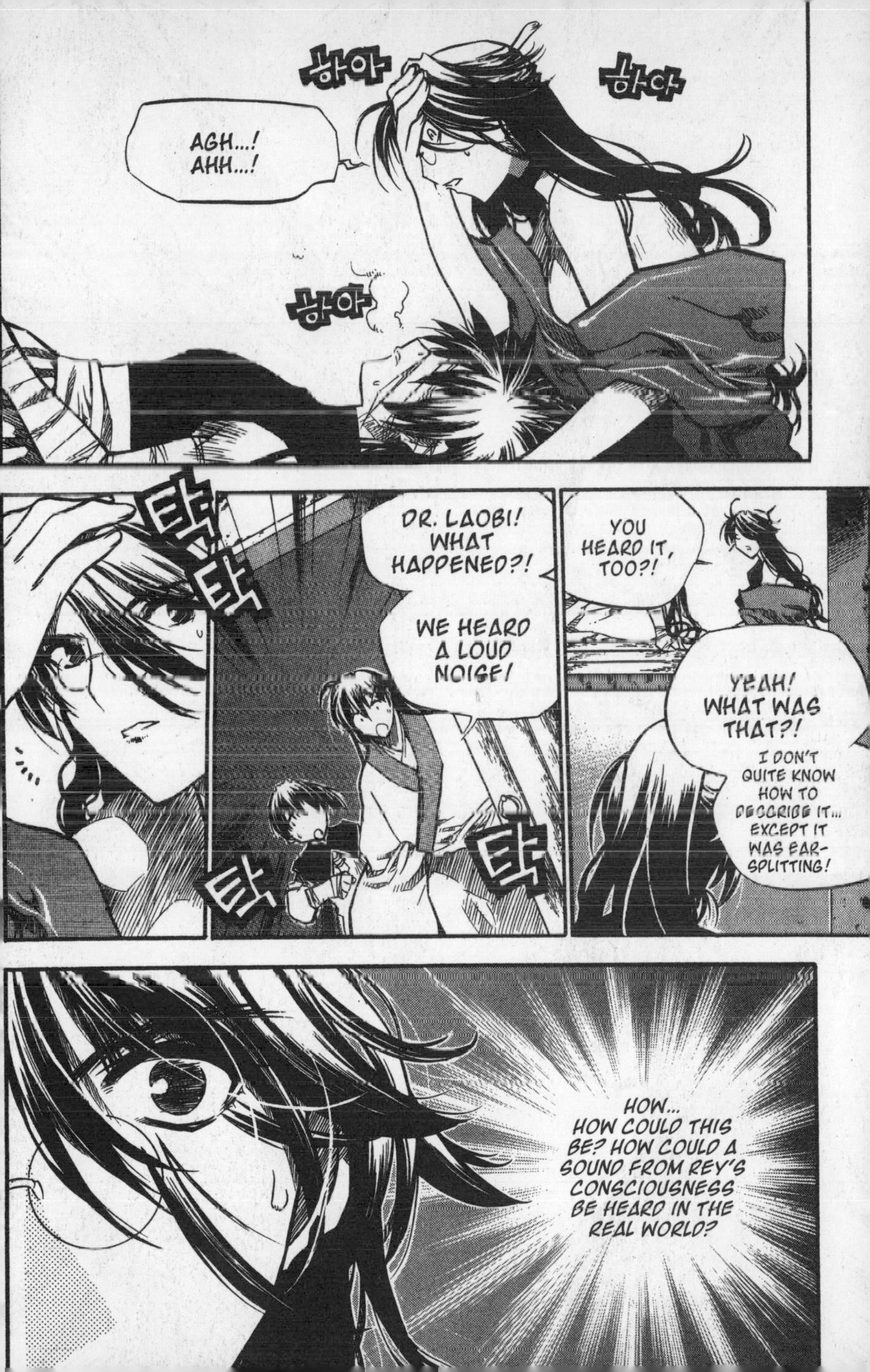
하아
하아
AGH...! AHH...!
하아
탁
탁
DR. LAOBI! WHAT HAPPENED?!
WE HEARD A LOUD NOISE!
탁
탁
YOU HEARD IT, TOO?!
YEAH! WHAT WAS THAT?!
I DON'T QUITE KNOW HOW TO DESCRIBE IT... EXCEPT IT WAS EAR-SPLITTING!
HOW... HOW COULD THIS BE? HOW COULD A SOUND FROM REY'S CONSCIOUSNESS BE HEARD IN THE REAL WORLD?

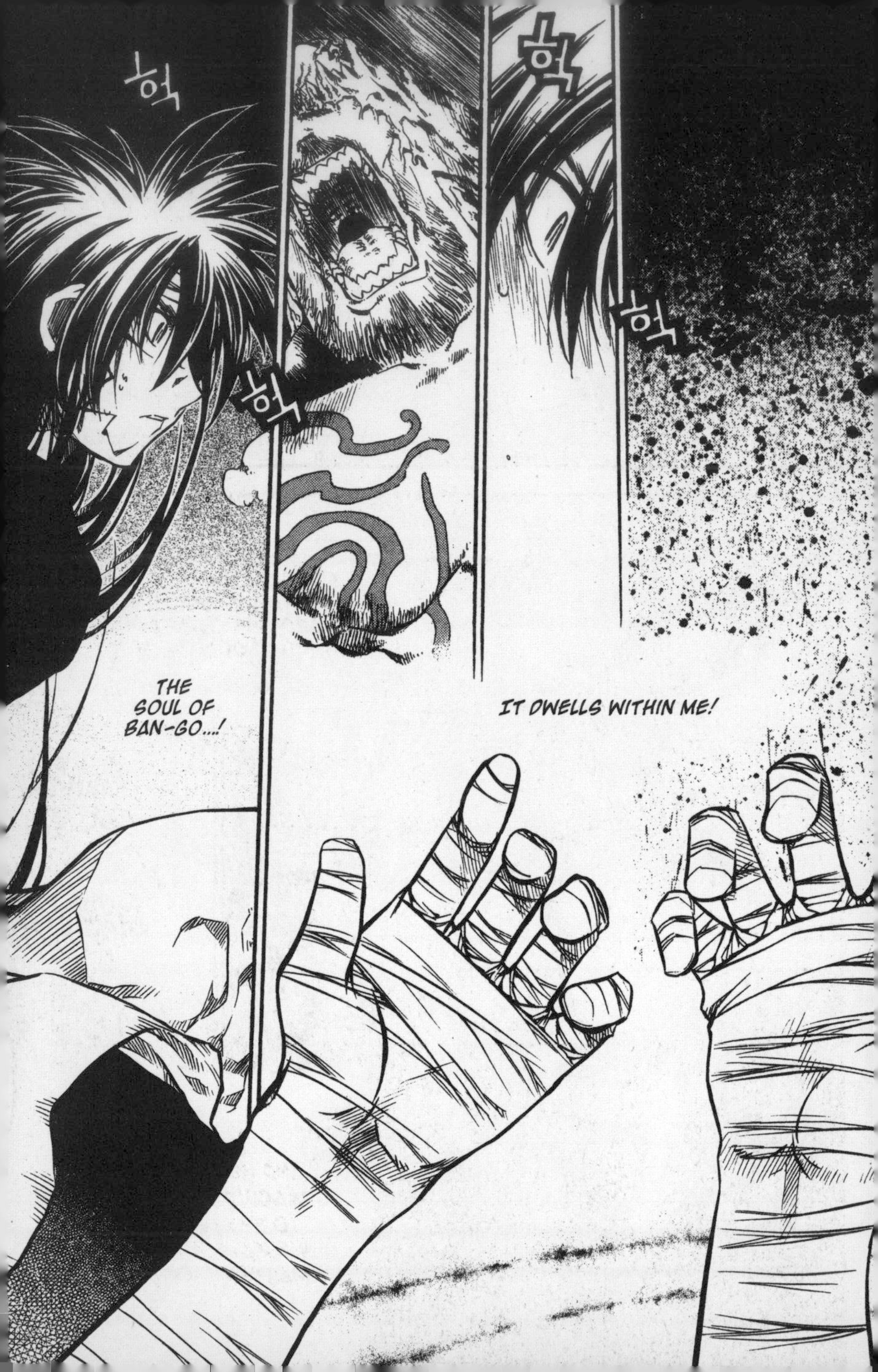
헉
헉
헉
헉
THE SOUL OF BAN-GO...!
IT DWELLS WITHIN ME!

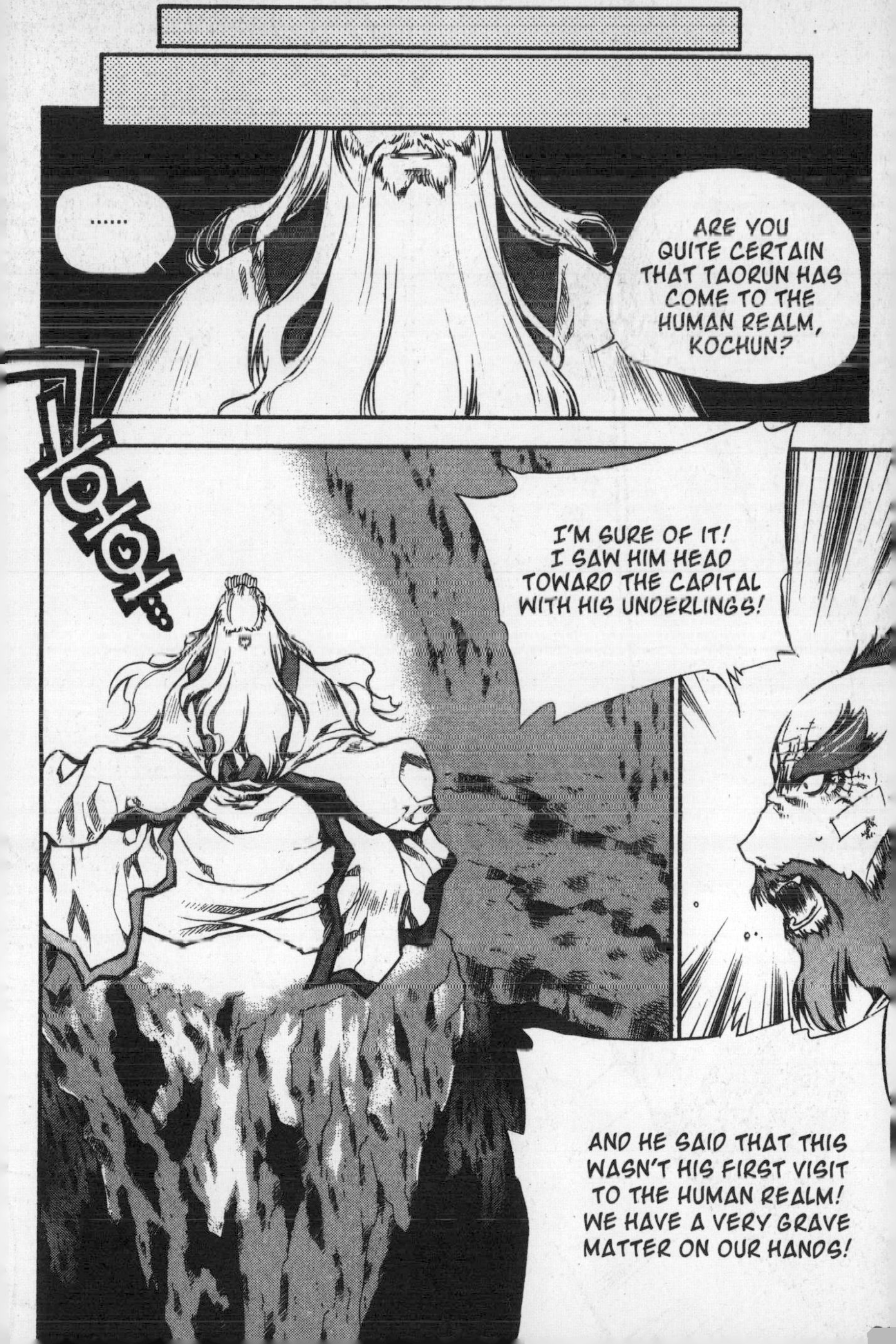
......
ARE YOU QUITE CERTAIN THAT TAORUN HAS COME TO THE HUMAN REALM, KOCHUN?
I'M SURE OF IT! I SAW HIM HEAD TOWARD THE CAPITAL WITH HIS UNDERLINGS!
AND HE SAID THAT THIS WASN'T HIS FIRST VISIT TO THE HUMAN REALM! WE HAVE A VERY GRAVE MATTER ON OUR HANDS!

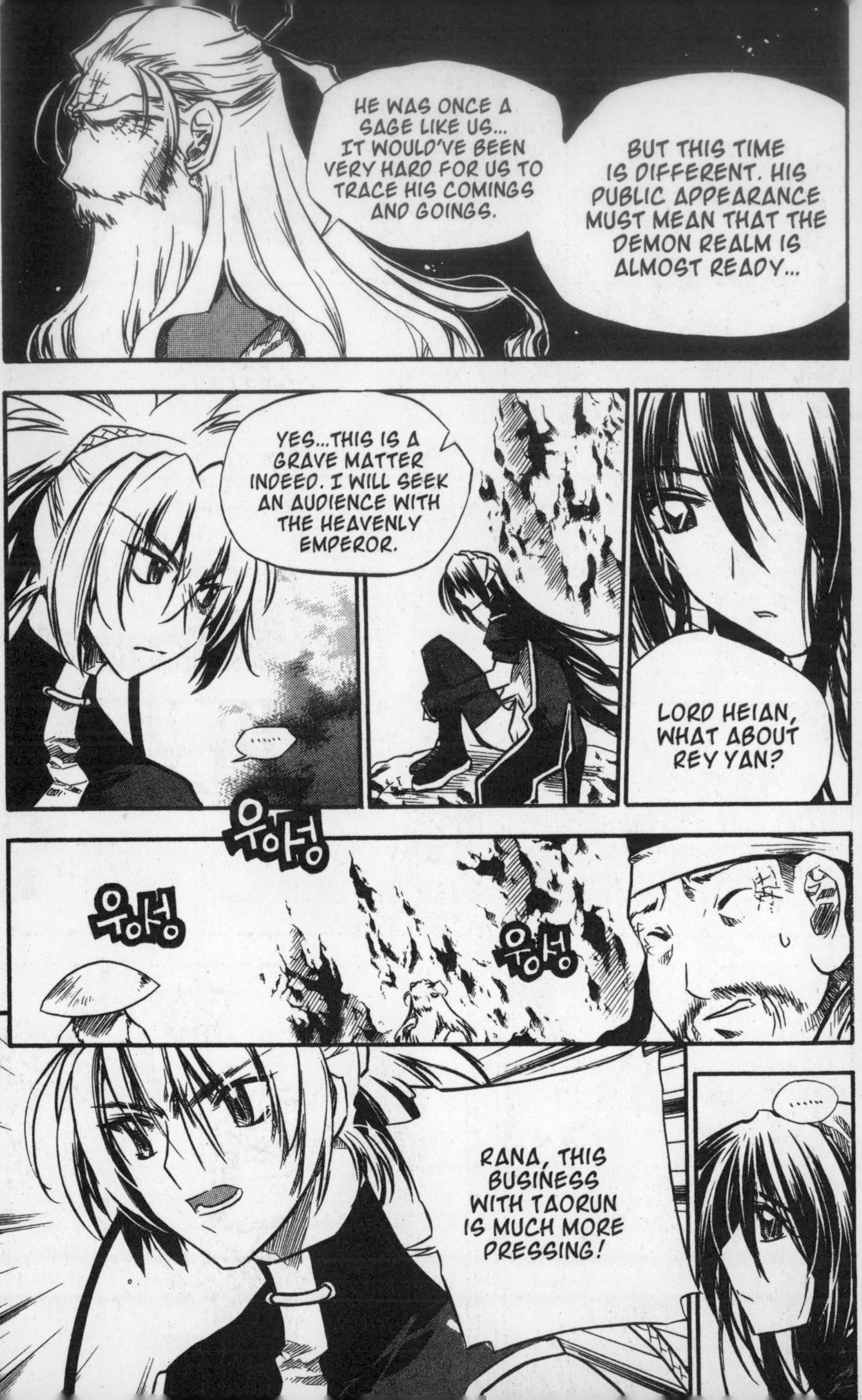
HE WAS ONCE A SAGE LIKE US... IT WOULD'VE BEEN VERY HARD FOR US TO TRACE HIS COMINGS AND GOINGS.
BUT THIS TIME IS DIFFERENT. HIS PUBLIC APPEARANCE MUST MEAN THAT THE DEMON REALM IS ALMOST READY...
YES...THIS IS A GRAVE MATTER INDEED. I WILL SEEK AN AUDIENCE WITH THE HEAVENLY EMPEROR.
......
LORD HEIAN, WHAT ABOUT REY YAN?
RANA, THIS BUSINESS WITH TAORUN IS MUCH MORE PRESSING!
......

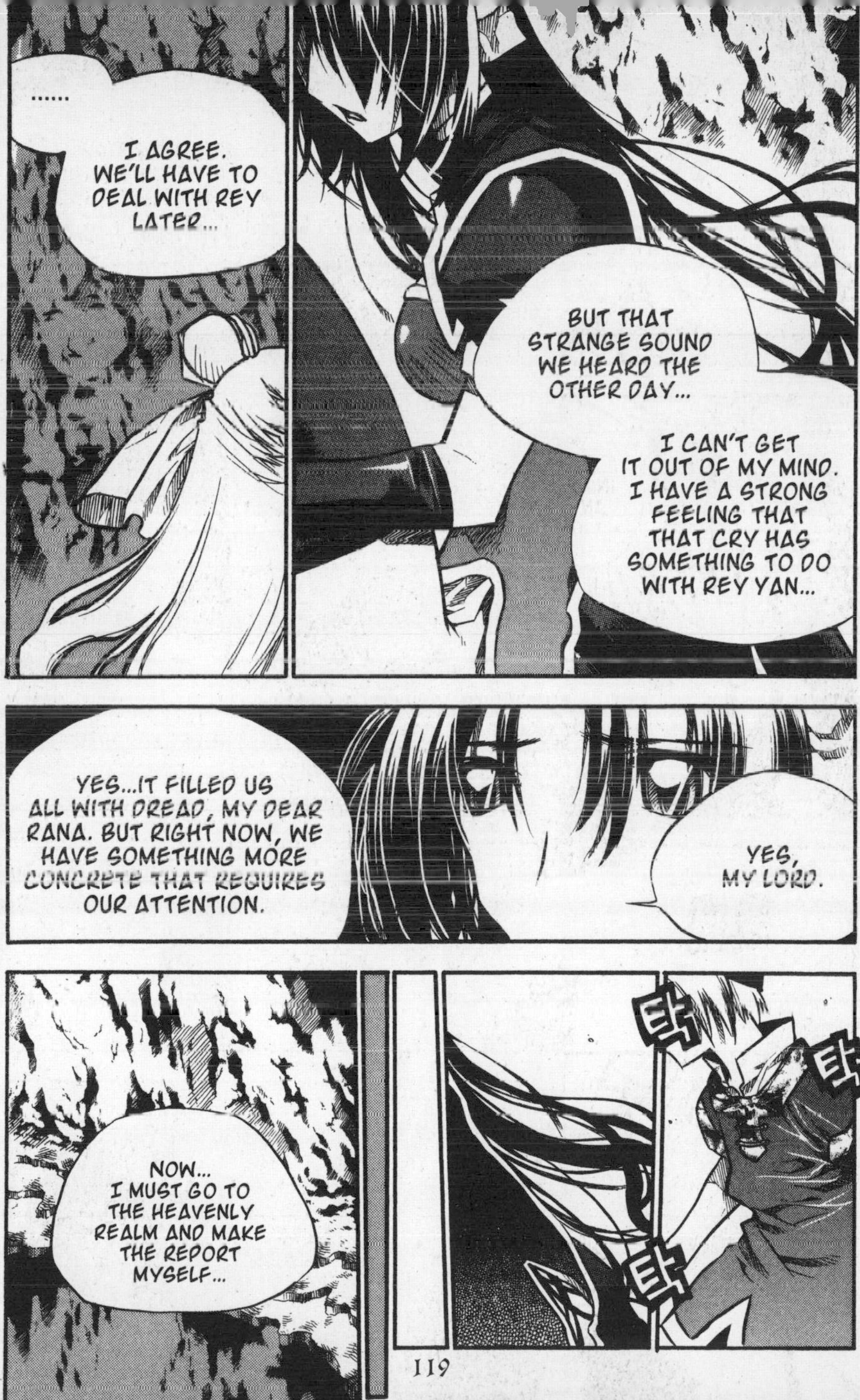
......
I AGREE. WE'LL HAVE TO DEAL WITH REY LATER...
BUT THAT STRANGE SOUND WE HEARD THE OTHER DAY...
I CAN'T GET IT OUT OF MY MIND. I HAVE A STRONG FEELING THAT THAT CRY HAS SOMETHING TO DO WITH REY YAN...
YES...IT FILLED US ALL WITH DREAD, MY DEAR RANA. BUT RIGHT NOW, WE HAVE SOMETHING MORE CONCRETE THAT REQUIRES OUR ATTENTION.
YES, MY LORD.
NOW... I MUST GO TO THE HEAVENLY REALM AND MAKE THE REPORT MYSELF...

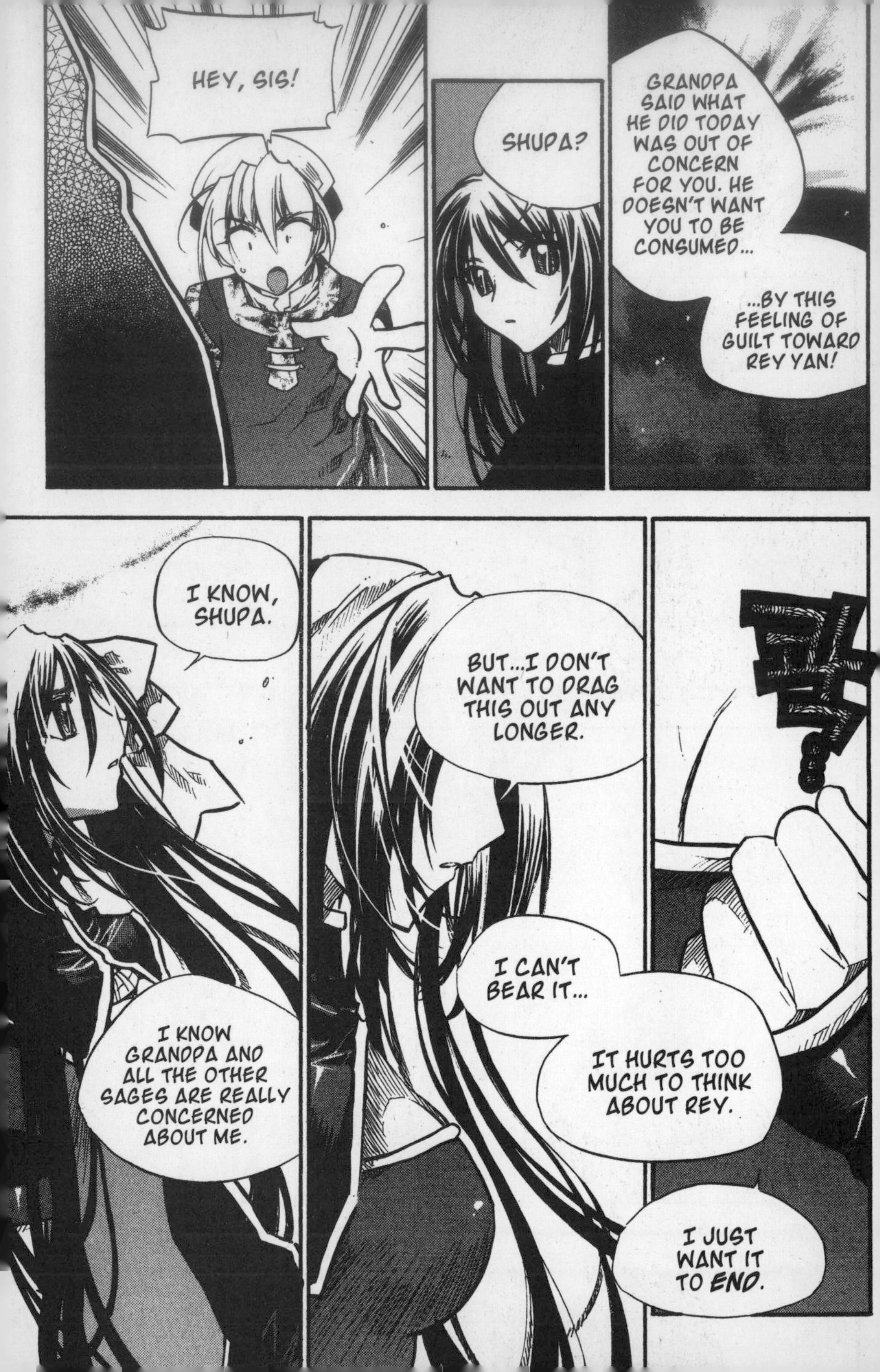
HEY, SIS!
SHUPA?
GRANDPA SAID WHAT HE DID TODAY WAS OUT OF CONCERN FOR YOU. HE DOESN'T WANT YOU TO BE CONSUMED...
...BY THIS FEELING OF GUILT TOWARD REY YAN!
I KNOW, SHUPA.
I KNOW GRANDPA AND ALL THE OTHER SAGES ARE REALLY CONCERNED ABOUT ME.
BUT...I DON'T WANT TO DRAG THIS OUT ANY LONGER.
I CAN'T BEAR IT...
IT HURTS TOO MUCH TO THINK ABOUT REY.
I JUST WANT IT TO *END*.

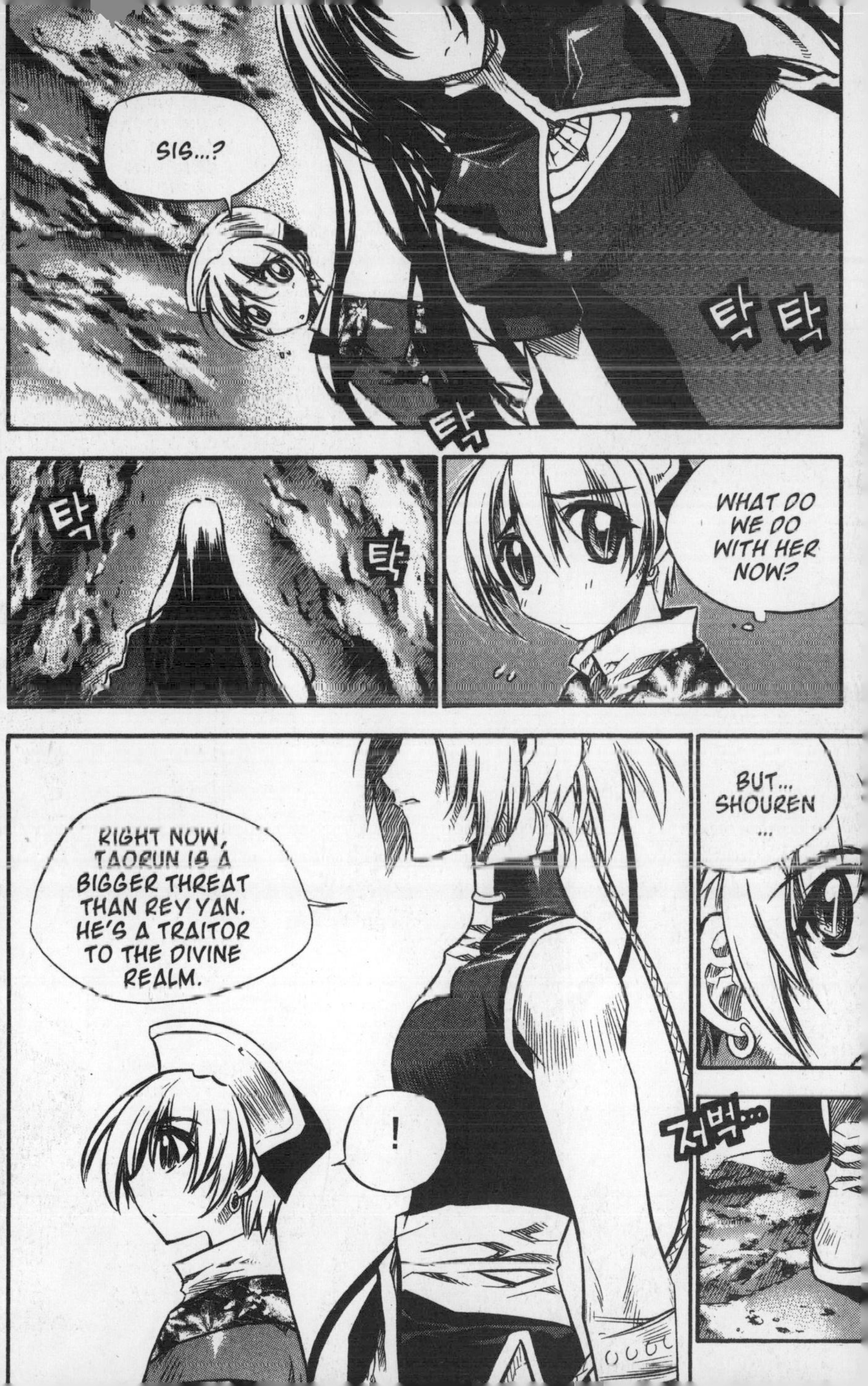
SIS...?
탁탁
탁
탁
탁
WHAT DO WE DO WITH HER NOW?
RIGHT NOW, TAORUN IS A BIGGER THREAT THAN REY YAN. HE'S A TRAITOR TO THE DIVINE REALM.
!
BUT... SHOUREN ...
저벅...

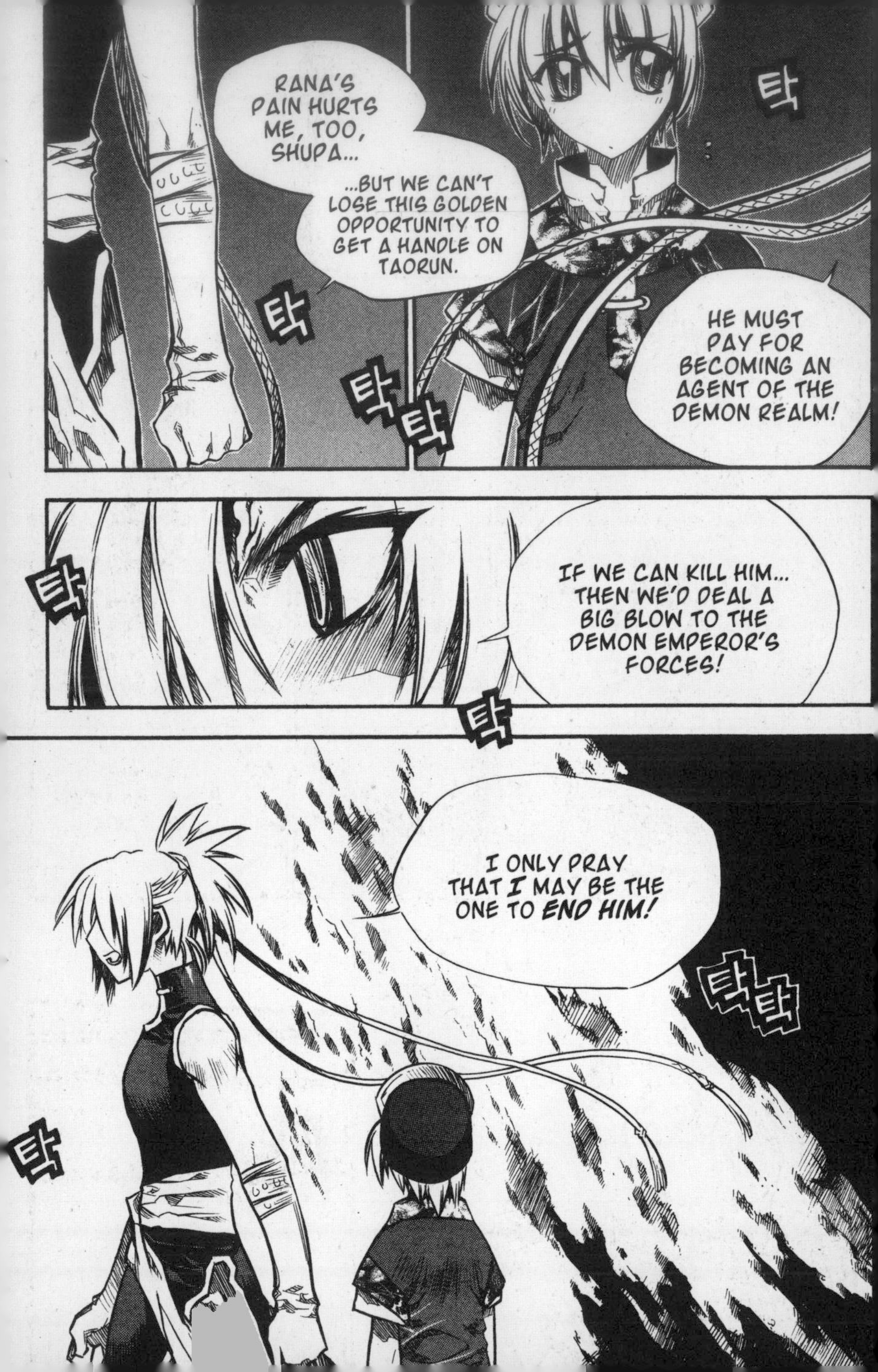
RANA'S PAIN HURTS ME, TOO, SHUPA...
...BUT WE CAN'T LOSE THIS GOLDEN OPPORTUNITY TO GET A HANDLE ON TAORUN.
탁
탁
탁
탁
HE MUST PAY FOR BECOMING AN AGENT OF THE DEMON REALM!
탁
IF WE CAN KILL HIM... THEN WE'D DEAL A BIG BLOW TO THE DEMON EMPEROR'S FORCES!
탁
I ONLY PRAY THAT *I* MAY BE THE ONE TO ***END HIM!***
탁탁
탁

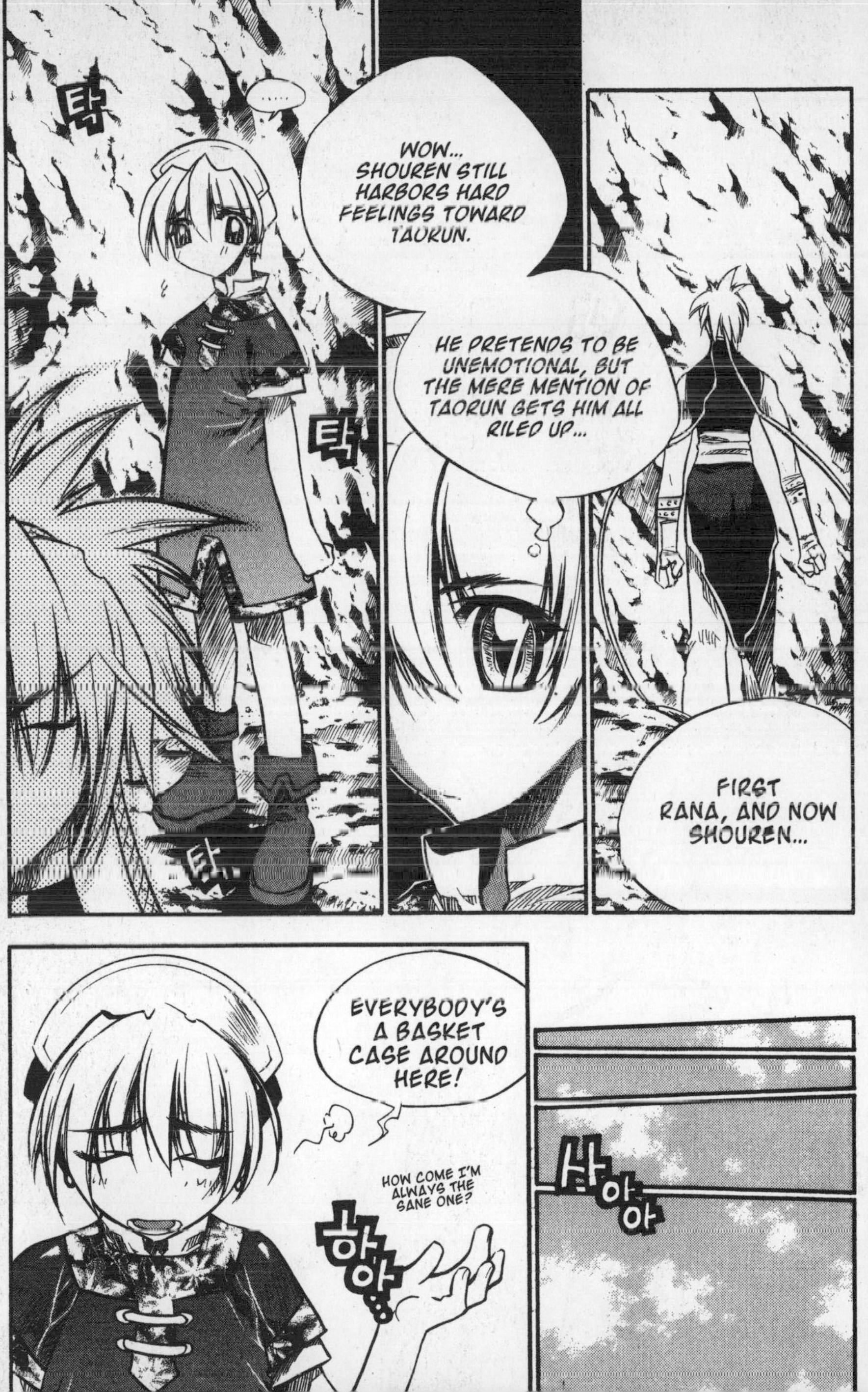
탁
.....
탁
탁
WOW... SHOUREN STILL HARBORS HARD FEELINGS TOWARD TAORUN.
HE PRETENDS TO BE UNEMOTIONAL, BUT THE MERE MENTION OF TAORUN GETS HIM ALL RILED UP...
FIRST RANA, AND NOW SHOUREN...
EVERYBODY'S A BASKET CASE AROUND HERE!
HOW COME I'M ALWAYS THE SANE ONE?
하아..

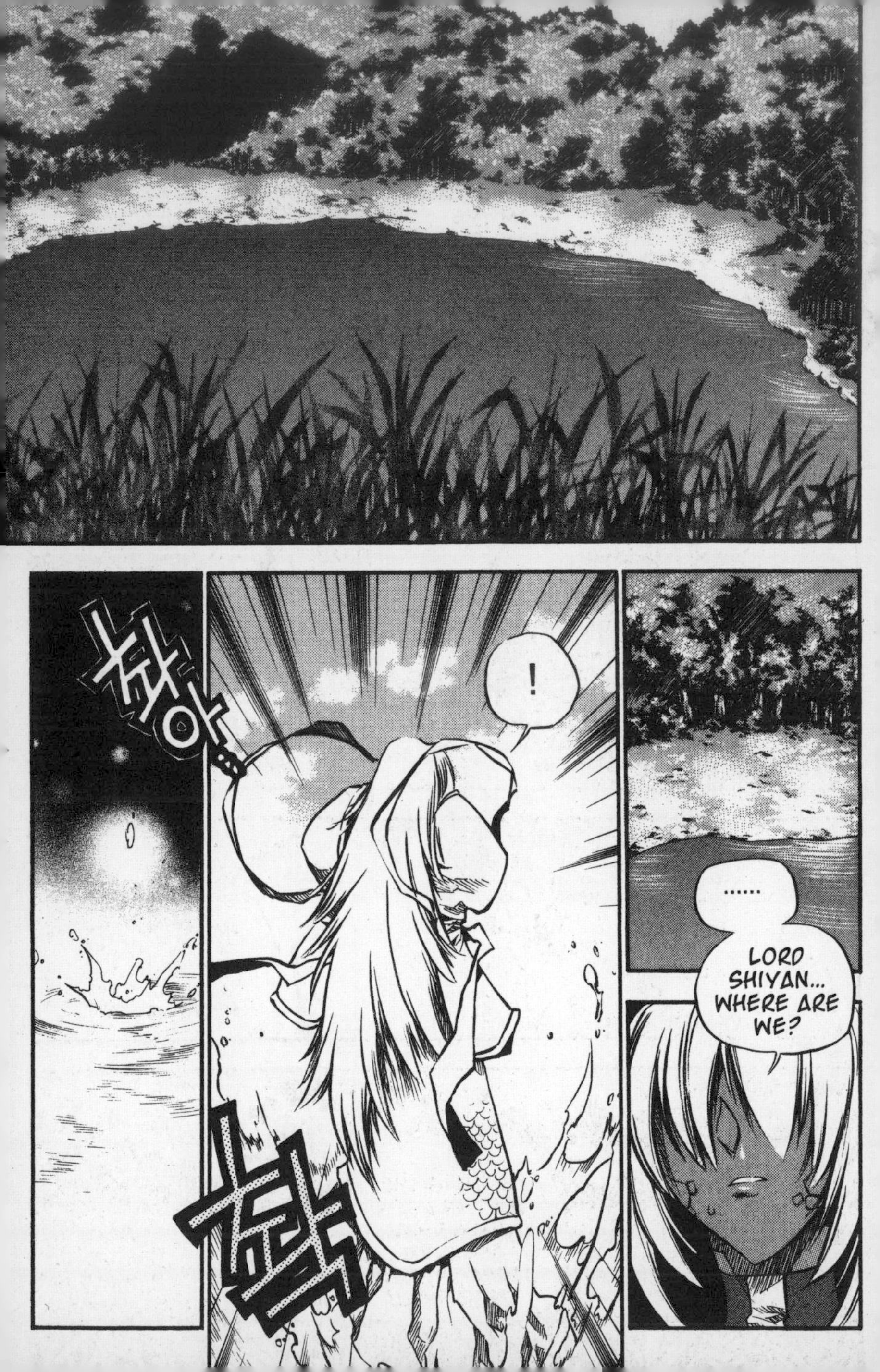

!
......
LORD SHIYAN... WHERE ARE WE?

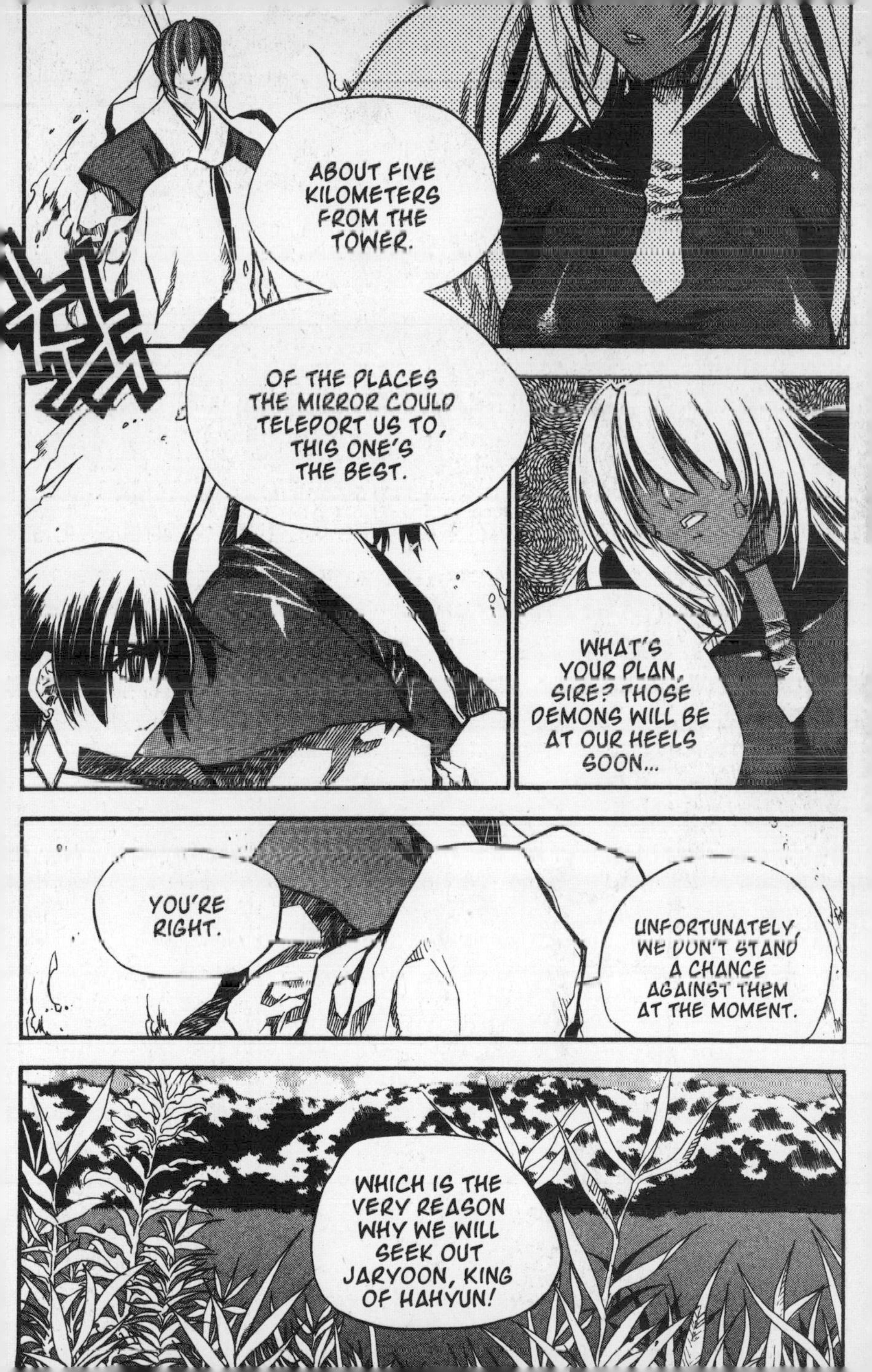
ABOUT FIVE KILOMETERS FROM THE TOWER.
OF THE PLACES THE MIRROR COULD TELEPORT US TO, THIS ONE'S THE BEST.
WHAT'S YOUR PLAN, SIRE? THOSE DEMONS WILL BE AT OUR HEELS SOON...
YOU'RE RIGHT.
UNFORTUNATELY, WE DON'T STAND A CHANCE AGAINST THEM AT THE MOMENT.
WHICH IS THE VERY REASON WHY WE WILL SEEK OUT JARYOON, KING OF HAHYUN!

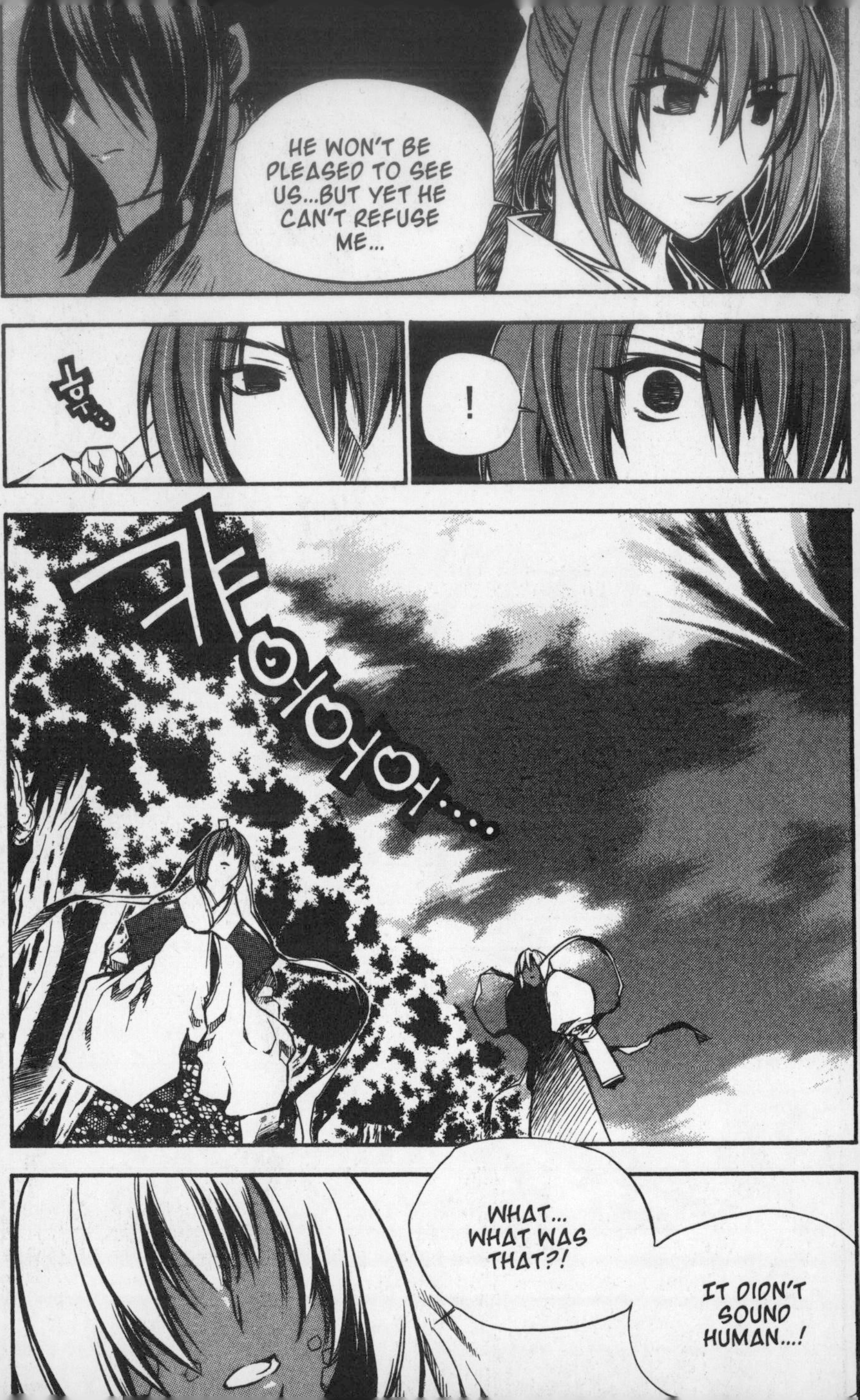
HE WON'T BE PLEASED TO SEE US...BUT YET HE CAN'T REFUSE ME...
!
WHAT... WHAT WAS THAT?!
IT DIDN'T SOUND HUMAN...!

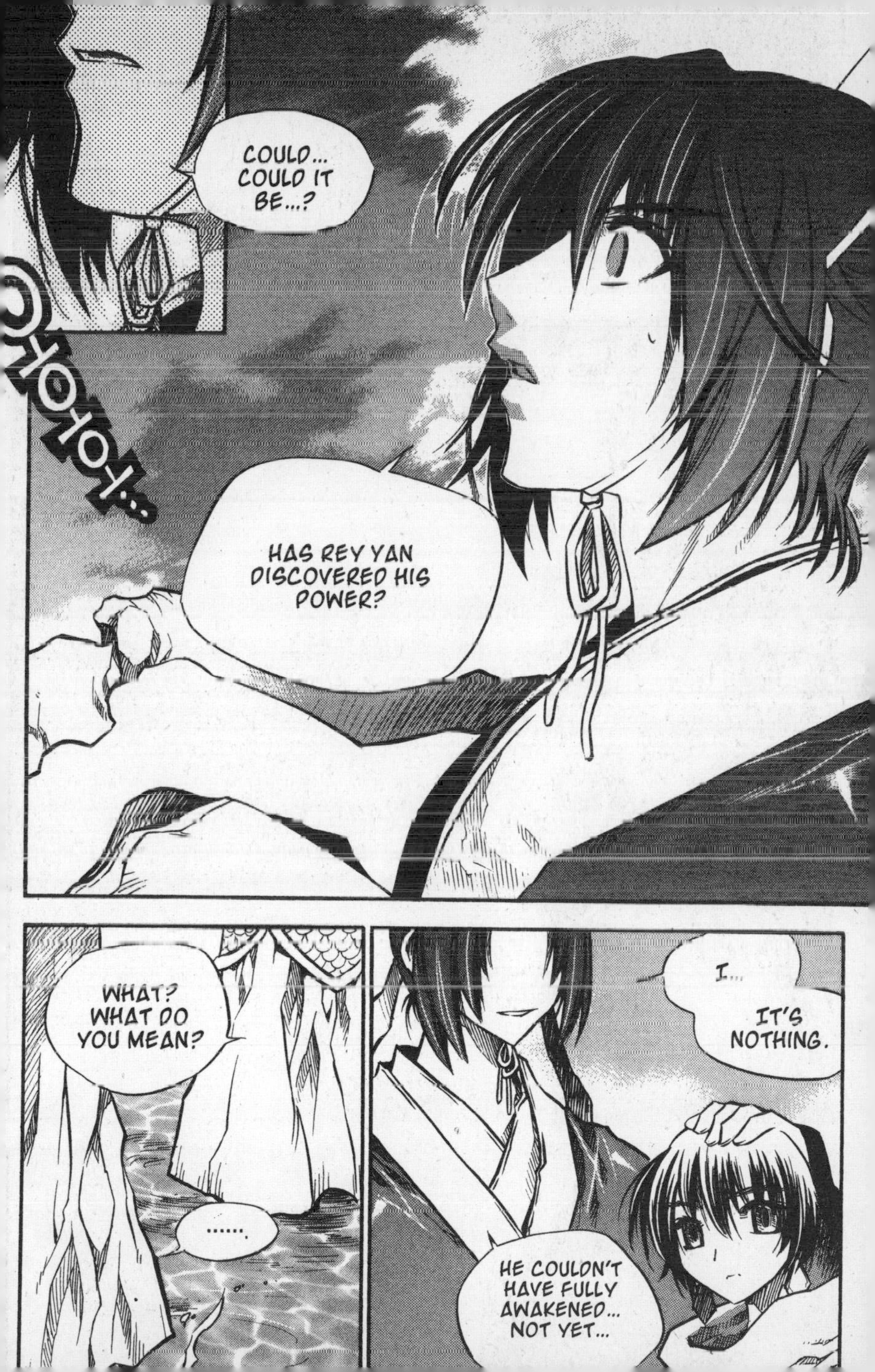
COULD... COULD IT BE...?
HAS REY YAN DISCOVERED HIS POWER?
WHAT? WHAT DO YOU MEAN?
....
I...
IT'S NOTHING.
HE COULDN'T HAVE FULLY AWAKENED... NOT YET...

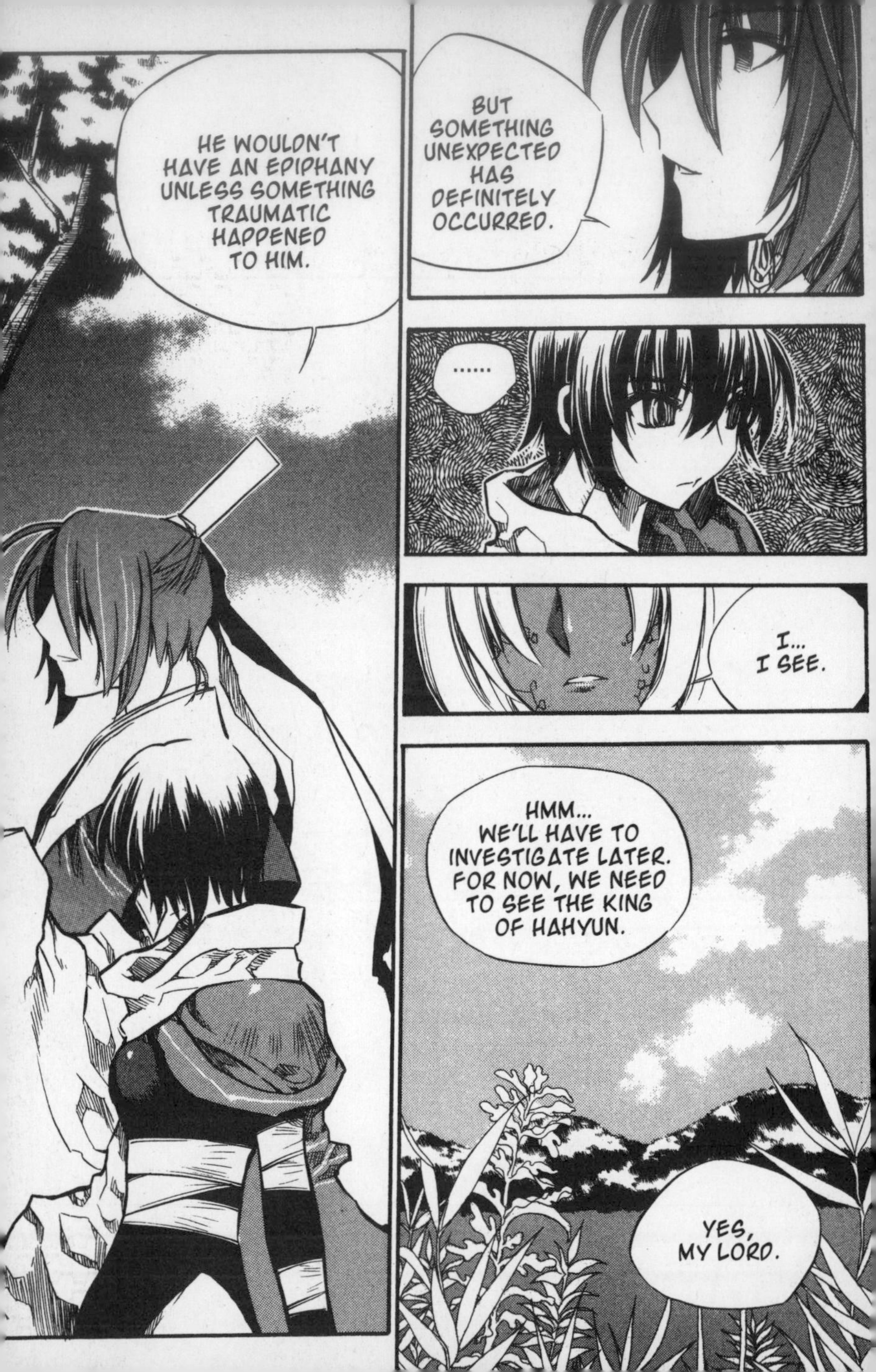
HE WOULDN'T HAVE AN EPIPHANY UNLESS SOMETHING TRAUMATIC HAPPENED TO HIM.
BUT SOMETHING UNEXPECTED HAS DEFINITELY OCCURRED.
......
I... I SEE.
HMM... WE'LL HAVE TO INVESTIGATE LATER. FOR NOW, WE NEED TO SEE THE KING OF HAHYUN.
YES, MY LORD.

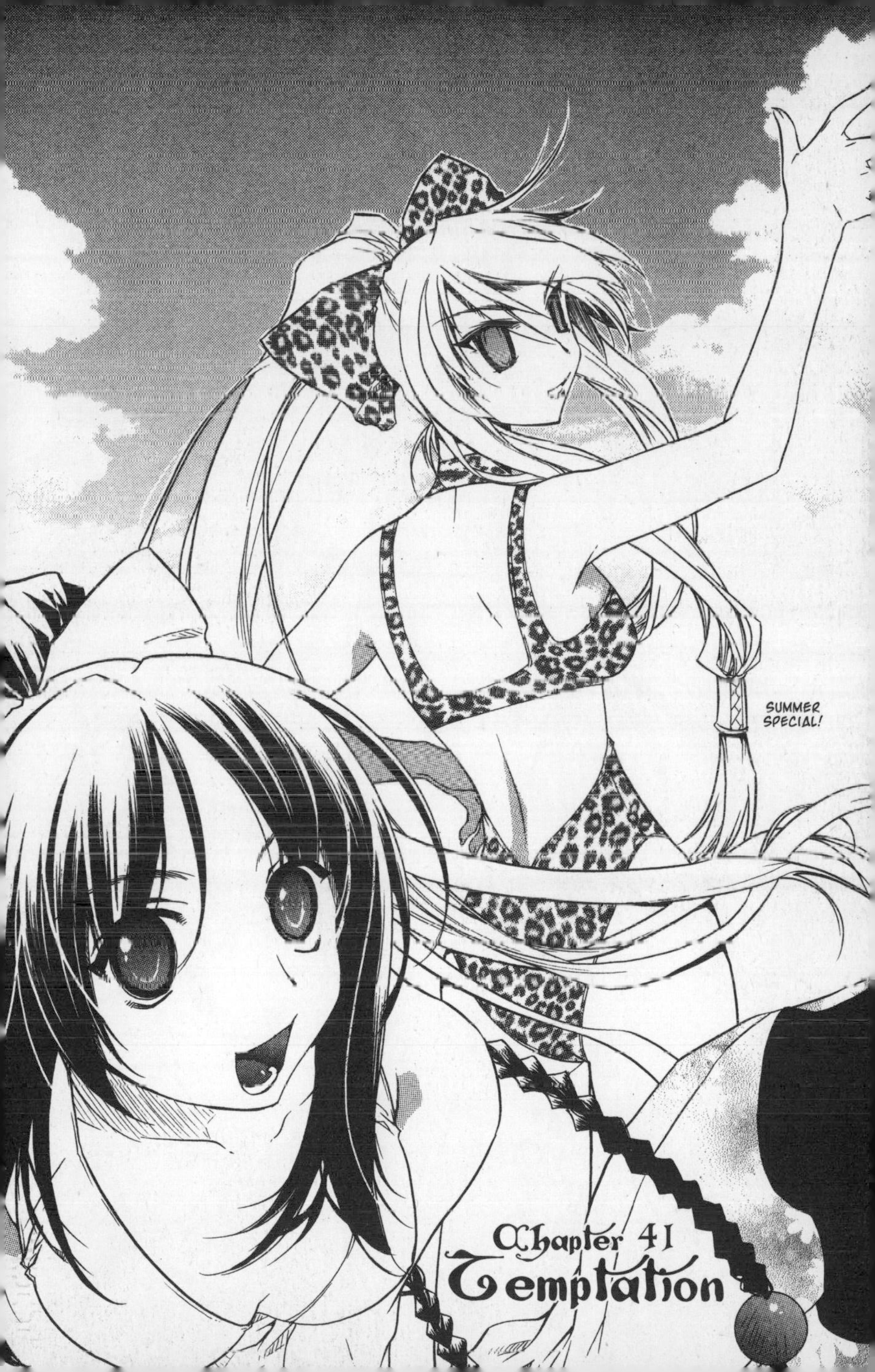
SUMMER SPECIAL!
Chapter 41
Temptation

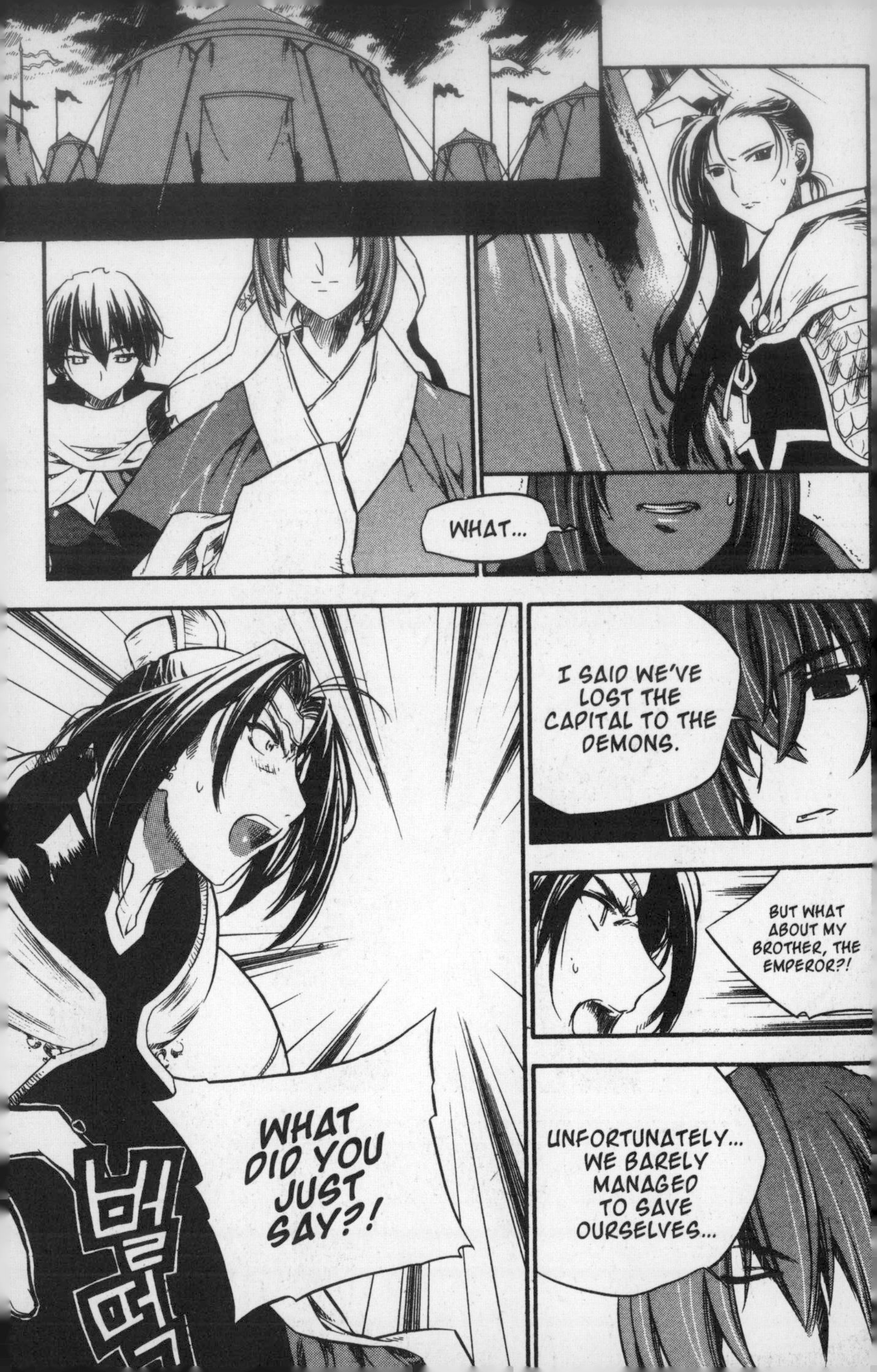
WHAT...
WHAT DID YOU JUST SAY?!
벌떡
I SAID WE'VE LOST THE CAPITAL TO THE DEMONS.
BUT WHAT ABOUT MY BROTHER, THE EMPEROR?!
UNFORTUNATELY... WE BARELY MANAGED TO SAVE OURSELVES...

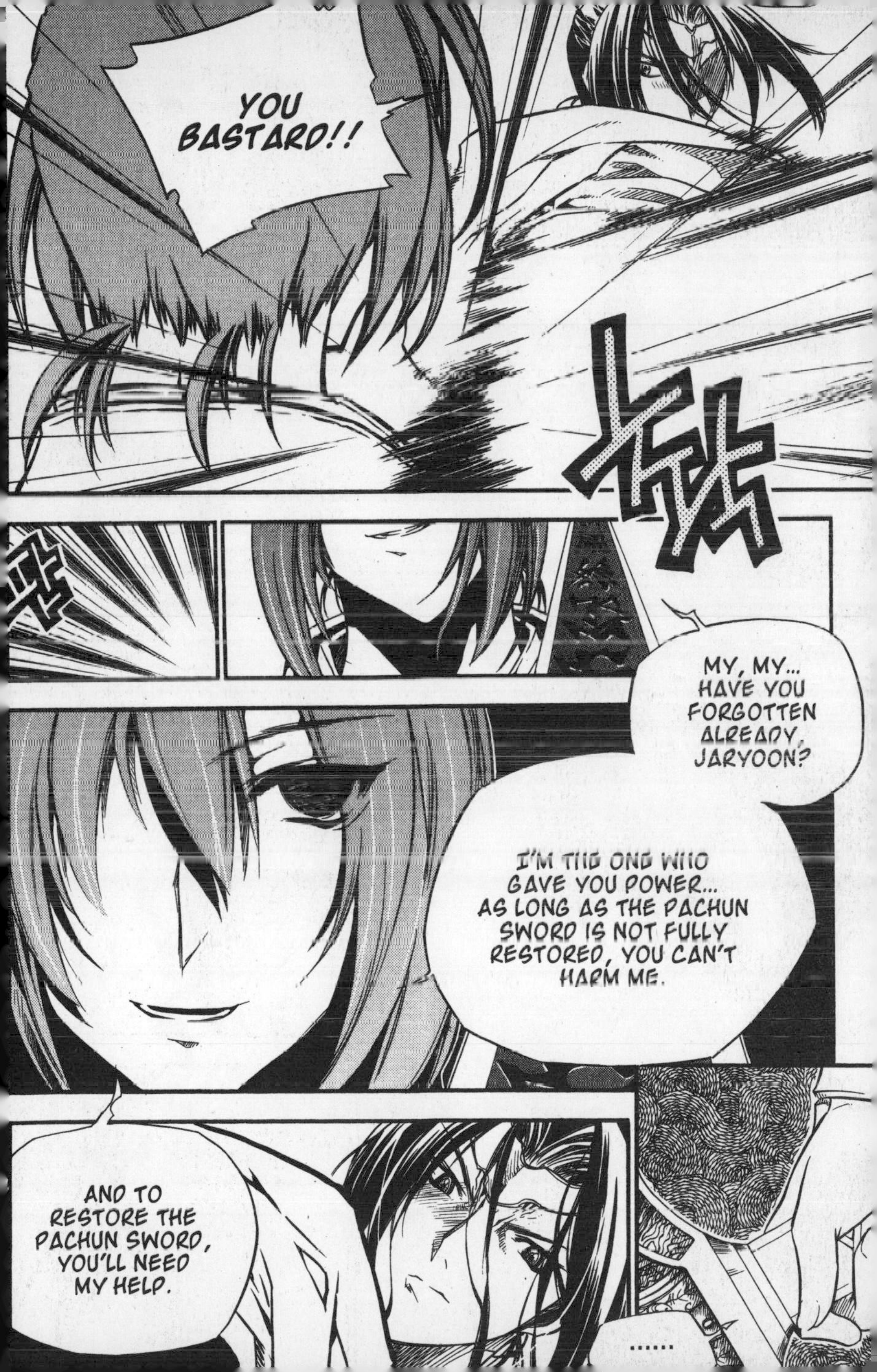
YOU BASTARD!!
MY, MY... HAVE YOU FORGOTTEN ALREADY, JARYOON?
I'M THE ONE WHO GAVE YOU POWER... AS LONG AS THE PACHUN SWORD IS NOT FULLY RESTORED, YOU CAN'T HARM ME.
AND TO RESTORE THE PACHUN SWORD, YOU'LL NEED MY HELP.
......

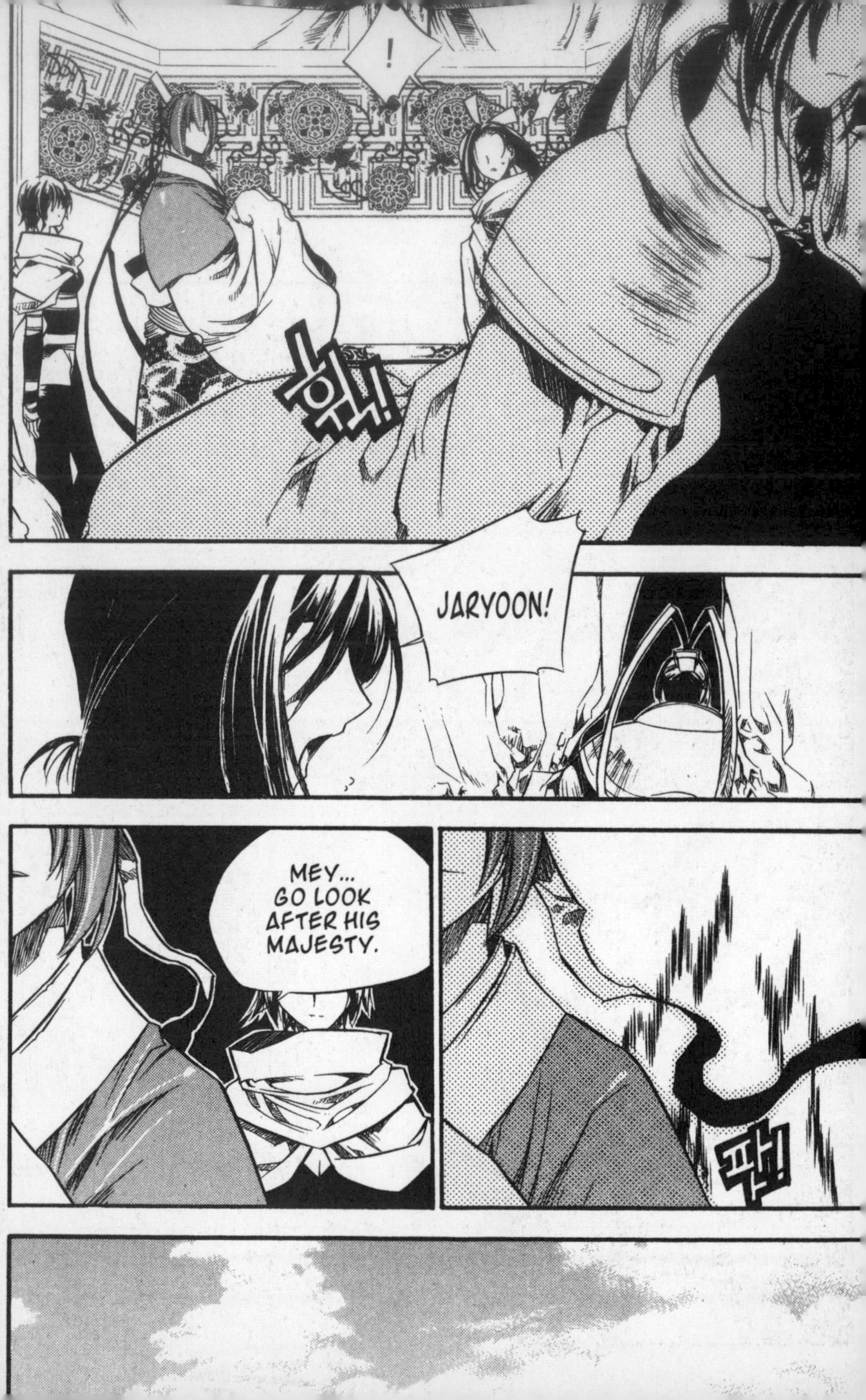
!
휙!
JARYOON!
MEY...
GO LOOK
AFTER HIS
MAJESTY.
팍!

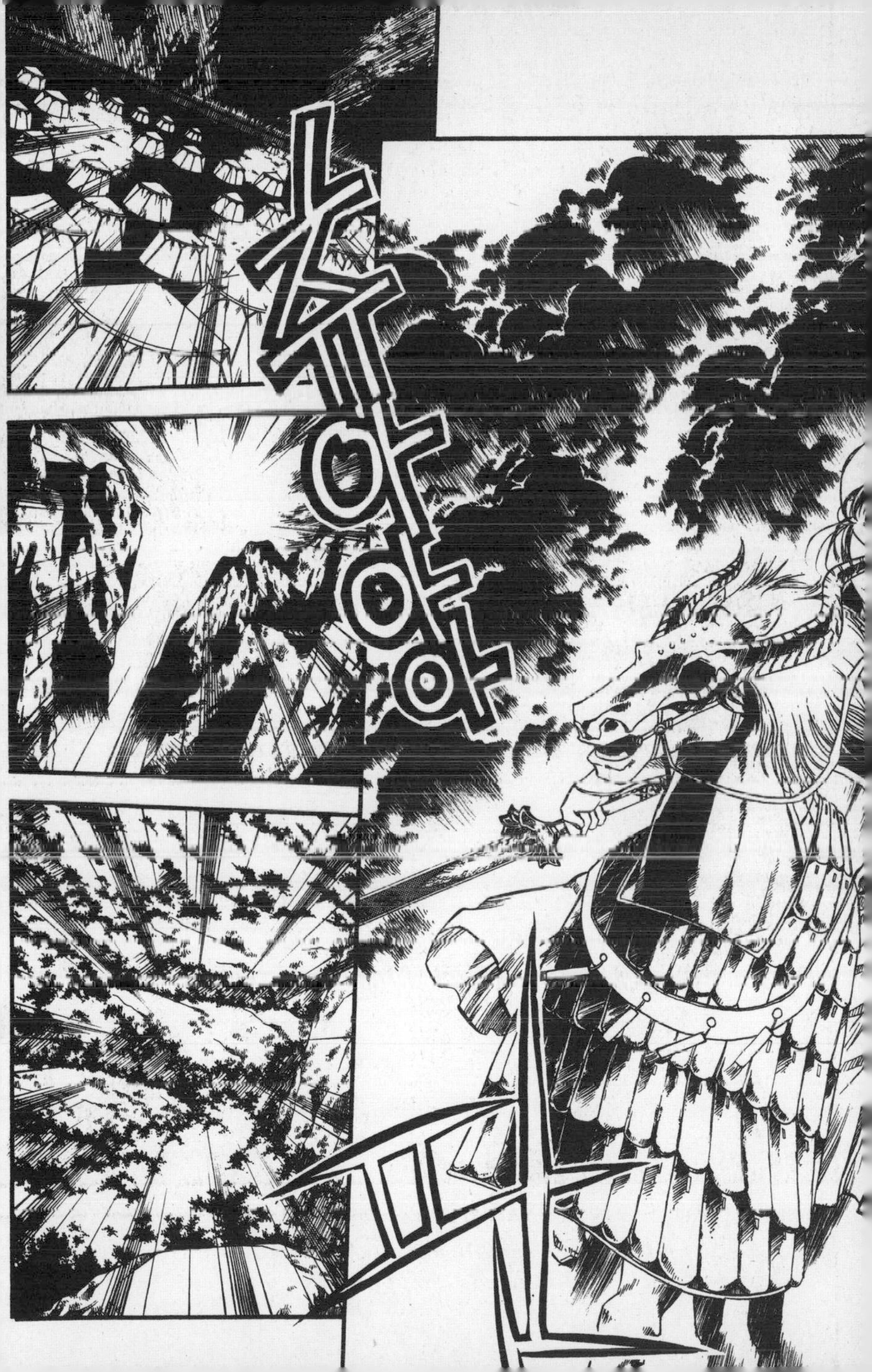
쏴아아아

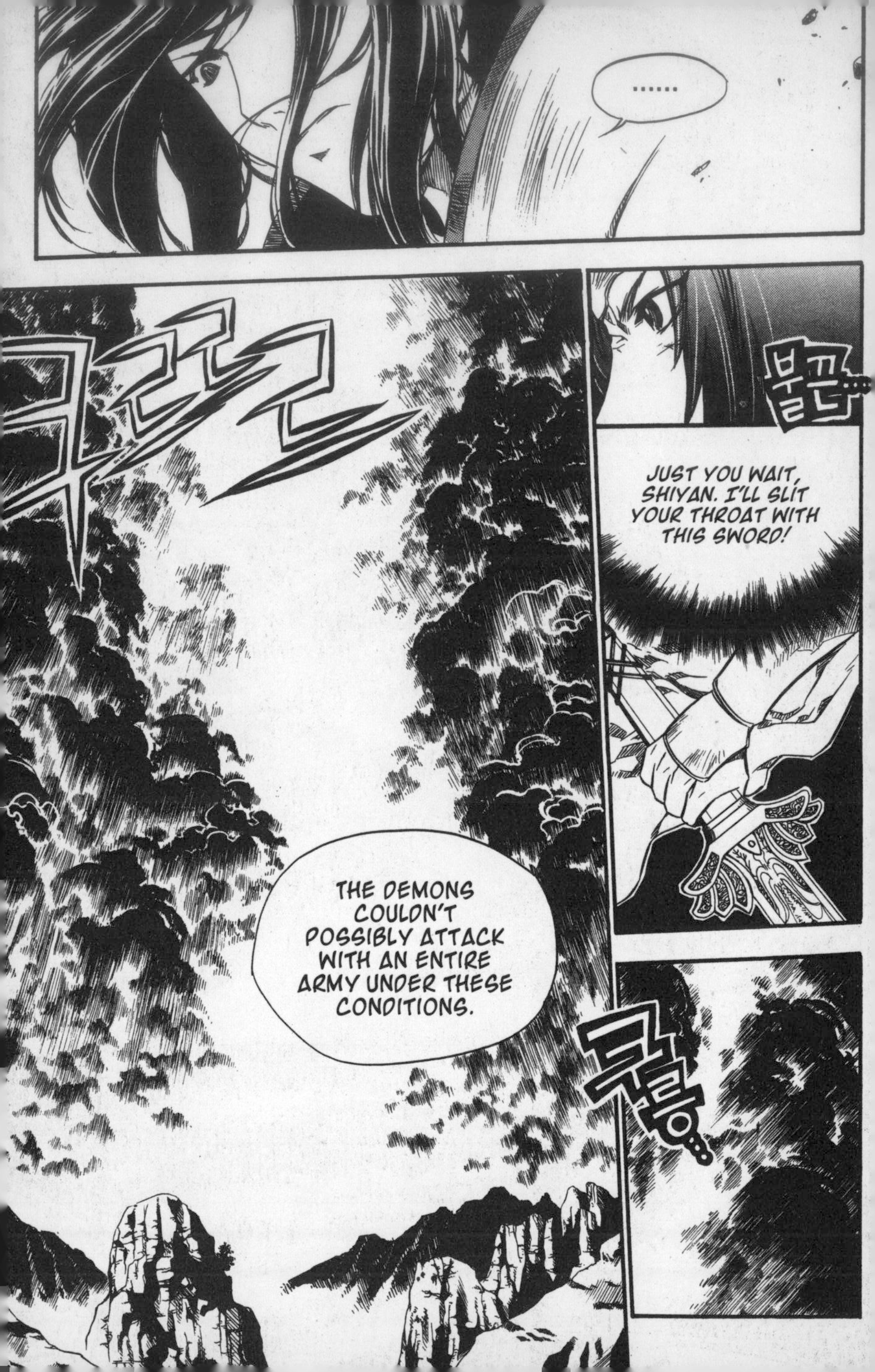
......
THE DEMONS COULDN'T POSSIBLY ATTACK WITH AN ENTIRE ARMY UNDER THESE CONDITIONS.
JUST YOU WAIT, SHIYAN. I'LL SLIT YOUR THROAT WITH THIS SWORD!

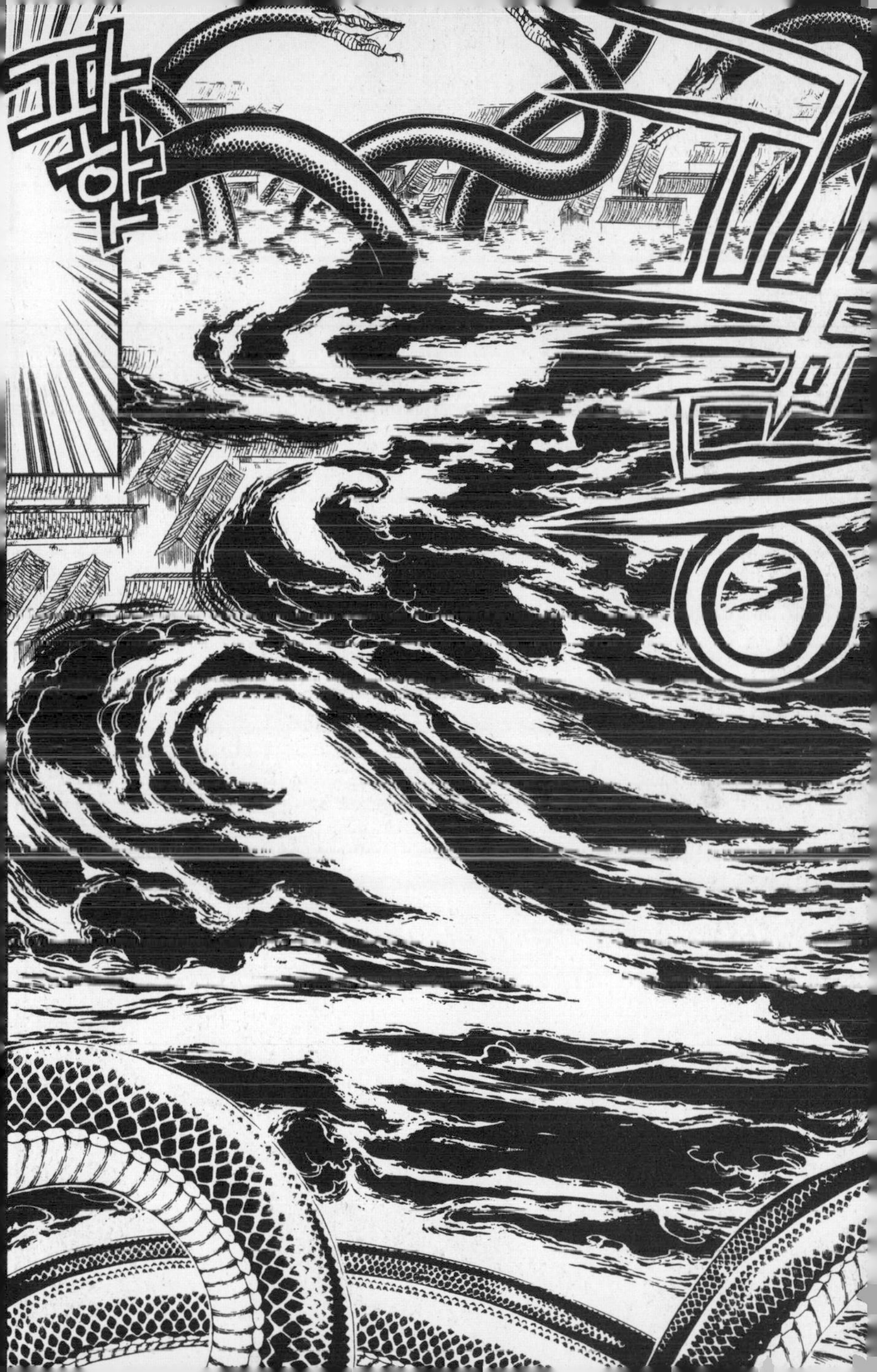
파아아

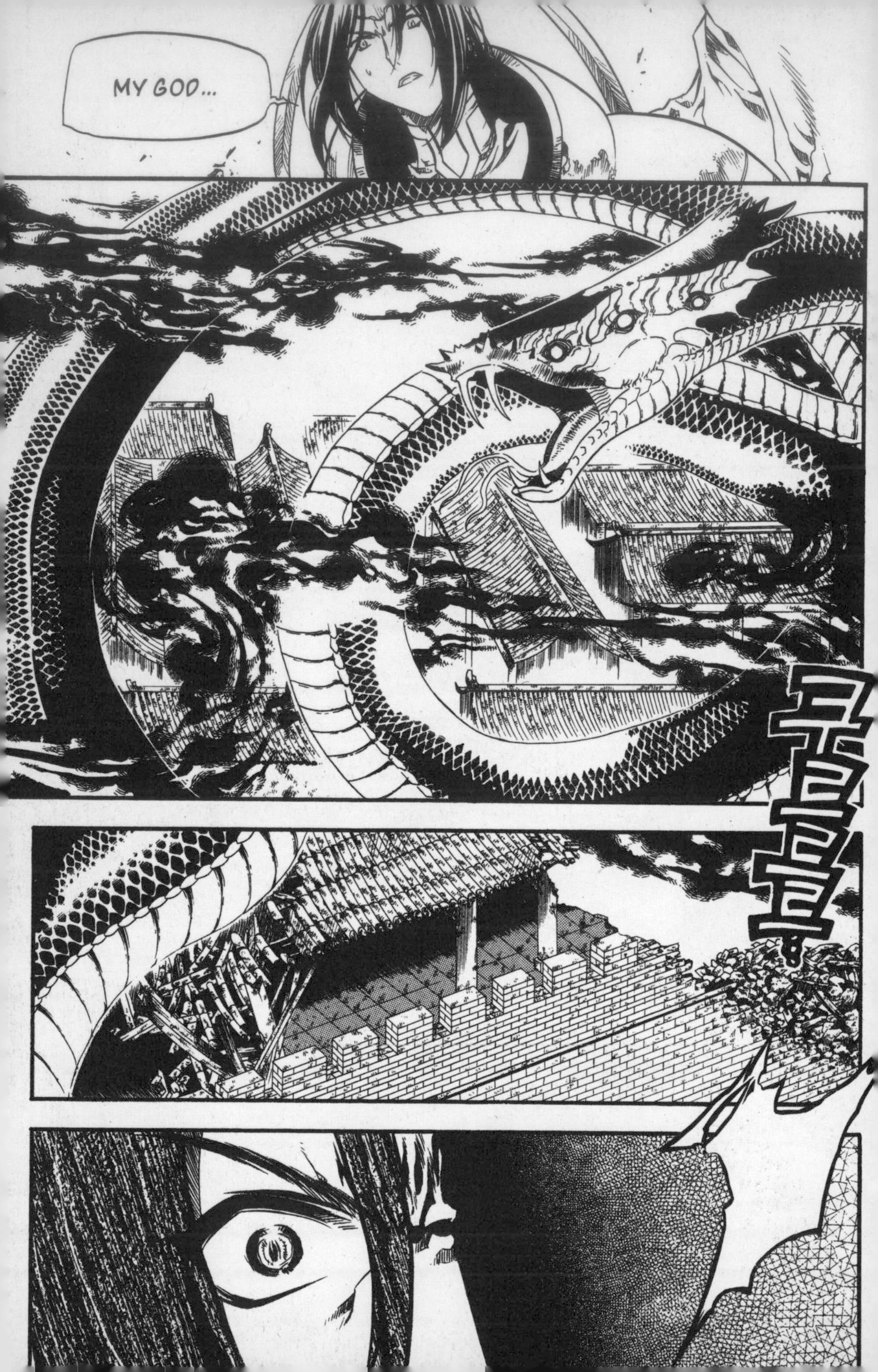
MY GOD...
쿠르르르!

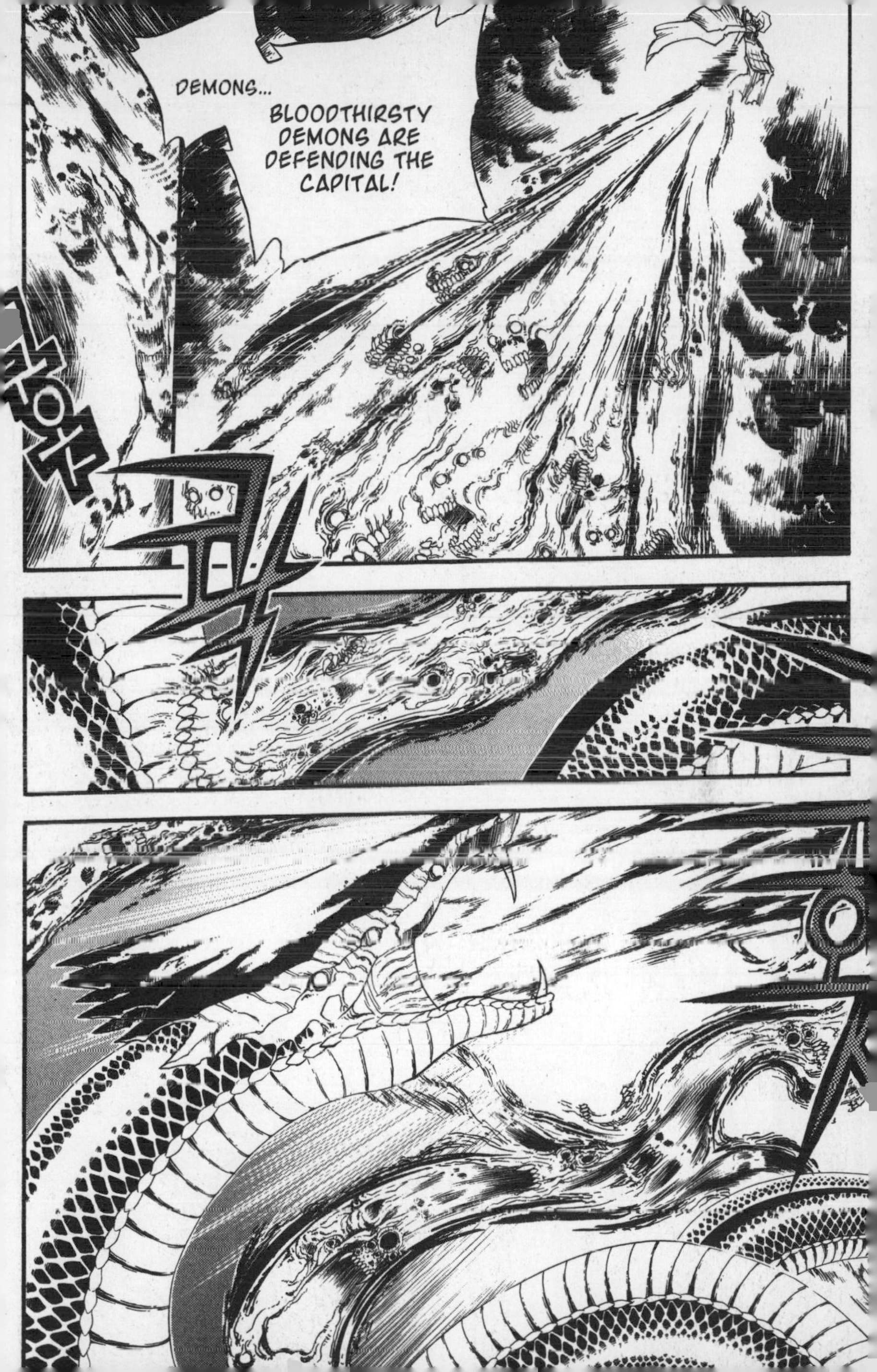
DEMONS...
BLOODTHIRSTY DEMONS ARE DEFENDING THE CAPITAL!

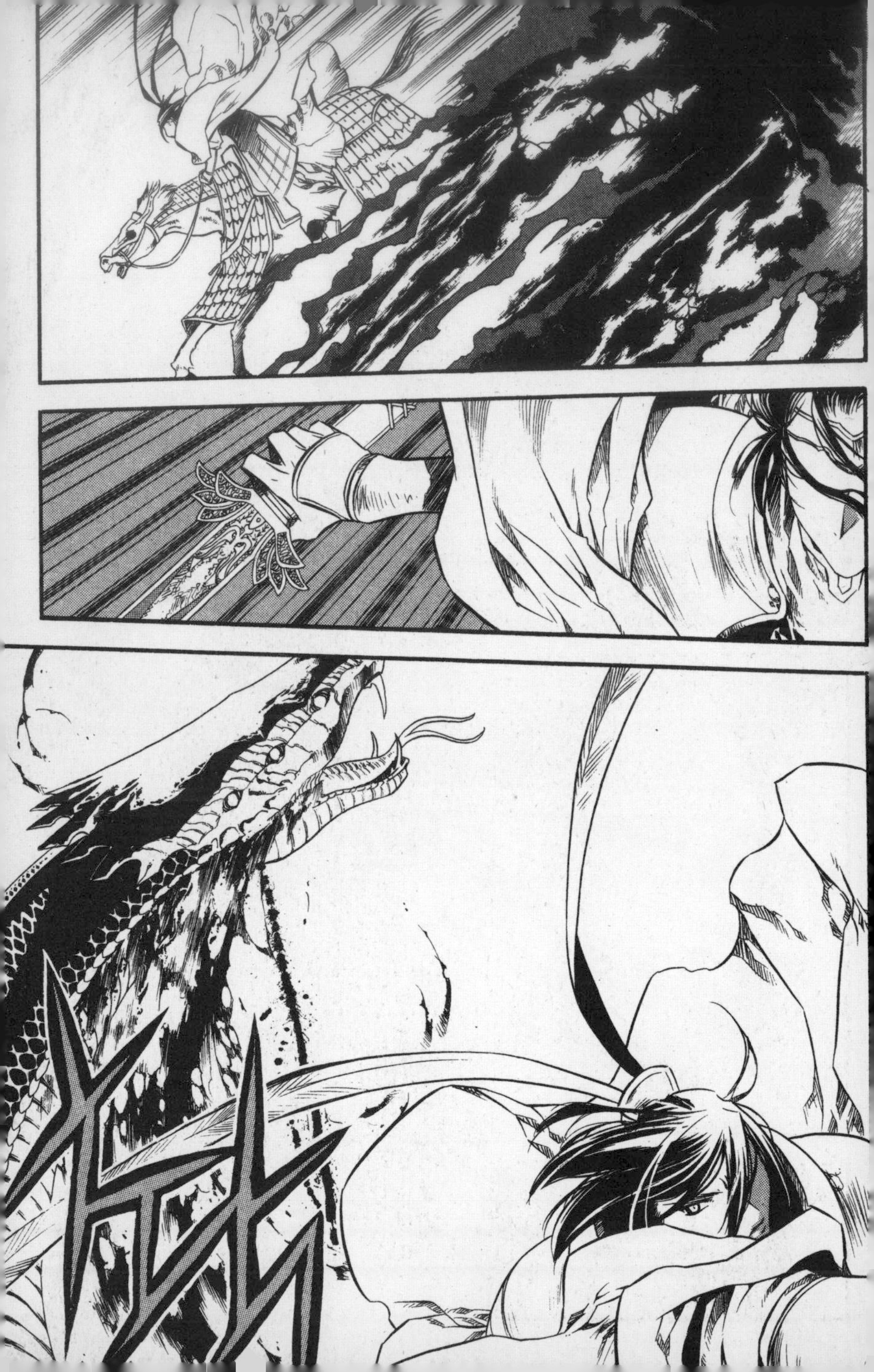

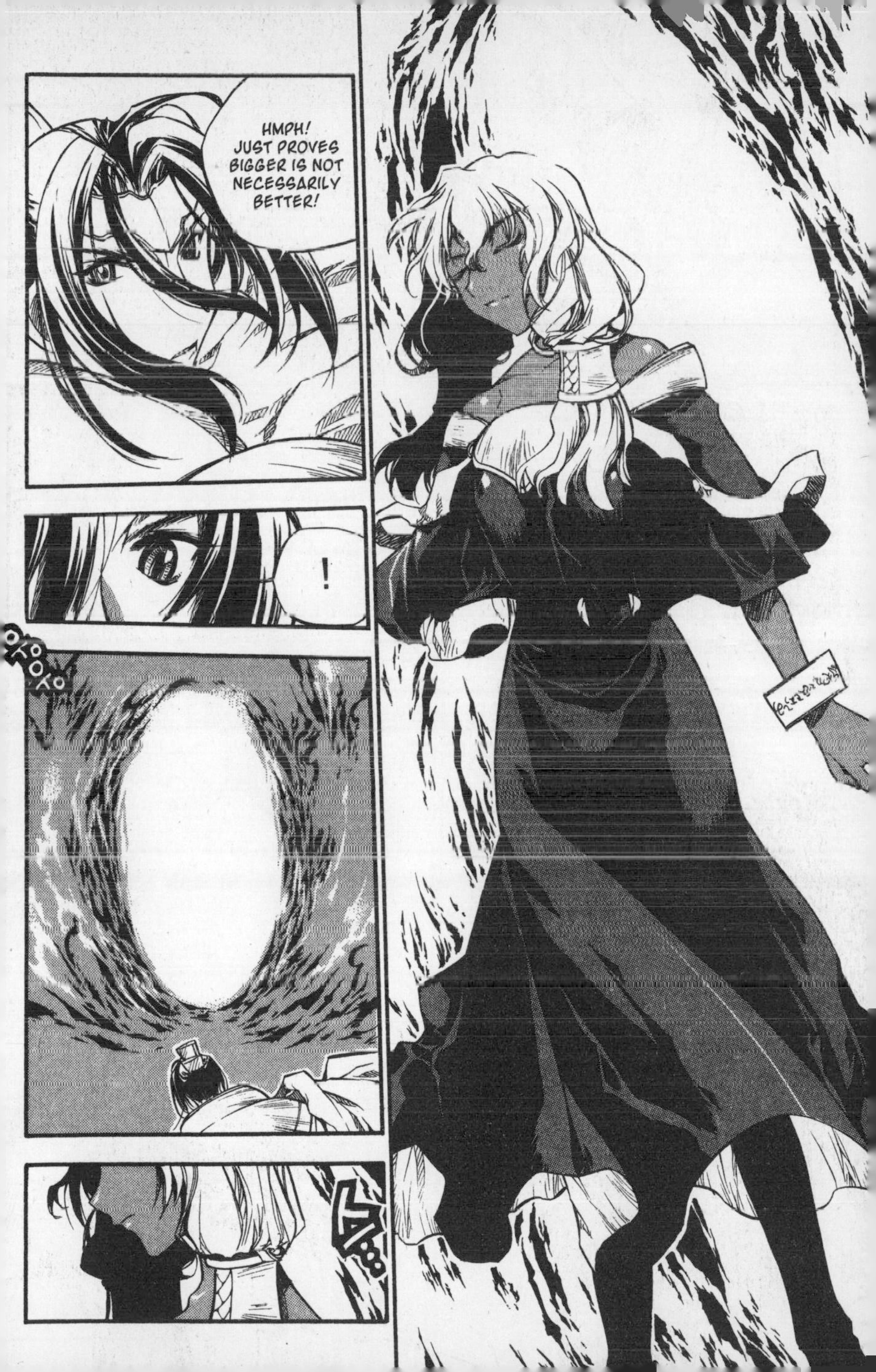
HMPH! JUST PROVES BIGGER IS NOT NECESSARILY BETTER!
!
OTOOTO

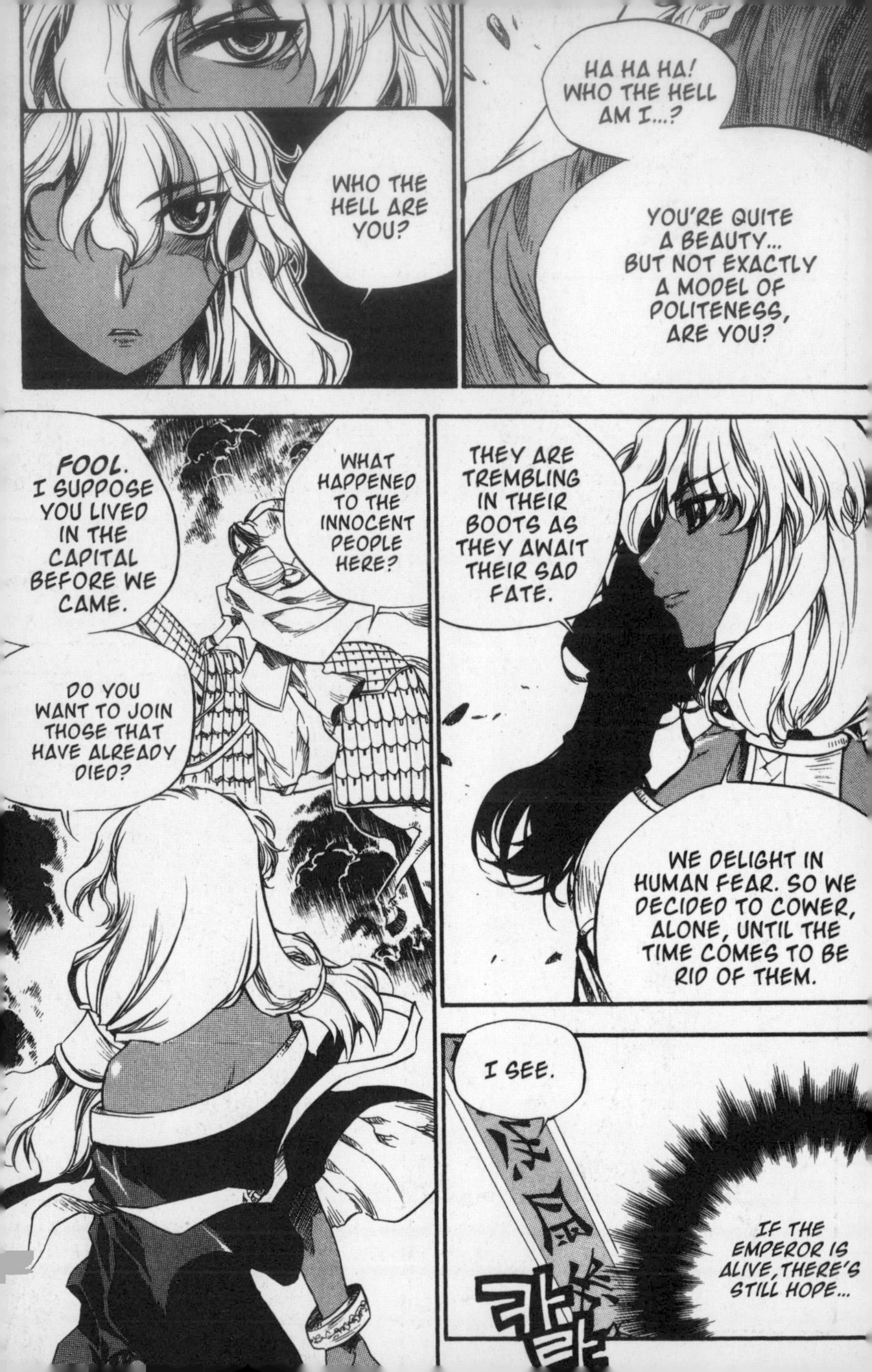
WHO THE HELL ARE YOU?
HA HA HA! WHO THE HELL AM I...?
YOU'RE QUITE A BEAUTY... BUT NOT EXACTLY A MODEL OF POLITENESS, ARE YOU?
FOOL. I SUPPOSE YOU LIVED IN THE CAPITAL BEFORE WE CAME.
WHAT HAPPENED TO THE INNOCENT PEOPLE HERE?
DO YOU WANT TO JOIN THOSE THAT HAVE ALREADY DIED?
THEY ARE TREMBLING IN THEIR BOOTS AS THEY AWAIT THEIR SAD FATE.
WE DELIGHT IN HUMAN FEAR. SO WE DECIDED TO COWER, ALONE, UNTIL THE TIME COMES TO BE RID OF THEM.
I SEE.
IF THE EMPEROR IS ALIVE, THERE'S STILL HOPE...

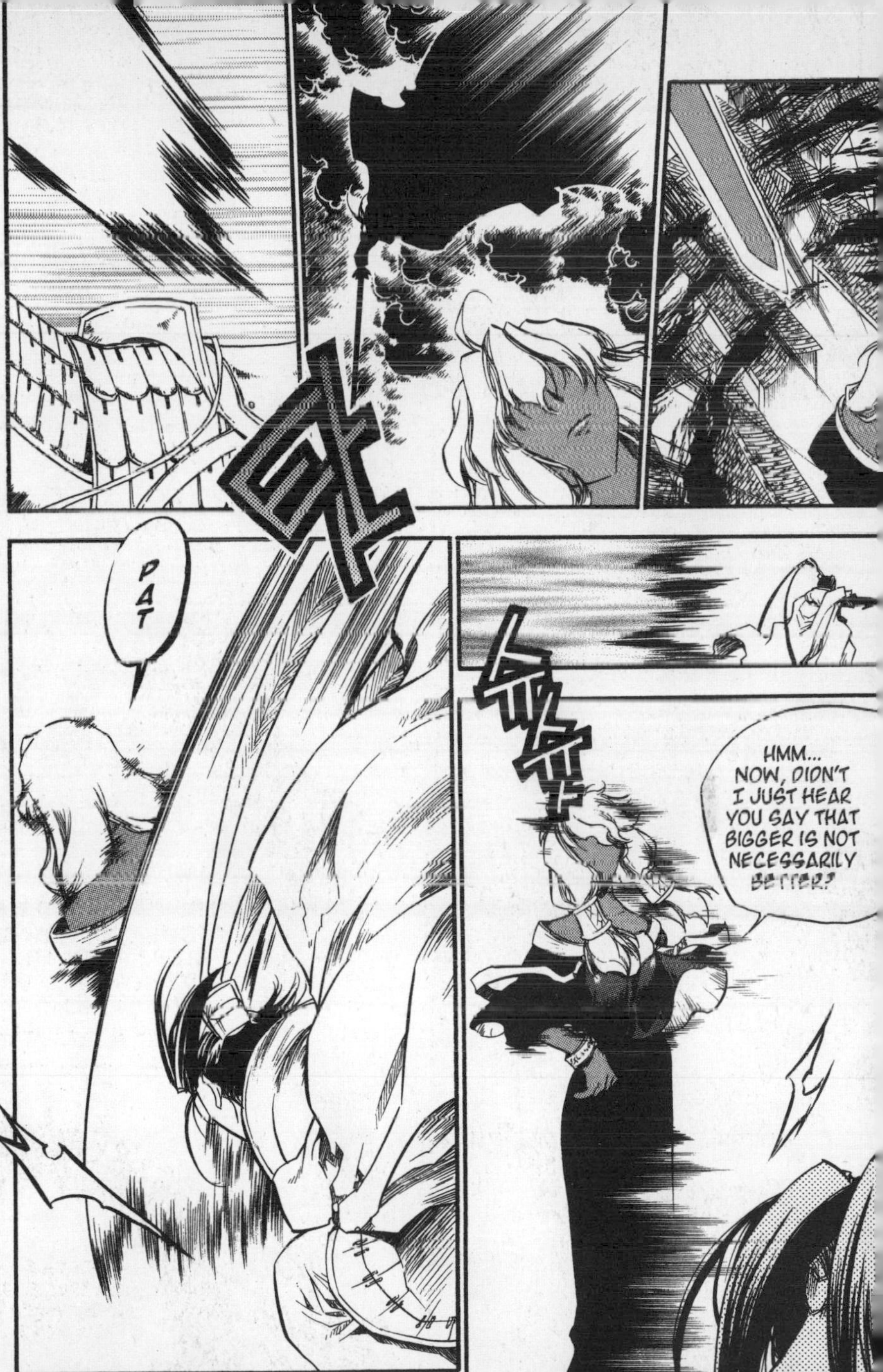
PAT
HMM... NOW, DIDN'T I JUST HEAR YOU SAY THAT BIGGER IS NOT NECESSARILY BETTER?

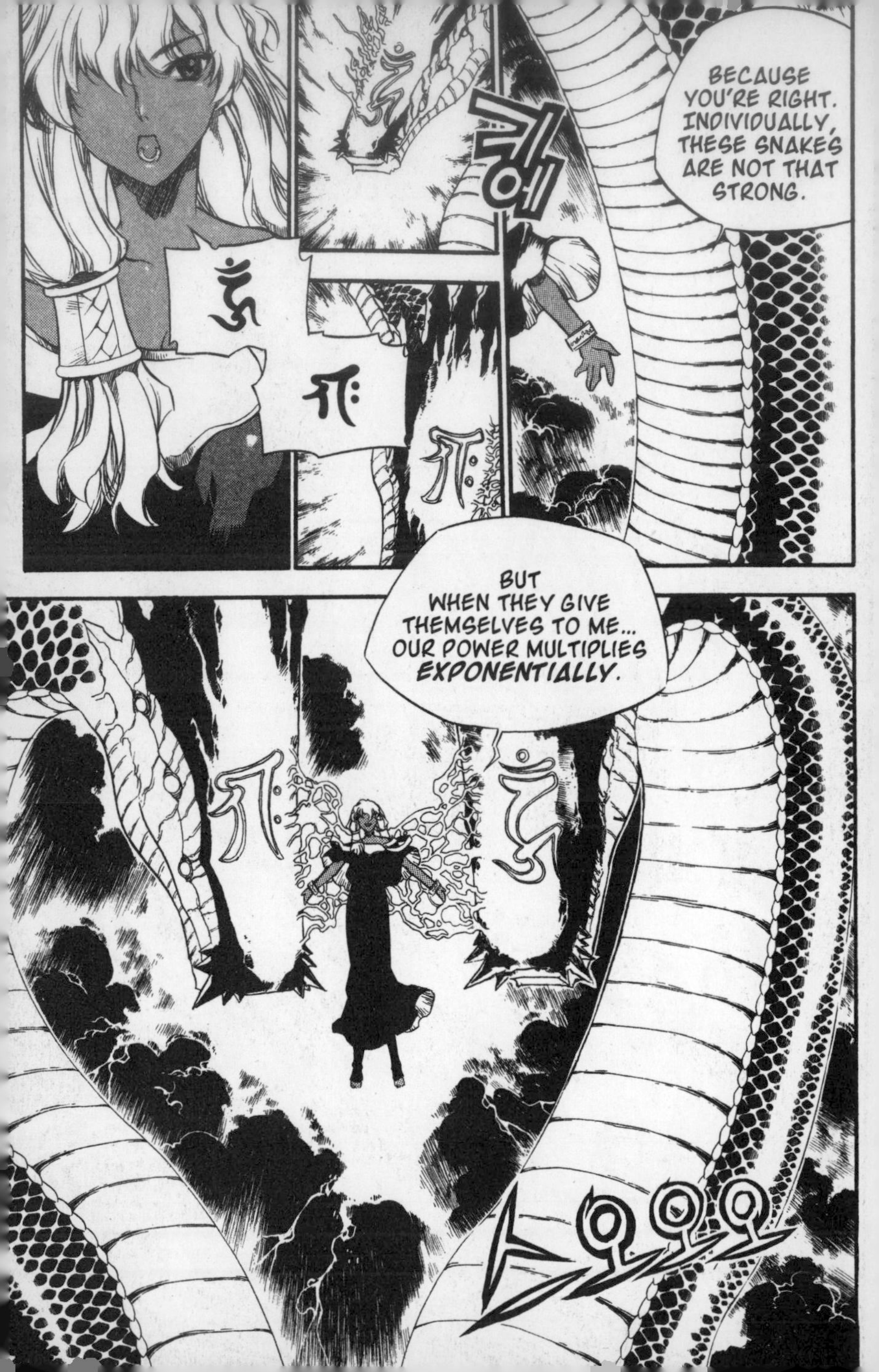
BECAUSE YOU'RE RIGHT. INDIVIDUALLY, THESE SNAKES ARE NOT THAT STRONG.
BUT WHEN THEY GIVE THEMSELVES TO ME... OUR POWER MULTIPLIES *EXPONENTIALLY*.

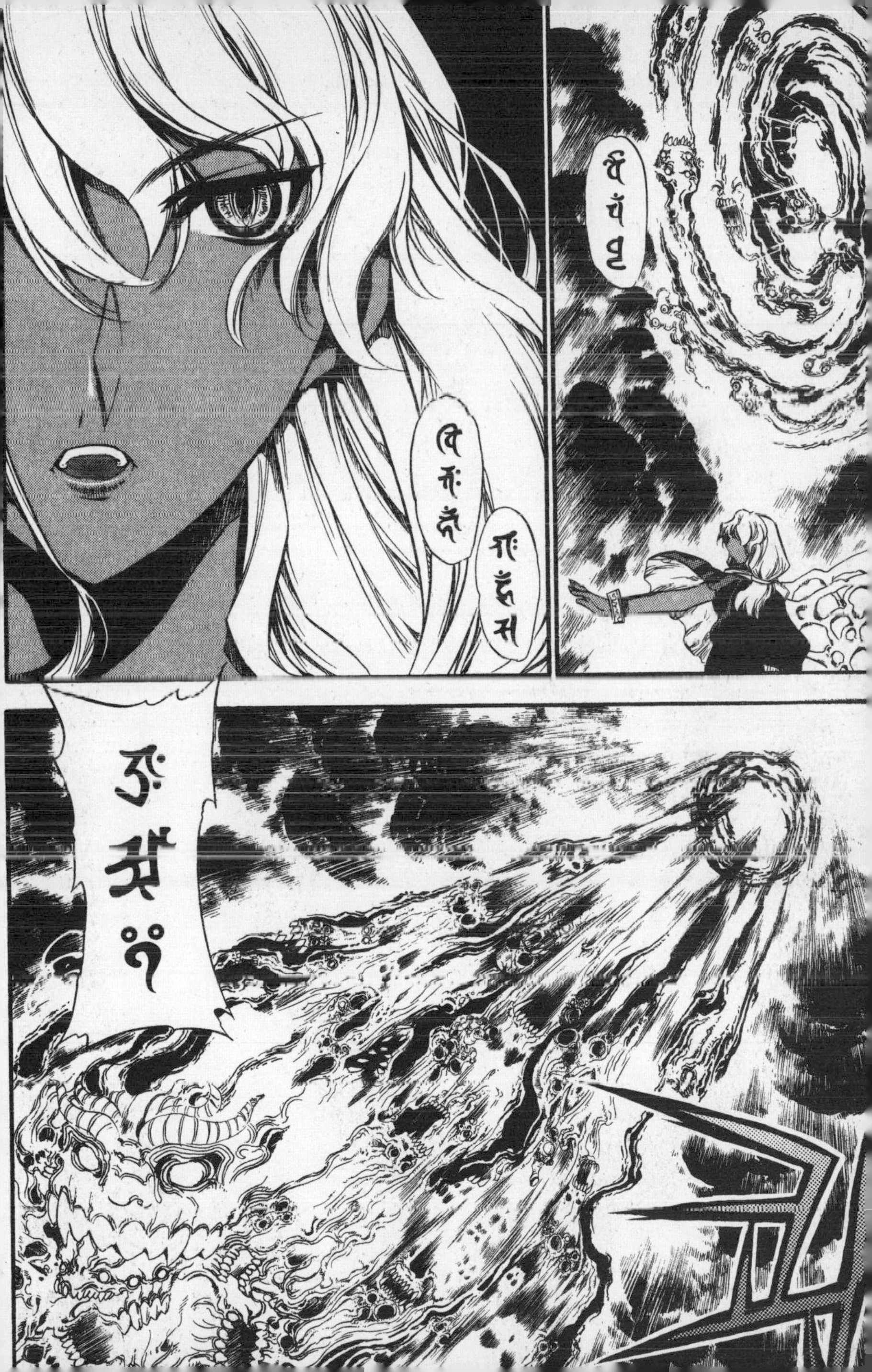

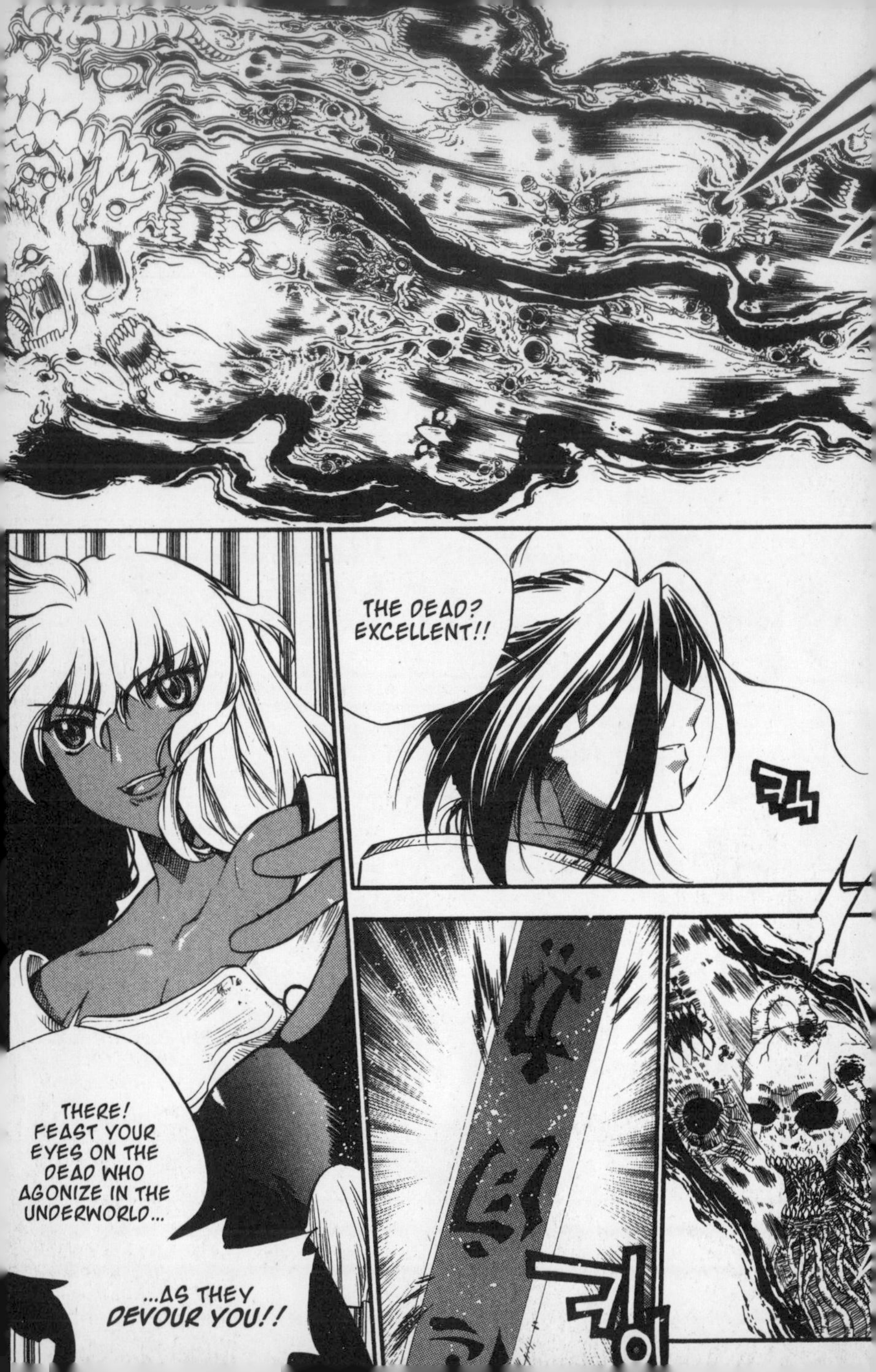
THERE! FEAST YOUR EYES ON THE DEAD WHO AGONIZE IN THE UNDERWORLD...
...AS THEY DEVOUR YOU!!
THE DEAD? EXCELLENT!!

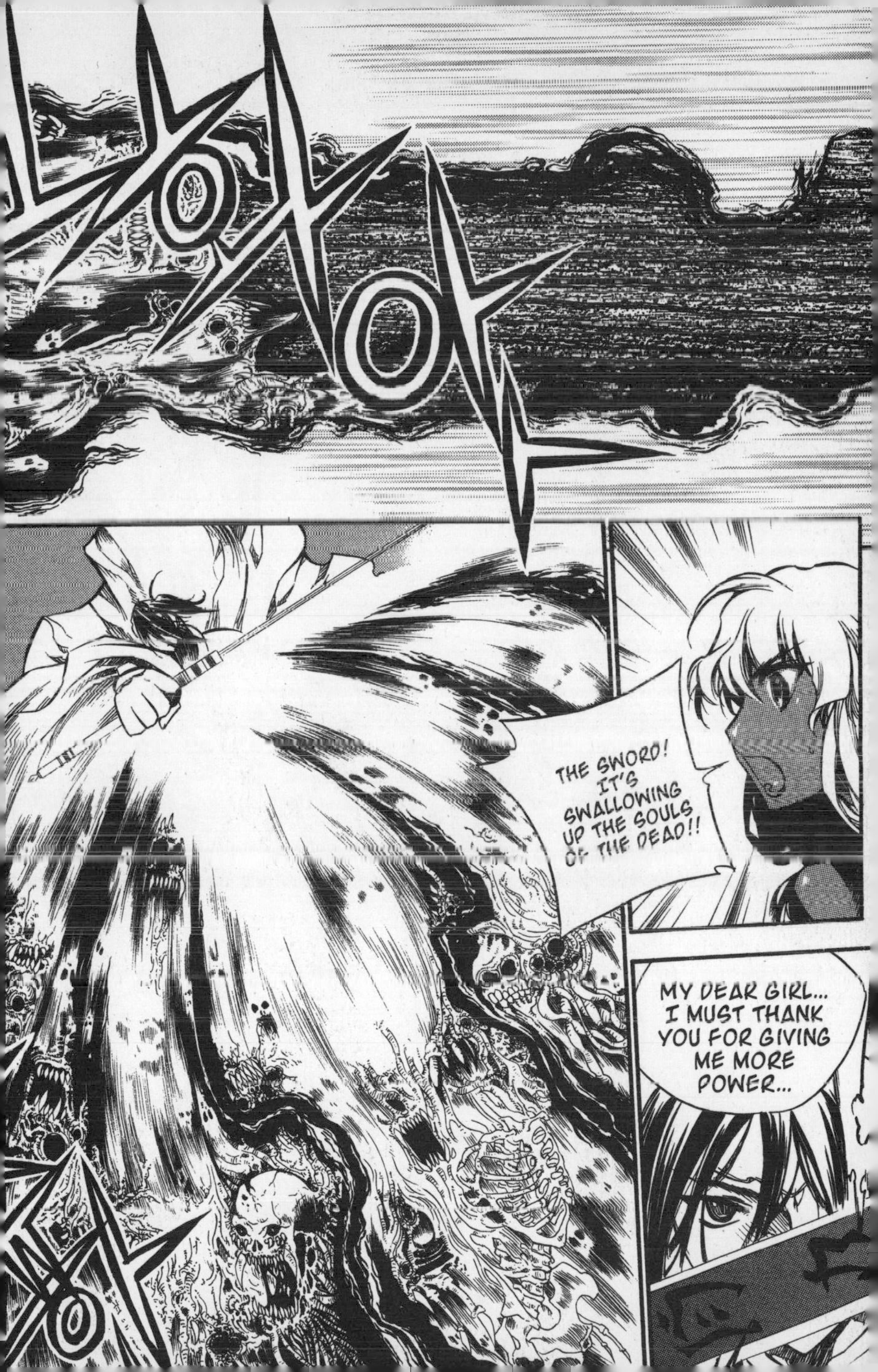
THE SWORD! IT'S SWALLOWING UP THE SOULS OF THE DEAD!!
MY DEAR GIRL... I MUST THANK YOU FOR GIVING ME MORE POWER...

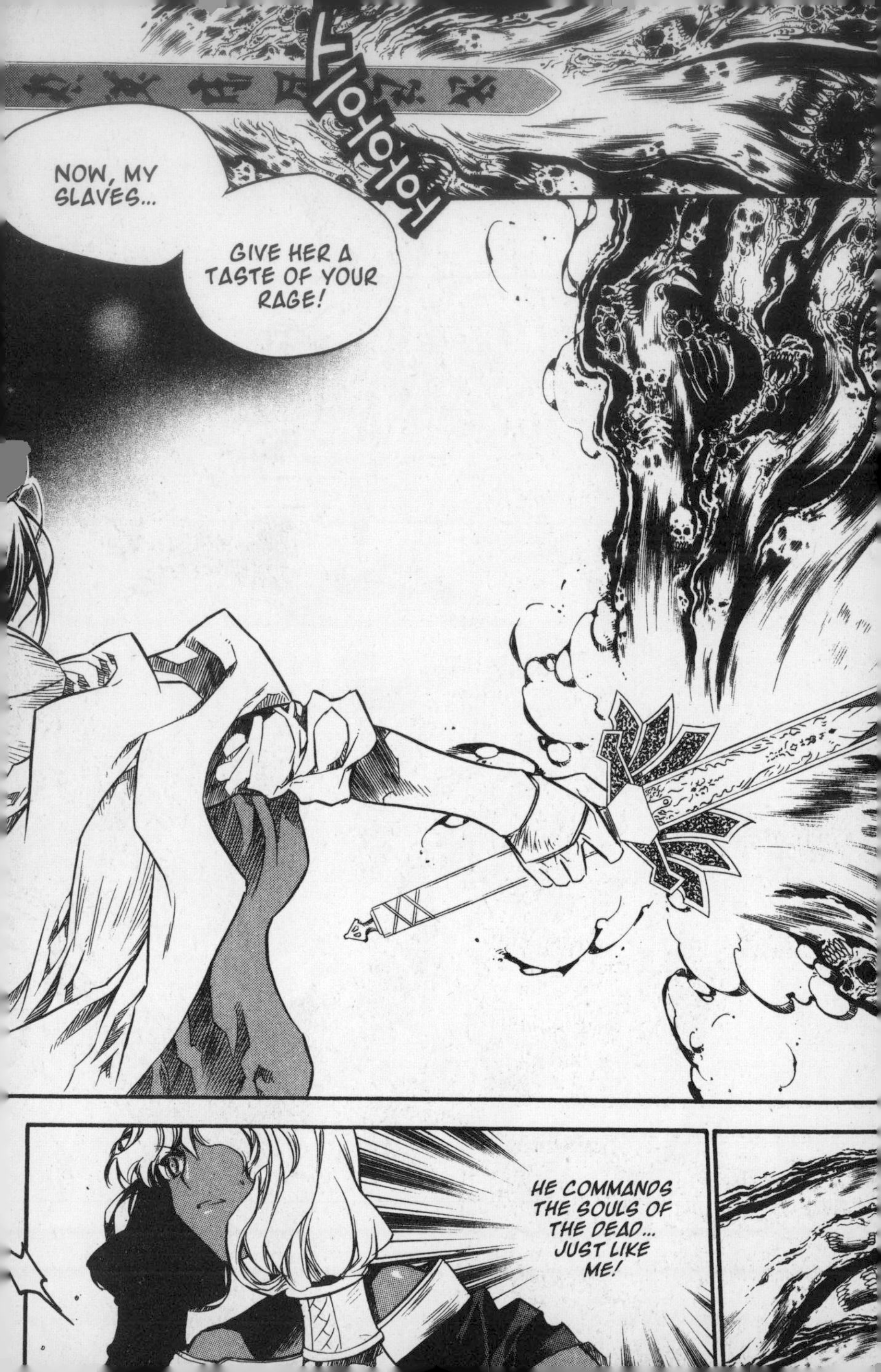
NOW, MY SLAVES...
GIVE HER A TASTE OF YOUR RAGE!
HE COMMANDS THE SOULS OF THE DEAD... JUST LIKE ME!

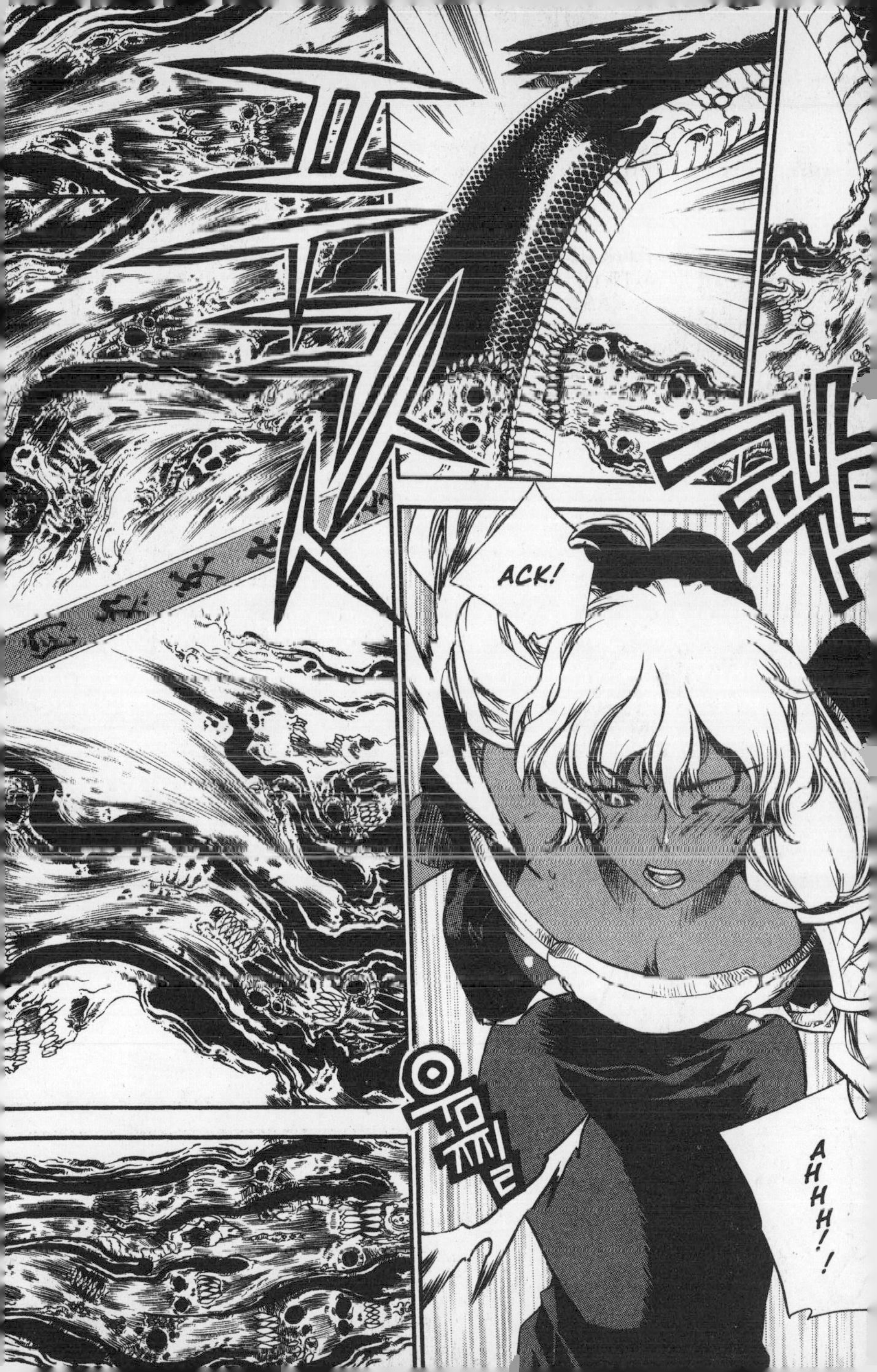
ACK!
AHHH!!

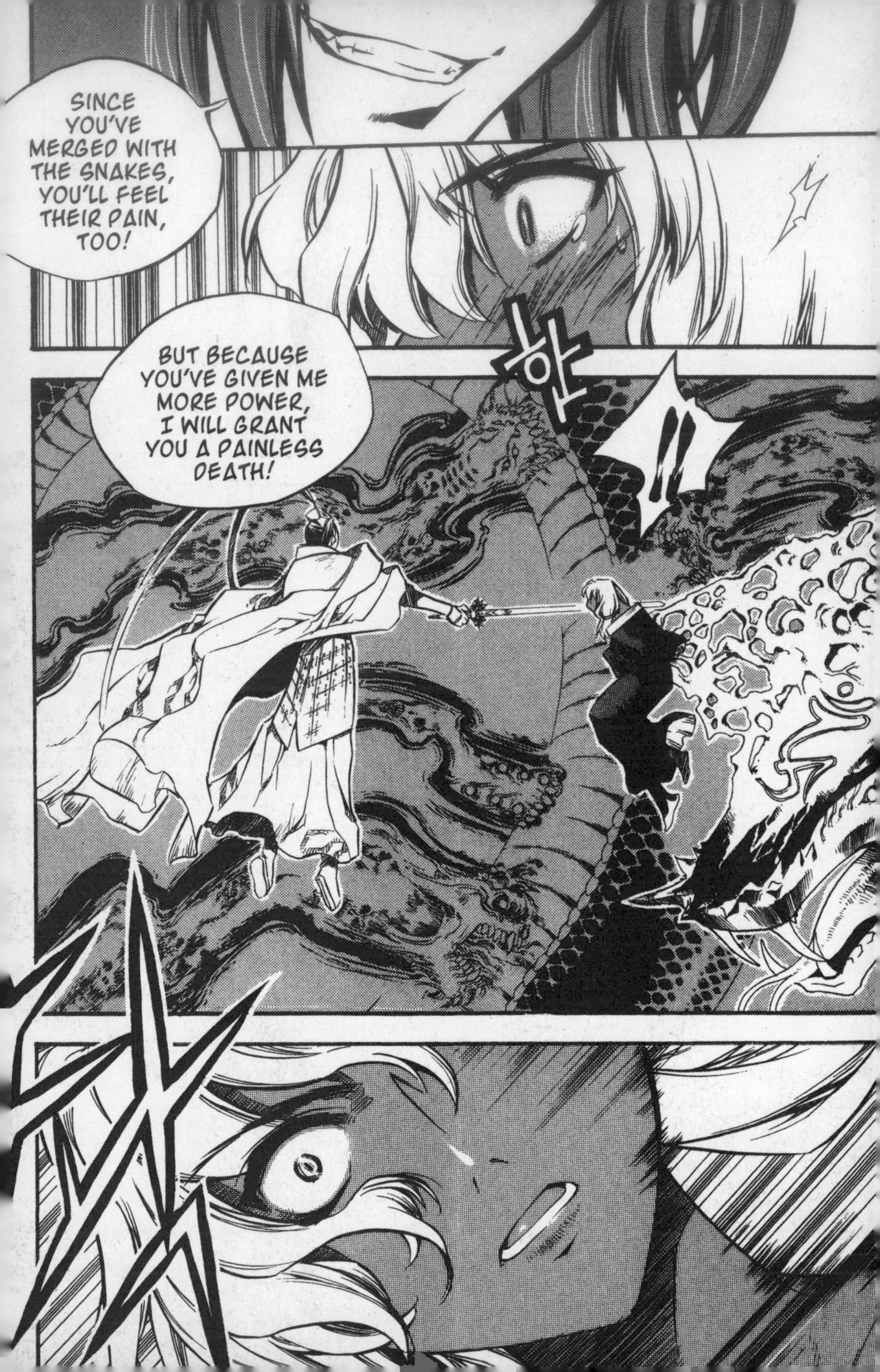
SINCE YOU'VE MERGED WITH THE SNAKES, YOU'LL FEEL THEIR PAIN, TOO!
BUT BECAUSE YOU'VE GIVEN ME MORE POWER, I WILL GRANT YOU A PAINLESS DEATH!
학
!!

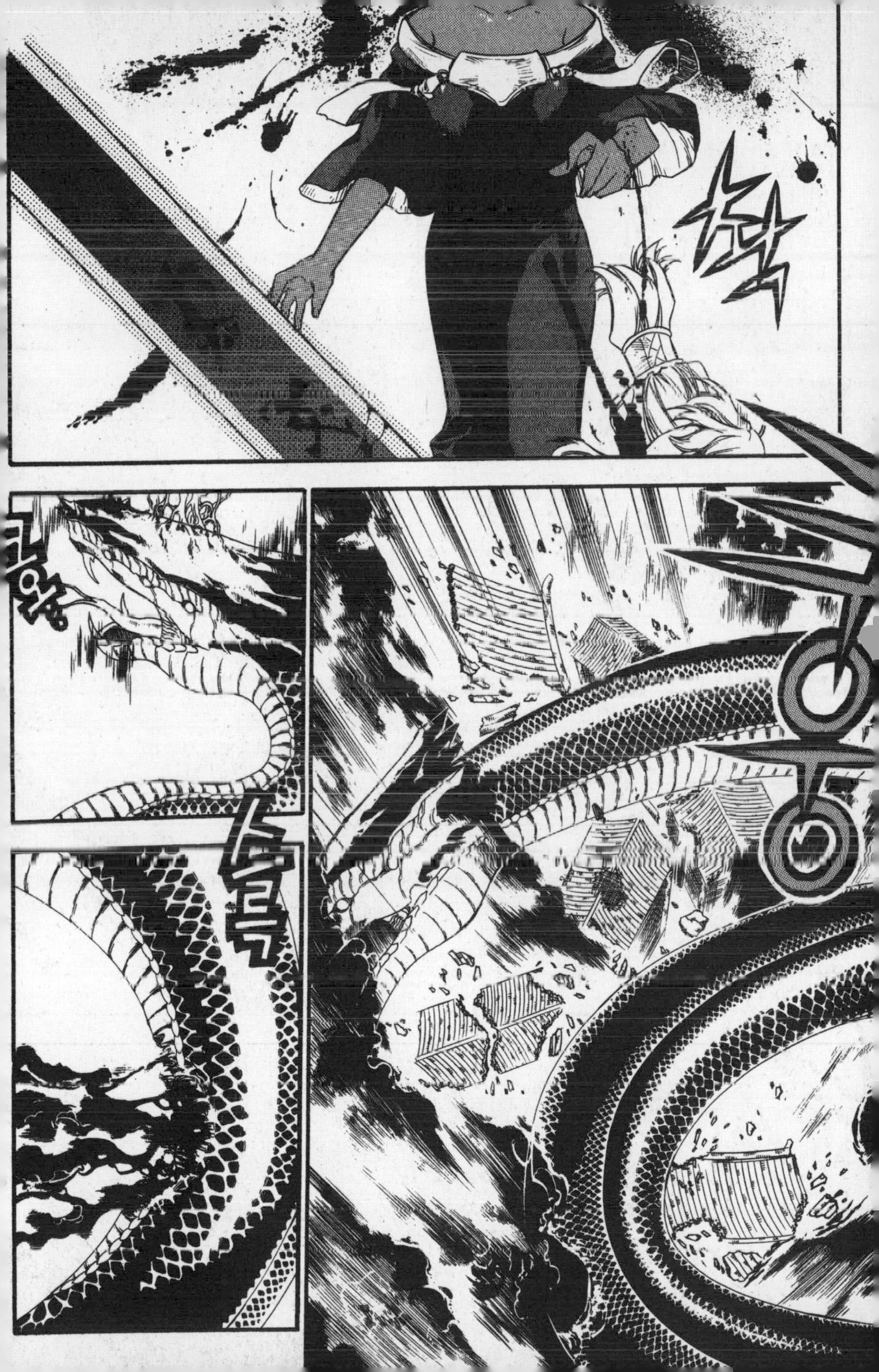
스륵

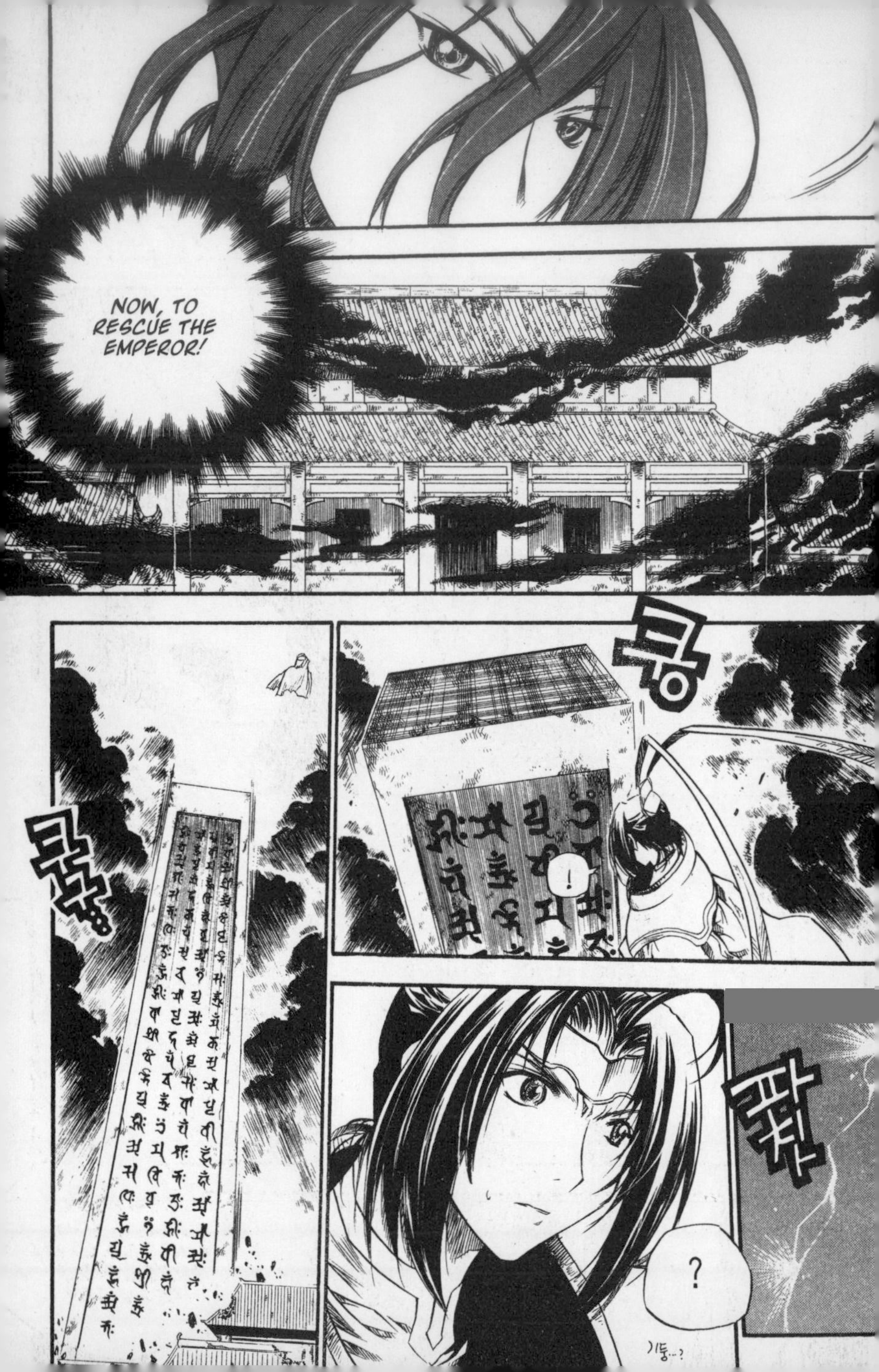
NOW, TO RESCUE THE EMPEROR!
쿵
!
?

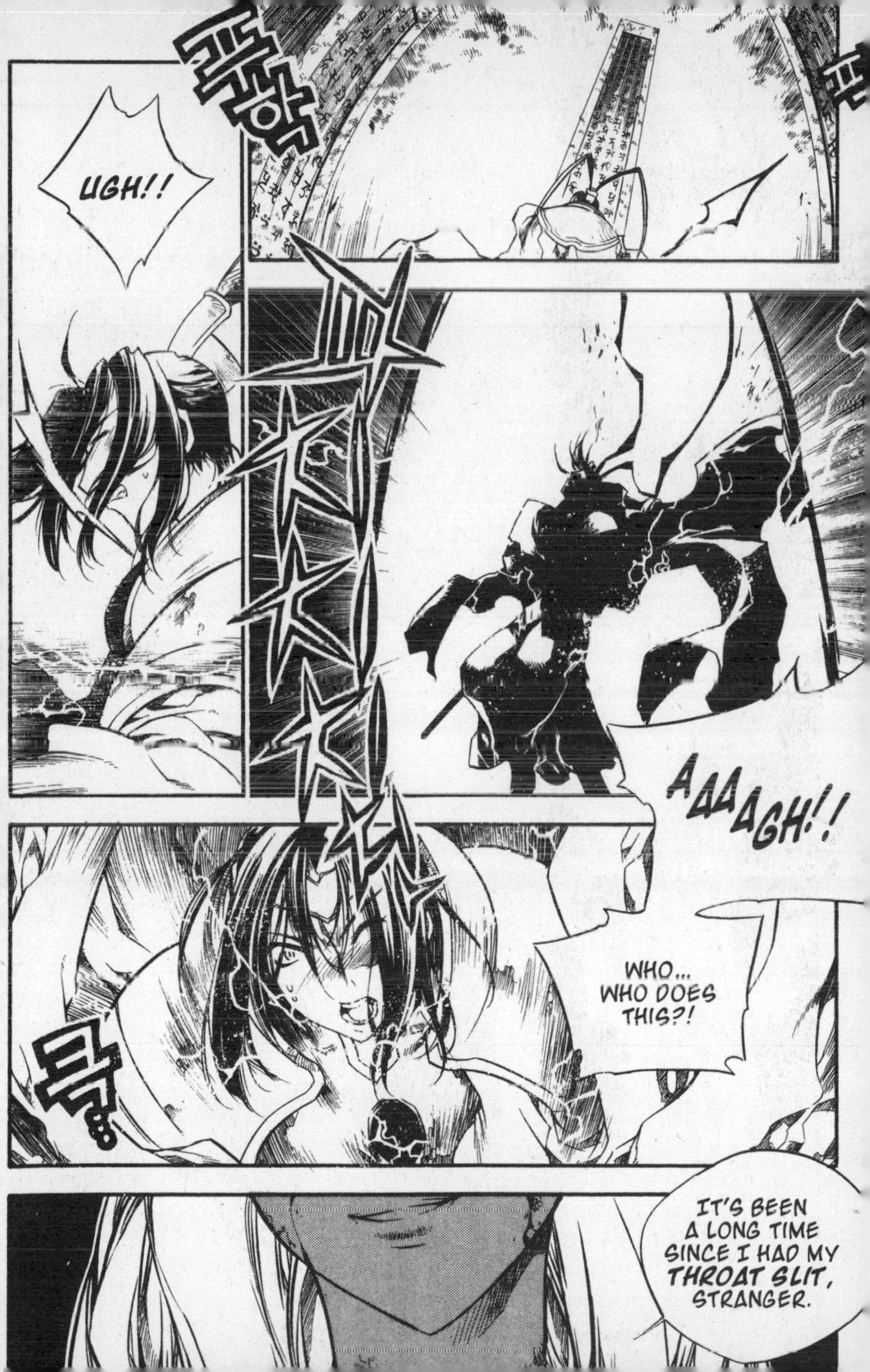
UGH!!
AAAAGH!!
WHO... WHO DOES THIS?!
IT'S BEEN A LONG TIME SINCE I HAD MY THROAT SLIT, STRANGER.

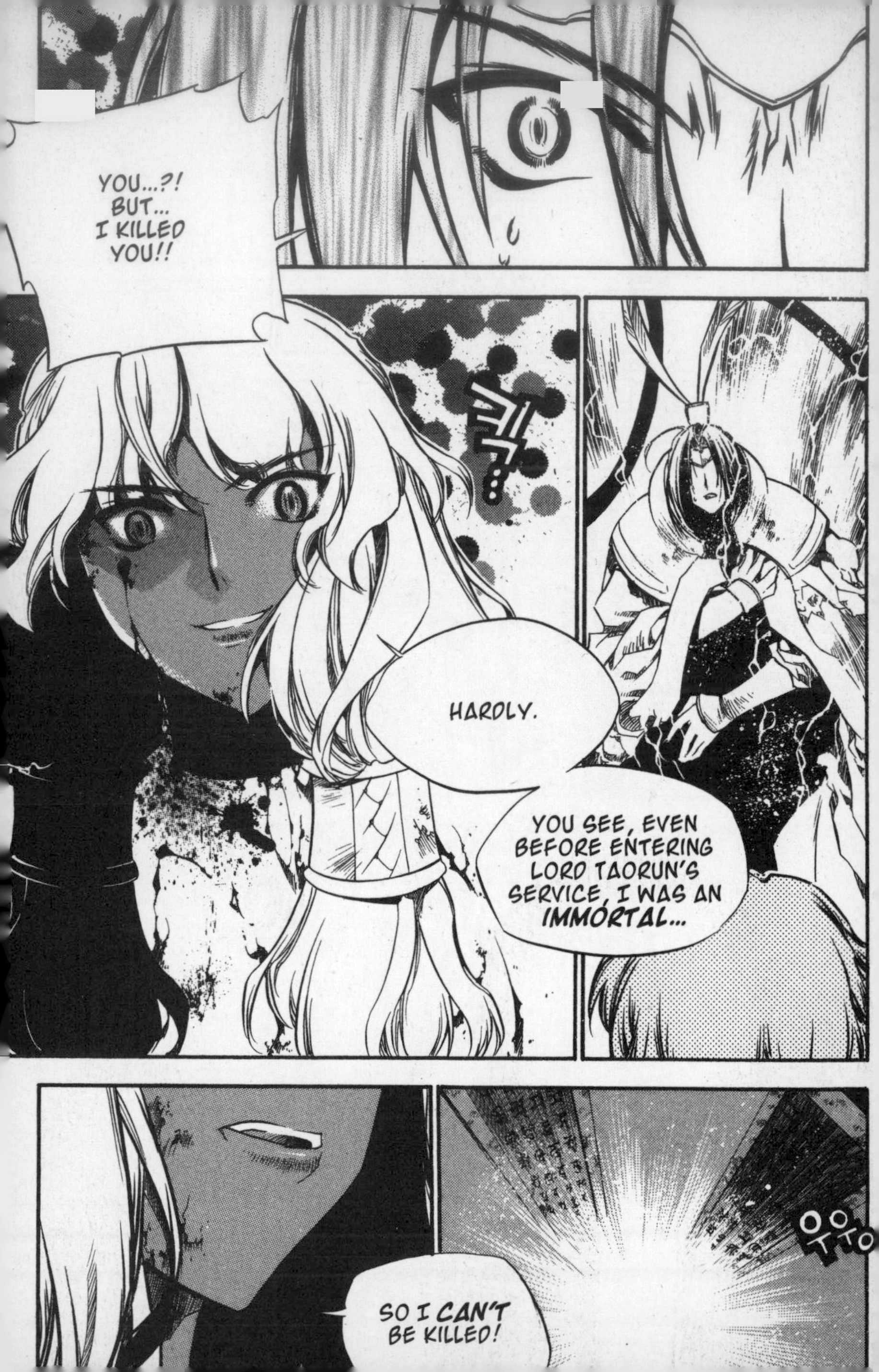
YOU...?! BUT... I KILLED YOU!!
HARDLY.
YOU SEE, EVEN BEFORE ENTERING LORD TAORUN'S SERVICE, I WAS AN **IMMORTAL...**
SO I **CAN'T** BE KILLED!

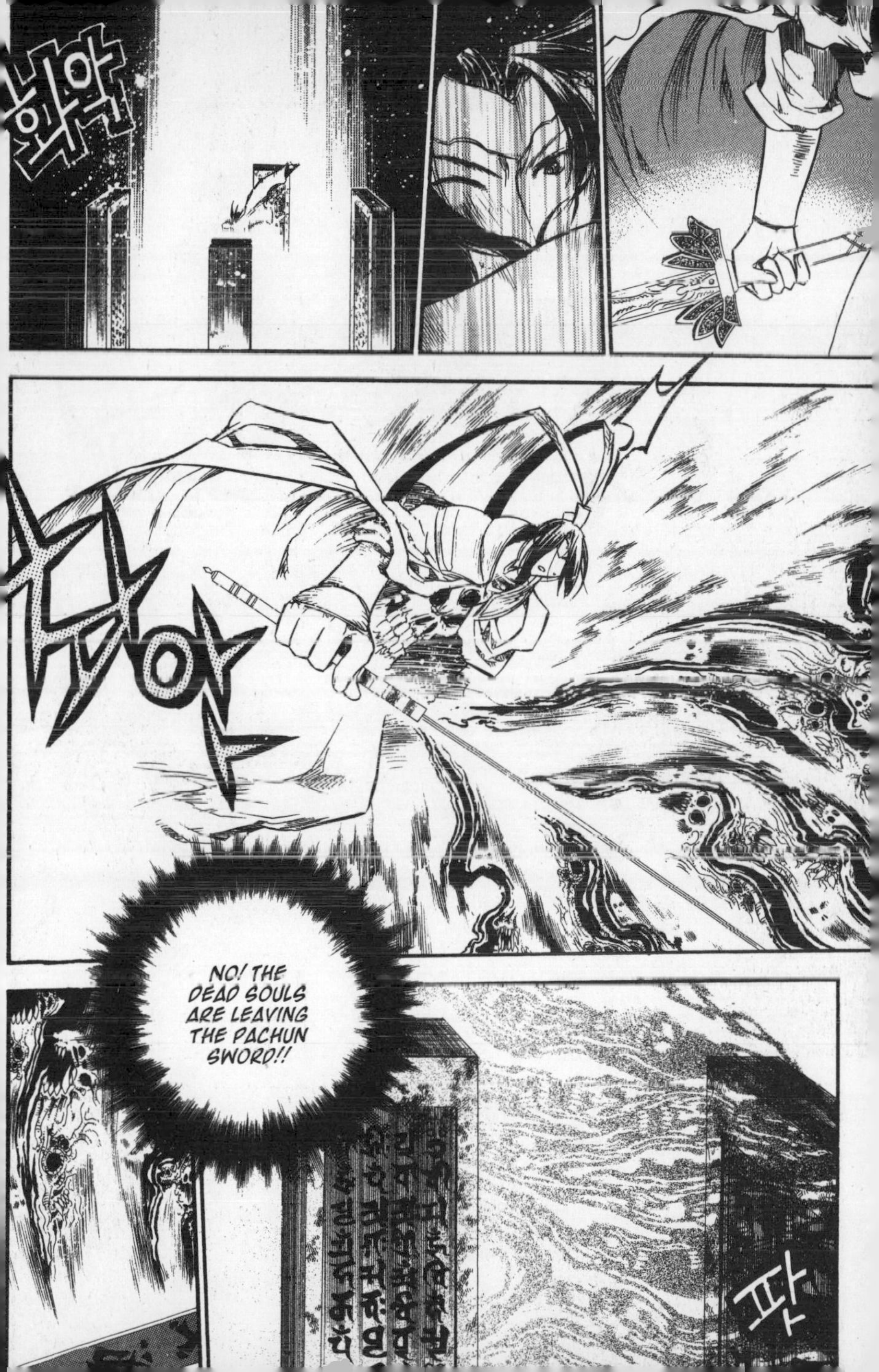
화악
NO! THE DEAD SOULS ARE LEAVING THE PACHUN SWORD!!
팍

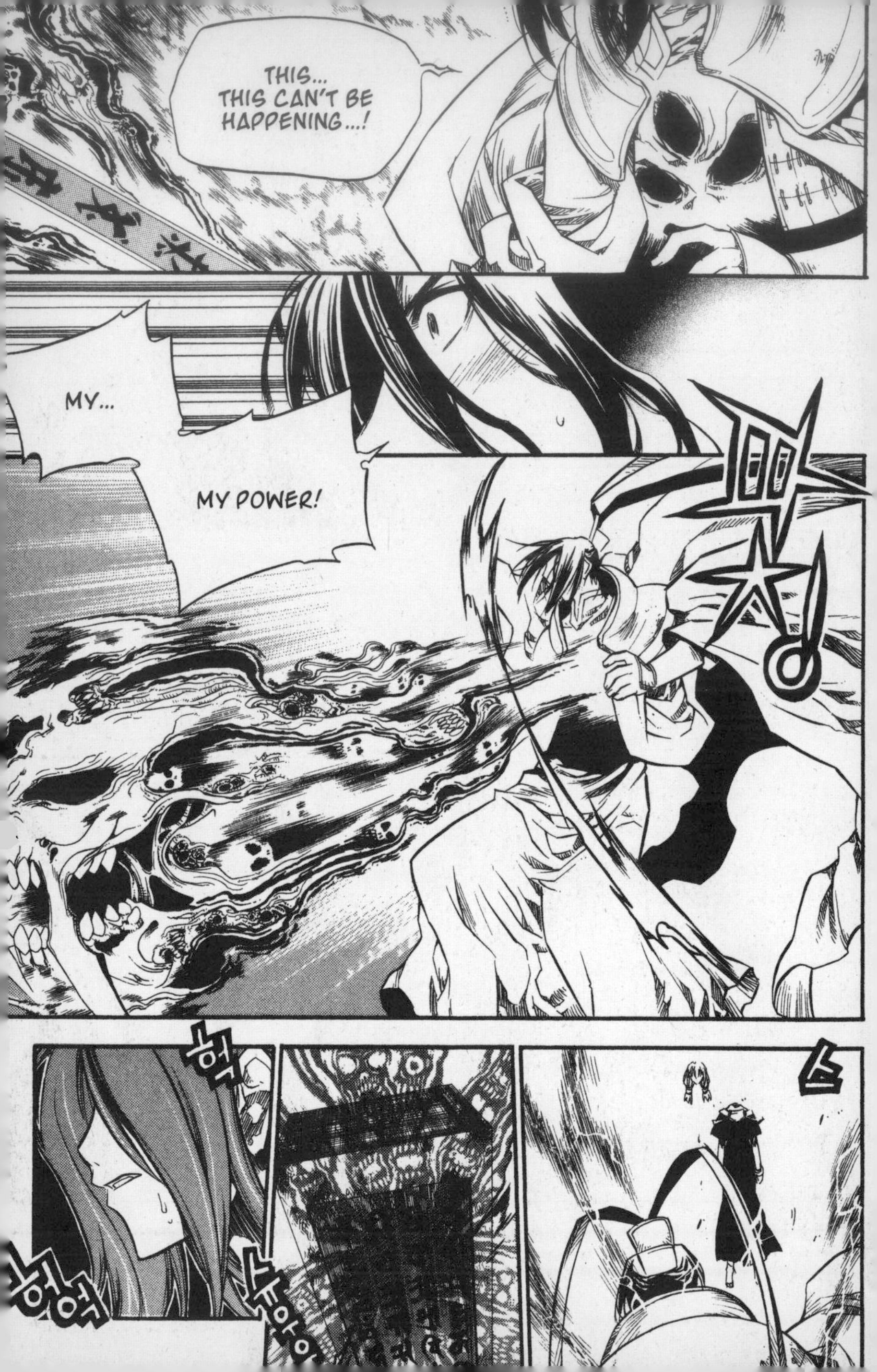
THIS... THIS CAN'T BE HAPPENING...!
MY...
MY POWER!
헉

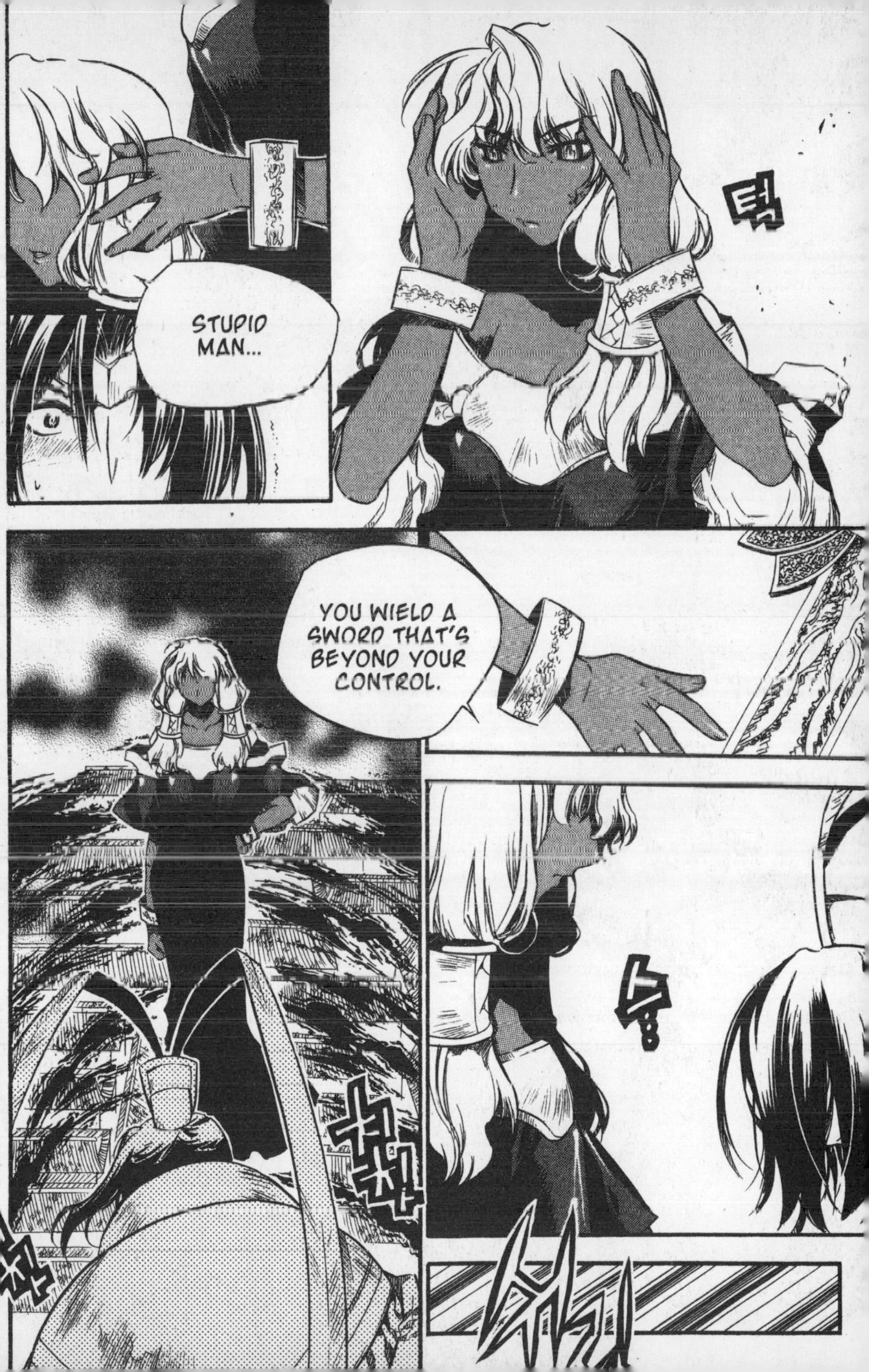
STUPID MAN...
YOU WIELD A SWORD THAT'S BEYOND YOUR CONTROL.

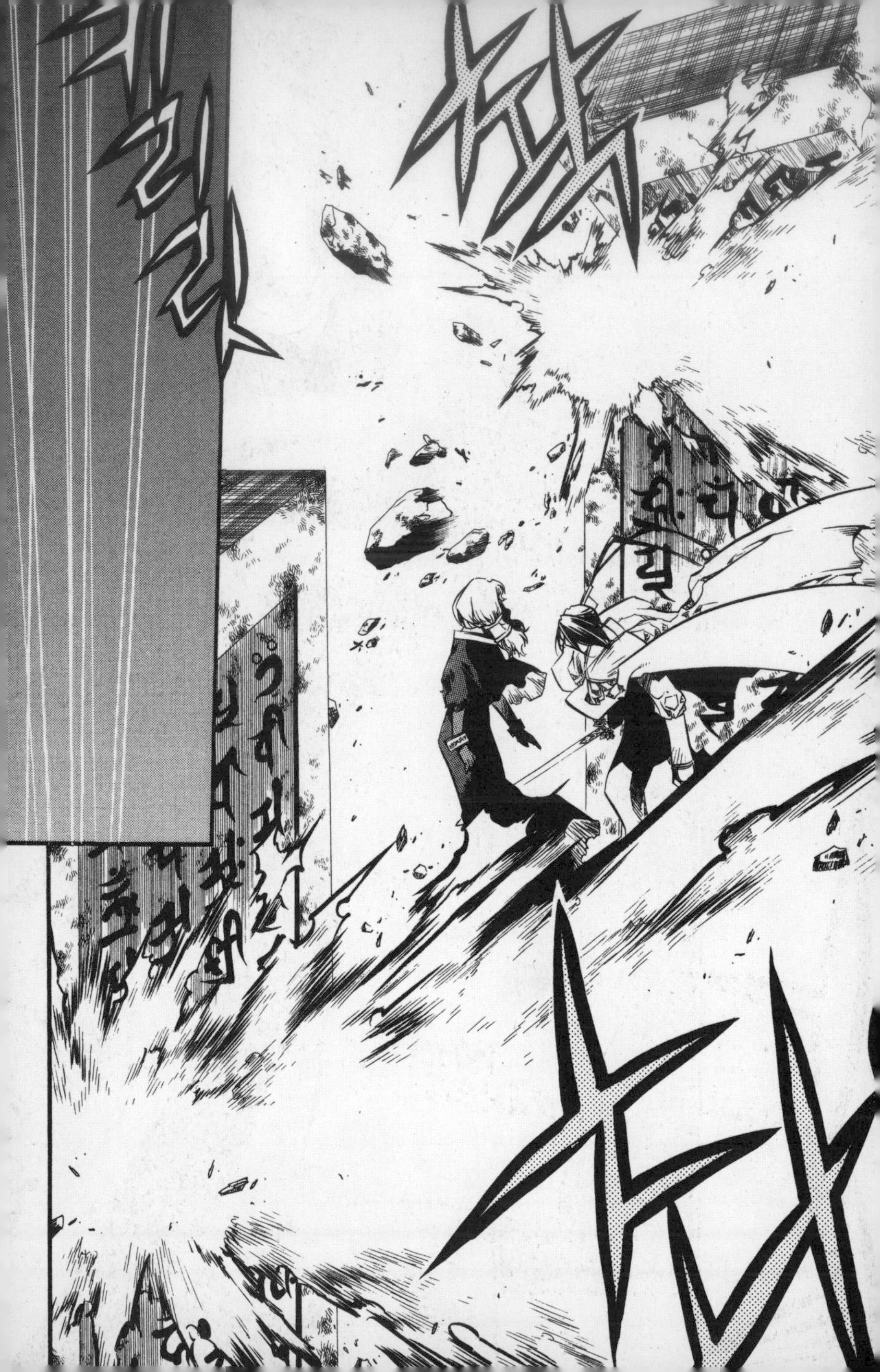

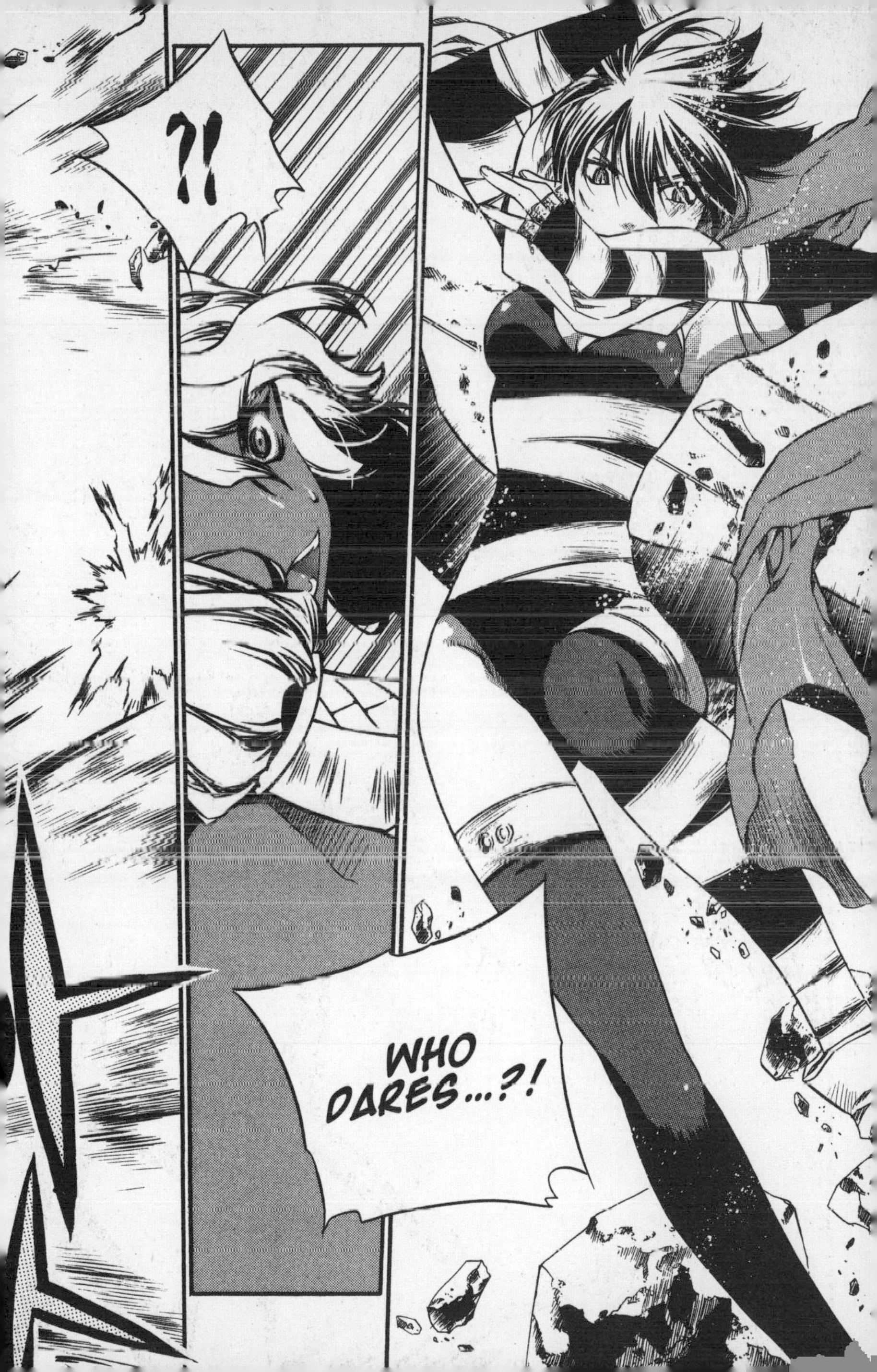
?!
WHO DARES...?!

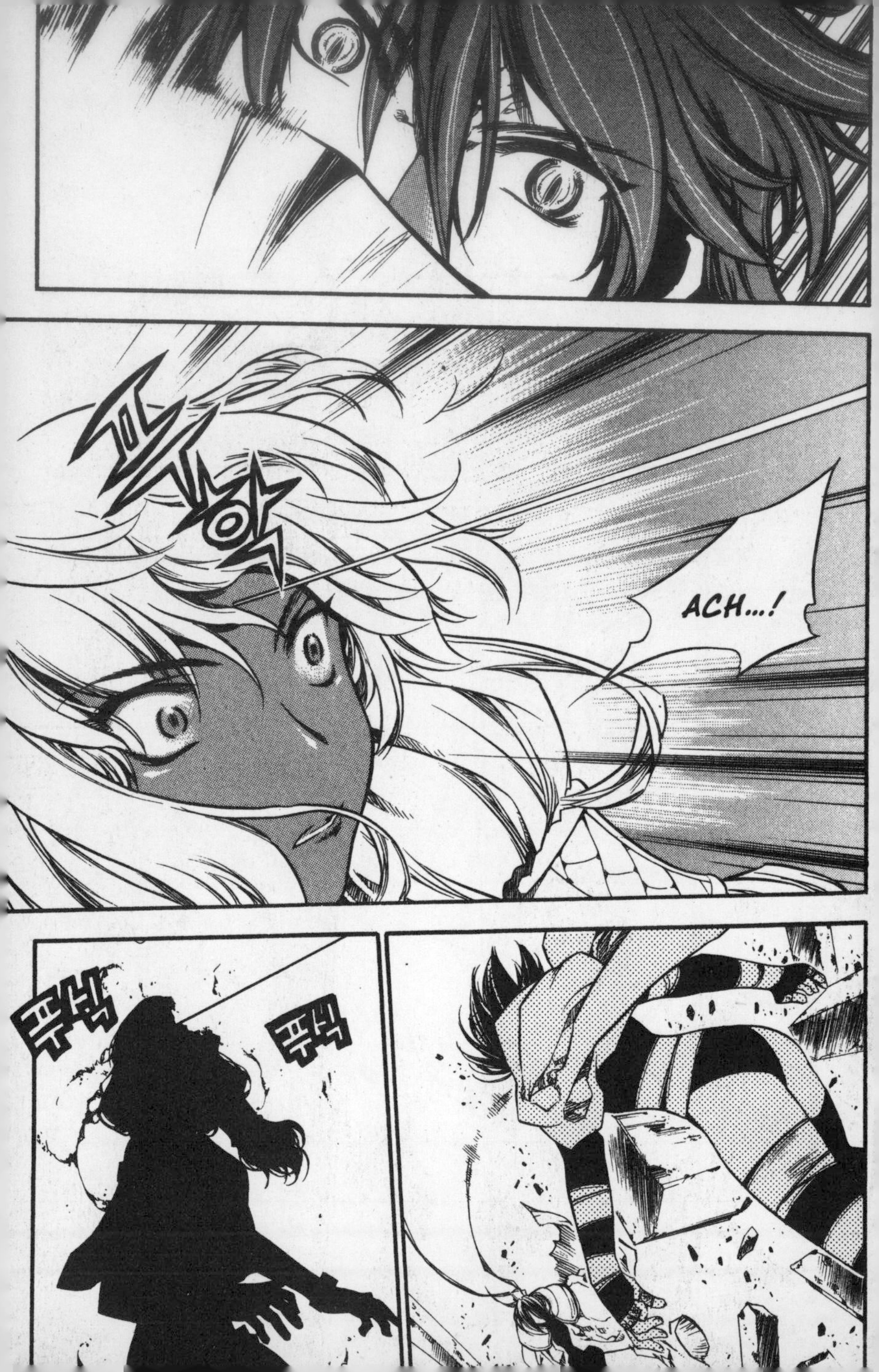
ACH...!

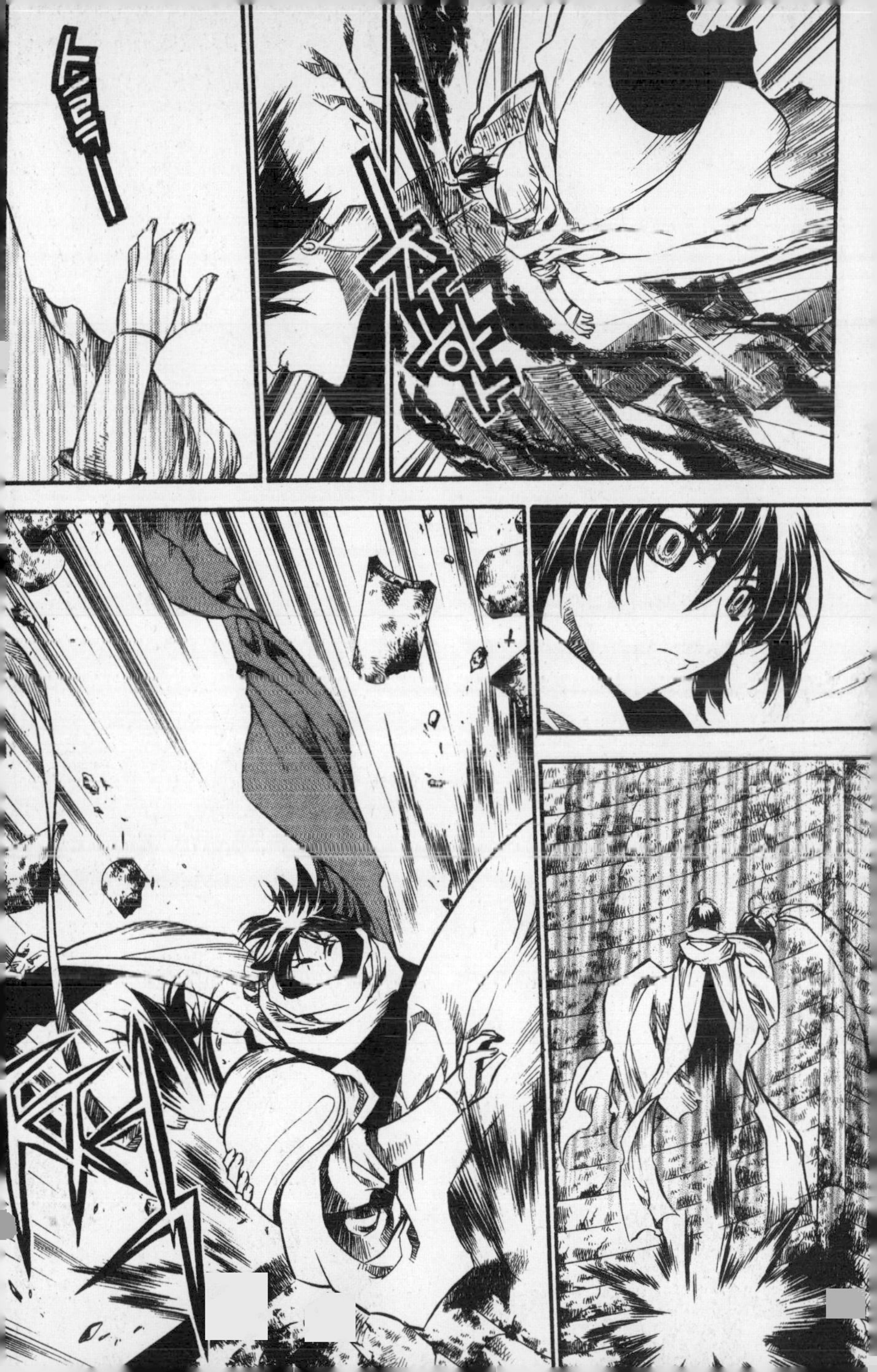

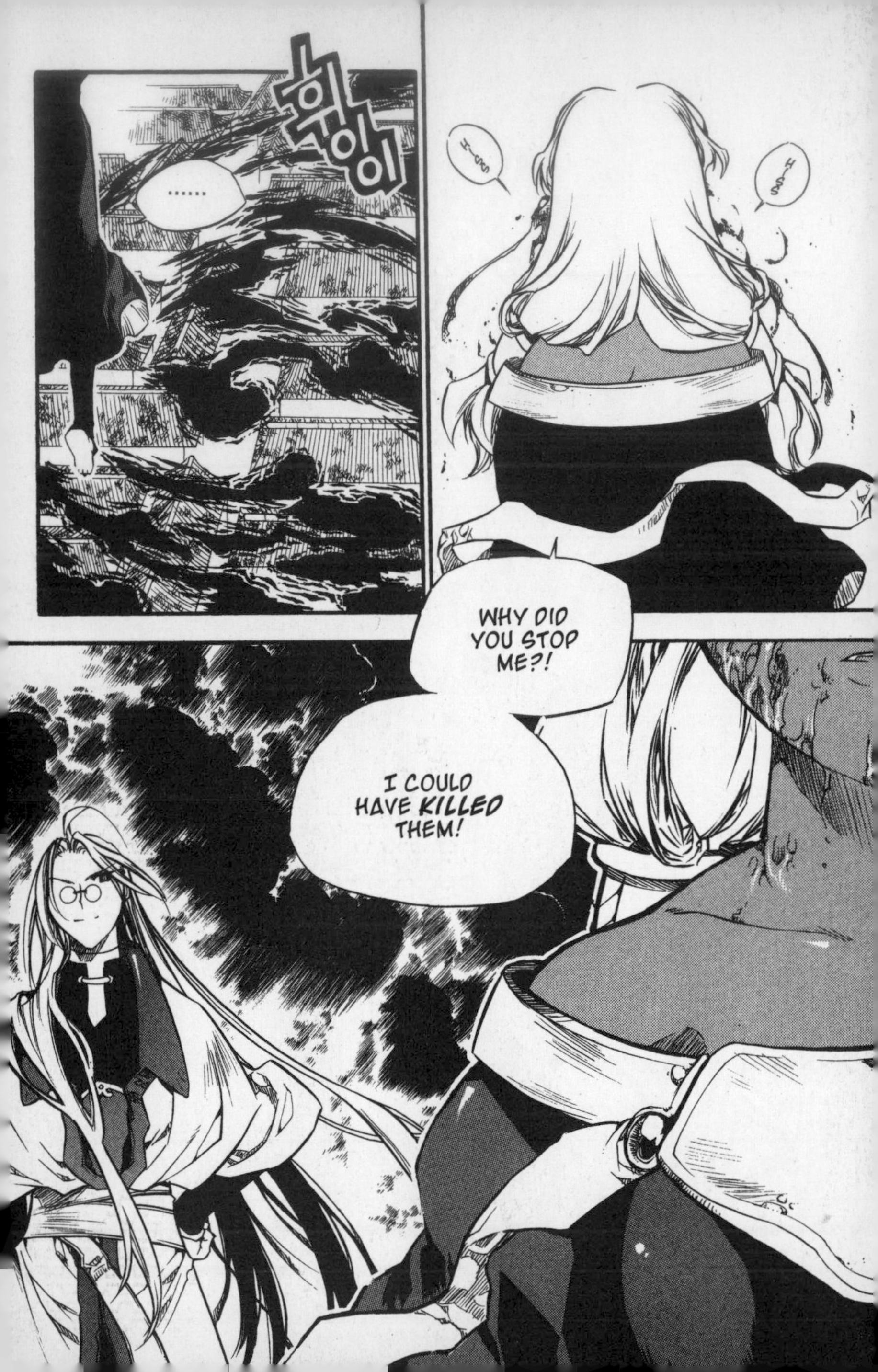
......
H-SS
HISS
WHY DID YOU STOP ME?!
I COULD HAVE KILLED THEM!

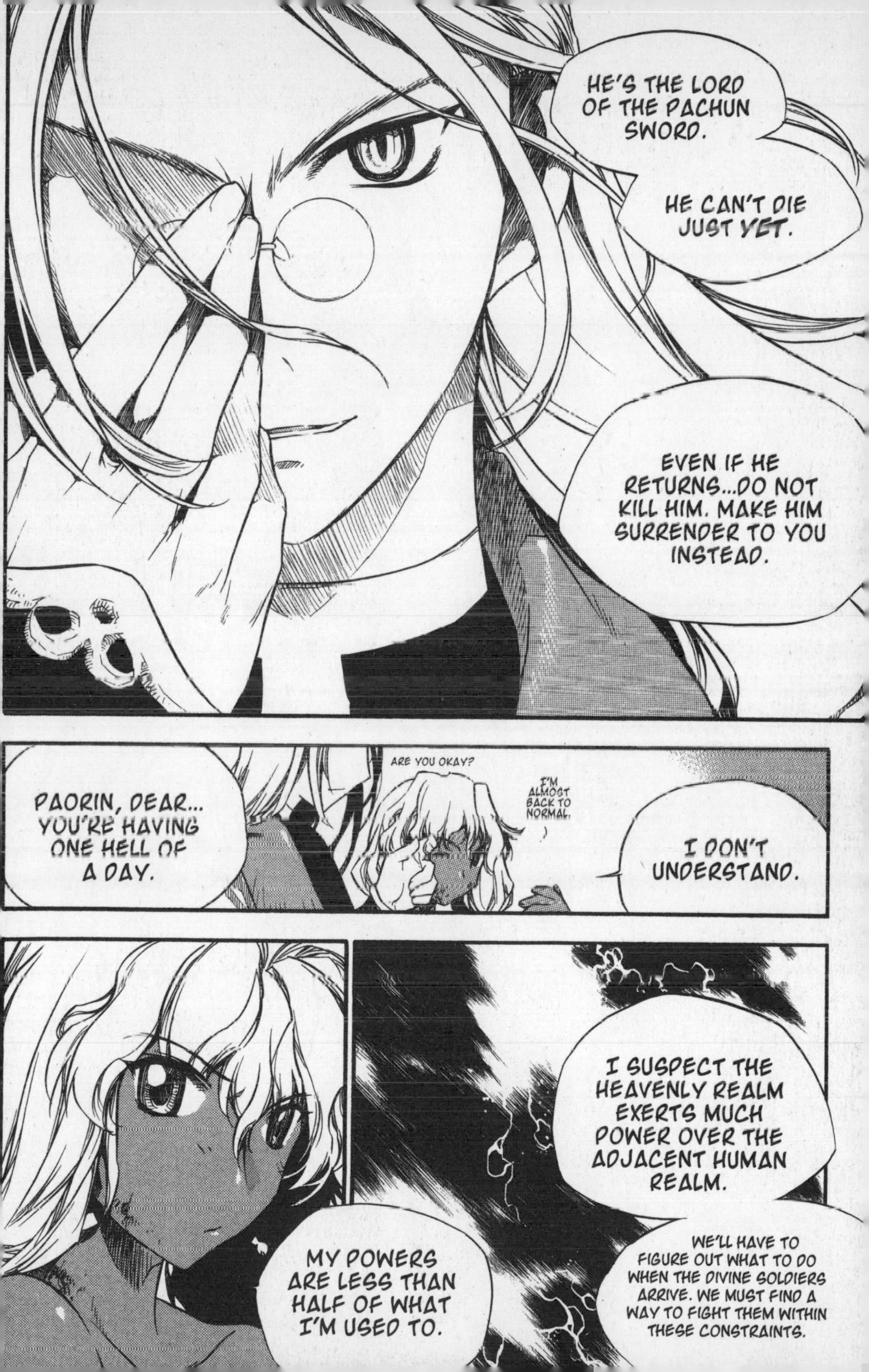
HE'S THE LORD OF THE PACHUN SWORD.
HE CAN'T DIE JUST YET.
EVEN IF HE RETURNS...DO NOT KILL HIM. MAKE HIM SURRENDER TO YOU INSTEAD.
PAORIN, DEAR... YOU'RE HAVING ONE HELL OF A DAY.
ARE YOU OKAY?
I'M ALMOST BACK TO NORMAL.
I DON'T UNDERSTAND.
MY POWERS ARE LESS THAN HALF OF WHAT I'M USED TO.
I SUSPECT THE HEAVENLY REALM EXERTS MUCH POWER OVER THE ADJACENT HUMAN REALM.
WE'LL HAVE TO FIGURE OUT WHAT TO DO WHEN THE DIVINE SOLDIERS ARRIVE. WE MUST FIND A WAY TO FIGHT THEM WITHIN THESE CONSTRAINTS.

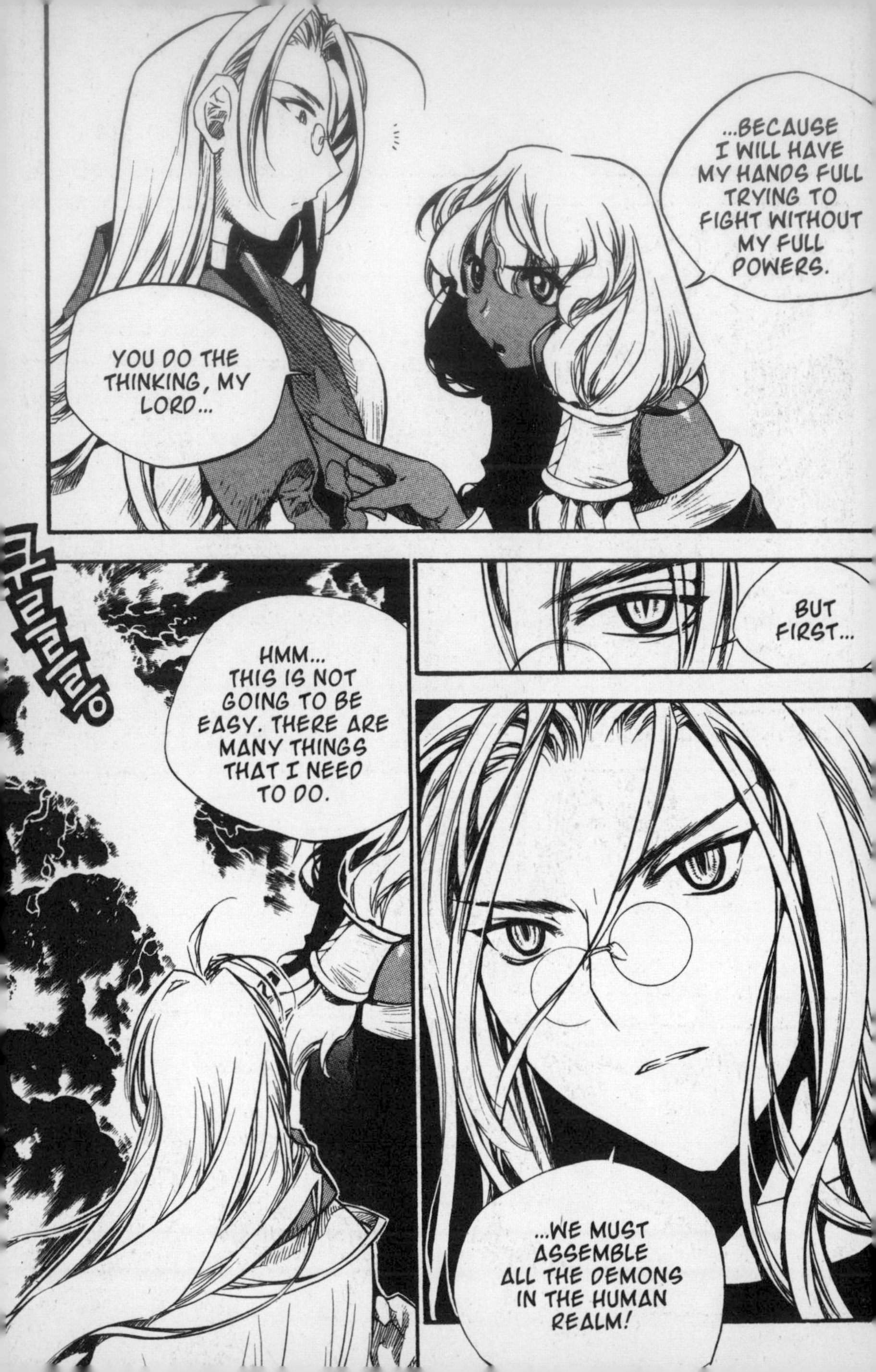
YOU DO THE THINKING, MY LORD...
...BECAUSE I WILL HAVE MY HANDS FULL TRYING TO FIGHT WITHOUT MY FULL POWERS.
쿠르르르릉
HMM... THIS IS NOT GOING TO BE EASY. THERE ARE MANY THINGS THAT I NEED TO DO.
BUT FIRST...
...WE MUST ASSEMBLE ALL THE DEMONS IN THE HUMAN REALM!

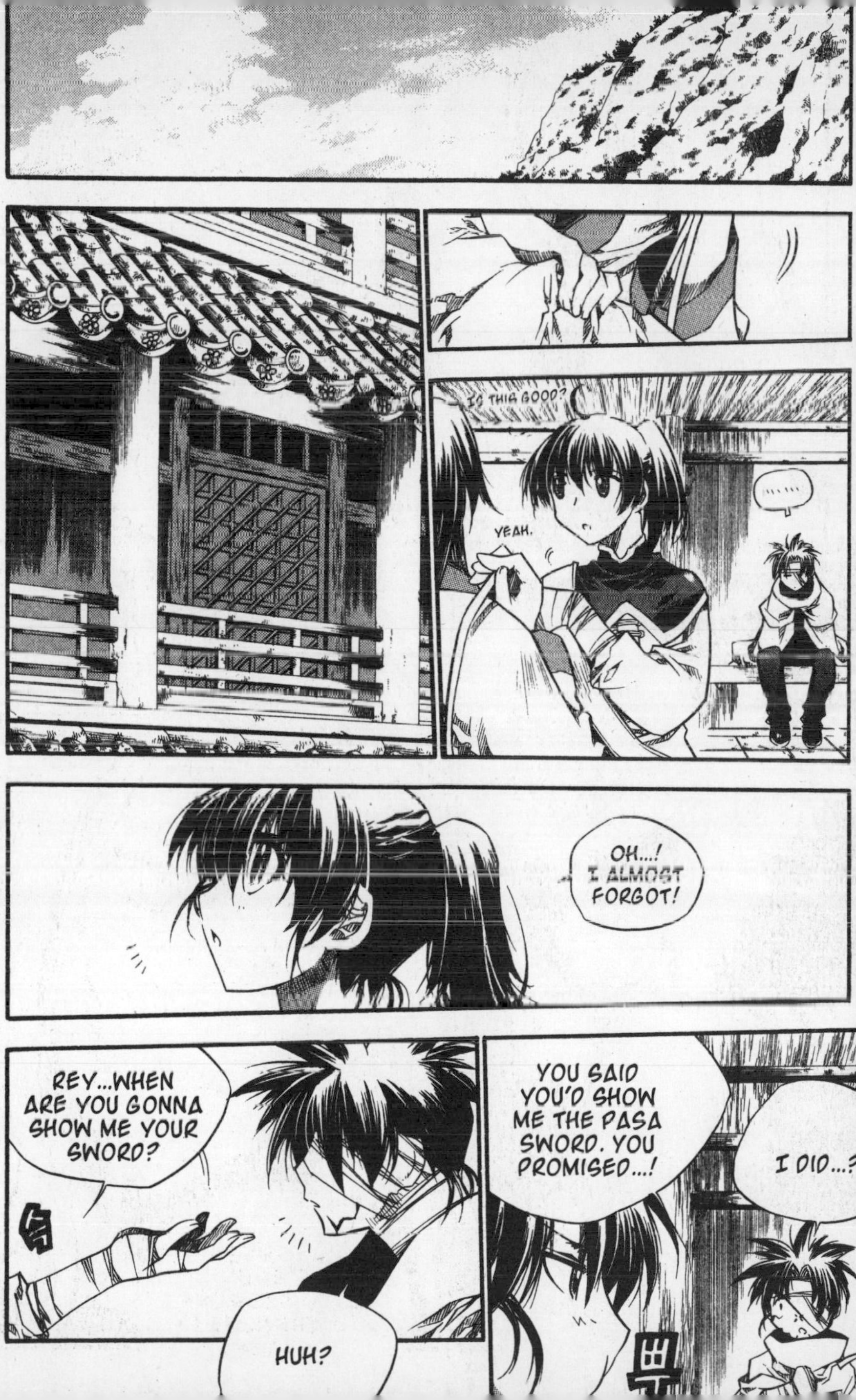
IS THIS GOOD?
YEAH.
......
OH...! I ALMOST FORGOT!
REY...WHEN ARE YOU GONNA SHOW ME YOUR SWORD?
HUH?
YOU SAID YOU'D SHOW ME THE PASA SWORD. YOU PROMISED...!
I DID...?

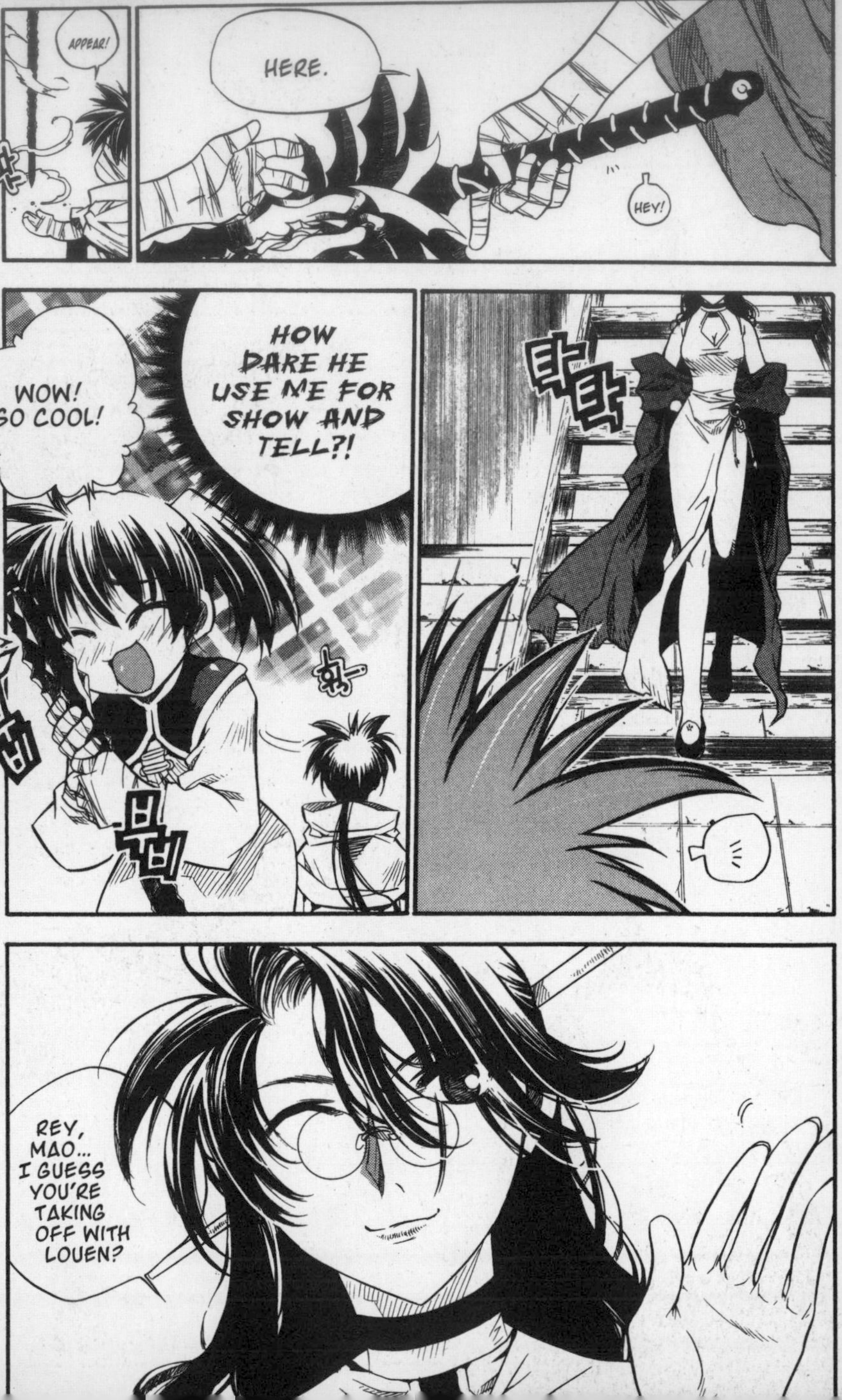
APPEAR!
HERE.
HEY!
WOW! SO COOL!
HOW DARE HE USE ME FOR SHOW AND TELL?!
탁탁
REY, MAO... I GUESS YOU'RE TAKING OFF WITH LOUEN?

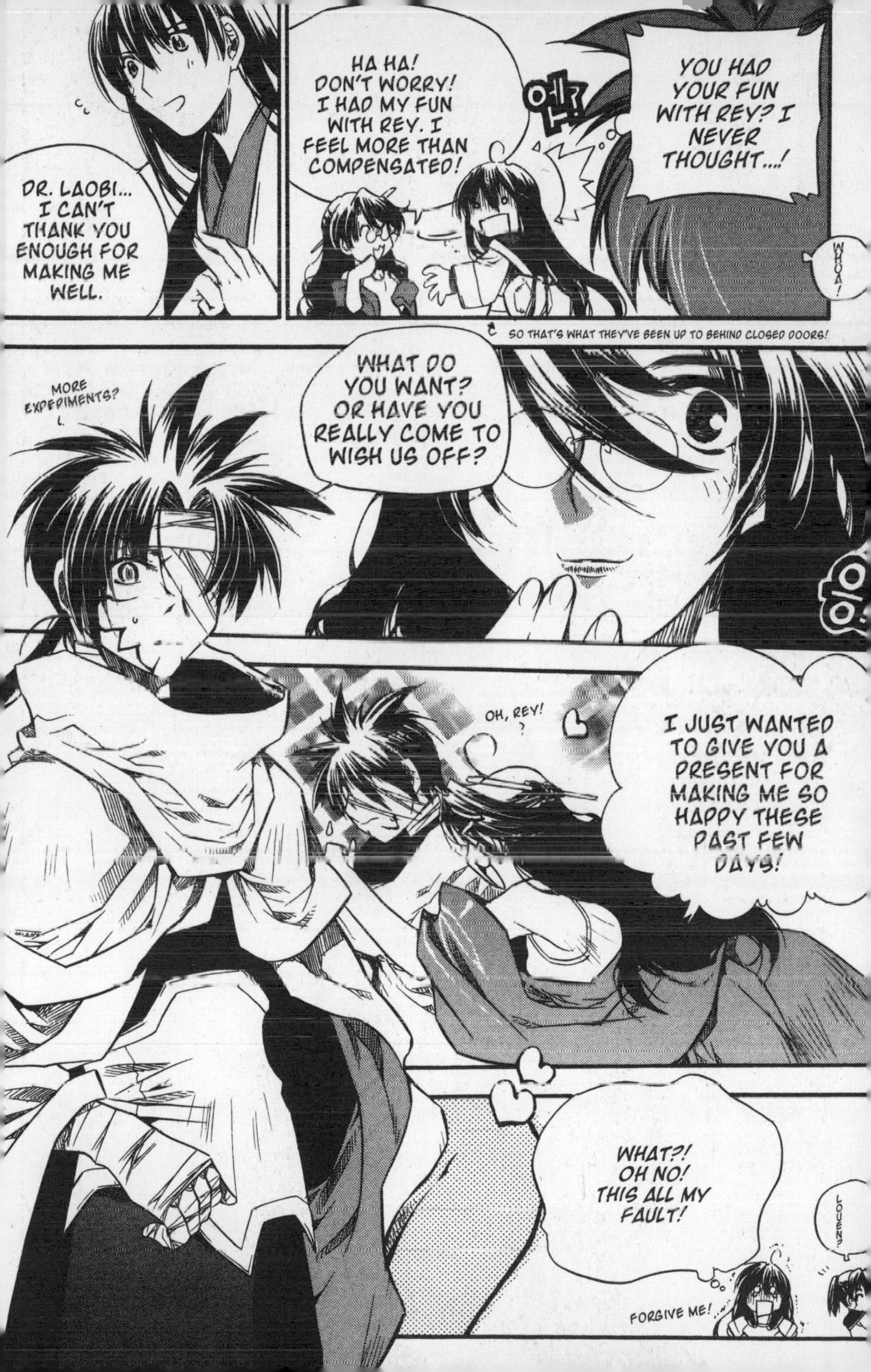
DR. LAOBI... I CAN'T THANK YOU ENOUGH FOR MAKING ME WELL.
HA HA! DON'T WORRY! I HAD MY FUN WITH REY. I FEEL MORE THAN COMPENSATED!
YOU HAD YOUR FUN WITH REY? I NEVER THOUGHT...!
WHOA!
SO THAT'S WHAT THEY'VE BEEN UP TO BEHIND CLOSED DOORS!
MORE EXPERIMENTS?
WHAT DO YOU WANT? OR HAVE YOU REALLY COME TO WISH US OFF?
OH, REY!
I JUST WANTED TO GIVE YOU A PRESENT FOR MAKING ME SO HAPPY THESE PAST FEW DAYS!
WHAT?! OH NO! THIS ALL MY FAULT!
LOVEN?
FORGIVE ME!

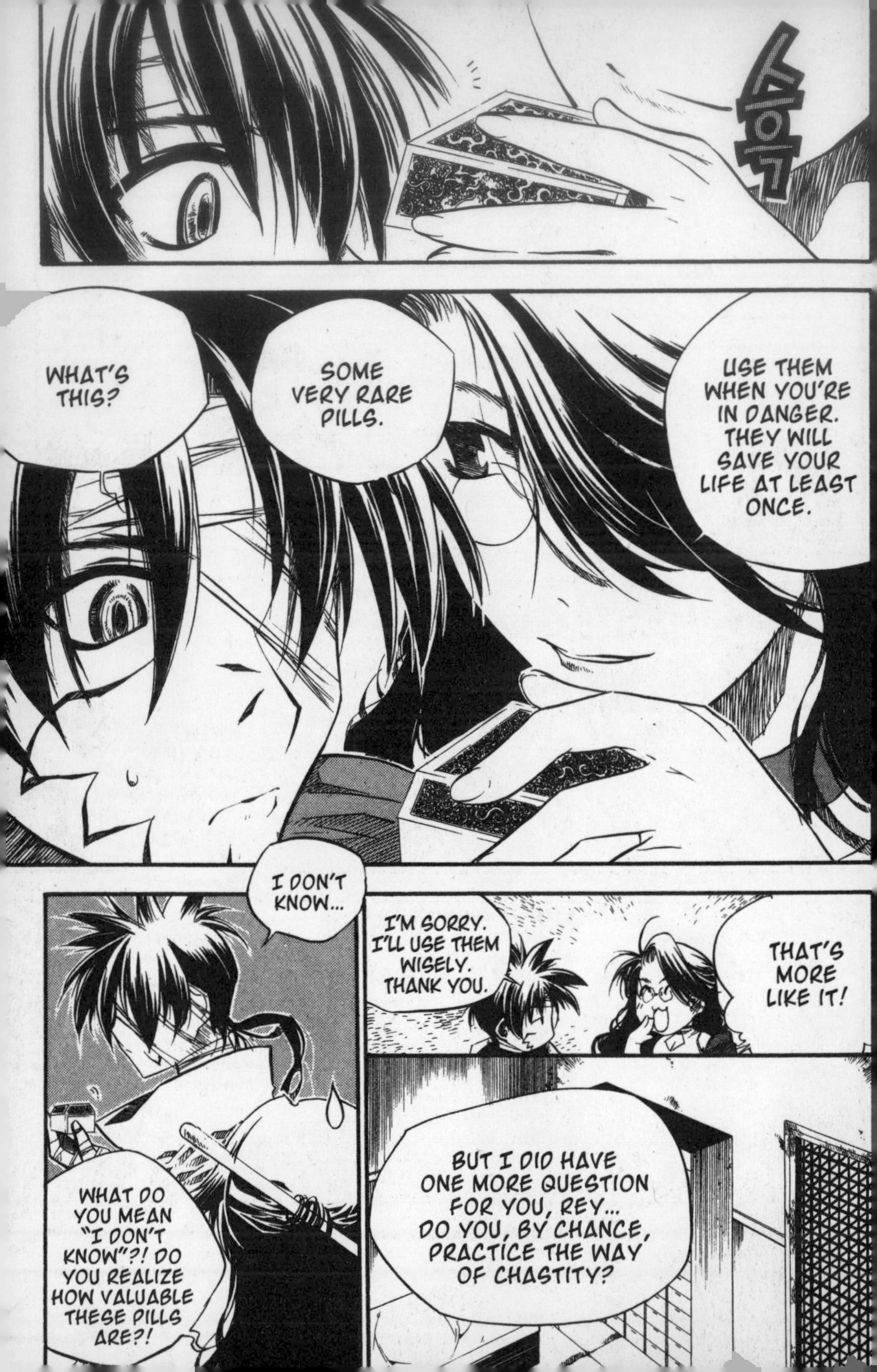
WHAT'S THIS?
SOME VERY RARE PILLS.
USE THEM WHEN YOU'RE IN DANGER. THEY WILL SAVE YOUR LIFE AT LEAST ONCE.
I DON'T KNOW...
WHAT DO YOU MEAN "I DON'T KNOW"?! DO YOU REALIZE HOW VALUABLE THESE PILLS ARE?!
I'M SORRY. I'LL USE THEM WISELY. THANK YOU.
THAT'S MORE LIKE IT!
BUT I DID HAVE ONE MORE QUESTION FOR YOU, REY... DO YOU, BY CHANCE, PRACTICE THE WAY OF CHASTITY?

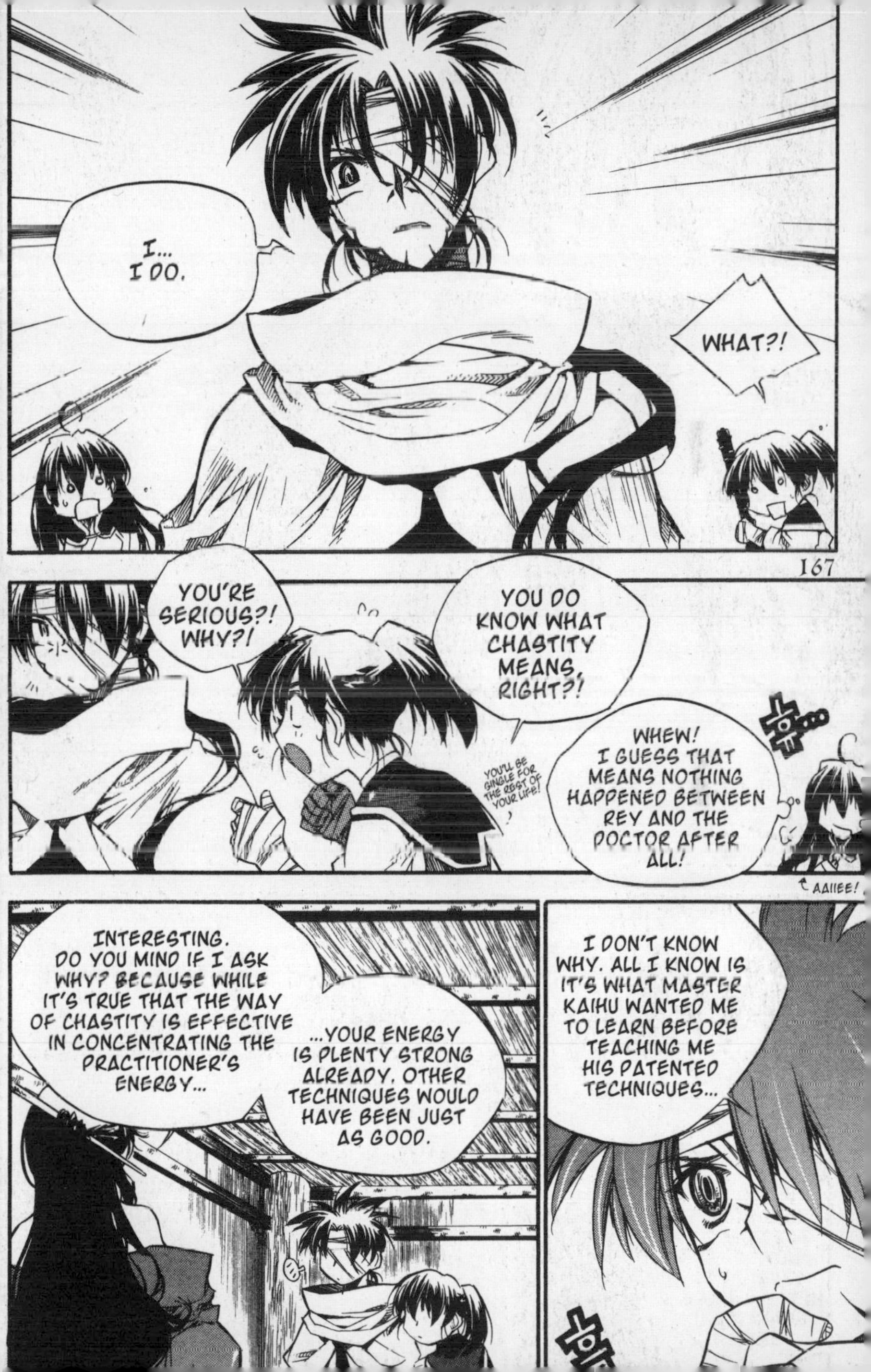
I... I DO.
WHAT?!
YOU'RE SERIOUS?! WHY?!
YOU DO KNOW WHAT CHASTITY MEANS, RIGHT?!
YOU'LL BE SINGLE FOR THE REST OF YOUR LIFE!
WHEW! I GUESS THAT MEANS NOTHING HAPPENED BETWEEN REY AND THE DOCTOR AFTER ALL!
AAIIEE!
INTERESTING. DO YOU MIND IF I ASK WHY? BECAUSE WHILE IT'S TRUE THAT THE WAY OF CHASTITY IS EFFECTIVE IN CONCENTRATING THE PRACTITIONER'S ENERGY...
...YOUR ENERGY IS PLENTY STRONG ALREADY. OTHER TECHNIQUES WOULD HAVE BEEN JUST AS GOOD.
I DON'T KNOW WHY. ALL I KNOW IS IT'S WHAT MASTER KAIHU WANTED ME TO LEARN BEFORE TEACHING ME HIS PATENTED TECHNIQUES...

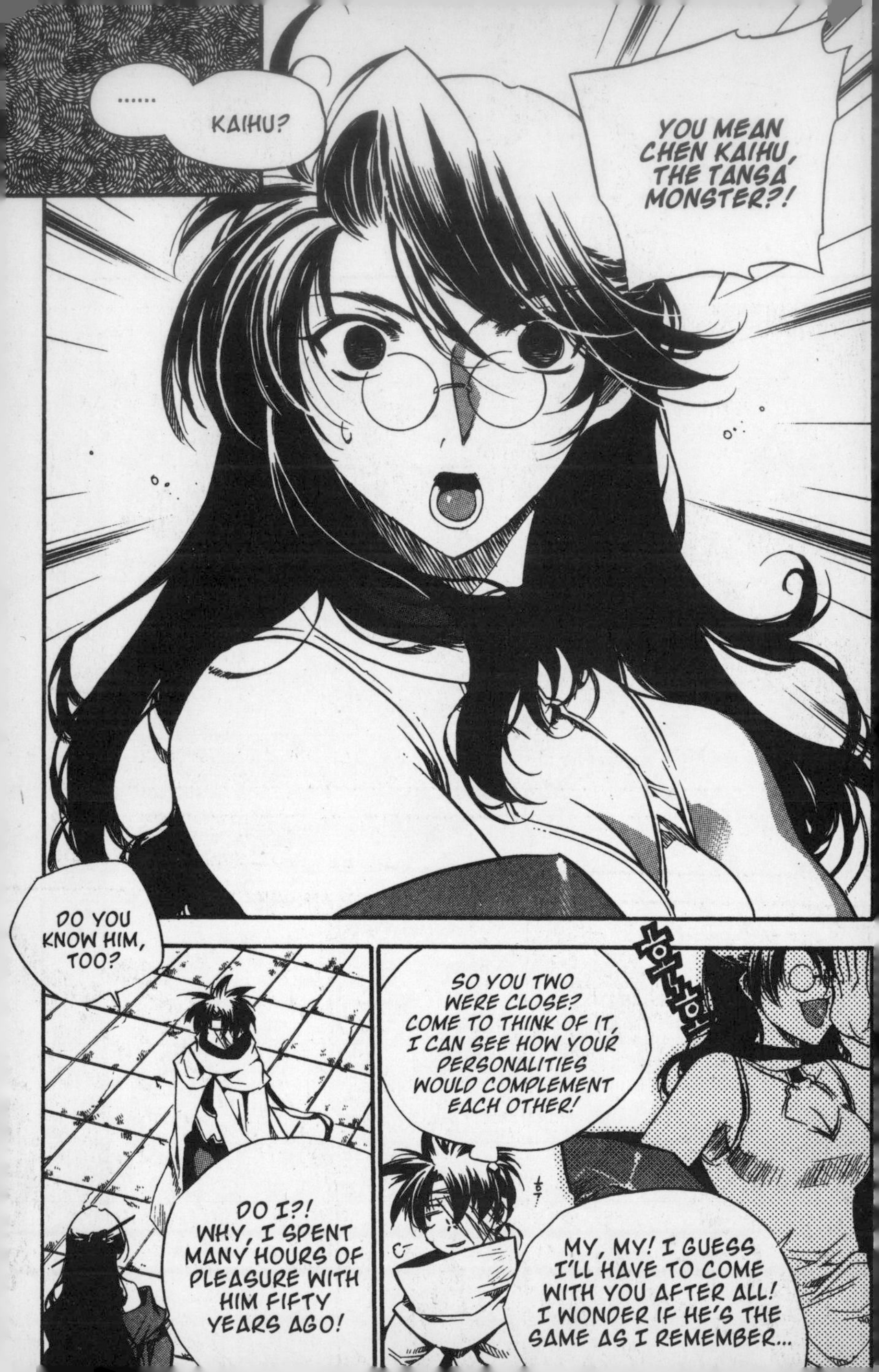

......
KAIHU?
YOU MEAN CHEN KAIHU, THE TANSA MONSTER?!
DO YOU KNOW HIM, TOO?
DO I?! WHY, I SPENT MANY HOURS OF PLEASURE WITH HIM FIFTY YEARS AGO!
SO YOU TWO WERE CLOSE? COME TO THINK OF IT, I CAN SEE HOW YOUR PERSONALITIES WOULD COMPLEMENT EACH OTHER!
MY, MY! I GUESS I'LL HAVE TO COME WITH YOU AFTER ALL! I WONDER IF HE'S THE SAME AS I REMEMBER...

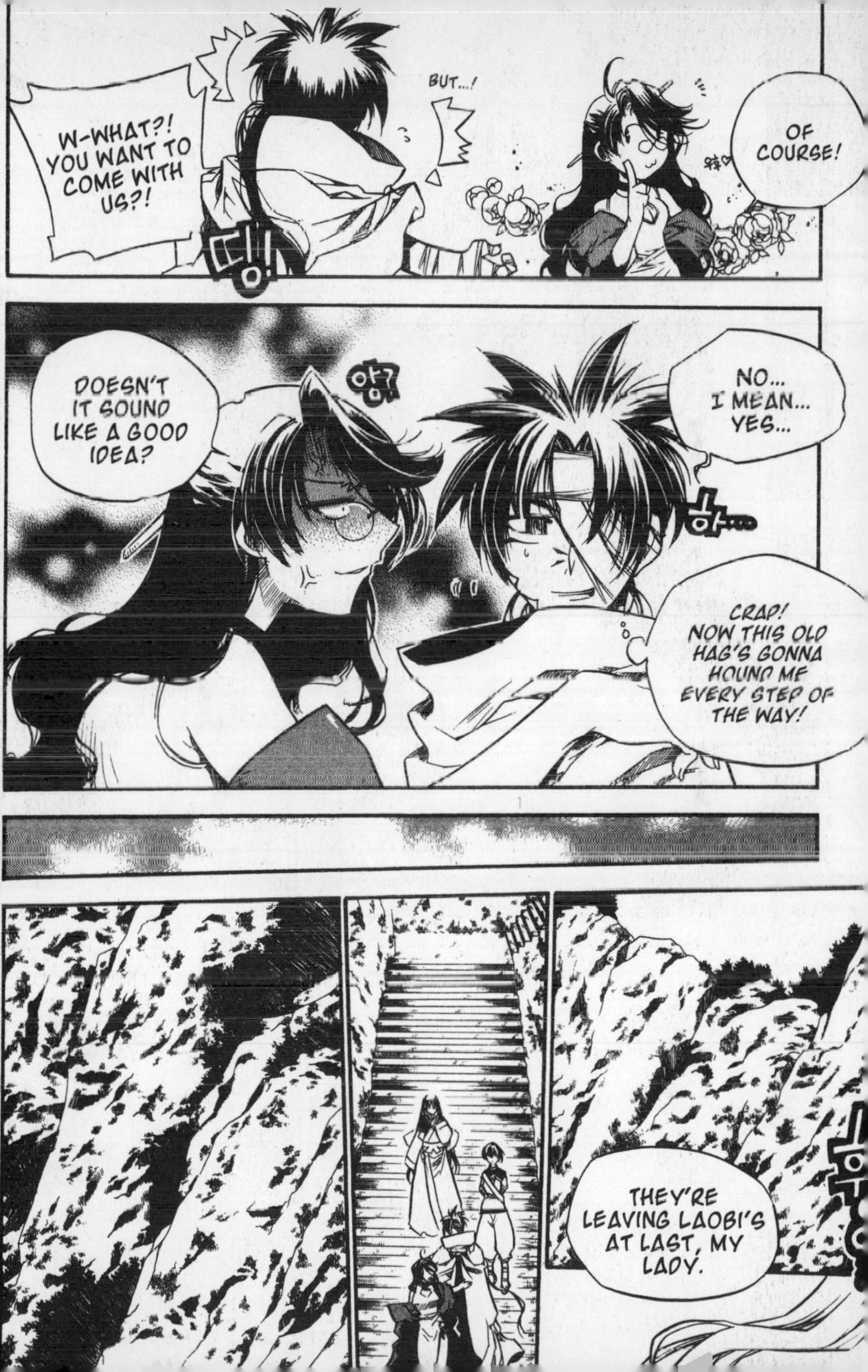
W-WHAT?! YOU WANT TO COME WITH US?!
BUT...!
OF COURSE!
DOESN'T IT SOUND LIKE A GOOD IDEA?
NO... I MEAN... YES...
하...
CRAP! NOW THIS OLD HAG'S GONNA HOUND ME EVERY STEP OF THE WAY!
THEY'RE LEAVING LAOBI'S AT LAST, MY LADY.

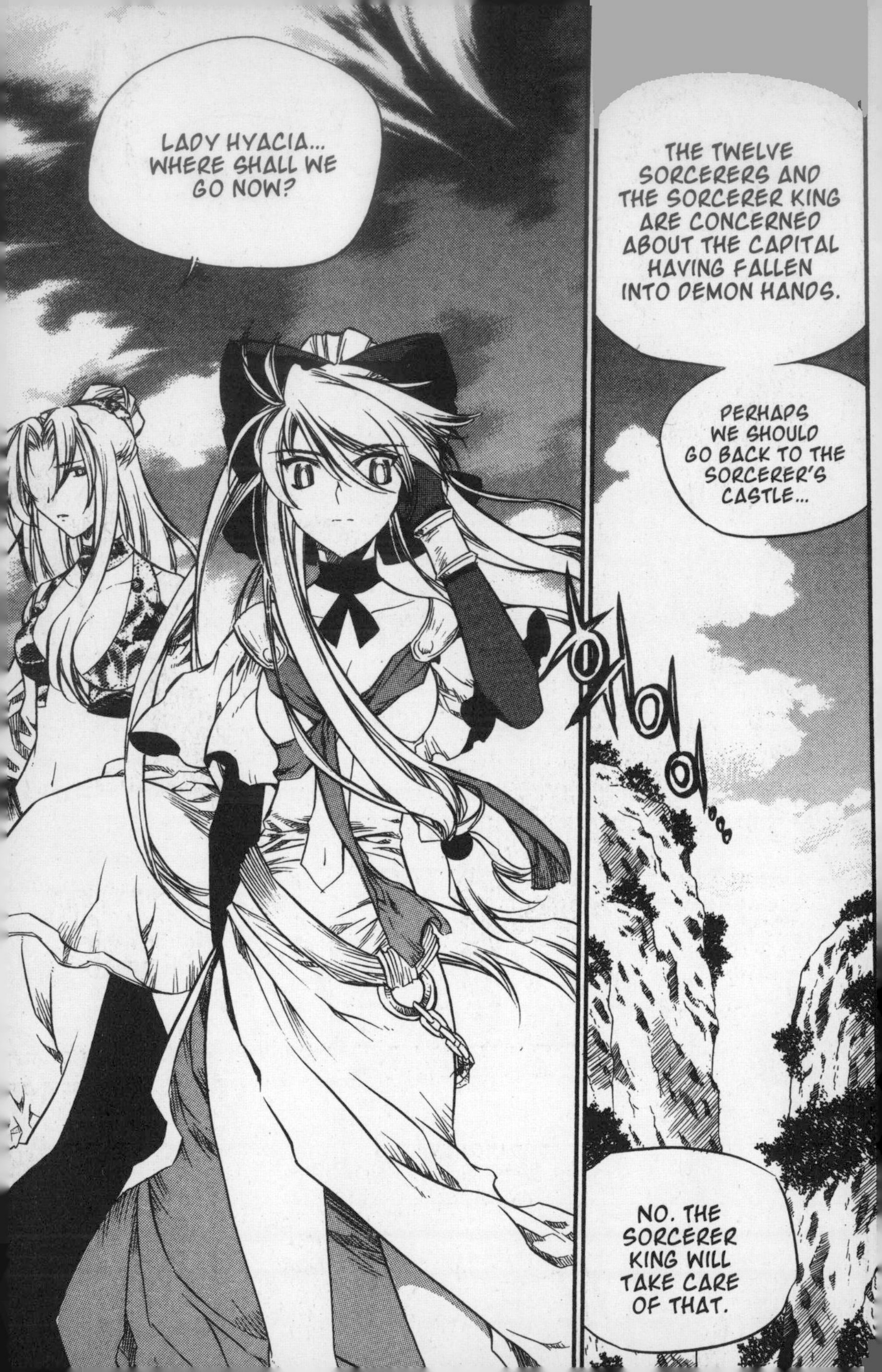
LADY HYACIA... WHERE SHALL WE GO NOW?
THE TWELVE SORCERERS AND THE SORCERER KING ARE CONCERNED ABOUT THE CAPITAL HAVING FALLEN INTO DEMON HANDS.
PERHAPS WE SHOULD GO BACK TO THE SORCERER'S CASTLE...
NO. THE SORCERER KING WILL TAKE CARE OF THAT.

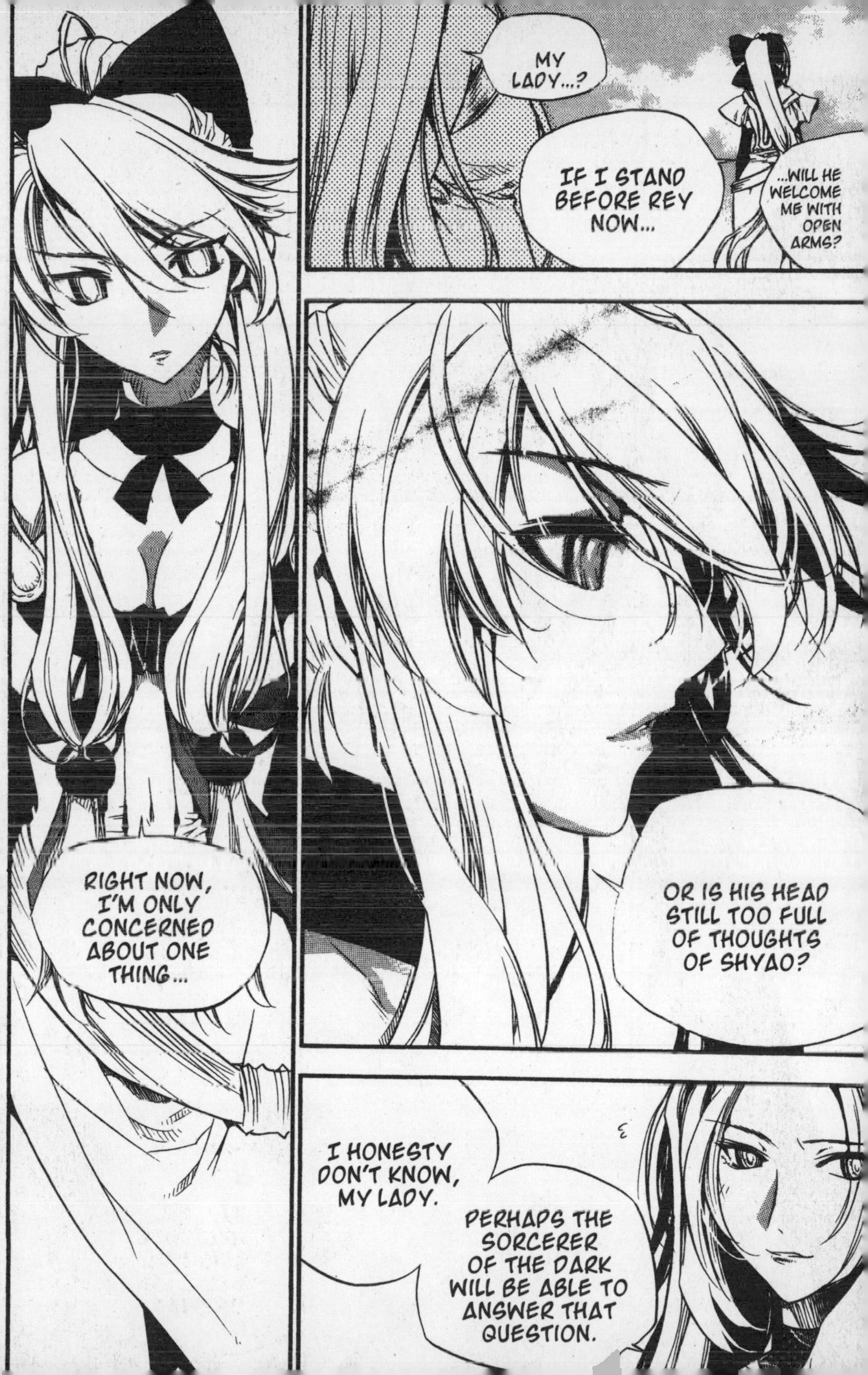
RIGHT NOW, I'M ONLY CONCERNED ABOUT ONE THING...
MY LADY...?
IF I STAND BEFORE REY NOW...
...WILL HE WELCOME ME WITH OPEN ARMS?
OR IS HIS HEAD STILL TOO FULL OF THOUGHTS OF SHYAO?
I HONESTY DON'T KNOW, MY LADY.
PERHAPS THE SORCERER OF THE DARK WILL BE ABLE TO ANSWER THAT QUESTION.

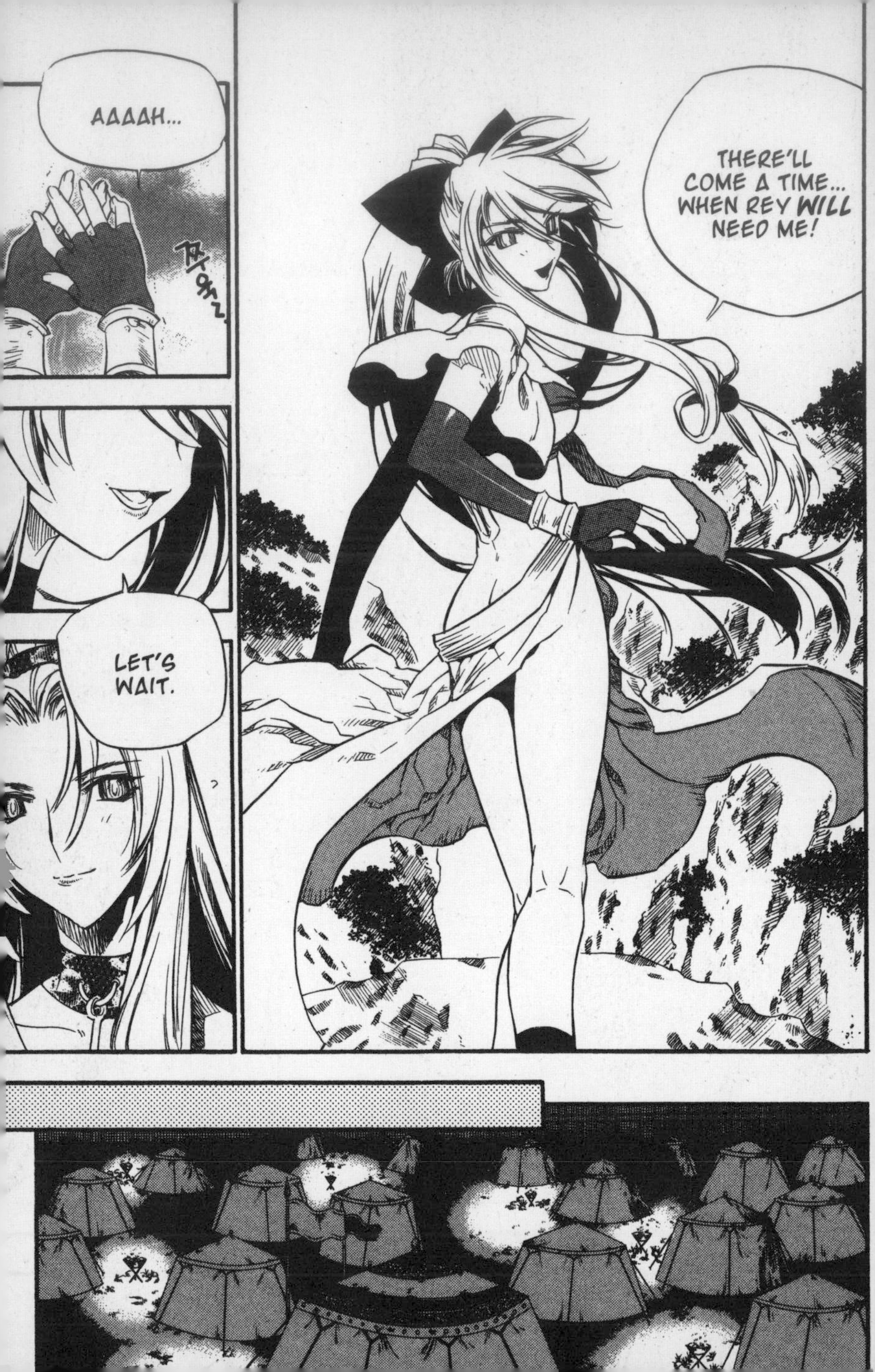
AAAAH...
LET'S WAIT.
THERE'LL COME A TIME... WHEN REY WILL NEED ME!

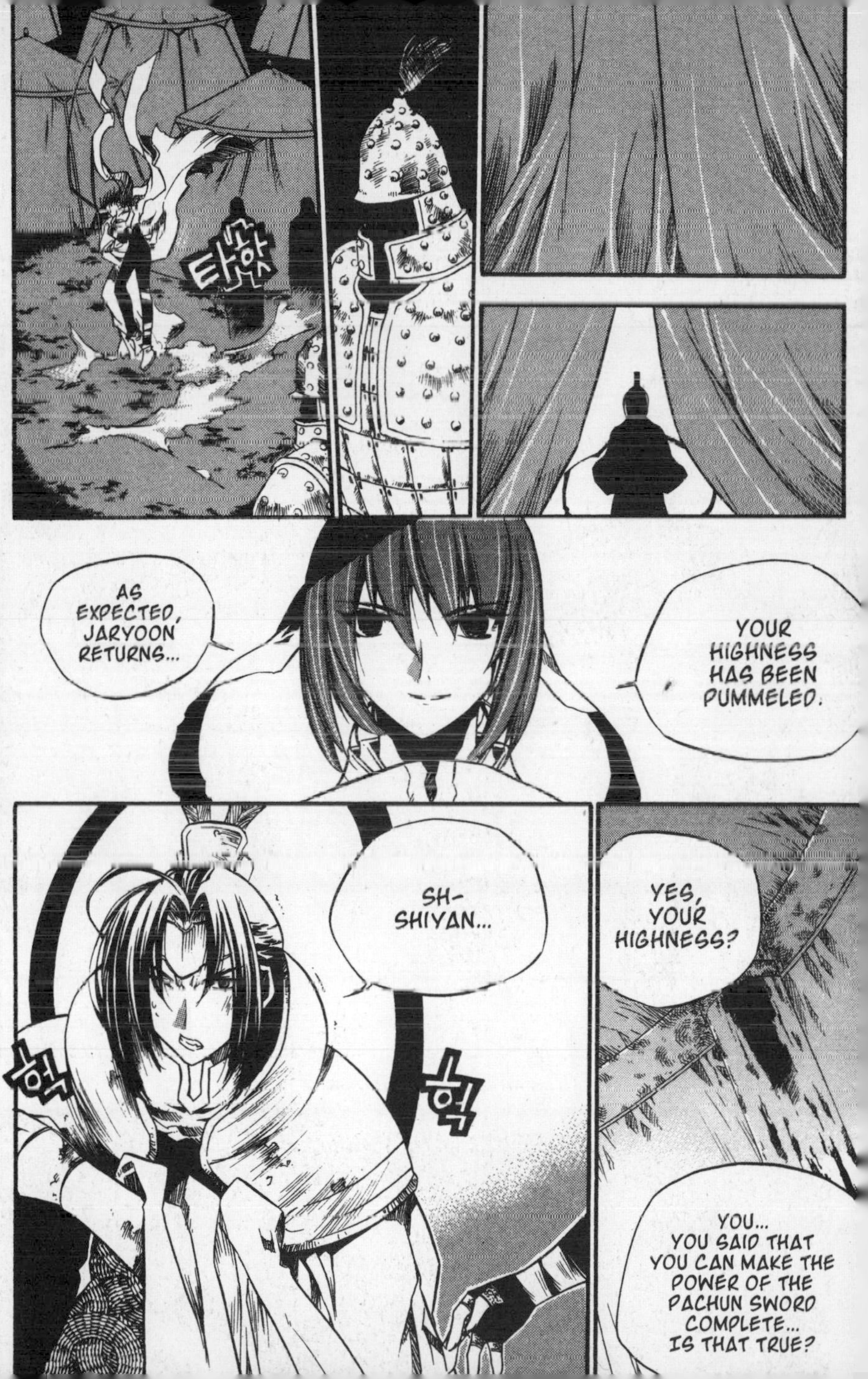
타앗
AS EXPECTED, JARYOON RETURNS...
YOUR HIGHNESS HAS BEEN PUMMELED.
헉
SH- SHIYAN...
헉
YES, YOUR HIGHNESS?
YOU... YOU SAID THAT YOU CAN MAKE THE POWER OF THE PACHUN SWORD COMPLETE... IS THAT TRUE?

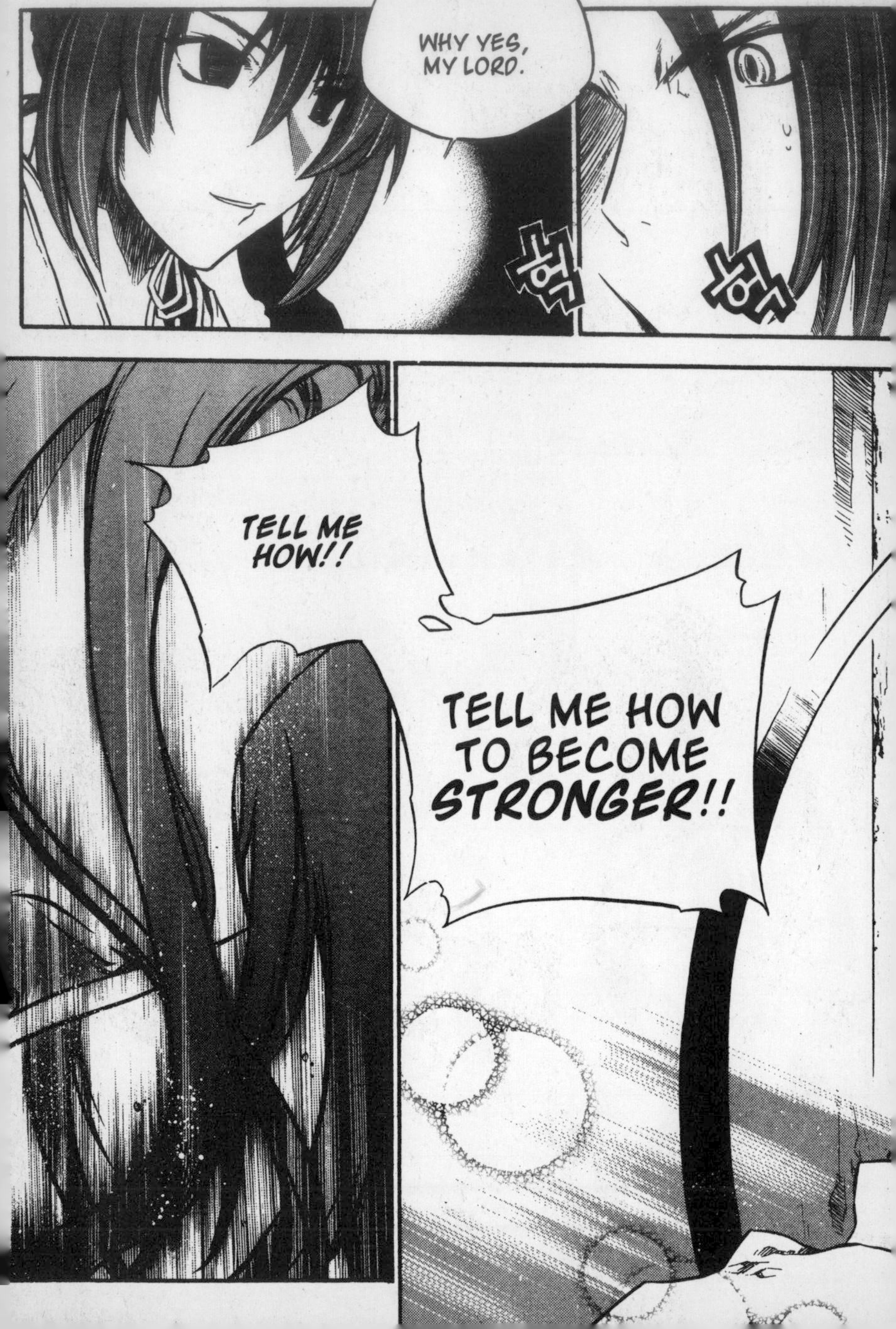
WHY YES, MY LORD.
TELL ME HOW!!
TELL ME HOW TO BECOME STRONGER!!

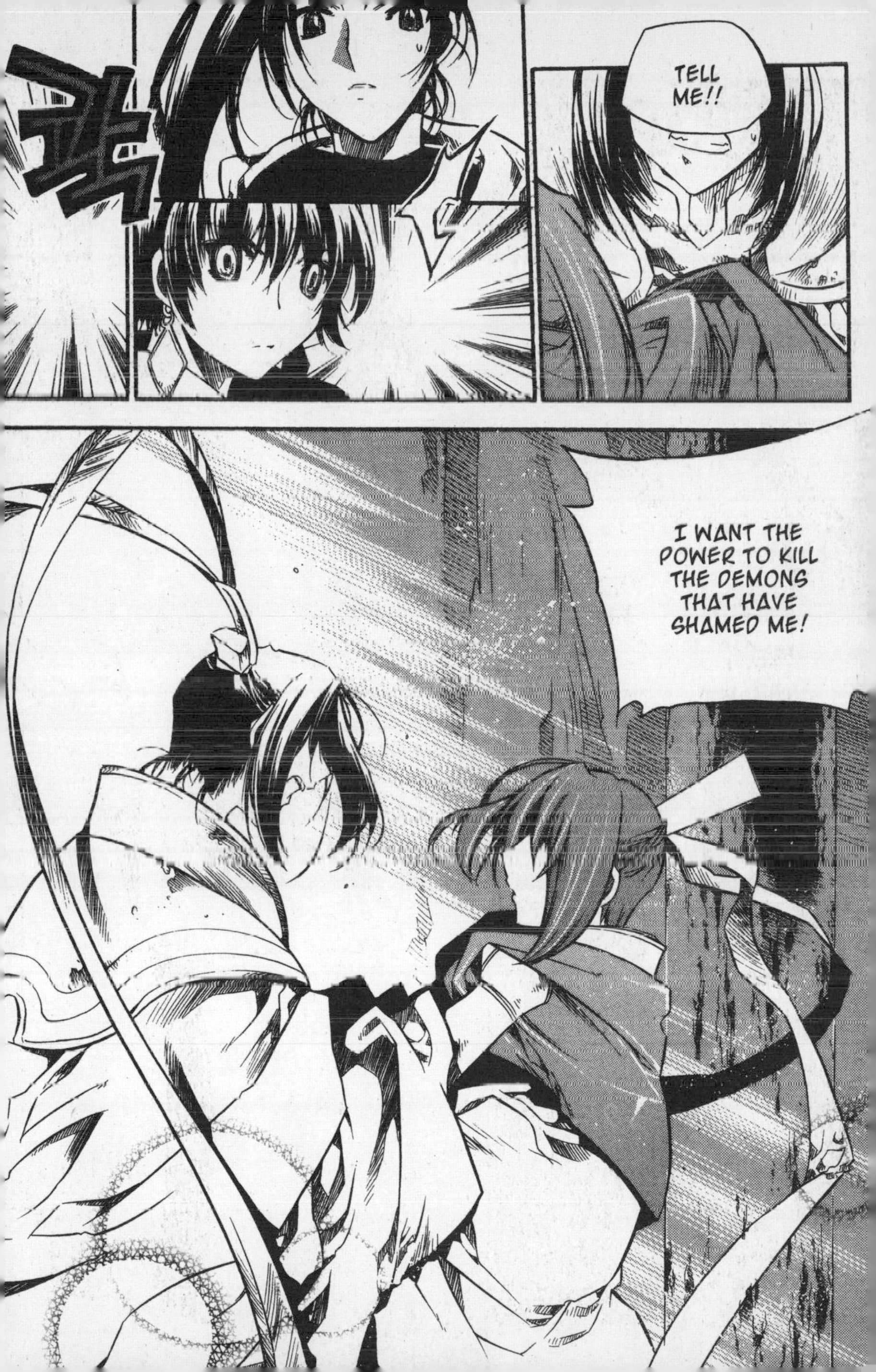
TELL ME!!
I WANT THE POWER TO KILL THE DEMONS THAT HAVE SHAMED ME!

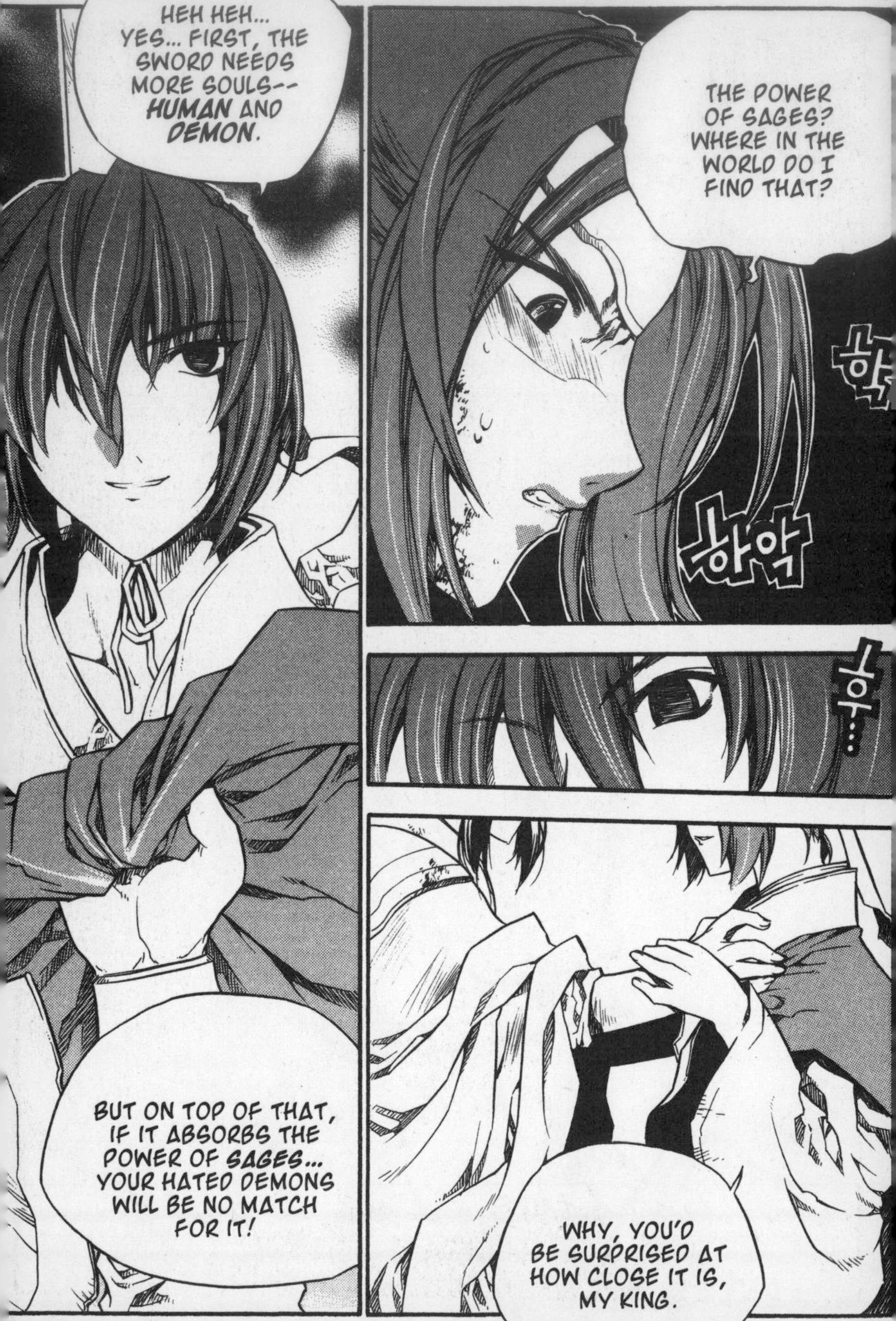
HEH HEH... YES... FIRST, THE SWORD NEEDS MORE SOULS-- **HUMAN** AND **DEMON**.
BUT ON TOP OF THAT, IF IT ABSORBS THE POWER OF **SAGES**... YOUR HATED DEMONS WILL BE NO MATCH FOR IT!
THE POWER OF SAGES? WHERE IN THE WORLD DO I FIND THAT?
하악
하악
후…
WHY, YOU'D BE SURPRISED AT HOW CLOSE IT IS, MY KING.

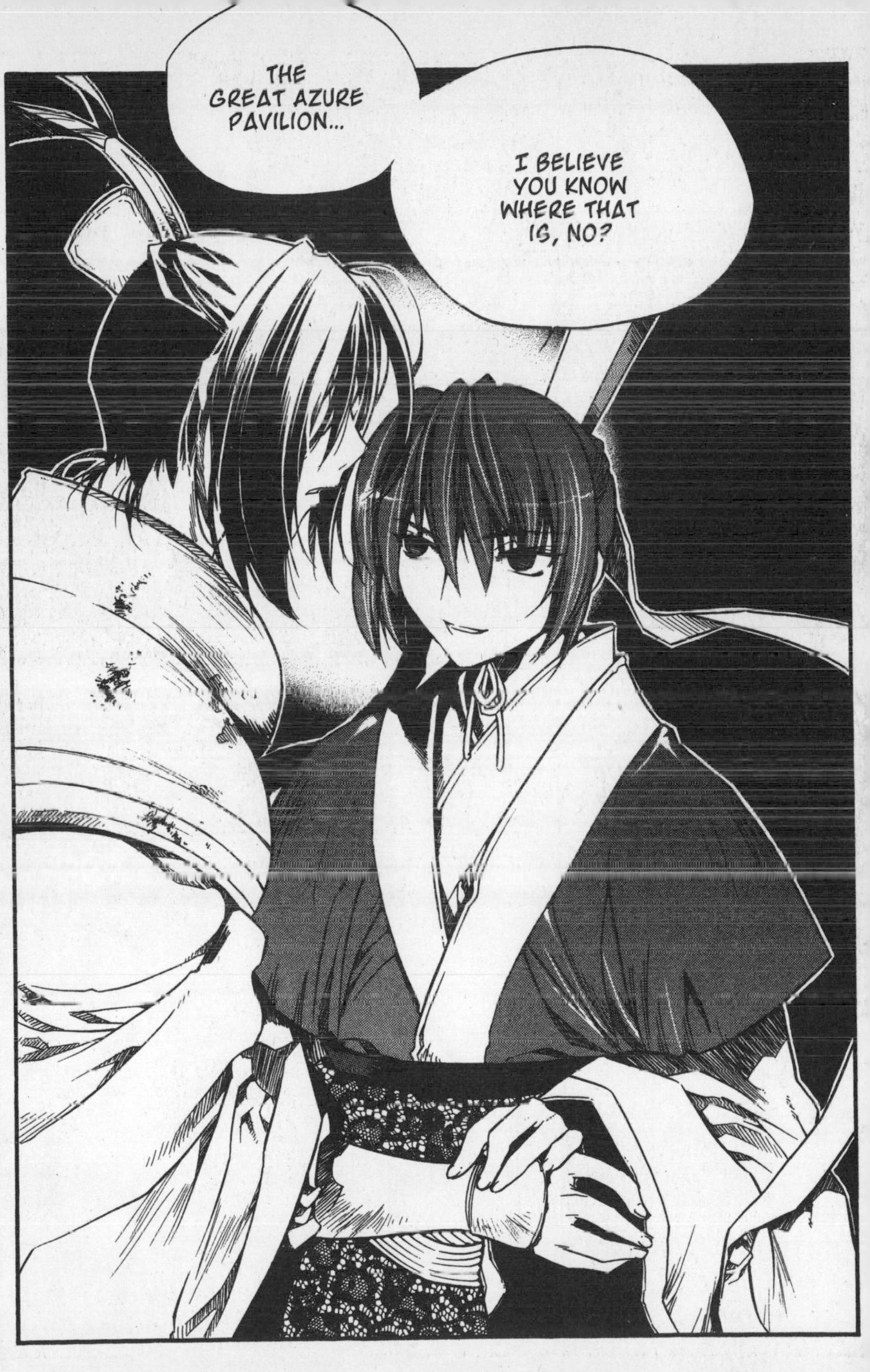
THE GREAT AZURE PAVILION...
I BELIEVE YOU KNOW WHERE THAT IS, NO?

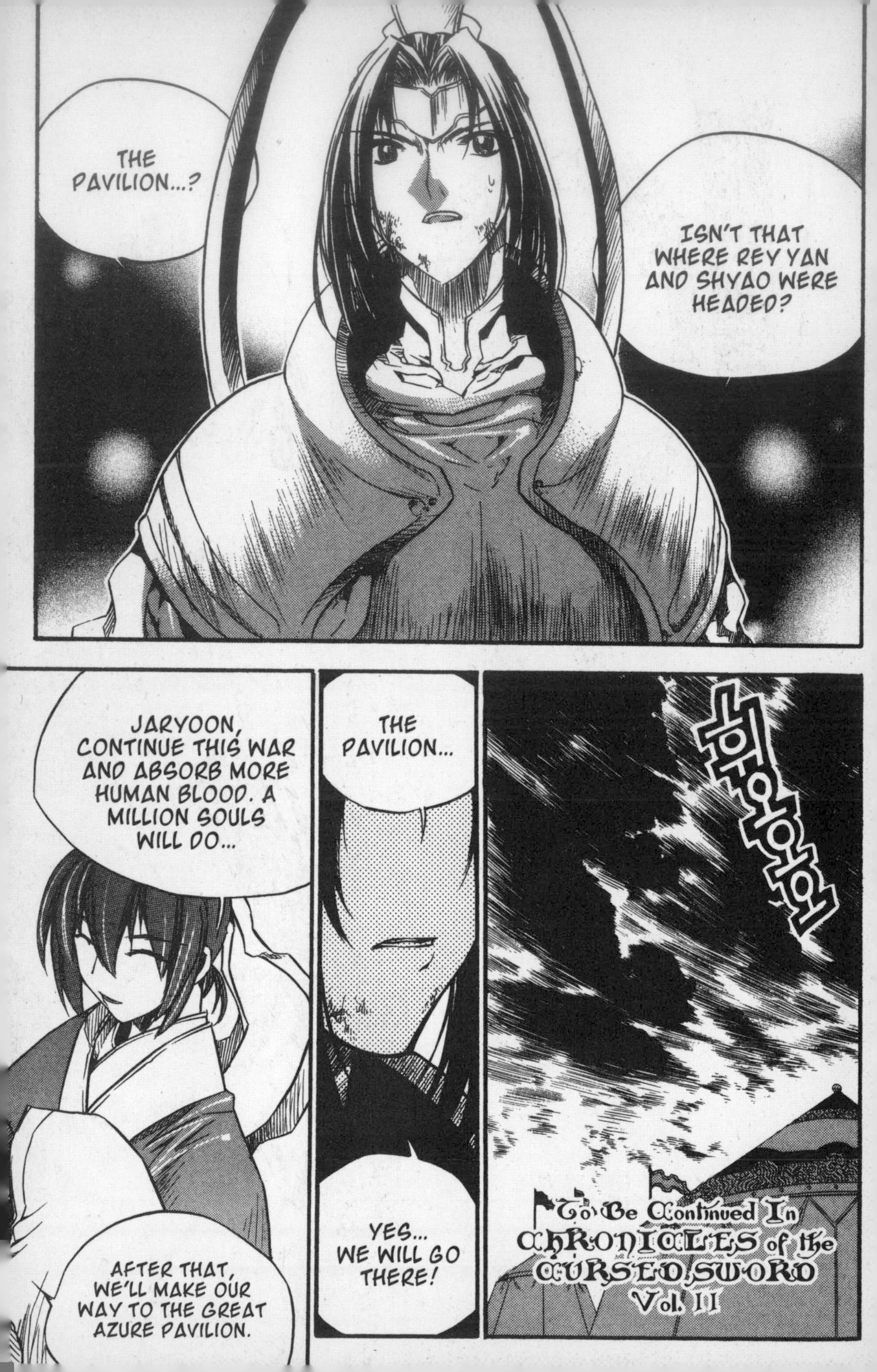
THE PAVILION...?
ISN'T THAT WHERE REY YAN AND SHYAO WERE HEADED?
JARYOON, CONTINUE THIS WAR AND ABSORB MORE HUMAN BLOOD. A MILLION SOULS WILL DO...
AFTER THAT, WE'LL MAKE OUR WAY TO THE GREAT AZURE PAVILION.
THE PAVILION...
YES... WE WILL GO THERE!
To Be Continued In CHRONICLES of the CURSED SWORD Vol. 11

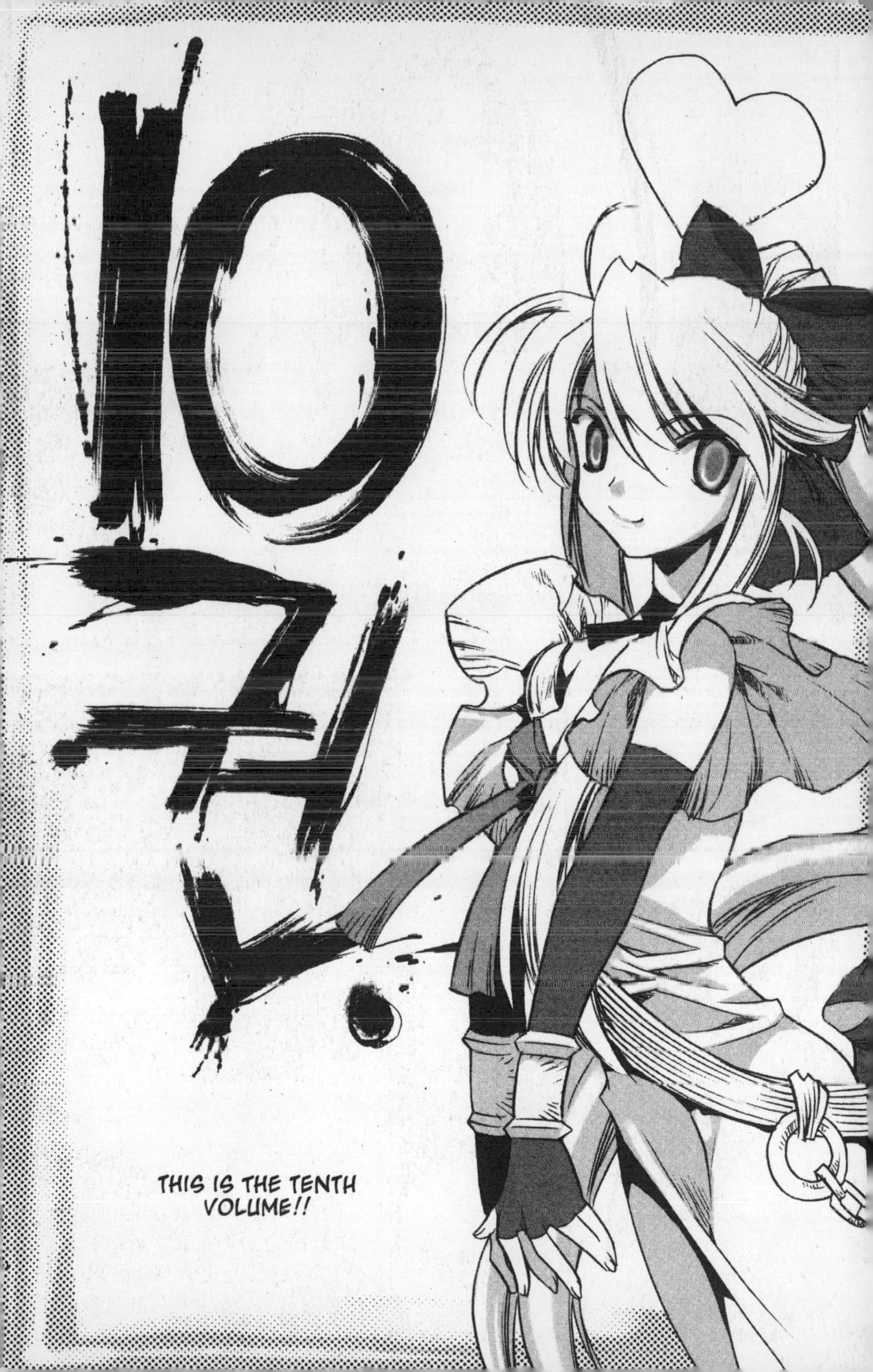
THIS IS THE TENTH
VOLUME!!

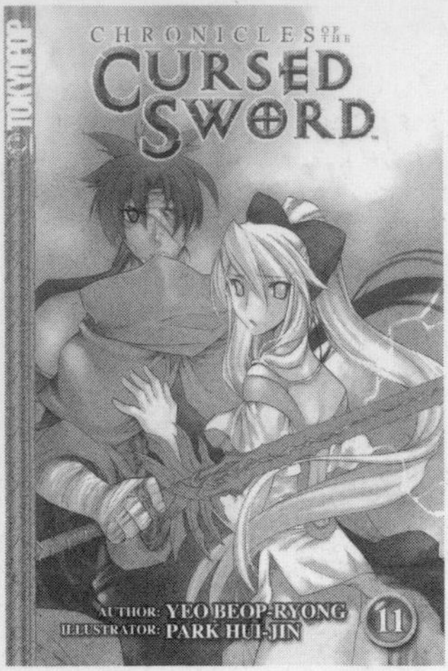
CHRONICLES OF THE
CURSED SWORD
TOKYOPOP
AUTHOR: YEO BEOP-RYONG
ILLUSTRATOR: PARK HUI-JIN
11

In preparation for the demon invasion on Human realm, the Demon Emperor is out to eliminate all potential threats...including Lady Hyacia. After being betrayed by her once-loyal subjects, Lady Hyacia is barely able to escape. However her body has only days to live if it is not reunited with her captive soul! Rey and his rag-tag team are in a race against time to save Lady Hyacia's life. Will they beat the clock? Will they even be able to save themselves?

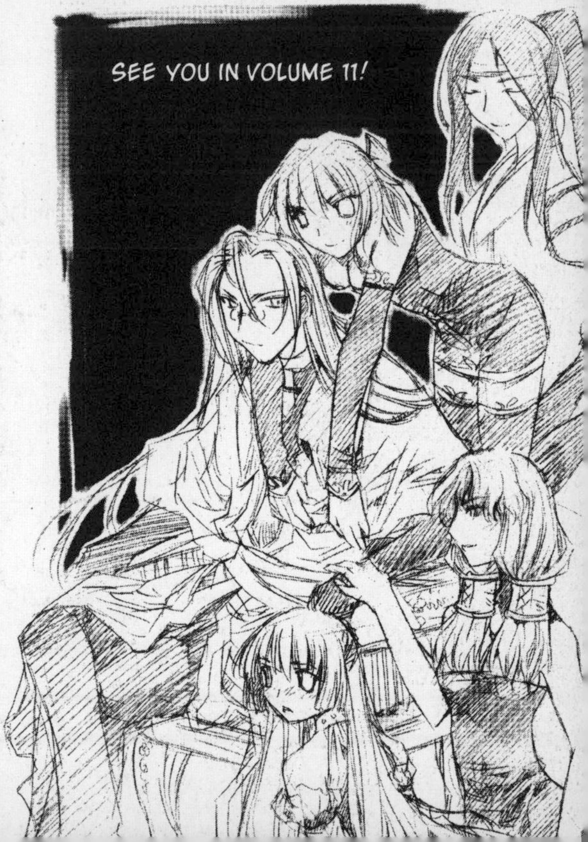
SEE YOU IN VOLUME 11!

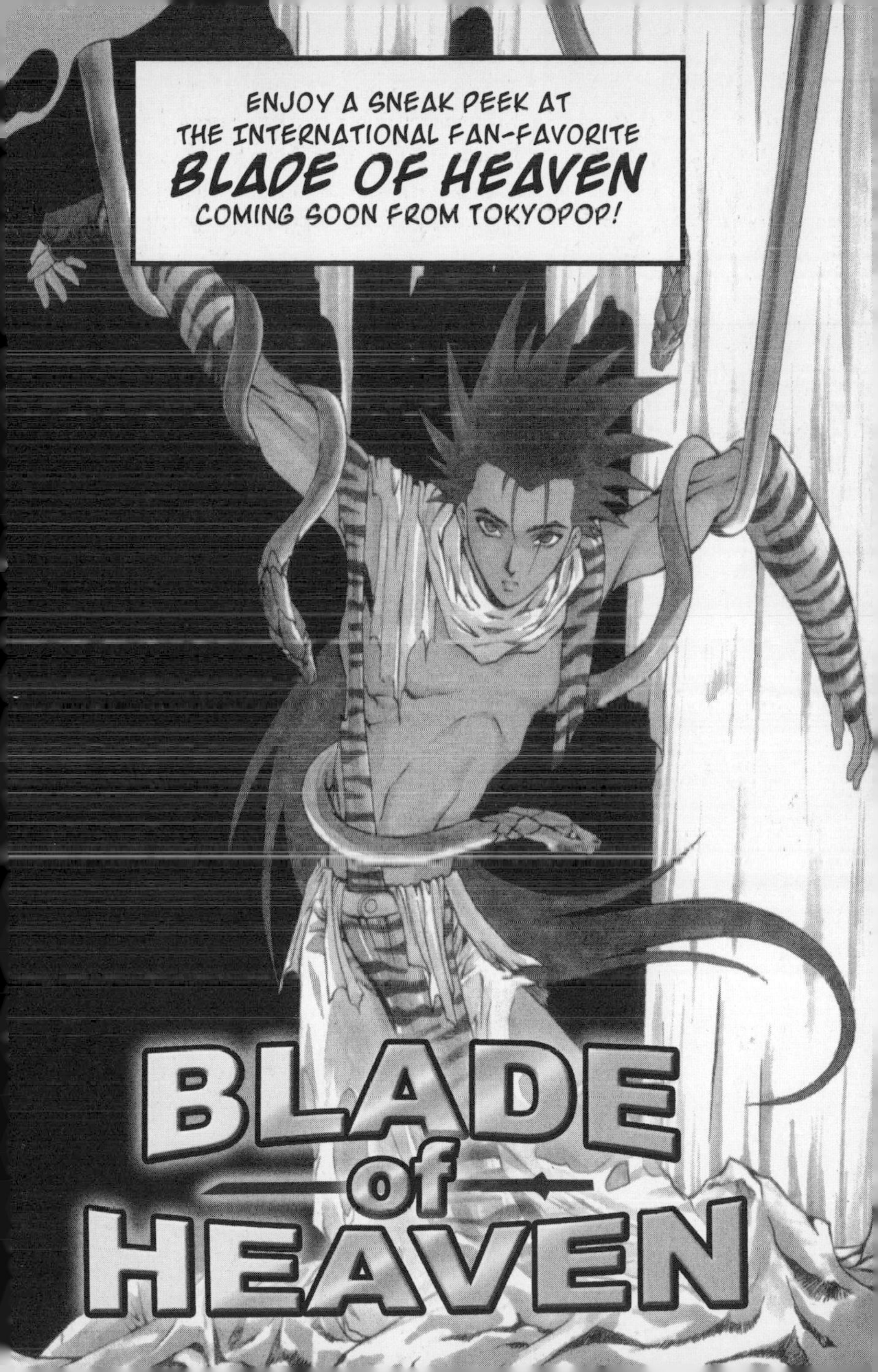

ENJOY A SNEAK PEEK AT
THE INTERNATIONAL FAN-FAVORITE
BLADE OF HEAVEN
COMING SOON FROM TOKYOPOP!
BLADE of HEAVEN

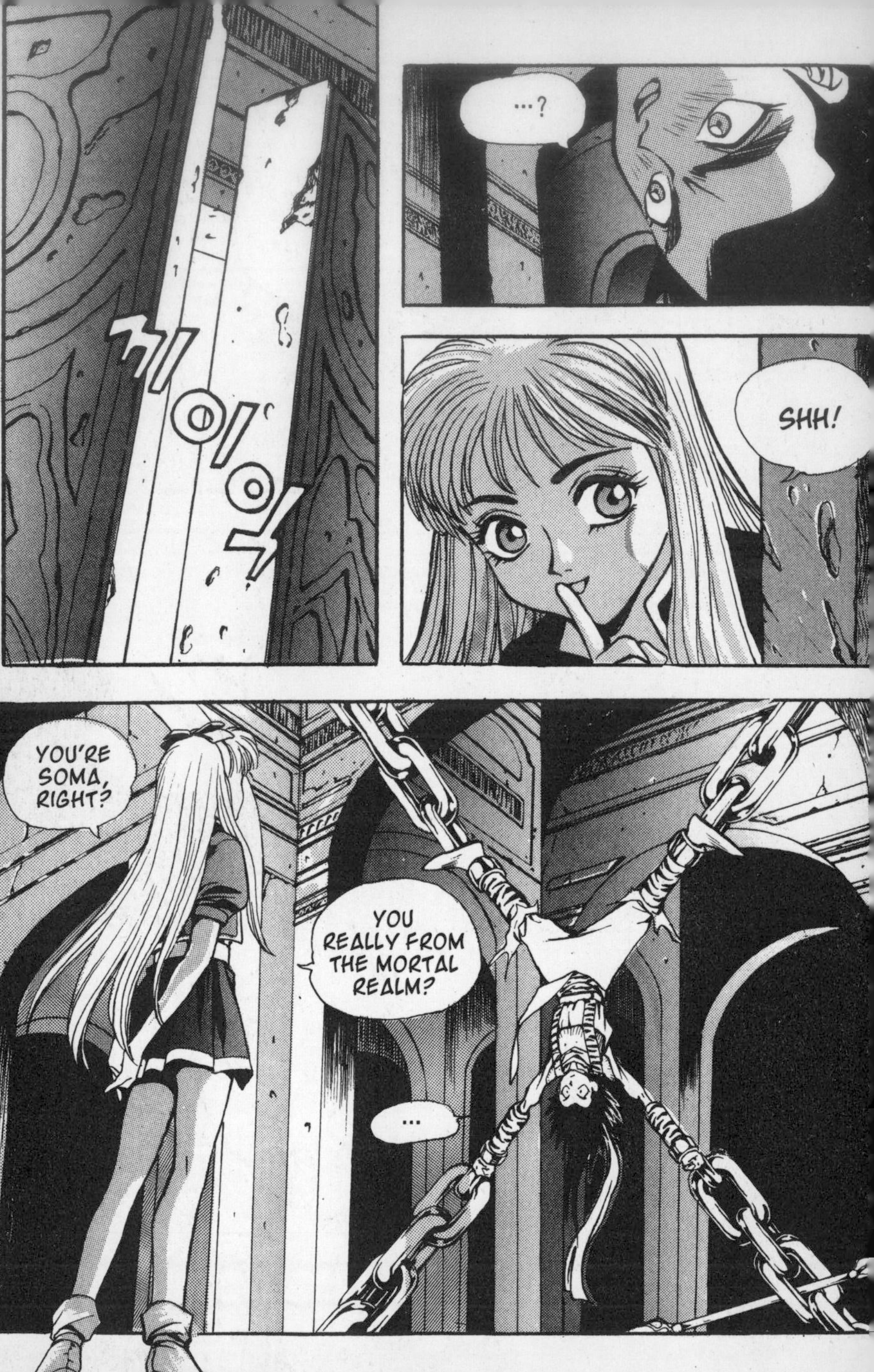
...?
SHH!
YOU'RE SOMA, RIGHT?
YOU REALLY FROM THE MORTAL REALM?
...

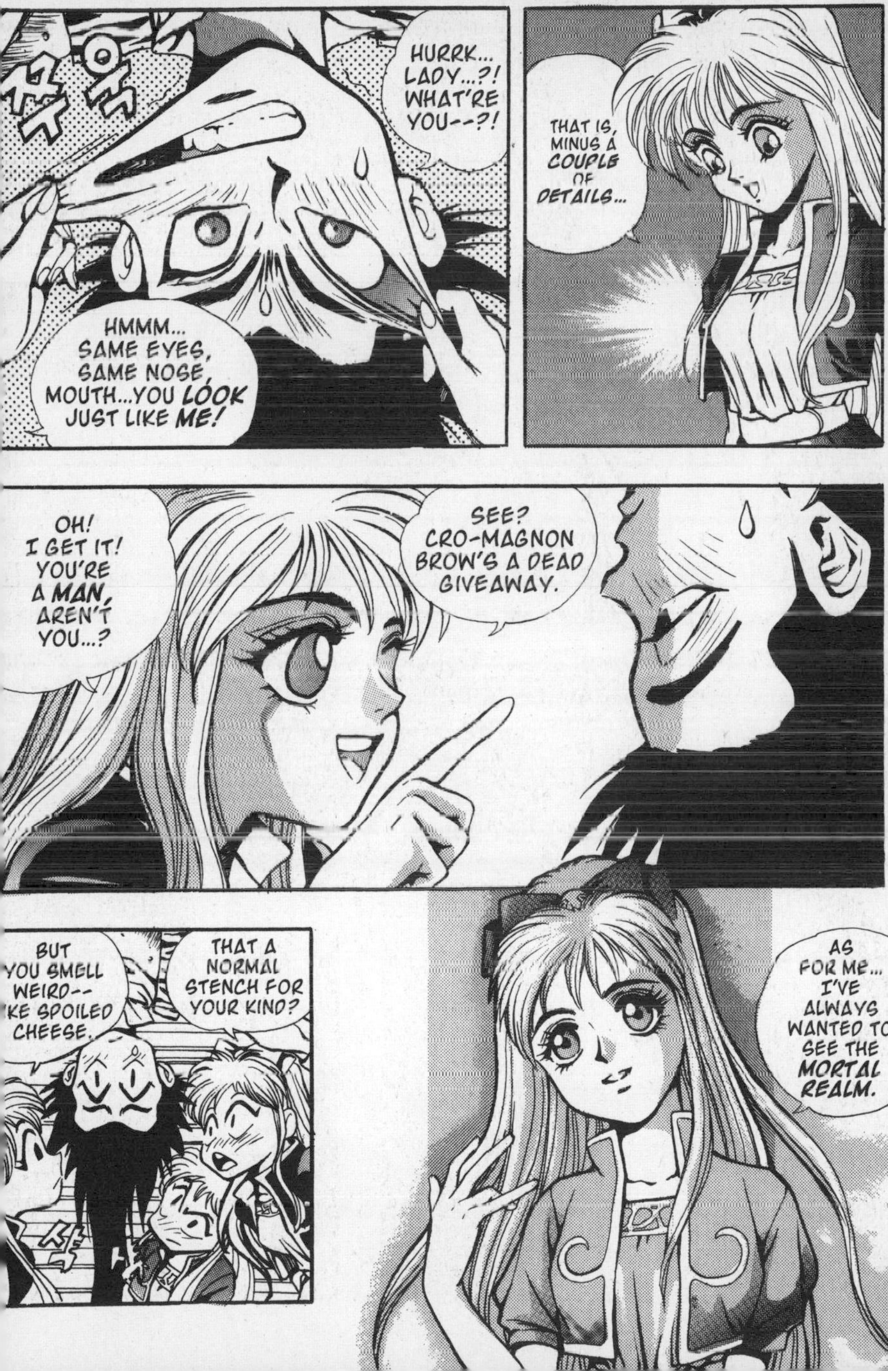
HURRK... LADY...?! WHAT'RE YOU--?!
HMMM... SAME EYES, SAME NOSE, MOUTH...YOU LOOK JUST LIKE ME!
THAT IS, MINUS A COUPLE OF DETAILS...
OH! I GET IT! YOU'RE A MAN, AREN'T YOU...?
SEE? CRO-MAGNON BROW'S A DEAD GIVEAWAY.
BUT YOU SMELL WEIRD-- KE SPOILED CHEESE.
THAT A NORMAL STENCH FOR YOUR KIND?
AS FOR ME... I'VE ALWAYS WANTED TO SEE THE MORTAL REALM.

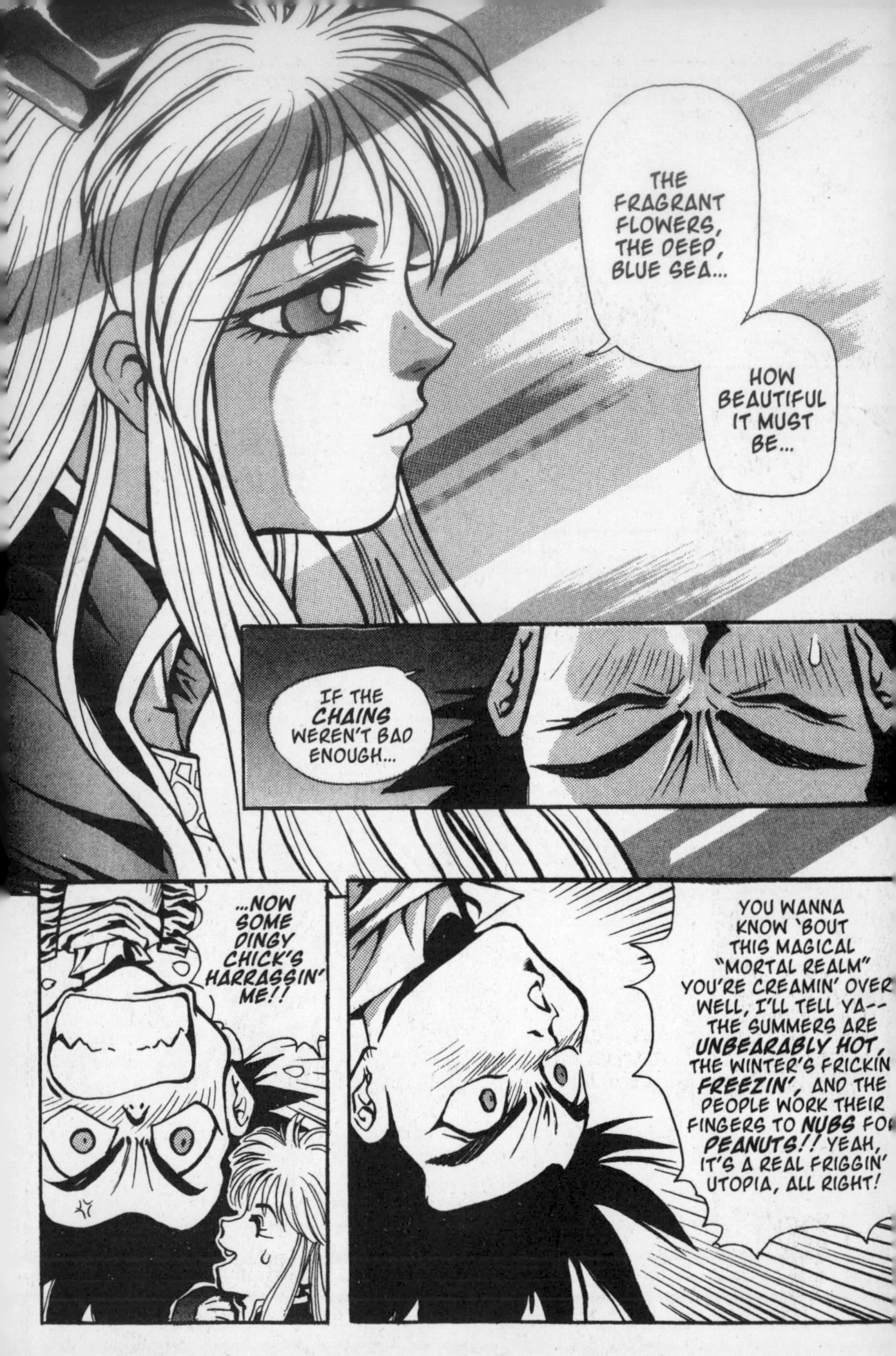
THE FRAGRANT FLOWERS, THE DEEP, BLUE SEA...
HOW BEAUTIFUL IT MUST BE...
IF THE CHAINS WEREN'T BAD ENOUGH...
...NOW SOME DINGY CHICK'S HARRASSIN' ME!!
YOU WANNA KNOW 'BOUT THIS MAGICAL "MORTAL REALM" YOU'RE CREAMIN' OVER WELL, I'LL TELL YA-- THE SUMMERS ARE UNBEARABLY HOT, THE WINTER'S FRICKIN FREEZIN', AND THE PEOPLE WORK THEIR FINGERS TO NUBS FOR PEANUTS!! YEAH, IT'S A REAL FRIGGIN' UTOPIA, ALL RIGHT!

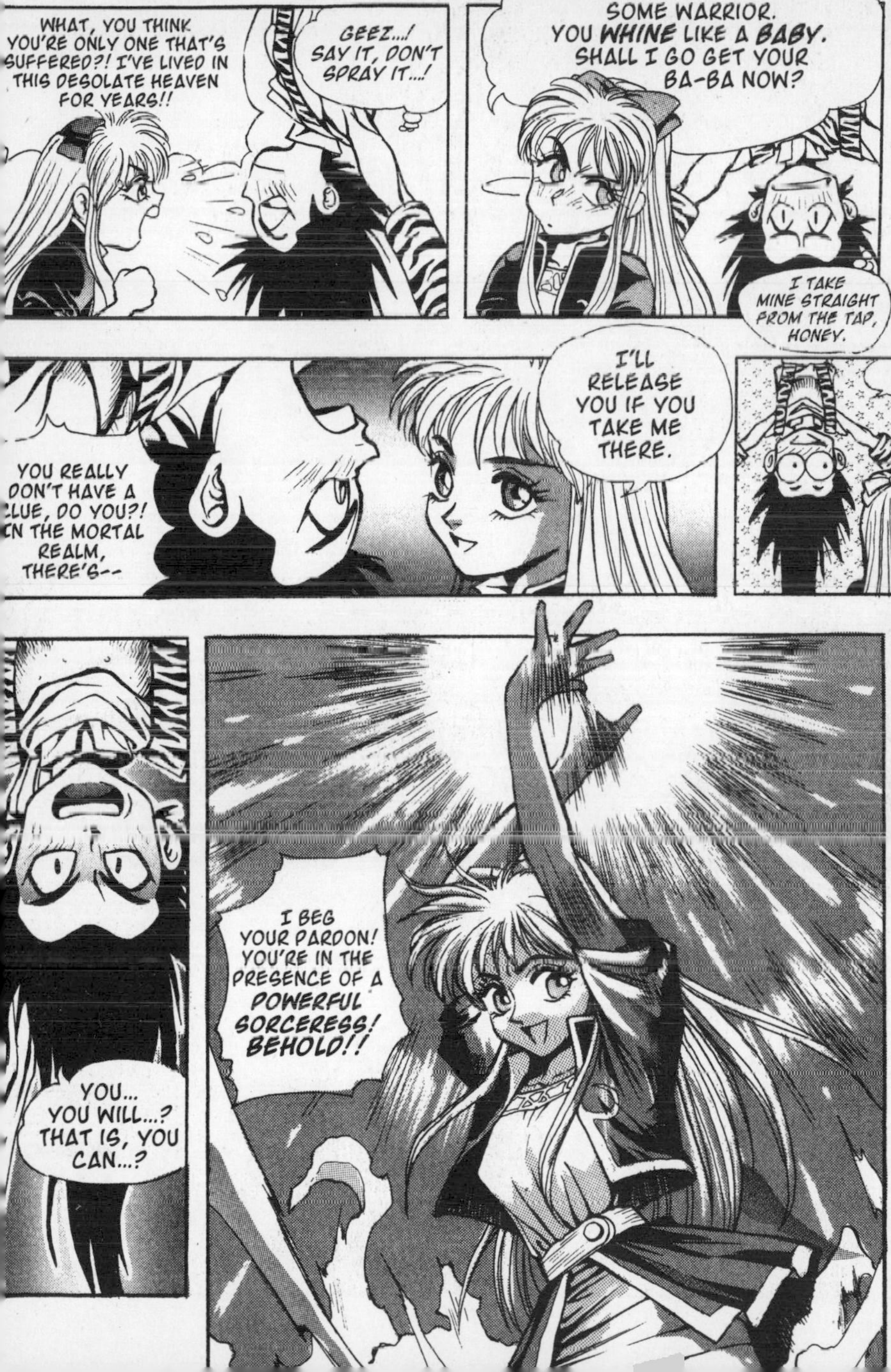
WHAT, YOU THINK YOU'RE ONLY ONE THAT'S SUFFERED?! I'VE LIVED IN THIS DESOLATE HEAVEN FOR YEARS!!
GEEZ...! SAY IT, DON'T SPRAY IT...!
SOME WARRIOR. YOU WHINE LIKE A BABY. SHALL I GO GET YOUR BA-BA NOW?
I TAKE MINE STRAIGHT FROM THE TAP, HONEY.
YOU REALLY DON'T HAVE A CLUE, DO YOU?! IN THE MORTAL REALM, THERE'S--
I'LL RELEASE YOU IF YOU TAKE ME THERE.
YOU... YOU WILL...? THAT IS, YOU CAN...?
I BEG YOUR PARDON! YOU'RE IN THE PRESENCE OF A POWERFUL SORCERESS! BEHOLD!!

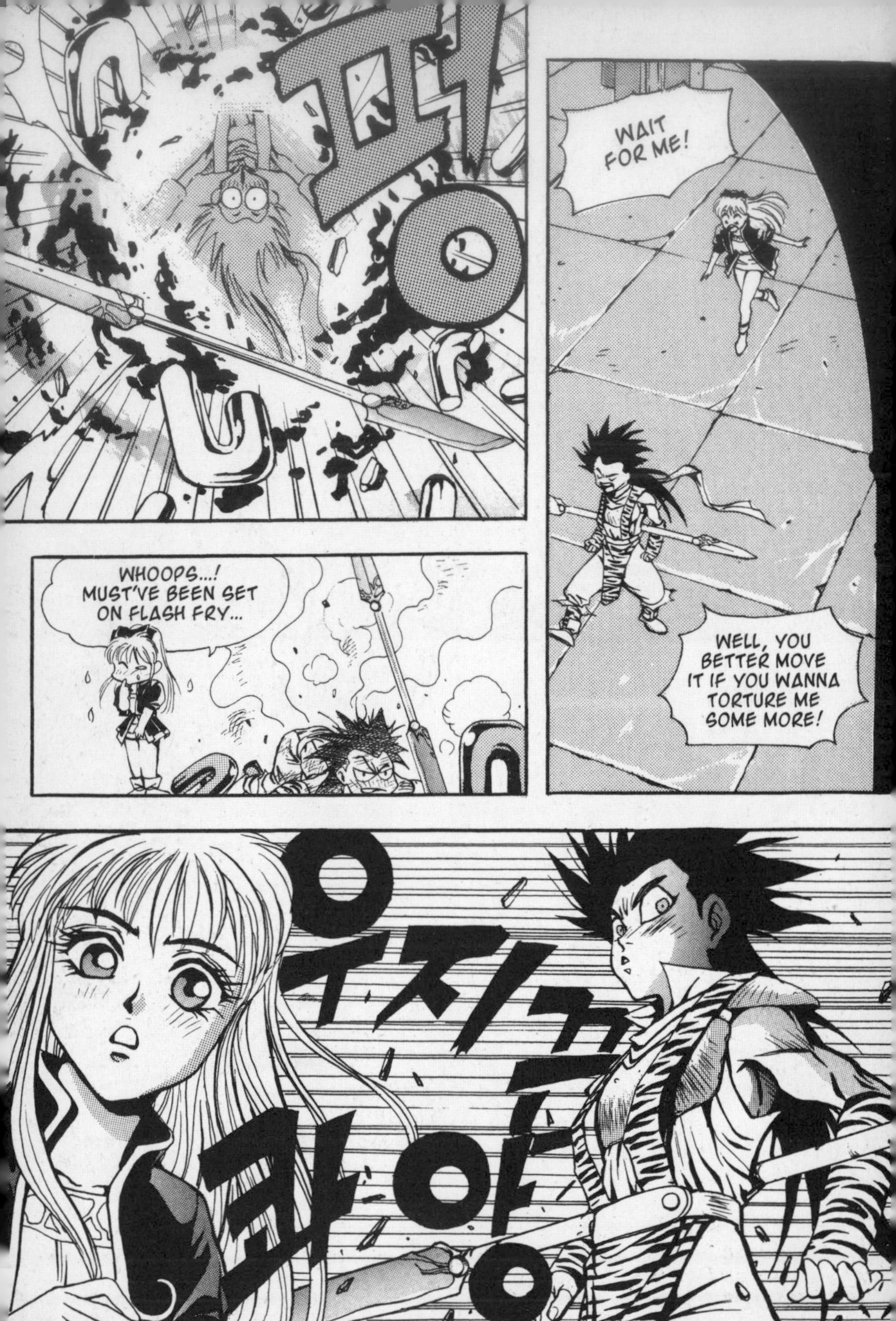
WHOOPS...! MUST'VE BEEN SET ON FLASH FRY...
WAIT FOR ME!
WELL, YOU BETTER MOVE IT IF YOU WANNA TORTURE ME SOME MORE!

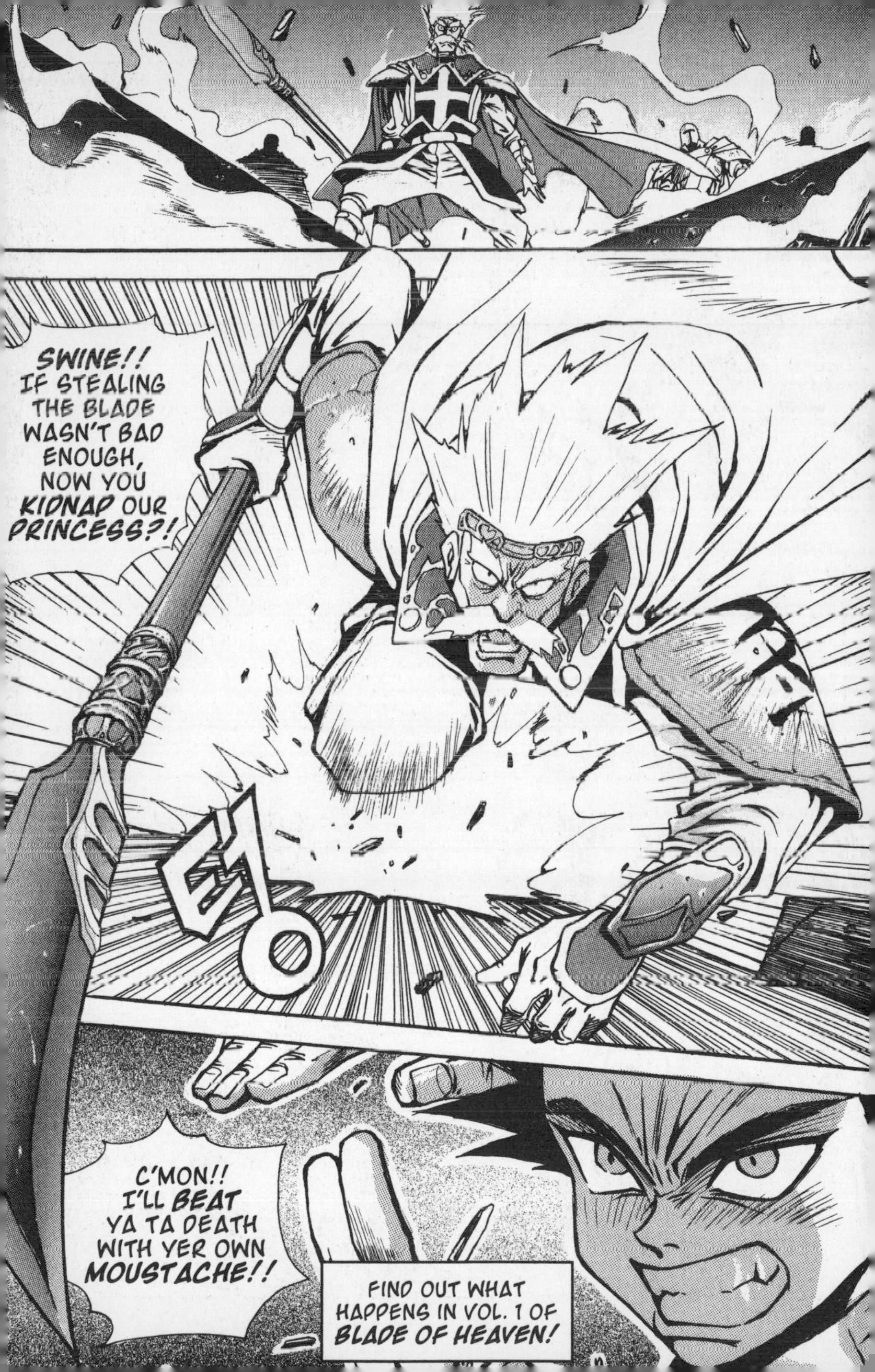
SWINE!! IF STEALING THE BLADE WASN'T BAD ENOUGH, NOW YOU KIDNAP OUR PRINCESS?!
C'MON!! I'LL BEAT YA TA DEATH WITH YER OWN MOUSTACHE!!
FIND OUT WHAT HAPPENS IN VOL. 1 OF BLADE OF HEAVEN!

ALSO AVAILABLE FROM TOKYOPOP®

MANGA

.HACK//LEGEND OF THE TWILIGHT
@LARGE
ABENOBASHI: MAGICAL SHOPPING ARCADE
A.I. LOVE YOU
AI YORI AOSHI
ALICHINO
ANGELIC LAYER
ARM OF KANNON
BABY BIRTH
BATTLE ROYALE
BATTLE VIXENS
BOYS BE...
BRAIN POWERED
BRIGADOON
B'TX
CANDIDATE FOR GODDESS, THE
CARDCAPTOR SAKURA
CARDCAPTOR SAKURA - MASTER OF THE CLOW
CHOBITS
CHRONICLES OF THE CURSED SWORD
CLAMP SCHOOL DETECTIVES
CLOVER
COMIC PARTY
CONFIDENTIAL CONFESSIONS
CORRECTOR YUI
COWBOY BEBOP
COWBOY BEBOP: SHOOTING STAR
CRAZY LOVE STORY
CRESCENT MOON
CROSS
CULDCEPT
CYBORG 009
D•N•ANGEL
DEARS
DEMON DIARY
DEMON ORORON, THE
DEUS VITAE
DIABOLO
DIGIMON
DIGIMON TAMERS
DIGIMON ZERO TWO
DOLL
DRAGON HUNTER
DRAGON KNIGHTS
DRAGON VOICE
DREAM SAGA
DUKLYON: CLAMP SCHOOL DEFENDERS
EERIE QUEERIE!
ERICA SAKURAZAWA: COLLECTED WORKS
ET CETERA
ETERNITY
EVIL'S RETURN
FAERIES' LANDING
FAKE
FLCL
FLOWER OF THE DEEP SLEEP
FORBIDDEN DANCE
FRUITS BASKET
G GUNDAM
GATEKEEPERS
GETBACKERS

GIRL GOT GAME
GRAVITATION
GTO
GUNDAM SEED ASTRAY
GUNDAM SEED ASTRAY R
GUNDAM WING
GUNDAM WING: BATTLEFIELD OF PACIFISTS
GUNDAM WING: ENDLESS WALTZ
GUNDAM WING: THE LAST OUTPOST (G-UNIT)
HANDS OFF!
HAPPY MANIA
HARLEM BEAT
HYPER POLICE
HYPER RUNE
I.N.V.U.
IMMORTAL RAIN
INITIAL D
INSTANT TEEN: JUST ADD NUTS
ISLAND
JING: KING OF BANDITS
JING: KING OF BANDITS - TWILIGHT TALES
JULINE
KARE KANO
KILL ME, KISS ME
KINDAICHI CASE FILES, THE
KING OF HELL
KODOCHA: SANA'S STAGE
LAGOON ENGINE
LAMENT OF THE LAMB
LEGAL DRUG
LEGEND OF CHUN HYANG, THE
LES BIJOUX
LILING-PO
LOVE HINA
LOVE OR MONEY
LUPIN III
LUPIN III: WORLD'S MOST WANTED
MAGIC KNIGHT RAYEARTH I
MAGIC KNIGHT RAYEARTH II
MAHOROMATIC: AUTOMATIC MAIDEN
MAN OF MANY FACES
MARMALADE BOY
MARS
MARS: HORSE WITH NO NAME
MINK
MIRACLE GIRLS
MIYUKI-CHAN IN WONDERLAND
MODEL
MOURYOU KIDEN: LEGEND OF THE NYMPH
NECK AND NECK
ONE
ONE I LOVE, THE
PARADISE KISS
PARASYTE
PASSION FRUIT
PEACH FUZZ
PEACH GIRL
PEACH GIRL: CHANGE OF HEART
PET SHOP OF HORRORS
PHD: PHANTASY DEGREE
PITA-TEN
PLANET BLOOD
PLANET LADDER

10.19.04T

ALSO AVAILABLE FROM TOKYOPOP

PLANETES
PRESIDENT DAD
PRIEST
PRINCESS AI
PSYCHIC ACADEMY
QUEEN'S KNIGHT, THE
RAGNAROK
RAVE MASTER
REALITY CHECK
REBIRTH
REBOUND
REMOTE
RISING STARS OF MANGA™, THE
SABER MARIONETTE J
SAILOR MOON
SAINT TAIL
SAIYUKI
SAMURAI DEEPER KYO
SAMURAI GIRL™ REAL BOUT HIGH SCHOOL
SCRYED
SEIKAI TRILOGY, THE
SGT. FROG
SHAOLIN SISTERS
SHIRAHIME-SYO: SNOW GODDESS TALES
SHUTTERBOX
SKULL MAN, THE
SNOW DROP
SORCERER HUNTERS
SOUL TO SEOUL
STONE
SUIKODEN III
SUKI
TAROT CAFÉ, THE
THREADS OF TIME
TOKYO BABYLON
TOKYO MEW MEW
TOKYO TRIBES
TRAMPS LIKE US
UNDER THE GLASS MOON
VAMPIRE GAME
VISION OF ESCAFLOWNE, THE
WARCRAFT
WARRIORS OF TAO
WILD ACT
WISH
WORLD OF HARTZ
X-DAY
ZODIAC P.I.

NOVELS

CLAMP SCHOOL PARANORMAL INVESTIGATORS
SAILOR MOON
SLAYERS

ART BOOKS

ART OF CARDCAPTOR SAKURA
ART OF MAGIC KNIGHT RAYEARTH, THE
PEACH: MIWA UEDA ILLUSTRATIONS
CLAMP NORTH SIDE
CLAMP SOUTH SIDE

ANIME GUIDES

COWBOY BEBOP
GUNDAM TECHNICAL MANUALS
SAILOR MOON SCOUT GUIDES

TOKYOPOP KIDS

STRAY SHEEP

CINE-MANGA®

ALADDIN
CARDCAPTORS
DUEL MASTERS
FAIRLY ODDPARENTS, THE
FAMILY GUY
FINDING NEMO
G.I. JOE SPY TROOPS
GREATEST STARS OF THE NBA
JACKIE CHAN ADVENTURES
JIMMY NEUTRON: BOY GENIUS, THE ADVENTURES OF
KIM POSSIBLE
LILO & STITCH: THE SERIES
LIZZIE MCGUIRE
LIZZIE MCGUIRE MOVIE, THE
MALCOLM IN THE MIDDLE
POWER RANGERS: DINO THUNDER
POWER RANGERS: NINJA STORM
PRINCESS DIARIES 2, THE
RAVE MASTER
SHREK 2
SIMPLE LIFE, THE
SPONGEBOB SQUAREPANTS
SPY KIDS 2
SPY KIDS 3-D: GAME OVER
TEENAGE MUTANT NINJA TURTLES
THAT'S SO RAVEN
TOTALLY SPIES
TRANSFORMERS: ARMADA
TRANSFORMERS: ENERGON

You want it? We got it!
A full range of TOKYOPOP
products are available now at:
www.TOKYOPOP.com/shop

10.19.04T

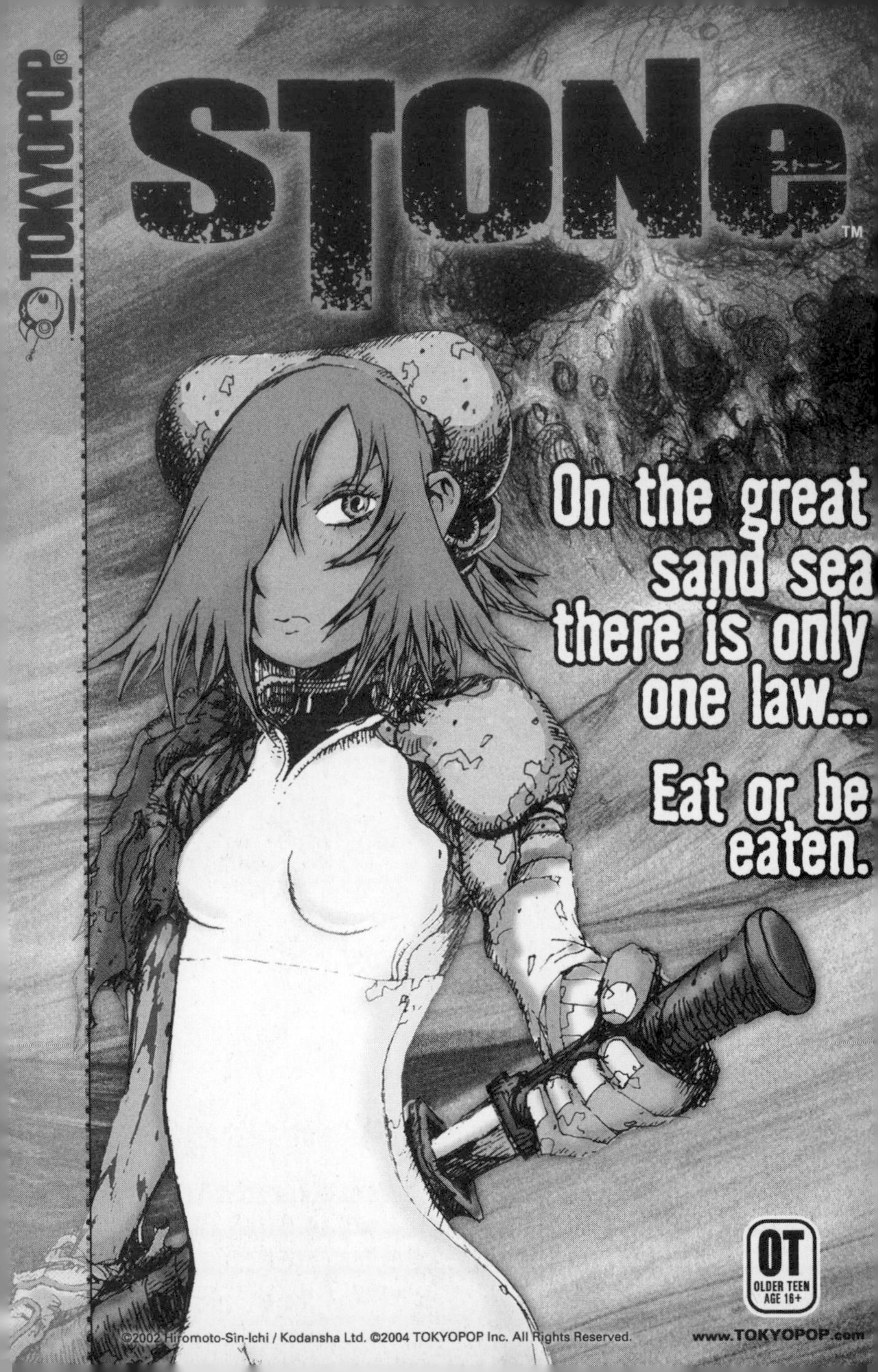
TOKYOPOP®
STONe™
ストーン
On the great sand sea there is only one law...
Eat or be eaten.
OT
OLDER TEEN AGE 16+
©2002 Hiromoto-Sin-Ichi / Kodansha Ltd. ©2004 TOKYOPOP Inc. All Rights Reserved.
www.TOKYOPOP.com

SGT FROG WANTS YOU!

SGT ✸ FROG
KERORO GUNSOU ™

A WACKY MANGA OF ALIEN FROGS & WORLD DOMINATION
BY MINE YOSHIZAKI

TEEN
AGE 13+

www.TOKYOPOP.com